HALIFAX

Town and City Histories

Titles in print or forthcoming include:

Town and City Histories

Series editor: Stephen Constantine

Halifax

John A. Hargreaves

John A. Hargreaves

With best wishes

to Jean.

Edinburgh University Press/
Carnegie Publishing

Dedication

To my wife Susan, our daughters Anne and Helen, our sons Paul and Stephen, my mother, Edna and in memory of my father Ronald (1917–1988)

Town and City Histories
Series Editor: Stephen Constantine

Halifax
John A. Hargreaves

© John A. Hargreaves, 1999

Published by Edinburgh University Press
22 George Square, Edinburgh
http://www.eup.ed.ac.uk
and Carnegie Publishing Ltd
Chatsworth Road, Lancaster

Typeset in Minion by
Carnegie Publishing
Printed and bound in Great Britain by
Cambridge University Press

British Library Cataloguing-in-Publication data
A catalogue record for this book is available from the British Library

ISBN 1 85331 217 7

The right of John A. Hargreaves to be identified
as the author of this work has been asserted
in accordance with the Copyright, Designs
and Patents Act 1988

Contents

Series Editor's Foreword

THE BOOKS in this series are designed and written with a broad readership in mind: local people interested to know how the character of their town has been shaped by major historical forces and the energies of their predecessors; newcomers and visitors curious to acquire a historical introduction to their new surroundings; general readers wishing to see how the sweeps of national and international history have manifested themselves in particular urban communities; and the scholar seeking to understand urbanisation by comparing and contrasting local experiences.

We live, most of us, in intensely urban environments. These are the products largely of the last two centuries of historical development, although the roots of many towns, of course, go back deep into the past. In recent years there has been considerable historical research of a high standard into this urban history. Narrative and descriptive accounts of the history of towns and cities can now be replaced by studies such as the TOWN AND CITY HISTORIES which investigate, analyse and, above all, explain the economic, political, social and cultural processes and consequences of urbanisation.

Writers for this series consider the changing economic foundations of their town or city and the way change has affected its physical shape, built environment and interests of those who wielded power locally and the structure and functions of local government in different periods are also examined, since locally exercised authority could determine much about the fortunes and quality of urban life. Particular emphasis is placed on the changing life experiences of ordinary men, women and children – their homes, education, occupations, social relations, living standards and leisure activities. Towns and cities control and respond to the values, aspirations and actions of their residents. The books in this series therefore explore social behaviour as well as the economic and political history of those who live in and helped make the towns and cities of today.

Stephen Constantine
University of Lancaster

Preface and acknowledgements

'In the same place where the wild boar made his repast on acorns, rich commerce smiles and industry and plenty make thousands happy!', reflected the anonymous author of a *History of the Town and Parish of Halifax*, published in 1789. How, when and why did such a transformation occur? Was Halifax's urban development entirely the product of the major economic and social changes which the town experienced from the late eighteenth century, as the anonymous author of the contemporary history appears to imply, or was it perhaps stimulated by an earlier phase of commercial expansion in the 300 years or so before the classic period of the Industrial Revolution? Indeed, what were the more distant origins of Halifax as a place of settlement and how did geography and environment shape its development as an urban centre? Moreover, how did the experience of industrial expansion and ultimately industrial decline affect the development of the town in the two centuries which followed the publication of this early anonymous history? Finally, how has the experience of history impacted upon the lives of those who live in Halifax and Calderdale today?

Although Halifax celebrated in 1998 the 150th anniversary of the granting of its municipal charter of incorporation, no full-length history has yet appeared attempting to explain the complex process by which 'a few straggling tenements built of wood, wattles and thatch' in the late medieval period developed into 'a town of a hundred trades' by the late Victorian period. Indeed, the last full-length history of Halifax for adult readers, John Crabtree's *Concise History of the Parish and Vicarage of Halifax*, appeared as long ago as 1836, a year before the accession to the throne of Queen Victoria in 1837 and twelve years before Halifax received its municipal charter in 1848. Moreover, Crabtree's history, like previous and subsequent histories, recognising that the fortunes of the town were inextricably linked with those of its hinterland, tended to focus more upon the history of the extensive parish of Halifax than on the history of the town itself. Even T. W. Hanson, the author of the most recent history of Halifax for children, *The Story of Old Halifax*, emphasised in 1920 that his narrative was 'not confined to the town of Halifax', but was 'also concerned with the tract of surrounding country' comprising the medieval parish of Halifax. Moreover, he concluded his story somewhat abruptly in the mid-Victorian period. His text therefore omits, for example, any reference to the origins and development of the institution which more than any other has been responsible for carrying the name of Halifax around the world and which remains today the largest private employer in the modern metropolitan district of Calderdale, namely the Halifax plc, formerly the Halifax Building Society.

This new history of Halifax, which takes account of research in the eighty years since Hanson wrote, attempts to distinguish the town from its periphery and to bring the account of the town's history up to the present, in the belief that history is essentially a continuing dialogue between present and past and that it is only possible to understand fully the present direction of our lives with a sense of historical perspective. The central aim of this new history of Halifax is, therefore, to enquire why Halifax exists today, in this place, with its distinctive built environment, with its prevailing economic, social, political and cultural characteristics, and with its current relationships with Calderdale, West Yorkshire, the United Kingdom and the world.

It might be considered presumptuous of a Lancastrian, a native of Burnley, some twenty miles to the west of Halifax, to attempt a history of a town in the heart of Pennine Yorkshire. However, the neighbouring towns and their modern metropolitan districts have much in common. Sharing a river with a common name and source, the Calder, and a prehistoric routeway, the Long Causeway, Burnley was a woollen town before it came to specialise in cotton weaving, while Halifax later diversified from woollen manufacture into worsted, cotton and silk production. Moreover, both towns have also had to discover new economic futures in the twentieth century as textiles have declined. Indeed, the extent of the post-industrial problems facing both towns was evident in their ranking in the bottom six of seventy-nine county boroughs according to rateable value per head of population in 1968. Coincidentally, Burnley was also considered for Business in the Community's pioneering partnership project in the 1980s before Halifax was finally selected.

My own association with Halifax arises from a family wartime connection during the period from 1940 to 1945. After the bombing of the Royal Engineers' barracks at Chatham by the Luftwaffe, my father's regiment moved to emergency bases in the West Riding, which included Ebenezer Sunday School, Halifax, where he was billeted before embarking for service in the Middle East. Later, at the end of the war, he returned to Shibden Hall, Halifax, prior to demobilisation in 1945. My mother became a regular visitor to Halifax during the war years and continuing friendships brought our family from Burnley to Halifax on a number of occasions in the 1950s. I also made an early educational visit to Shibden Hall with a party from Burnley Grammar School during this period. Following my marriage in 1972, I came to live in Halifax, where my wife was training as a midwife at Halifax General Hospital and where all four of our children were subsequently born. It is appropriate therefore that this book should be dedicated to members of my family who have helped to connect me with this place where I have now lived happily for nearly three decades.

My interest in the history of Halifax has also been fostered by membership of the Halifax Antiquarian Society, of which I have been secretary since 1986 and editor of its *Transactions* since 1992. It was always the ambition of the society's founding fathers in 1900 to produce a history of Halifax and I am delighted to have been able to contribute to the realisation of that ambition as the society approaches the celebration of the centenary of its foundation in the year 2000. I have found the numerous volumes of the society's *Transactions*, published annually since 1900, invaluable in researching this book and am indebted to the many authors, living and dead, for their exploration of so many aspects of local history. My understanding of the history of Halifax has also been developed through numerous discussions with individual members of the society and other local residents who have shared with me their knowledge of local history. I particularly wish to thank Donald Haigh and Alan Betteridge for their helpful comments on preliminary drafts of particular chapters of the book; A. J. Petford and P. M. Buckley for their careful drawing of the maps; Doreen Baxter, Emma Beaumont and Eureka, Ian Beesley, Stephen Gee, David Gilchrist and the Halifax plc, Sir Ernest Hall, David Hanson and the *Halifax Courier*, Nigel Herring and Calderdale Leisure Services, Andrew Lomax, Pat Sewell and the West Yorkshire Archive Service, Lord Somerleyton, Irene Spencer and Geoffrey Washington for assistance in supplying a variety of interesting illustrations and Colin Spencer for passing on to me his local history files. I am also grateful to a number of individuals from within the local community who gave me extended interviews which provided me with a range of invaluable twentieth-century perspectives on key themes. They included Sir James Birrell, Michael Ellison, Canon Robert Gibson, Sir Ernest Hall, Richard de Z. Hall, Chris Johnstone, Alan Machin, Alice Mahon MP, Gerard Norrie, Michael Scott and Wilfred Sharp.

I am also indebted to a number of other individuals for their advice and encouragement. My former tutors at the University of Southampton, Professor Colin Platt and Professor Paul Harvey commented perceptively upon Chapters two and three. Dr Steve Hindle of the University of Warwick, who provided me with valuable insights into current research on the sixteenth and seventeenth centuries at a revision course for teachers in Cambridge, also commented constructively on Chapter three. Professor Keith Laybourn of the University of Huddersfield, who with the late Dr David Wright supervised my Ph.D. thesis on 'Religion and society in the parish of Halifax, c.1740–1914', shared with me his extensive knowledge of the inter-war years. My colleague, Mrs S. Riaz, kindly answered a number of enquiries about multi-cultural issues. My brother, Professor Ian Hargreaves, former editor of *The Independent* and *The New Statesman*, made many stimulating observations particularly on twentieth-century themes. Dr Stephen Constantine, the series editor, provided challenging and helpful advice at every stage of this volume's evolution and Nicola Carr of Edinburgh University Press patiently guided the book towards publication. Finally, I wish to record my gratitude to my wife, Susan and family, Anne, Helen, Paul and Stephen for their constant support throughout the long period during which I have been engaged in researching and writing this book.

John A. Hargreaves

Tables

CHAPTER ONE

Introduction: geography and environment

'All Halifax history depends on Halifax geography', the novelist Phyllis Bentley (1894–1977) observed astutely in her introduction to a volume commemorating the centenary of Halifax's incorporation as a municipal borough in 1948.[1] Similarly, local geographer, John Ogden, introducing the newly-designated long-distance footpath, the Calderdale Way, concluded in 1978 that Halifax had 'by a complex interaction of geography and history' developed from a small medieval community 'on the banks of a minor Calder tributary, the Hebble Brook' into 'the major settlement' within the modern metropolitan borough of Calderdale.[2] A study of the urban development of Halifax reaffirms the aptness of these observations, for an awareness of the geographical constraints and environmental opportunities presented by the Calderdale landscape is a prerequisite to an understanding of the complex economic, social and political history of the town and its hinterland.

The modern metropolitan district of Calderdale, of which Halifax, situated towards its eastern perimeter on the mid-valley terrace of the Hebble Brook, is the administrative and urban centre, is located predominantly in the millstone grit area of the extreme west of the county of West Yorkshire. It forms part of the rolling central Pennine plateau, which dips gently towards the east as it enters the lower coal measures. Geologically, the Pennine plateau in the west consists of alternate strata of coarse sandstones or gritstones and relatively narrow bands of shale or mudstone, generally covered by a raw peat soil. The lower coal measures in the east are made up of alternate strata of finer sandstone and shale. The plateau is drained by the rivers Calder and Ryburn and their tributary moorland becks, tumbling down narrow, steep-sided valleys. Descending eastwards, through ruggedly beautiful countryside, from its source at an altitude of 764 feet on the crest of the Pennines high above Todmorden, the Yorkshire Calder intersects the dale to which it gives its name, before continuing its 44 mile course eastwards to its confluence with the Aire at Castleford.

The impervious nature of the bedrock, the poor quality of the topsoil, the rough inhospitable terrain, and the cold and wet climate probably deterred invaders and settlers in the period up to 1500, when its geographical remoteness ensured that Halifax remained a relatively insignificant Pennine

Figure 1.1
Halifax: location.

backwater. By creating conditions which militated against extensive arable farming, however, these geographical and environmental features also stimulated the development of the textile industry as a supplementary economic activity to subsistence agriculture in Calderdale towards the end of the medieval period. This transformation was assisted by another geographical advantage, a proliferation of swift-flowing moorland streams, which provided abundant supplies of soft water for the dyeing and finishing of woollen cloth. Corn mills were easily adapted or converted for water-powered fulling, the process by which woollen cloth was pounded, scoured and textured by heavy wooden stocks. A distinctive dual economy of farming and textiles thereby emerged in the upland settlements of this remote Pennine valley. This stimulated the development of Halifax as the dominant commercial and urban centre for its periphery in the later medieval period and provided the basis for the town's remarkable rise to regional prominence in the early modern period as a manufacturing and marketing centre of woollen cloth.[3]

However, geographical factors also subsequently hindered the development of both internal and external transport and communications systems, from turnpike and waterway to railway, tramway and motorway. An impenetrable shield of hills encompassing Halifax from north-east to south-east presented a formidable barrier for eighteenth- and nineteenth-century turnpike, waterway and railway engineers. This allowed neighbouring Bradford, which established earlier connections to the expanding canal and railway network, to achieve pre-eminence as a regional textile marketing centre after 1800.[4] Moreover, Halifax derived relatively limited supplies of coal from its location on the western edge of the Yorkshire coalfield until the development of a waterway link between the town and the Calder and Hebble Navigation in 1828 enabled cheap supplies to be transported into the town from further afield. This encouraged the dependence of Halifax and its hinterland on water power and delayed the adoption by local

Figure 1.2   Halifax and the Hebble Valley viewed from the north. This late twentieth-century aerial photograph reveals the concentration of industrial development along the valley floor of the Hebble Brook. The former Crossley carpet manufacturing mill complex at Dean Clough occupies a vast site on the northern edge of the town centre extending for over half a mile along the line of the modern A629 Halifax–Keighley Road. The shield of hills skirting the eastern edge of the town centre which determined the direction of Halifax's urban expansion is clearly visible. The thickly wooded slopes now form a spectacular backdrop to the town centre, when viewed from ground level. The blackened structure of Halifax Parish Church stands in the distance, beyond the modern flyover which totally obscures the Victorian North Bridge over the Hebble Brook. (Photograph courtesy of the *Halifax Courier*)

Figure 1.3
Halifax: relief.

entrepreneurs of coal-fired, steam-powered machinery. Halifax was therefore slower to develop as a centre of large-scale manufacturing industry
than some other West Yorkshire towns, notably Bradford and Leeds. However, in consequence, Halifax developed a more diversified economic base
than many similar sized towns, which enabled it to absorb some of the
impact of economic recession in the nineteenth and twentieth centuries.
Meanwhile, the steep gradients and rugged physical terrain of an urban
location which J. B. Priestley later described as the hilliest for any town of
its size in England, ensured that Halifax remained a predominantly pedestrian town until the development of electric tramways and motorised
transport after 1898.[5]

There were other disadvantages inherent in the town's location. The
range of hills encompassing the north-eastern and south-eastern perimeter
of Halifax imposed constraints on its economic and spatial development
as an urban centre. This produced a pattern of predominantly westward
urban expansion in the eighteenth and nineteenth centuries and ultimately
set limits on the town's urban growth in the early twentieth century, when
all the potential development land within the orbit of the town centre had
been acquired for industrial or residential purposes. Later industrial estates
and business parks tended, therefore, to be located around the periphery
of the town and at nearby Brighouse and Elland. This changed from the
1980s, however, when the modern telecommunications revolution allowed
greater flexibility of location for a burgeoning service sector, including the
re-occupation of some previously abandoned multi-storeyed factories and
warehouses close to the centre of the town. There were nevertheless some

Figure 1.4   The Hebble Valley and Dean Clough viewed from the south. The Hebble Brook, which provided water power for the early mills situated along its course, is clearly visible in the foreground as it emerges from beneath the massive Dean Clough industrial complex. The mill in the foreground of this 1985 photograph still bears the evocative sign of H. Fletcher and Co. Ltd Slubbing Dyers and Melange Printers. Halifax began to develop from the late medieval period as a centre for the dyeing, finishing and marketing of woollen cloth. The Akroyds were the first to employ steam-powered machinery at their worsted mills on the Hebble from the 1820s. (Photograph courtesy of Ian Beesley)

advantages of location which favoured the physical appearance of the town. Plentiful supplies of locally quarried stone enabled the development of a distinctive built environment in Halifax and its hinterland, although in-dustrial pollution diminished its appeal until the implementation of clean air legislation and stone cleaning programmes in the late twentieth century.[6]

Moreover, the geographical constraints which had sometimes impeded the economic and urban development of Halifax, also helped to foster a strong spirit of both individualism and community. Elements of the history and culture of popular radicalism, liberalism, conservatism and socialism all came to be represented in local politics, which after the turbulent years of economic and social dislocation in the mid-Victorian period ultimately inclined more towards consensus than conflict. Cultural values were shaped by many influences, including a tradition of philanthropy, mutual im-provement and voluntary service, which derived much of its impetus from the strong Puritan and Nonconformist presence in the town which had emerged during the Reformation and Evangelical Revival, and which remained a vibrant force within the community into the twentieth century. In the late twentieth century, however, religious and cultural diversity was broadened by an influx of immigrants from the Indian sub-continent, seeking employment in the town's declining textile industries. During this period, Halifax became, in many respects, a model of post-industrial society, pioneering new forms of partnership between the public, private and voluntary sectors. It also turned some of the former disadvantages of its geographical location into new economic opportunities by exploiting the growing appeal of its spectacular natural environment and unique built environment to a growing tourist market.

CHAPTER TWO

A Pennine backwater:
Halifax before 1500

What evidence is there for the occupation, settlement and function of the site on which the modern town of Halifax developed in the many centuries up to 1500? When did the settlement start to develop into an urban centre, with what economic purpose and with what social, political and cultural characteristics? How did its early development affect its later physical shape, built environment, urban character and its relationships with its surrounding settlements?

Before the Conquest

There is very little evidence of human habitation and settlement on the site of the modern town of Halifax before the Norman Conquest. This is perhaps not surprising as lowland sites before the tenth and eleventh centuries were generally densely wooded and poorly drained, and early settlers therefore tended to favour more elevated sites. Mesolithic microliths, obliquely-blunted flint implements from the Middle Stone Age, provide the earliest evidence of human activity, but principally on the rising moor-land around the future site of Halifax. Here, around 10,000 years ago, early hunters, operating from such base camp locations as Ringstone Edge Moor to the south-west and Nab Water on Oxenhope Moor to the north-west, followed herds of red deer and other wild animals into the higher reaches of the Central Pennines. Archaeological evidence, supported by a series of radiocarbon determinations, suggests increasing numbers of hunters visited and exploited both the animal and vegetable resources of the Yorkshire Pennines by the later Mesolithic period. Calderdale finds range from scatters of flints to more substantial upland gritstone sites on the Midgley, Ovenden, Saltonstall and Warley Moors. Untypically, they also include an isolated lowland gravel site at Halifax, which was discovered in the early 1970s below the clay floor of an excavated thirteenth-century house in Gaol Lane. The finds, comprising a microlith, quartzite hammerstone and nearly two dozen very rough, unretouched flakes and blades, dating perhaps from the sixth millennium BC, provide the earliest evidence of human activity on the site of the town of Halifax.[1]

Traces of Neolithic and Bronze Age occupation and passage have been discovered, but again at high altitudes along the route of the ancient trans-Pennine trackway, later known as the Long Causeway, linking the Halifax and Burnley areas. Neolithic, leaf-shaped flint arrowheads, used in hunting and possibly also in warfare, have also been discovered at former Mesolithic sites on the exposed uplands around Ringstone Reservoir, Midgley Moor, Blackstone Edge, Great Manshead Hill, March Hill, Waystone Edge and Windy Hill, suggesting possible re-use of previously occupied sites. The discovery of plano-convex flint knives, a polished-edge convex scraper and other artefacts provides evidence of a Neolithic occupation site at Holdsworth in North Halifax, while the discovery of flint axes over a wider area suggests the exploitation of the surrounding woodland. More extensive evidence of settlement has been uncovered from the Bronze Age along the terraces of the valleys of the Calder and its tributaries, for example, cinerary urns with cremations at Warley, Ovenden and Rastrick. A plain, thin-butted copper axe was found at Hipperholme between 1828 and 1831 and a small, thick-butted bronze flat axe was discovered at an upland site at Norland, to the south-west of Halifax, in 1984. Hunting appears to have remained important in the Bronze Age, the discovery of arrowheads at Mesolithic sites, for example Manshead, Ringstone Edge Moor, Inchfield and Langfield Moor, suggesting either continuity of occupation or Bronze Age re-use of sites. But evidence of sustained settlement from this period on the site of Halifax is still absent.[2]

Archaeological evidence of Iron Age settlement and Roman occupation in Calderdale is even less extensive, and there is still no evidence of any activity during this period on the site of the town of Halifax itself. Several Iron Age enclosures have been identified in Calderdale at Kirklees Park, Ovenden Moor, Norland and Meg Dyke, Barkisland. The latter, a rectangular enclosure with a double rampart, possibly formed one of a group of defensive Iron Age earthworks in the South West Pennines. The Revd John Watson, the celebrated eighteenth-century historian of Halifax, who claimed the distinction of having first discovered the Roman forts at Slack, near Huddersfield, and Castleshaw in Saddleworth, failed to detect the remains of any Roman fort within the parish of Halifax. Moreover, the traditional association of the paved trans-Pennine moorland road over Blackstone Edge with the Romans is now discredited, and the presumed course of the Manchester to Ilkley Roman road through the parish of Halifax south of the Calder has also been questioned. However, it seems likely that a Roman road, constructed during the second century AD linking Ilkley with Manchester, did pass through Soyland, south-west of Halifax. In addition, in 1955 the claim of the topographer Roger Dodsworth (1585–1654) for the existence of a Roman site just within the Halifax parish boundary at Fixby was confirmed by the rediscovery of a Roman tile kiln in Grimscar Wood. It has also been suggested that a hoard of Coritanian and early first-century Roman coins discovered at Lightcliffe between 1828

Figure 2.1 Roman altar from Thick Hollins, Bank Top, Greetland. This early third-century votive altar discovered in April 1597 at Greetland, some two miles south of Halifax, now forms part of the Cotton Collection in the Cambridge University Museum of Archaeology and Anthropology. It was dedicated by Titus Aurelius Aurelianus and his family to Victoria Brigantia and the Deities of the Two Roman Emperors and is one of a number of apparently isolated Roman finds from this vicinity of Halifax. (Photograph courtesy of Halifax Antiquarian Society)

and 1831, may have been deposited by refugees from the Claudian invasion. Other coin finds dating from the third and fourth centuries are considered to represent activity related to contemporary altars, including an altar dedicated by Titus Aurelius Aurelianus to Victoria Brigantia and the deities of the two Roman Emperors, discovered at Greetland in 1597 and preserved at Cambridge University since 1750. And yet no evidence has been discovered of either military or civilian settlements in the immediate vicinity of Halifax, suggesting that this still remained largely unpopulated.[3]

Little is known about Halifax and its periphery even in the six centuries between the end of the Roman period and the Norman Conquest. It is possible to identify a number of key changes in the political control of the area in which the future site of Halifax was situated during the pre-Conquest period. After the Roman withdrawal from Britain, a number of independent kingdoms emerged in the fifth century, including the British kingdom of Elmet, which, by the early seventh century, encompassed the modern county divisions of South and West Yorkshire. Literary sources reveal that Elmet reached its zenith in the second half of the sixth century, offering strong resistance to English expansion from the East Riding kingdom of Deira. However, following the formation of the kingdom of Northumbria, by the union of Deira and Bernicia, Elmet was annexed by Edwin of Northumbria in 617. Despite intermittent clashes between Northumbria and Mercia, which resulted in Mercian domination of Northumbria from 633–634 and 641–654, Northumbria ultimately regained its independence until the Danish invasions of the late ninth century. It remained under Danish control until the defeat of Eric Bloodaxe in 954. Thereafter, it was ruled by earls appointed by the kings of Wessex. But evidence of the impact of these political changes on settlement in Halifax and its environs is very sparse.[4]

William the Conqueror's pioneering Domesday survey reveals that a number of outliers or berewicks within the Calder Valley formed part of a pre-Conquest royal manor of Wakefield, but remains tantalisingly silent about whether these encompassed Halifax itself. However, modern scholarship has tended to emphasise the deficiencies of the Yorkshire Domesday survey, which was apparently compiled hastily. Its shortcomings may reflect the ignorance of the new Norman lords and their officials about their possessions. By what has been most plausibly explained as a clerical error in the recording of the nine constituent outliers of the manor of Wakefield in the Yorkshire Domesday survey, there is apparently no reference to Halifax. While nine outliers are enumerated within the royal manor of Wakefield, only eight are listed, namely: *Sandala* (Sandal Magna), *Sorebi* (Sowerby), *Werlafeslei* (Warley), *Micleie* (Midgley), *Wadesuurde*

Figure 2.2 The parish of Halifax before 1842.

(Wadsworth), *Crubetonestun* (Cruttonstall in Erringden), *Langefelt* (Lang-field) and *Stanesfelt* (Stansfield). Recognising the omission of Halifax from the list and reluctant to challenge the accuracy of the awesome Domesday survey, T. W. Hanson (1877–1967), and some other local historians of earlier generations mistakenly assumed that Halifax must have been represented by the suffix of *Werlafeslei*, an entry split between two lines of text in the original manuscript. However, close scrutiny of the original manuscript in 1935 by H. P. Kendall (d. 1937) revealed that the suffix *feslei*, although appearing on a separate line of text from its prefix, retained the lower case. Comparison of the entry with other early recorded forms of the name established conclusively that the combined prefix and suffix represent Warley, an extensive township which contained a large number of settlements in the Middle Ages. The absence also of a reference to Heptonstall has led recent scholars, more aware of the deficiencies of the Yorkshire Domesday record than their predecessors, to account for the discrepancy between the specified number of berewicks and the list of recorded names by suggesting that the sub-manor of Halifax-cum-Heptonstall was omitted from the list in error.[5]

There is also some evidence to suggest that Halifax might have formed part of a pre-Conquest ecclesiastical structure centred upon the ancient minster church of Dewsbury, since payments of tithes from Halifax to Dewsbury Parish Church are recorded in a fourteenth-century endowment deed. But archaeological evidence for an early Christian presence in the area is rare. At Rastrick, a chapelry within the later parish of Halifax, a fragment of a tenth- or early eleventh-century Anglian carved stone cross has survived, but there is no such evidence from the site of Halifax itself. The Yorkshire Domesday survey records relatively few churches in the poorer western part of the county, but the omission of a specific reference to a church does not necessarily imply that no such church existed, since Domesday does not provide a comprehensive record of ecclesiastical structures. However, whether the two unspecified churches and three priests referred to in the survey had any connection with Halifax remains a matter for speculation.[6]

Place name evidence of early settlement, which must necessarily be used with caution since it also derives from post-Conquest documentation, may nevertheless provide some tentative clues to pre-Conquest patterns of occupation and settlement within Calderdale. Calder is a Celtic river name signifying 'rapid stream'; Exley, a hybrid name deriving from the Celtic *egles* and the Anglo-Saxon *leah*, possibly denotes the site of an Elmetian church; while, Walsden, deriving from Old English descriptions of the British, possibly indicates a valley settlement which retained a recognisable British character after the English occupation of Elmet. Other compound names with Old English suffixes such as: *land* (land), *worth* (enclosure), *feld* (unenclosed land), *denu* (valley), *shaw* (wood) and *leah* (forest clearing) may reflect an English ascendancy. Local examples of these include: Elland (land by the river); Illingworth (Illa's enclosure), Holdsworth (Halda's enclosure); Langfield (long stretch of open country); Hebden (briar valley), Mixenden (dung-hill valley), Ovenden (the upper reaches of a valley), Shibden (sheep valley); Blackshaw (black wood); Midgley (midge-infested wood or clearing), Bentley (clearing overgrown with bent grass), Brearley (clearing overgrown with briar), Coley (cold, exposed clearing) and Wheatley (clearing used for growing wheat). Moreover, the sparsity of later Anglo-Scandinavian and Scandinavian names may confirm a continuing English ascendancy in Halifax. Erringden (Eric's valley) and Greetland (land strewn with boulders), exemplifying the former, and Sowerby (farm-stead on sour ground) and Mankinholes (Mancan's hollow), exemplifying the latter, probably derive from Norse immigration in the tenth century and possibly denote later north-facing settlements on the south bank of the Calder.

    A number of extraordinarily fanciful, highly influential, but entirely unsatisfactory explanations have been provided by William Camden (1551–1623), John Watson (1725–83), Dr T. D. Whitaker (1759–1821) and other antiquaries for the etymology of the name of Halifax, which has existed in its modern form only since the early twelfth century. Professor A. H. Smith's derivation of 'an area of coarse grass in a nook of land or amongst rocks' from the Old English *halh* (a nook of land) and *gefeaxe* (coarse grassland) is now preferred to such derivations as 'holy hair', 'holy face' and 'holy ways', based upon the Old English *halig* (holy), interwoven with legendary stories.[7]

    So, archaeological, documentary and place-name evidence for the pre-Conquest development of Halifax remains skeletal and its interpretation problematic, making it difficult to assess the extent of settlement by 1066. It would appear, however, that pre-Conquest settlement of Halifax had not been very extensive, possibly constrained by the sort of geographical factors implicit in its place name derivation as 'an area of coarse grass in a nook of land or amongst rocks'.[8]

Medieval Halifax

The nature of the impact of the Norman Conquest and the extent of the devastation wreaked on the fragile pre-Conquest settlement of Halifax by William the Conqueror's harrying of the rebellious north in 1069–70 are now impossible to assess, and historians have emerged sharply divided in their interpretation of the available evidence. The antiquary John Lister, analysing the lay subsidy returns of 1379, concluded in 1906 that 'the fact that this part of the country was desolated and laid waste by William the Norman would, to a large extent, account for its sparse population and poverty in the days of King Richard II', while more recently, the Domesday historian Michael Wood has maintained that the inhabitants of Yorkshire were 'marked for generations by fire and sword' after the harrying. Traditionally, the impact of the harrying was measured by the incidence in the Domesday survey of land classified as waste, comprising half the townships in Yorkshire, and the scale of the decline in the value of the land since 1066. In the manor of Wakefield, for example, the value of land was estimated to have declined by 75 per cent, from £60 to £15 since the reign of Edward the Confessor. However, W. E. Wightman has argued that since the manor of Wakefield, which contained large stretches of woodland, still had one third of its potential arable land under the plough in 1086, the drop in land value 'is not necessarily sufficiently severe in Yorkshire conditions to suggest any significant retreat in cultivation'. Moreover, since demesne arable farming was mainly concentrated in the fertile lowland townships of Wakefield and the outlier Sandal Magna, while much of the manorial woodland was situated in the Upper Calder Valley, it seems reasonable to conclude that Calderdale's geographical remoteness enabled Halifax to escape relatively unscathed what has been described as 'the most fearful genocide in the history of England'.[9]

If Domesday reveals little or no arable demesne land in Calderdale in 1086, there is evidence of the subsequent exploitation of the area for pasture. The ancient Forest of Sowerbyshire, which extended westwards across Calderdale from Halifax to the Lancashire border, appears to have been used initially by the manorial lords primarily for hunting, but increasingly it was opened up for both cattle rearing and sheep pasture. Moreover, as cattle farms or vaccaries were leased to tenants, some were even converted from pasture into arable farmland. Until the end of the thirteenth century, peasant farmers principally cultivated oats, a cereal crop better suited to the cool, damp climatic conditions than other grains. They farmed in open fields on the hillside terraces, at heights of 700–1,000 feet, fertilising the land by pasturing their livestock in common on the open-field strips after the crops had been harvested. However, the Wakefield manorial records reveal an abandonment of this custom when the cultivated area was extended by the assarting or clearing of the valley slopes below the main terraces, particularly during the early fourteenth century. This

Figure 2.3   Medieval grave cover, south porch, Halifax Parish Church, c.1150. A pair of cropper's shears inscribed alongside the elongated calvary cross on the tombstone provides the earliest surviving evidence of the textile industry in the parish of Halifax. The shears were used for trimming the surface of the woollen cloth after the cloth had been fulled. During the later medieval period Halifax emerged as a finishing centre for the local woollen industry. (Photograph courtesy of J. G. Washington)

process was stimulated either by the poor fertility of the cultivated soil or the pressure of population growth on the land.[10]

There is also growing evidence of textile production as a supplementary economic activity throughout Calderdale from the twelfth century. The earliest evidence of textile manufacture in Halifax is a twelfth-century grave cover bearing a crude representation of cropper's shears. Land charters confirm that cloth making was developing in Halifax during the thirteenth century, and the Wakefield Court Rolls from 1274 record both a range of textile occupational names such as websters (weavers), listers (dyers) and walkers (fullers) and the existence of features in the landscape associated with the finishing processes of woollen cloth, notably fulling mills in Warley in 1286, Sowerby in 1296, Halifax in 1306, Hebden Bridge in 1347, Heptonstall in 1382 and a tentercroft in Halifax in 1414.[11]

Halifax, with relatively poor soil, may have been slower to develop both arable cultivation and textile manufacture than some of its neighbouring settlements. The lay subsidy returns of 1334 certainly reveal considerably lower taxation assessments for Halifax than for the upland settlements of Calderdale, where more land had recently been brought into cultivation. Moreover, Halifax was also assessed at a significantly lower rate in 1334 than the manorial vills in the fertile lowland around Wakefield, where arable farming had been more extensively practised since the eleventh century, and the older textile producing centres of the county such as Ripon. Halifax was also slow to develop as a commercial centre, unlike neighbouring Elland, which having acquired a market charter during the reign of Edward II (1307–27) appears to have been a busier commercial centre than Halifax in the early fourteenth century. However, incidental evidence in the manorial records of tolls and penalties imposed for the concealment of forestallers suggests that Halifax was beginning to emerge as an unlicensed marketing centre for its periphery during this period.[12]

Table 2.1. *Lay Subsidy Returns, 1334 and 1379*

	1334		1379	
Halifax and Heptonstall	11s.	0d.	12s.	8d.
Sowerby and Soyland	16s.	0d.	12s.	8d.
Warley	16s.	0d.	8s.	0d.
Midgley	13s.	0d.	7s.	4d.
Wadsworth	16s.	0d.	13s.	0d.
Stansfield	16s.	0d.	13s.	0d.
Langfield	14s.	0d.	7s.	4d.
Wakefield	120s.	0d.	95s.	8d.

Sources: B. Jennings, *Pennine Valley* (Smith Settle, Otley: 1992), p. 42; J. Lister and J. H. Ogden, *Poll Tax (Lay Subsidy), 1379* (Halifax Antiquarian Society, Halifax: 1906), p. 39.

Both Halifax and its neighbouring settlements suffered a severe setback as a result of the Black Death, a catastrophic pandemic spread by fleas and rats which reached England from Asia in June 1348. Conservative estimates suggest a mortality rate of 33 to 40 per cent in Sowerby and Warley from the deadly bubonic plague, which had engulfed virtually the whole of the British Isles by December 1349. It has been calculated that in the Upper Calder Valley 40 to 50 per cent of land holdings were vacated by plague victims in 1349–50, when land clearance also came to an abrupt halt. In Halifax itself, plague claimed the lives of two successive vicars, Thomas Gaytington and Richard Ovenden, within the space of two months in 1349. There is also unequivocal evidence in the manorial rolls of a migration of labour from the parish in 1352, in contravention of the Statute of Labourers of 1351. Moreover, a return of 'the great pestilence' in 1361–62 claimed the life of another vicar of Halifax, John Stamford, and further plague epidemics in 1369 and 1375 also took their toll. Estimates of population derived from the lay subsidy returns and an early rental suggest a mere 220 souls resident in Halifax by 1379, rising to perhaps 313 by 1439.[13]

Halifax, like the other Calderdale settlements, appears to have recovered slowly from the impact of plague in the second half of the fourteenth century, when the village community contained few wealthy residents and manifested very little status differentiation within its social structure. Most Halifax women, for example, brewed their own ale at home, as the manorial records show many suffering penalties for doing so in contravention of statutory regulations. In 1379 none of the Halifax taxpayers was valued at more than a groat, the lowest levy in this graduated poll tax assessment, although only one beggar was granted exemption. Richard Robertson, lessee of the manorial fulling mill; John Milner, the tenant of the corn mill; and Robert Lister, the sole dyer within the town authorised by the lord of the manor, were all taxed at the same level as the rest of the non-mendicant inhabitants. Moreover, of the thirty-three property owners listed in a rental of 1439, no fewer than fifteen have been identified in the manorial rolls as serving terms of office as constable. The rental also reveals that one of the largest landowners in the village in 1439, Richard Peck, a silversmith, actually resided at Owram Hall in the neighbouring township of Southowram. The manorial tenant paying the highest rent in 1439 was Richard Lister, who held the property rented by Robert Lister in 1379, together with a number of other properties, including the pinfold, a compound for stray animals. His son and brother held shares in the fulling mill at North Bridge, where the family dyed cloth.[14]

Archaeological excavation of late-medieval housing sites in Halifax reveals predominantly simple, low-walled, one-roomed, open-hearthed, single-storeyed accommodation, built with timber, stone, rubble and clay. These dwellings are in marked contrast to the spacious, late-medieval, timber-framed yeomen clothier houses situated outside the township, with their massive timber-and-plaster firehoods and other lavish fittings. There are no finer surviving examples of such homes in England than these, apart from the Wealden houses of the prosperous yeomanry of Kent, confirming the view that living standards within Halifax itself were generally inferior to those of yeomen clothiers residing within its rural periphery. The predominance of northern gritty-wares among the pottery fragments recovered from the excavations of Halifax housing for this period further reinforces this impression of a lack of conspicuous consumption in Halifax itself.[15]

A 1439 rental for the township of Halifax, indicating the allotment of furlong strips or selions in the arable fields, reveals that by the early fifteenth century open-field arable cultivation was practised in the town fields. By the late fifteenth century, however, Halifax was gaining a growing reputation for the making and marketing of textiles. The ulnager's accounts, that is the records of fees paid to crown officials for measuring and sealing finished cloth, reveal that by 1469 the parish of Halifax was second only to Ripon in cloth production, contributing almost one third of the West Riding's total output of cloth. By 1473, Halifax had even outstripped Ripon, producing the highest total of cloth for the West Riding, five times the output of Leeds and eight times the output of Bradford. Moreover, the provision of spacious workshop and storage facilities in the aisled houses of yeomen clothiers in the Halifax area from the second half of the fifteenth century confirms the development of an organised system of textile production from the late fifteenth century.

The explanation of this success has been traditionally attributed to cheaper labour costs in the newer Pennine industrial centres, which were not subject to guild regulation; an abundance of fast-flowing, soft water for fulling; and the evolution of a highly cost-effective dual economy of textiles and farming in the Calder Valley in the late fifteenth century, which will be examined more fully in the next chapter. These developments also coincided with a more favourable economic climate for cloth exports following the Treaty of Utrecht in 1474 and peace with France in 1475. By this period, it appears that Halifax had become a centre for cloth finishing for a dependent rural periphery: no fewer than eight out of seventeen Halifax cloth tradesmen indicted at Lancaster in 1467, following an affray in Burnley, were engaged in fulling.[16]

Besides cloth production, other forms of economic activity were in evidence within Halifax's rural periphery. Manorial records and slag deposits provide evidence of a number of medieval iron-working sites in the Upper Calder Valley, and coal appears to have been mined for both domestic and industrial purposes from the thirteenth century. In 1274, Richard Nailer was granted permission to dig for coals at Hipperholme 'for forging'. Early fourteenth-century forges were located at Rastrick, Hipperholme and Erringden, and excavation and fieldwork has identified several medieval bloomery sites, including slag found beneath the floor of a late fifteenth-century timber-framed house at Boothtown, Northowram, and as surface deposits at Cinderhills, Siddal and Southowram. An innovative tilt or trip hammer, designated an 'oliver' in the manorial roll, was in operation in Warley in 1349. There is also evidence of a stone quarrying industry concentrated on the township of Northowram in the fourteenth and fifteenth centuries.[17]

This increasing economic activity stimulated the development of Halifax as a commercial centre in the late fifteenth century. The reference in the Lancaster indictments of 1467 to four tailors, three butchers, two glovers, two smiths, a mercer, weaver and cobbler in addition to seventeen cloth tradesmen, provides a snapshot of the commercial life of Halifax by this period. It reveals considerable commercial expansion since 1439 when a town rental specified one solitary shop, though both documents probably fail to reflect the full extent of commercial activity in Halifax in their respective periods. By 1470, John Lister, recognising that the increased economic activity within the parish had implications for Halifax's commercial development, proclaimed the 'fortunes of the place were to all intents and purposes made'. Modern research has tended to confirm Lister's conclusion.[18]

The emergence of Halifax as a commercial centre during the medieval period also owed much to its development as a centre of manorial and ecclesiastical administration. This helped to establish a number of connections between Halifax and its surrounding periphery. The combined manor of Halifax-cum-Heptonstall, a sub-manor of the royal manor of Wakefield, appears to have been granted by Henry I (1100–35) in 1106 to William de Warenne (d. 1138), second earl of Surrey, whose distinctive gold and blue chequered arms were later incorporated into the Halifax corporate seal. The sub-manor was later granted, with the advowson for the church, to Lewes Priory in East Sussex some time between 1106 and the issuing of a confirmation by William de Warenne, third earl of Surrey (d. 1148), in 1147. The principal seat of the earls of Warenne, who held the manor of Wakefield until the fourteenth century when it reverted to the crown, was located at Sandal Castle, and the nearby town and borough of Wakefield became the centre of manorial administration. However, the Wakefield manorial court travelled on circuit twice a year, usually in May and October. After 1274, the Wakefield court rolls record that it sat in Halifax at the Moot Hall, where it not only dealt with the administration of the demesne lands in the Upper Calder Valley, but also held court leet or tourn sessions, examining cases of criminal infringement of statutory or manorial law. These latter sessions, presided over by the earl's bailiff, heard cases involving tenants, both servile and free, of both the manor and the sub-manor. Territorial administration within the sub-manor was dealt with in separate sessions at the Moot Hall, presided over by the proctor of the monastic lords of the rectorial manor.

In addition, the earls of Warenne, as lords of the manor of Wakefield, enjoyed infangthief jurisdiction, that is the right to carry out summary trial and execution of thieves caught in the bailiwick of Sowerbyshire. The establishment of a prototype guillotine, or gibbet, as it was known locally, gained notoriety for the town, with some sixty-three recorded executions between 1286 and 1650. An apocryphal beggars' litany prayed: 'From Hull, Hell and Halifax, good Lord deliver us'. The regular meetings of the manorial courts, the occasional executions, and the obligation for demesne tenants to pay suit at the manorial corn and fulling mills provided opportunities for manorial tenants and members of their families to visit Halifax, thereby developing connections between the town and its immediate periphery.[19]

Although Halifax remained an outpost of manorial administration throughout the medieval period, by the twelfth century the township had also become the religious centre of a vast parish extending westwards across the Upper Calder Valley from Rastrick in the east as far as Stansfield and the Lancashire border, containing 23 townships and becoming second only in size to the Lancashire Pennine parish of Whalley. The black-robed monks of Lewes, a Benedictine community of the great Cluniac family (whose Sussex priory, founded in 1077 by William de Warenne (d. 1088), first earl

Figure 2.4 Halifax Moot Hall. The Wakefield Court Rolls confirm that meetings of the courts of the manor of Wakefield and sub-manor of Halifax-cum-Heptonstall were held in the Halifax Moot Hall from the late-thirteenth century. The building, which was originally timber-framed, was situated to the north-west of Halifax Parish Church in Nelson Street. During the medieval period, it was surrounded by a large common field called the Hallynge. By the 1920s, it was being used as a joiner's shop. It was demolished in 1956. (Photograph courtesy of S. Gee)

Figure 2.5 Halifax Gibbet. During the period from 1286 to 1650 some 63 felons were beheaded on the Halifax Gibbet, a prototype guillotine, under the infangthief jurisdiction of the lords of the manor of Wakefield in the bailiwick of Sowerbyshire. By 1856, according to William Camden, Halifax had become famous 'by reason of a law there whereby they behead straight-ways whosoever are taken in stealing'. This engraving shows the blade about to be released by a horse tethered to the scaffold. The original blade has been preserved at the Bankfield Museum and in 1974 a replica of the scaffold was erected on the original site of the executions in Gibbet Street. (Photograph: J. A. Hargreaves Collection)

of Surrey, was subsequently endowed with rents and fines from the de Warenne's Yorkshire estates, including the sub-manor of Halifax-cum-Heptonstall) had built the Norman church at Halifax around 1120. The church was administered largely by absentee rectors appointed by the Warennes in the twelfth and thirteenth centuries. Among them were such distinguished figures as John Talvace, friend of Archbishop Thomas Becket and later Archbishop of Lyons; Hubert Walter, later Archbishop of Canterbury; and William Champvent, later Bishop of Lausanne. The monks eventually obtained a papal bull permitting the appropriation of the rectory and the creation of a vicarage, which assigned the great tithes to the monks as rectors and the small tithes to the vicar. In 1272 Halifax received its first vicar, Ingelard Turbard, who undertook to reside in the vicarage provided for him.

By the late thirteenth century at least two parochial chapelries existed within the parish at Elland and Heptonstall, with chaplains appointed and paid by the vicar, and two other chapels-of-ease were created within the parish in the second half of the fifteenth century at Ripponden and Luddenden, with perpetual curates appointed by the vicar but paid by the chapelry. However, the requirement for attendance at the parish church for baptisms, marriages and burials and the celebration of mass on all feast days, the payment of customary dues, alms and tithes to the mother church, and the development of fairs associated with the patronal festival of St John the Baptist, established further connections between Halifax and its periphery.[20]

Manorial and ecclesiastical exigencies also contributed to the development of a route network centred upon Halifax, which further stimulated the commercial development of the town. The Wakefield Gate, sections of which have been preserved as a footpath, descended over the shoulder of Beacon Hill and crossed Clark Bridge into Halifax. It provided links for

Figure 2.6   The Wakefield Gate at Dark Lane between Hipperholme and Halifax photographed by W. B. Crump in 1924. This surviving section of the medieval route from Wakefield to Halifax followed the line of the most gradual incline up the ridge from Hipperholme to Halifax, descending into Halifax over the shoulder of Beacon Hill down Old Bank via Bank Bottom and Clark Bridge. The route continued past the Parish Church and through Woolshops, the Shambles and Old Market, carrying traffic from the manorial estates in Wakefield to the Upper Calder Valley, including hunting parties destined for the deer park in Erringden. As the textile trade developed supplies of raw wool and finished cloth were carried by pack-horses along the same route, which was also used by Sir Thomas Fairfax's troops after their disastrous defeat at the battle of Adwalton Moor in 1643. Condemned by Daniel Defoe in the early eighteenth century as 'so steep, so rugged, and sometimes too slippery' and 'exceedingly troublesome and dangerous' it was eventually replaced by new turnpike roads in 1741 and 1824. (Photograph courtesy of H. Armitage)

the major demesne holdings in the Upper Calder Valley, which included the important hunting grounds and cattle farms in Erringden Park, with the commercial and administrative centre of the manor at Wakefield. The road also formed part of an important trans-Pennine route, in particular for the transportation of salt from Cheshire to Yorkshire. There are also numerous references in the manorial rolls to kirkgates, early routes to the parish church, from such outlying townships as Hipperholme, Northo-wram, Southowram and Shelf, demonstrating the important influence of the church on the medieval road system. One route from Coley, still called Kirk Lane, joined the Wakefield Gate south of Hipperholme, and other routes from Hipperholme and Southowram crossed the Hebble by Clark Bridge, which derived its name from the constant traffic of clergy visiting the parish church during this period.[21]

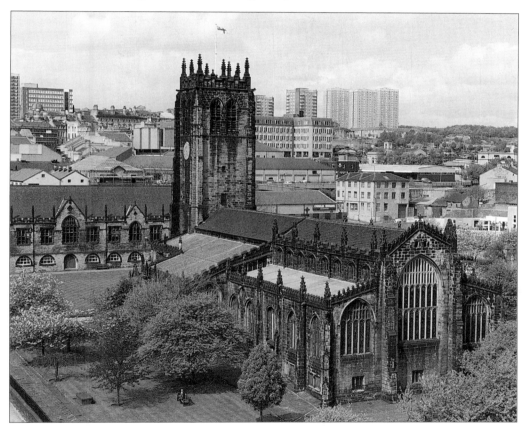

Figure 2.7   Halifax Parish Church of St John the Baptist, photographed from the east in 1994. Halifax Parish Church has been described by the architectural historian Peter Ryder as 'without a doubt the largest and most impressive of the late medieval churches in the county'. A sizeable early medieval church of probable cruciform construction was remodelled in phases in the perpendicular style during the fifteenth century, commencing with the rebuilding of the nave in 1437 and culminating in the construction of the huge west tower between 1450 and 1480. Sir George Gilbert Scott and his son John Oldrid Scott undertook a major restoration of the building in 1879. (Photograph courtesy of J. G. Washington)

Archaeologists now believe that the road and field layout of the medieval settlement of Halifax probably pre-dated the Norman Conquest, but how did the physical appearance of Halifax change in the period between 1066 and 1500? Settlement at Halifax followed an east-west axis, extending from the early focus of settlement around the church up the hillside to Cow Green, the likely site of Halifax Green. The open fields were laid out to the north and south of this axis. Rented tenements, or tofts, were built along the highway, each with a permanently allocated croft to the rear, and the open field beyond. Archaeological excavations between 1970 and 1975 revealed housing of late thirteenth-century construction on the south side of Northgate behind Woolshops. This was of high density and un-planned, and perhaps represents a period of late thirteenth-century expansion. However, this housing appears to have been demolished around 1300, perhaps following destruction by fire, when the precursors of Wade Street, Ann Street and Gaol Lane were laid out in typical grid plan devel-opment characteristic of growing settlements elsewhere during this period, such as Wakefield. After 1350, however, the village contracted dramatically, almost certainly as a consequence of the Black Death, and the new streets of tenements were abandoned.

Unfortunately, insufficient documentary evidence exists to corroborate the archaeological indicators of urban expansion in the late thirteenth century. However, taxation returns from the late fourteenth century, a rental of 1439 and a sixteenth-century manuscript recording the early reminiscences of John Waterhouse of Shibden (who died in 1540, aged 97) reveal a relatively small settlement. Waterhouse recalled 'a few straggling tenements built of wood, wattles and thatch', comprising some thirty-two houses, forty-four rented tenements and a cottage, nestling around the church, vicarage and market place, and extending westwards towards Cow Green. Robert Otes had a shop and some land at the west end of the churchyard, which had only recently been taken from the waste. The Moot Hall, a small timber-framed building, occupied a site to the north-west of the church, surrounded by the large common field called the Hallynge. The manorial fulling mill was situated further north, near North Bridge, and the manorial corn mill a short distance downstream, near Clark Bridge. The Mulcture Hall, where tolls were collected for corn ground at the mill, probably stood on a site to the north-east of the church, and the residence of the bailiff was east of the Hebble Brook at Bailey Hall. Two of the common fields, Blakelegynge and Southfeld, lay to the south of the church, the former in grass and the latter, accessed via Southgate, under the plough in 1439. The Neytherfeld, another large unenclosed common field, extended down to the 'miln-goit' and the Hebble Brook, while the Northfeld and Sydelynge lay on rising ground to the north-west.

Later in the fifteenth century, as cloth production began to expand within the parish, the market appears to have been moved westwards to

Figure 2.8
Pre-Reformation
font canopy,
Halifax Parish
Church, 1981. The
fifteenth century
font, situated at
the west end of
the nave, is
surmounted by an
intricately carved
wooden canopy,
which originally
would have been
painted in different
colours. Its design
incorporates the
carved York rose,
suggesting that it
originated before
the accession of
the Tudor dynasty
in 1485. In 1645
the font was
removed by
Scottish soldiers,
but the canopy
was preserved and
returned to the
church in 1661.
(Photograph
courtesy of
J. G. Washington)

a new site away from the church. The church itself, like other contemporary East Anglian churches, for example Blythburgh in Suffolk, was considerably enlarged in a magnificent perpendicular rebuilding, presumably in order to offer more spacious accommodation for the growing population of the parish. One architectural historian has claimed that it is 'without a doubt the largest and most impressive of the late medieval churches in the county' and it was certainly the most prominent building in Halifax by the end of the fifteenth century. The late thirteenth- and early fourteenth-century construction had apparently re-utilised considerable amounts of stone from the earlier Anglo-Norman building, including some chevron-moulded voussoirs, which are scattered around the building, but the fifteenth-century rectangular remodelling left little evidence of the fourteenth-century cruciform church, apart from a three-bay length of masonry in the north wall of the north aisle. Rebuilding of the nave appears to have commenced in 1437 and the construction of the huge west tower was completed over a thirty-year period from mid-century: the elderly John Waterhouse, later recalled that he had 'with many more children stood upon the first stone of the steeple'.[22]

By 1500, then, Halifax, while little more than a village in size and population, was developing into an exceptionally prosperous industrial village capable of supporting, with its rural periphery, a huge parish church. It was also beginning to display some of the characteristics of an urban centre, in a period otherwise widely characterised by urban stagnation or decline. Although documentary evidence for the settlement of Halifax only appears in the early twelfth century, archaeological and place-name evidence suggests intermittent occupation of the site and its hinterland from prehistoric times and continuity of settlement from before the Norman Conquest. During the twelfth and thirteenth centuries, Halifax emerged as a centre of ecclesiastical and manorial administration and increasingly during the later medieval period as a commercial and cloth finishing centre for the dispersed settlements of its rural periphery. However, for most of the period up to 1500 Halifax remained a Pennine backwater, due partly to the remoteness of its geographical location and partly to the devastating impact of the Black Death and other epidemics after 1349. Moreover, unlike Bradford and even neighbouring Elland, Halifax did not acquire a market charter during this period. Nevertheless, during the second half of the fifteenth century there was evidence of commercial expansion and Halifax became poised to achieve its later regional prominence in the early modern period.

CHAPTER THREE

'The inhabitants do altogether live by cloth making': Halifax and its hinterland, 1500–1750

Halifax and the regional economy

The population of the township of Halifax grew from a mere 313 in 1439 to perhaps 2,600 by 1566, 4,400 in 1641–2 and 5,000 in 1743. Moreover, it is also evident that during this period the population of the parish of Halifax, covering a wider area, grew even faster, from about 1,000 in 1439 to 8,500 by 1548, 20,000 in 1630 and 31,000 in 1743, since the township's share of the parish population decreased from nearly one third in the mid-sixteenth century, to barely over one-fifth in the mid-seventeenth century to around one-sixth in the mid-eighteenth century. This growth rate was considerably higher than the national average, especially during the period from 1650 to 1750, but was not steady. There were setbacks caused, for example, by epidemics of sweating sickness in 1551, typhus fever in 1587–88 and bubonic plague in 1631 and 1645.[1] But there were also spectacular periods of growth which attracted contemporary comment. The Elizabethan antiquary, William Camden, recalled that some inhabitants of the parish had boasted to him in the early 1580s that the parish population of some 12,000 people amounted to 'more men and women than other living creatures' and the journalist and novelist, Daniel Defoe, recorded in 1725 that the parish population had 'increased one fourth, at least, within the last 40 years'.[2] In addition, analysis of birth and death rates from parish registers and patterns of migration from poor law settlement certificates and removal orders suggests that migration into the area rather than natural increase was the principal cause of population growth during the late seventeenth and early eighteenth centuries.[3]

This chapter will seek to explain why increasing numbers of immigrants were attracted to the parish of Halifax after 1500, identifying the key elements within the regional economy and analysing how they contributed to the growth of Halifax as an urban centre for its hinterland. As the parish recovered from the impact of plague and pestilence from the late fifteenth century, it did not return to a precarious medieval agrarian economy but developed a more sustainable dual economy of textiles and farming, while

Figure 3.1
Halifax, 1500–1750.

the township of Halifax developed as the commercial and service centre for its increasingly prosperous rural periphery. Both contemporaries and modern historians have professed amazement that a major cloth making industry developed in the bleak inhospitable countryside of the Upper Calder Valley, with its relatively poor access to wool supplies and cloth markets. William Camden, writing in 1586, trumpeted the achievement as one of the wonders of the Tudor Age, while a modern historian of Yorkshire, Professor David Hey, writing in 1986, pronounced it 'the Halifax miracle'.[4]

Various environmental, social and economic explanations have long been adduced to account for the astonishingly rapid growth of cloth making from an initially low level in the rural hinterland of Halifax in the late fifteenth and early sixteenth centuries, in contrast to its decline in the older urban centres of the county such as Beverley, Ripon and York. In 1561, a York corporation minute book recorded ruefully the exodus of the city's weavers to Halifax, Leeds and Wakefield, where they had conveniently-situated 'water mills', a plentiful supply of cheap labour and fuel 'which is in this city very dear and wanting'. The Upper Calder Valley, with its higher than average rainfall and precipitous terrain, was particularly well-endowed with soft water for scouring and dyeing, and fast-flowing streams to power the fulling mills, as well as an abundance of peat and timber for fuel. Here, heavy wooden hammers pounded the woven cloth with fuller's earth to bond its fibres together and to clean it. This was the earliest application of mechanisation to the manufacture of woollen cloth, an industry which was otherwise slow to adopt technological innovation.[5]

Moreover, in the remote uplands of Calderdale, entry into the industry was not governed by the restrictive guild regulations which dominated the textile industries of the declining urban centres, and it required relatively little initial capital investment. It was possible for spinners and weavers with limited capital resources to purchase spinning wheels and looms for use in their own homes, since the cost of such basic equipment was considerably lower than local contemporary average prices for livestock. Labour costs were also cheap, because most of the Calderdale clothiers relied on the labour of their own families, supplemented occasionally by that of apprentices and journeymen. A kersey, the staple cloth of the Halifax area from the fourteenth century, could conveniently be woven in the interval of time between the weekly cloth markets, thus providing a regular income from a small investment in the raw wool, which was purchased in small quantities at the markets from 'broggers' or wool dealers.[6]

Historians have also emphasised the significance of demographic, tenurial and psychological factors, operating in conjunction with climate and topography, as explanations for the rapid growth of the textile industry in the Upper Calder Valley. Professor Joan Thirsk and others have observed that a flexible system of partible or divisible inheritance developed as an alternative to primogeniture in the remote uplands of the manor of Wakefield. These equitable bequests of land between the surviving sons of customary manorial tenants meant that younger sons remained within the locality after marriage. However, this created a pressure of population on the means of subsistence in an agriculturally unproductive area and stimulated the early development of weaving to supplement family incomes. Moreover, it has also been suggested that the perennial struggle with an intractable environment fostered a spirit of 'unyielding industry', which was further reinforced by Puritan preaching during the English Reformation.[7]

Perhaps the most reliable indicator of the timing and pace of the acceleration of industrial production is the steady expansion of fulling capacity in the Upper Calder Valley from the early fifteenth century. The rate of expansion quickened from the early sixteenth century, so that by 1640 there were an estimated eighteen to twenty fulling mills in the parish of Halifax. An examination of late fifteenth- and early sixteenth-century taxation returns, manorial records, chantry surveys and the distribution of aisled houses confirms the growing prosperity of parts of the parish and supports the proposition of Herbert Heaton, the historian of the Yorkshire woollen and worsted industries, that Halifax parish, rather than anywhere else in Yorkshire, was the stronghold of the textile industry from the fifteenth century onwards. Bequests for the improvement of highways; the rebuilding of bridges in stone; the construction of paved packhorse causeways; the provision of additional 'free chapels'; the casing of existing timber-framed houses in stone and the building of impressive new stone residences provide further evidence of increasing trade, traffic and prosperity in the Calder Valley during the sixteenth and early seventeenth centuries.[8]

The primary textile products manufactured in the Upper Calder Valley during this period were kerseys, cheap coarse narrow woollen cloths used particularly for hose, outer garments and, increasingly from the late seventeenth century, for military uniforms. Wills from the early sixteenth century contain numerous references to textile materials and equipment, by which time the market industry was well established. During the sixteenth century, as the woollen trade of Kersey in Suffolk decayed, the Upper Calder Valley became the largest producer of kersey cloths in England, exporting them all over western Europe via the port of Hull. Occasionally, however, there were complaints about the quality of local cloth, especially as a consequence of overstretching on tenters or mixing short fibre flocks with the longer-fibred wool normally used. For example, in 1533 a commission set up by Henry VIII to enquire into this malpractice led to the fining of 282 clothiers from the parish of Halifax.[9]

When the national economy entered a period of relative decline about half way through the reign of Henry VIII from which it did not recover until midway through the reign of Elizabeth, statutes of 1545 and 1552 tried to eliminate middlemen dealing in wool in order to minimise the cost of the product to the consumer. However, such middlemen occupied an essential role in the pattern of industrial organisation in Calderdale, and Halifax became one of the few districts to secure formal exemption from the effects of the legislation. The preamble to the 1555 Halifax Act proclaimed famously that the inhabitants of the parish 'altogether do live by cloth making' and explained that the majority of inhabitants being unable

> to keep a horse to carry wool, nor yet to buy much wool at once, had ever used only to repair to the town of Halifax ... and there to buy from the wool driver some a stone, some two, and some three or four, according to their ability, and to carry the same to their houses some three, four, five or six miles off, upon their heads and backs, and so to make and convert the same either into yarn or cloth, and to sell the same and so to buy more wool.[10]

The legislative protection enabled the woollen industry to prosper. In 1588 a correspondent informed the Vicar of Leeds that 'at Halifax there is no cloth made but yard broad kerseys', adding that they wove a fine wool, mostly from Lincolnshire, selling their coarse wool 'to the men of Rochdale'. Moreover, it also enabled Halifax to continue to grow as a marketing centre for both its hinterland and a wider region.[11]

During the second half of the seventeenth century local manufacturers diversified into worsteds, cloth woven from long wools, imported from Lincolnshire and Leicestershire along the Aire and Calder Navigation, for reasons which have never fully been explained. It is possible that the change was stimulated by stagnating markets for coarser woollen cloth or by Norfolk merchants putting out work for spinning in the parish in the later seventeenth century, encouraging local clothiers to experiment with worsted weaving. Increasing amounts of worsted equipment and cloth certainly appear in local inventories after 1690. By 1706, Joseph Holroyd, a local clothier, was engaged in a large trade in bays, cloth with a worsted warp and a woollen weft, and in 1715 an indenture of apprenticeship reveals that James Haggas was bound apprentice with John Jackson of Halifax to learn the art of weaving shalloons, light worsted fabrics. A decade later when Daniel Defoe, the foremost industrial commentator of the age, visited Halifax he estimated that the parish was producing 100,000 pieces of shalloons yearly. However, expansion of worsted production during this period remained sporadic. In 1738 Samuel Hill, the Soyland clothier, wrote despondently that he was 'perfectly sick of the little or no hopes of the shalloon business', but by 1747 he had achieved a remarkable annual turn-over of over £35,000, exporting cloth to Amsterdam, Rotterdam, Utrecht, Antwerp, Bremen and St Petersburg. By 1750, then, Halifax was not only an important centre for the manufacture of woollen kerseys, but also the most important worsted manufacturing centre in the West Riding and by 1770 worsted production in Halifax and its hinterland had reached the same level as that of Norwich.[12]

The increasing preoccupation with textile manufacture meant that ag-riculture eventually came to be regarded as a mere supplement to income and that clothiers came to depend upon their sales of cloth to buy food, hence making the area less self-sufficient and more concerned with external trade. Commenting on the scale of farming in the parish of Halifax by the early eighteenth century, Daniel Defoe observed that 'they scarce sow corn enough for their cocks and hens'. Notwithstanding his observation that 'every manufacturer generally keeps a cow or two, or more, for his family', he concluded also that 'as to beef and mutton, they feed little or none', obtaining the bulk of their provisions 'from other parts of the country'.[13] Average landholdings in the parish remained small through-out the sixteenth and seventeenth centuries and the enclosure movement during this period did not result in a substantial increase in land under cultivation. Indeed, by the sixteenth and seventeenth centuries much of the corn consumed by the community was probably imported, although testamentary evidence reveals that oats and rye were grown locally. Many land deeds during this period also refer to a kitchen garden, supplying peas, beans and other vegetables for the family, and bequests were also often made of hives and swarms of bees. Sixteenth-century wills reveal that cattle were grazed in the township of Halifax and at least one chapman, Isaac Bates of Halifax, became interested in cattle farming as an investment, for in his will of 1608 he noted that he had spent £40 on cows and heifers. Some thirty other wills provide evidence of extensive sheep farming, and sheep and pigs are frequently referred to in presentments made at the manor courts. Animals were pastured on the steeper hillsides and the common pastures around the developing town of Halifax, although by the mid-eighteenth century most of the township of Halifax was systematically enclosed, including Halifax Moor.[14]

Land within Halifax's rural periphery was also increasingly exploited, however, for its coal and mineral deposits during the sixteenth and seventeenth centuries. There is evidence of coal mining at Hipperholme, Northowram, Ovenden, Shelf and Sowerby, where natural drainage assisted both open-cast and underground mining operations. In 1582 Queen Elizabeth I granted all the coal held by the crown in Northowram and a mine in Sowerby to Henry Farrer of Midgley. The manorial court in

Figure 3.2   Horse gin, West Riding Folk Museum, Shibden Hall. Daniel Defoe observed horses carrying coal from hilltop seams when he travelled through Halifax in the early eighteenth century and in 1726 a horse gin was evidently in use at Shibden to wind coal up to the surface. The twentieth-century museum reconstruction shows a shire horse from Stone Trough Brewery harnessed to a capstan so that as the horse moved round in a circle the winding machinery rotated raising the coal from the mine. (Photograph courtesy of H. Armitage)

October 1608 ordered that coalpits alongside the road in Wakefield Bank be filled in by Christmas because 'man and horse cannot travel but in great danger', and in the following year requested the inhabitants of Shelf 'to fill or fence about their pits'. Occupational analysis of marriage records if the mid-seventeenth century has also identified approximately three per cent of males in the parish of Halifax as colliers. Moreover, the probate inventory of Charles Best, yeoman clothier, of Woodend, Hipperholme, who died in 1723, reveals that he was in both farming and working 'coal pits on Norwood Green'. Later, Defoe observed horses carrying coal from hilltop seams, and in 1726 a horse gin was evidently in use at Shibden to wind coal up to the surface.[15]

Conveniently located reserves of quality gritstone and sandstone sustained the Great Rebuilding, which occurred earlier and was more prolonged in Calderdale than in other parts of West Yorkshire and stimulated the development of skills in masonry which local craftsmen utilised far beyond the parish of Halifax. In 1579 slate-stones were being quarried at Northowram by Edward Carey, and references abound in manorial records and churchwardens' accounts to stone delivery within the locality. Further afield, Halifax builders, notably John Akroyd (1556–1613) and John Bentley (1574–1615) were responsible for construction work for John Savile at Bradley Hall and Methley Hall and, under the patronage of Sir Henry Savile, at Oxford, including work on the Bodleian Library and on the fellows' quadrangle at Merton College. Nearer home, prosperous clothiers such as James Murgatroyd of Warley built a succession of impressive houses in the vernacular style, including Haigh House, Warley (1631); Yew Tree (1643), Ovenden Wood (1643) and Kershaw House, Midgley (1650).[16] Local clay and coal was also utilised in the seventeenth century in the development of a regionally important earthenware industry and a distinctive local pottery industry in Calderdale, the latter centred on Howcans, near Ovenden. So Halifax and its hinterland, although predominantly identified with cloth making after 1500, remained an area of diversified economic activity.[17]

There is, however, no evidence of the primary production of iron in Calderdale during the period 1500–1750, even though growing supplies of iron equipment such as cropping shears and tenterhooks were required by textile workers. Charcoal blast furnaces (which gradually replaced medieval bloomeries from the fifteenth century) at Holme in Cliviger and at Colnebridge, outside the parish, supplied Calderdale ironworkers. The forge at Colnebridge was of monastic origin, but later became part of the extensive Spencer syndicate, a partnership which dominated the iron industry of West Yorkshire and held the local monopoly of iron production during the seventeenth and eighteenth centuries. But there is some evidence of secondary iron production in Calderdale during this period. Grace Bolton of Skircoat, widow of Laurence Bolton, shearmaker, in her will of 1594 entrusted her brother Robert with the task of training her two sons in 'the

craft and science of making and setting shears'. There is also evidence of
nail-making at Halifax in the seventeenth century and wire drawing at
Brighouse in the early eighteenth century.[18]

County rate assessments reveal the growing prosperity of Halifax over
its parochial out-townships by the end of the sixteenth century as the town
developed into the market centre for a range of goods produced regionally,
especially textiles. In an attempt to gain revenue from the expanding local
economy, the Waterhouse family of Shibden Hall had provided Cloth Halls
for the town by the late sixteenth century, which were described in a lease
of 1562 as 'Greater and Lesser Blackwell Halls' and pre-dated the Cloth
Halls of Leeds, Bradford and Huddersfield. By the early seventeenth century
Halifax, which was granted permission to hold a wool market in 1617, was
the sole commercial centre in the parish. It was subsequently described as

Figure 3.3   Shibden Hall, Halifax, 1996. The original timber-framed house was built by William Otes in
the early fifteenth century and remained in the Otes family for the remainder of the century. In 1505 it
passed through marriage to the Saviles and in 1522 to the Waterhouses, in whose possession it remained
until 1612. The Waterhouses collected tithes for the Priors of Lewes and their lay successors after the
dissolution of the monasteries. They ultimately became lords of the sub-manor of Halifax-cum-Heptonstall
and one of the wealthiest and most influential local families in the sixteenth century, when the house was
modified and extended to the rear. Sections of the south front were encased in stone in the seventeenth
century and a tower and right wing added by Anne Lister in the early nineteenth century. (Photograph
courtesy of J. G. Washington)

a market town in quarter sessions records and besides providing markets for cloth and wool, it already provided an extensive and growing market for provisions. Indeed, one contemporary, James Ryder, had written to Lord Burghley in 1589: 'it is incredible how far the town of Halifax excels York in uttering much and good meat'.[19]

By the early seventeenth century, Halifax was clearly becoming a commercial rival not only of older urban textile manufacturing centres such as York but also newer industrial centres such as Leeds and Wakefield. Indeed, when bills were introduced into Parliament in 1621 and 1626 to make the river Calder navigable to Halifax, they were blocked following intervention by the City of York, supported by the other two market towns. The failure to improve the Calder was a setback for the economic expansion of Halifax, since access to the town by road was often difficult. When Halifax clothiers sent in petitions of support for the improvement of the Aire and Calder Navigation in 1698, they stressed the poor condition of the pre-turnpiked roads, complaining that 'they are forced to stay two months sometimes until the roads are passable to market and many times the goods receive considerable damage through the badness of the roads by overturning.'[20] Celia Fiennes (1662–1741), an experienced traveller, was discouraged from visiting Halifax in 1698 because the roads to it were 'so stony and difficult', and Daniel Defoe later provided a graphic description of some of the problems he encountered on leaving the town:

> We quitted Halifax not without some astonishment at its situation, being so surrounded with hills and those so high, as ... makes the coming in and going out of it exceedingly troublesome, and indeed for carriages hardly practicable ... particularly the hill which they go up to come out of the town eastwards towards Leeds ... which ... is so steep, so rugged, and sometimes so slippery, that, to a town of so much business as this, 'tis exceedingly troublesome and dangerous.[21]

Remarkably, however, the commercial development of Halifax continued apace, despite the problems of accessibility. The 1686 War Office returns of the number of guest beds and stabling in towns and villages throughout England reveal that Halifax with 130 beds and stabling for 306 horses had more accommodation for visitors than Ripon, Thirsk, Richmond and Pontefract.[22] Indeed, Defoe himself acknowledged that 'multitudes of people' crowded into the town on a market-day both 'to sell their manufactures' and 'to buy provisions'. He concluded that 'so great is the confluence of people hither, that except Leeds and Wakefield, nothing in all the north of England can come near it'.[23] The network of local and regional packhorse routes continued to sustain the development of Halifax as a commercial and service centre for its hinterland, but new turnpike links with the town and a wider region were also developed in the early eighteenth century. In 1735 the Rochdale-Elland turnpike via Halifax became the first stretch of turnpiked road in West Yorkshire and one of the earliest turnpike schemes in England. In 1740–41 further turnpike links were established between Leeds and Elland, between Leeds, Bradford and Halifax and between Wakefield and Halifax.[24]

Social structure, occupations and living standards

The development of Halifax as a commercial and service centre for its rural hinterland during the period from 1500 to 1750 shaped the social structure, occupations and living standards of the emerging urban community. There evolved within the market town a relatively undifferentiated social structure with a substantial nucleus of middling people, only a limited gentry presence, a declining proportion of labourers, and fluctuating numbers of poor.

The Saviles of Thornhill and Rufford Abbey, owners of almost half the townships of the parish of Halifax, had moved away to residences on their other geographically less remote estates by the end of the sixteenth century. Moreover, since they owned very little land in the township of Halifax, they played a less significant role in the development of the town than they did in either Leeds or Wakefield. Other local gentry families who held land in the township of Halifax during this period, including the Farrers of Midgley, the Gledhills of Barkisland, the Lacys of Brearley, the Sunderlands of High Sunderland, and the Waterhouses and Listers of Shibden Hall, also preferred to reside around the town's rural periphery rather than in the town itself. Indeed, the wealthiest resident in the town by the mid-sixteenth century was Dr Robert Holdsworth, the last vicar of Halifax to be appointed by the Cluniac Priors of Lewes to the rich benefice of Halifax in 1526. He was brutally murdered by intruders at the vicarage, which had been broken into by robbers on no fewer than four previous occasions. He died possessed of fifteen houses, six cottages and a personal estate of 250 acres. However, his prosperous family background, his alleged misappropriation of charitable funds designed for the benefit of the parish, and his involvement in local gentry feuds made him very untypical of other parochial clergy during the early modern period. Following the dissolution of the monasteries, the rectory sub-manor of Halifax-cum-Heptonstall passed eventually to the Waterhouses of Shibden Hall in 1545 and subsequently to the Ingrams of Temple Newsam in 1609. Both these families were far more conspicuous than the Saviles in the commercial exploitation of their land and properties in the town, particularly Sir Arthur Ingram (1565–1642), but in no sense was Halifax a town socially dominated by the landed gentry in the early modern period.

In the lay subsidy return for 1545, fewer individuals from the township of Halifax were taxed than from the parochial out-townships of Sowerby and Warley, and by 1588 Northowram had also more individuals liable for

Figure 3.4
Barkisland Hall.
This magnificent
three-storeyed
prodigy house was
completed in 1638
by John and Sarah
Gledhill, whose
initials are
inscribed upon the
porch. John
Gledhill's father,
Thomas, was one
of the highest
taxpayers in the
township of
Barkisland and had
been granted a
coat of arms in
1612. His wife,
Sarah, was the
daughter of
William Horton of
the Howroyd,
Barkisland. The
doorway is flanked
by Doric and Ionic
fluted columns and
surmounted by a
rose window, one
of only four which
have survived in
Calderdale. The
parlours in the
wings and many of
the upper
chambers, with
their multi-light
mullions and
transoms, were
heated by fire-
places served by a
large number of
flues. Richard
Gledhill was later
knighted by the
Earl of Newcastle
and served in the
royalist army in the
Civil War, but was
killed at Marston
Moor in July 1644.
(Photograph
courtesy of Halifax
Antiquarian Society)

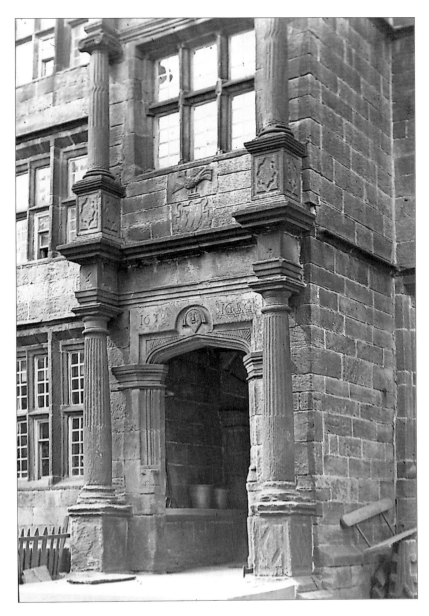

tax than Halifax. By the reign of Charles I even townships like barren Langfield were ranking with Halifax in the amount of subsidy paid. A similar pattern also emerges from other sources, including parish assessments for the relief of the poor and fines for distraint of knighthood. In 1630, of 215 members of the West Riding gentry fined for distraint of knighthood by Charles I, no fewer than 37 per cent were from the parish of Halifax, an emerging Puritan stronghold. However, none of the wealthiest landed proprietors within the parish resided in the township of Halifax, which furnished the crown with a mere £90 of the total fines for the parish, which amounted to £1,034 6s. 8d. Of the seven Halifax landowners incurring fines, Thomas Blackwood, who had built a house on Halifax Moor in 1617, was the wealthiest, contributing £20 to the royal coffers, followed by Robert Exley, Richard Barrowclough and Nathaniel Waterhouse, who each suffered fines of £13 6s. 8d., confirming that the town was not dominated by a wealthy elite during the sixteenth and seventeenth centuries.[25]

Indeed, a study of local wills from the period 1558 to 1640 reveals a higher concentration of butchers, shoemakers, tanners and glovers in the social and occupational structure of the township of Halifax than in the parochial out-townships. However, most urban artisans were engaged in the cloth trade, outnumbering the yeomen, who were somewhat higher up the social scale. Moreover, between 1609 and 1663 the tenurial structure of the manor changed dramatically due to the enfranchisement of copy-holders. Of around 200 copyholders in the manor in the late 1580s over 150 had been enfranchised by the late 1650s, indicating an enhancement of the legal and social standing of many of the town's inhabitants during the first half of the seventeenth century. Indeed, a rental of 1702 contains very few references to copyhold property and Dr Alan Betteridge has concluded that 'the number of freeholders in relation to copyholders may have been greater in Halifax, at least during the early seventeenth century, than in many northern communities', suggesting that the town of Halifax was dominated more by independent artisans or freeholders than gentry families.[26]

Marriage records suggest that approximately half of those above the status of labourer in Halifax in the mid-seventeenth century were involved in the cloth trade, clothiers and tailors predominating. Indeed, by the 1690s only 9 per cent of those whose occupations are recorded in their wills worked outside the textile industry or the basic craft and provision trades such as carpentry, masonry and baking. These included a chapman, nailer, clockmaker, innkeepers, linen drapers, mercers, apothecaries, shoemakers and tailors. By the mid-eighteenth century, however, while over half the trades remained connected with textiles, there had been a dramatic fall in the number of clothiers in the town. A growing proportion of croppers, however, reflected the development of the town as a cloth finishing centre, while a rising number of woolcombers, provided an index of the growth of the worsted industry since the mid-seventeenth century. The decline of the small independent clothier may have been indicative of a trend towards increased specialisation within the textile industry under the control of a wealthier and economically more dominant entrepreneurial class, of whom Samuel Hill (1677–1759) of Soyland, who left an estate valued at £20,000, was the most outstandingly successful local example. The emergence of shoemakers, masons, joiners and carpenters as more significant occupa-tional groups was undoubtedly a product of the growth of Halifax as a service centre in the early eighteenth century. Moreover, an increase in the number of non-traditional craft occupations recorded in local wills reflects a rising demand for a wider range of consumer goods from the residents of Halifax and its hinterland. Occupations such as innkeeper, cordwainer, linen draper, grocer and shopkeeper were relatively common by the mid-eighteenth century, but more unusual trades such as breeches maker, saddler and staymaker were also making an appearance.[27]

In addition, churchwardens' accounts plus literary and testamentary sources reveal a growing professional class, which included apothecaries, doctors, schoolmasters, ministers of religion, lawyers and a coroner, arising from the development of Halifax as a service centre for a wider community during this period. The main business of local lawyers, many of whom were primarily scriveners, was conveyancing and wills. For example, John Hargreaves and his son of the same name, who practised in Halifax in the late seventeenth century, were very active in drawing up wills and deeds, but did not undertake more complicated legal work. During the eighteenth century, however, both the number of lawyers practising in the parish and the range of services that they offered increased dramatically. The number of schoolmasters and bookkeepers also increased, but it was not until the late 1730s that any of the surviving commercial account books show the influence of a bookkeeper's diligence. The growth of the professions and growing prosperity of the middling sort has led Dr John Smail to conclude that in Halifax 'by the mid-eighteenth century there was a self-conscious middle class demanding and receiving local political power and social prestige and transforming the social world in which they lived'.[28]

Marriage registers suggest that labourers constituted the town's largest single occupational group in the mid-seventeenth century, some of whom, no doubt, on occasions became dependent on charity or poor relief. Vagrants also created problems from time to time. Manorial officials in the 1530s and 1580s and parochial officials in the 1620s were concerned about the influx of vagrants into the town, and during the 1630s pauper children were being sent to Halifax from as far afield as Westmorland to serve apprenticeships. There were also periods when the number of paupers within the town reached alarming proportions. At the peak of an epidemic of bubonic plague in October 1645, the West Riding justices of the peace allotted the sum of £66 13s. 4d. for Halifax and Northowram, recognising that 'there are 1,632 poor people that live upon charity'. Moreover, in 1664, the hearth tax returns for the township of Halifax reveal no fewer than 41 per cent of householders exempted from the tax on grounds of poverty. However, later the poor were less in evidence. When Defoe visited Halifax in the early eighteenth century, he observed that there was 'not a beggar, not an idle person to be seen, except here and there an almshouse, where people ancient, decrepit, and past labour might be found'. In the mid-eighteenth-century labourers still formed the largest occupational group

Figure 3.5   The Oak Room, Old Cock Hotel, Southgate, Halifax. A rare survival of an Elizabethan room from a northern town. Originally a town house built in the 1580s by William Savile of Copley following his marriage to Isabel Lacy in 1575, the Old Cock has been an inn since 1668. The central feature of the impressive oak-panelled chamber is an elaborately carved oak overmantel, dated 1581, with inlaid panels set inside arcades separated by grotesque caryatids. The Savile arms flanked by royal supporters in the plasterwork over the fireplace was probably added in the 1630s. The room is lit by a large transomed window of 20 lights infilled with colourful stained glass. David Hartley the notorious counterfeiter was arrested in this room in 1769 and the meeting which gave birth to the Halifax Permanent Benefit Building Society was held here in December 1852. (Photograph courtesy of Halifax plc)

in the town, although their numbers in relation to the total population had apparently declined.[29]

Evidence from property deeds, hearth tax returns and wills suggests some differentiation in the quality of housing in Halifax in the early modern period. The townhouse of a more prosperous artisan of the sixteenth century normally consisted of a parlour, a shop, an entrance with rooms above and a basement, but from the late sixteenth century as the population grew an increasing number of property deeds included references to the division of houses into several apartments. Husbandmen would have leased small cottages, perhaps incorporating barns, or small houses with two or three rooms on the ground floor and upper chambers reached by a ladder. Labourers would have lived in single-storey cottages of one or two rooms. The hearth tax returns of 1664 reveal that the township of Halifax contained no fewer than 30 per cent of houses with three or more hearths, including 7 per cent with six or more, indicating fairly spacious living accommodation of at least seven to nine rooms. However, they also disclose that Halifax possessed the second largest number of poorer quality non-chargeable houses in the parish offering more limited accommodation.[30]

Nevertheless, Dr John Smail has argued that compared with other communities such as the Essex village of Terling, the hearth tax returns of 1664 suggest that Halifax's social structure was relatively undifferentiated and that the probate inventories confirm a relatively homogeneous material culture across a broad social spectrum. Basic household furnishings such as tables, chairs, stools, cooking utensils, show some slight variations in value amongst the deceased, but the inventories reveal a fairly widespread ownership of luxury goods in late seventeenth-century Halifax. Out of a total of 292 inventories from the period between 1690 and 1699, almost a third owned clocks and linen, a quarter owned glass cases and mirrors and a sixth owned white plate. Some items, however, appeared only in the inventories of the wealthier members of the community. Only three house-holds, for example, owned chairs upholstered with 'russia leather', only nine had curtains on their windows, and only seven had maps decorating their walls.[31]

The pattern of births, marriages and deaths recorded in the parish registers suggests that Halifax and its hinterland suffered sharp rises in mortality as a result of epidemics in the sixteenth and early seventeenth centuries. An outbreak of typhus fever in Halifax during 1587–8 resulted in a dramatic rise in the number of burials, which remained at three or four times the monthly average for a period of four months and, in the space of five months, a bubonic plague epidemic in 1645 claimed no fewer than 529 victims in Halifax and Northowram. Although epidemics may have been less serious after the 1680s, the limited data obtained from tombstone inscriptions for the period 1701 to 1760, reveal that infant mortality was dramatically high even for the better off, with more than 25 per cent of deaths occurring in children under five. Within the age-group 25–45, mortality was slightly higher among women than men. However, women who survived beyond the child-bearing age tended to live longer than their male contemporaries, who often died in their early sixties. Very elderly members of the community were rare, although small numbers of both sexes survived into their seventies and eighties. However, the mean age at death in these records of 35.1 years probably accounts for the large proportion of orphans in local society during this period. Local residents who survived into adulthood, however, appeared healthy to contemporary observers. The Revd Thomas Wright, a curate at Halifax Parish Church, writing in 1738, remarked that 'the air is fresh and sharp, but good and wholesome, as may be seen by the clear and sound complexion of the natives'.[32]

Religion and politics

William and Sarah Sheils have argued that 'in Halifax and its hinterland the Reformation years were disruptive ones' since the dissolution of the chantries and the disendowment of the extensive network of proprietary chapels-of-ease in the vast parish in 1548 'posed considerable problems for the inhabitants of Halifax', diminishing the pastoral provision which had been built up over the previous century. Changes in religious belief and practice affected the local community in many different ways during the period 1500–1750, when religion undoubtedly became the most keenly contested issue in the locality. Halifax as the centre of ecclesiastical admin-istration for its hinterland inevitably became the focal point for much of this religious controversy, which spilled over into Civil War fighting in the

1640s. Moreover, the restoration of the monarchy in 1660 produced an uneasy settlement between the Established Church and Protestant Non-conformity, which ensured the continuation of religious divisions and social tensions in Halifax throughout the period up to 1750.[33]

One of the leading figures of the pre-Reformation Church, William Rokeby, Vicar of Halifax (1502–21) and Archbishop of Dublin (1511–21), who had celebrated mass at Westminster Abbey when Thomas Wolsey received his cardinal's hat in 1515 and officiated at the baptism of Mary Tudor in 1516, returned to Halifax to die in 1521. He left instructions that his heart be entombed in a lead casket beneath the chancel of Halifax Parish Church and made a bequest for the building of a chantry chapel on the north side of the church. In 1535, Dr Robert Holdsworth, Vicar of Halifax 1525–56, who, in accordance with his father's wish, had built another chantry on the south side of Halifax Parish Church, allegedly declared in the year following Henry VIII's breach with Rome: 'if the king reign any space he will take all that ever we have ... and therefore I pray God send him a short reign'. He was the last Vicar of Halifax to be appointed by the Prior of Lewes. In 1537 the Cluniac priory was dissolved and its estates, including the rectory sub-manor of Halifax and Heptonstall, transferred to Thomas Cromwell. On Cromwell's disgrace and execution they passed, with the advowson, to Anne of Cleves and then to the crown, when Henry's marriage to Anne was dissolved.[34]

If minor changes to the preambles of Halifax wills after 1526 reflect changing scribal practice, those of William Holmes and Robert Thomson, drafted in 1538, reveal a deliberate Protestant emphasis. Both rejected the intercession of the saints, commending their respective souls 'unto Christ Jesu, my maker and redeemer, in whom, and by the merits of whose blessed passion, is all my whole trust of clean remission of all my sins'. In 1538, Holdsworth, a theological conservative and worldly pluralist, submissively placed an English Bible in Halifax Parish Church and began the Halifax Parish Registers. But in the same year Robert Ferrar, prior of Nostell and a native of the parish of Halifax, writing to Thomas Cromwell, bemoaned the lack of Protestant preachers in Halifax and other West Riding towns, despite the fact that 'the people were hungrily desirous to hear and learn'. However, an erosion of belief in the importance of masses for the dead is revealed in the private dissolution of some chantry foundations and con-fiscation of their endowments before 1548. These included the endowment of the Frith chantry in Halifax Parish Church, which was lost to Sir Edmund Ackroyd, who took possession of the lands supplying it in 1539.[35]

After 1538 the proportion of Halifax wills omitting reference to the Virgin and saints rose sharply, confirming a growing Protestant commitment amongst the laity. The lengthy preamble to the will of Edward Hoppay of Skircoat, drafted in 1548, early in the reign of Edward VI (1547–53), included the affirmation that 'touching the wealth of my soul, the faith that I have taken is sufficient, as I believe, without any other man's work or works'. This provides one of the earliest provincial occurrences of a radical Protestant statement of belief and incontrovertible evidence of the impact of Protestant teaching and Bible-reading upon a middle-aged or elderly yeoman of modest means residing near Halifax. Traditionally, historians have attributed the emergence of Halifax as a radical Protestant centre to the survival of a strong Lollard tradition in the geographically remote parish. But the evidence for this has always been elusive. It now seems more likely that Protestantism travelled with merchants and tradespeople from cosmopolitan centres like London and Hull to market towns and manufacturing centres like Halifax and its hinterland, where it spread within local communities through kinship networks. Protestantism seems particularly to have rooted in Halifax families with textile connections such as the Maudes and the Bests, who were well established in the community, possessing lands and producing clerical sons.[36]

Holdsworth dutifully closed the chantries in the parish church and the proprietary chapelries throughout the parish following the enactment of the Chantries Act of 1548. The absence of churchwardens' accounts makes it impossible to measure the financial implications of the Act in Halifax, but William and Sarah Sheils have concluded that 'the principal inhabitants of Halifax were deprived of an important outlet for their individual and corporate social energies' which was not restored until the preaching ministry of John Favour and his Puritan protégés 'touched the charitable wellsprings' of the local community in different political circumstances after 1590. However, the switch to an English liturgy on Easter Day, 1549, little over a month after the publication of Archbishop Thomas Cranmer's first English prayer book, was considered sufficiently momentous to be recorded in the baptismal registers and probably helped to develop an increasing awareness of the Reformation changes among those sections of the community not versed in Latin.[37]

During the Catholic reaction of Mary Tudor's reign (1553–58), when Holdsworth readily restored the Latin mass, the parish of Halifax began to display an increasingly militant Protestantism. The church courts at York heard of a succession of heretical offences ranging from 'looking down at the time of the elevation of the sacrament during the mass and refusing holy water' to tearing down the crucifix and forcibly removing the reserved sacrament from the parish church. However, A. G. Dickens has expressed surprise at the relatively small number of cases of heresy from Halifax presented in the ecclesiastical courts under Mary, concluding that the clothiers of Halifax, like the closely-knit merchant community of Hull, 'avoided giving away much detailed evidence to contemporary persecutors and modern historians'. But Robert Ferrar, a former chaplain of both Cranmer and Protector Somerset, went to the stake at Carmarthen in 1555 for refusing to renounce his 'heresies, schisms and errors' and there were several local protests against the re-introduction of the mass, for example in July 1554, when the host was stolen from Halifax Parish Church.[38]

In the decade following the death of Mary Tudor in 1558 local will formulations tended towards religious neutrality, since the Elizabethan church settlement, embodied in the acts of supremacy and uniformity of 1559, was accepted with minimal opposition in the parish. In 1559, shortly after the accession of Elizabeth I (1558–1603), when James Pilkington, Regius Professor of Divinity at Cambridge and an eminent Protestant reformer, preached at Halifax Parish Church, 'the congregation listened with joy'.

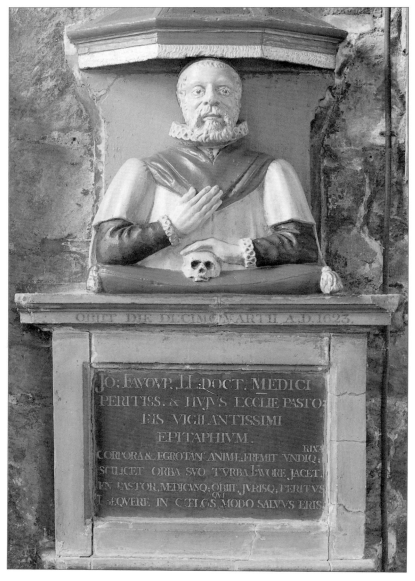

Figure 3.6   Dr John Favour (1556–1623). His ministry as Vicar of Halifax from 1593 to 1623 promoted the growth of Puritanism in the parish and an upsurge in charitable benefactions and bequests, including the endowment of Heath Grammar School. His celebrated *Antiquity triumphing over Novelty*, published in 1619, which condemned 'all new and late upstart heresies' was dedicated to his ally, Archbishop Tobias Matthew of York. His alabaster monument on the south wall of Halifax Parish Church, photographed in 1981, portrays the vicar in his pulpit, dressed in canonicals and ruffle, his left hand resting on a skull. (Photograph courtesy of J. G. Washington)

Catholic recusancy and repeated absence from communion were rare within the parish, and in 1569–70 the parish remained famously loyal to the Queen during the Catholic rebellion of the northern earls, which sought to re-establish the Catholic religion and secure the succession of the Catholic Mary Queen of Scots. This allegiance was later attributed by Archbishop Grindal to the effect of sustained Puritan preaching in the local 'exercises' or 'prophesyings'.[39]

After a temporary lapse, monthly mid-week 'exercise-days' were revived by the celebrated Puritan Dr John Favour, Vicar of Halifax from 1593 to 1623, when 'multitudes of hearers' regularly flocked to listen to visiting preachers from near and far. Dr Favour, a former Oxford civil lawyer and fervent Calvinist preacher, published in 1619 his celebrated *Antiquity triumphing over Novelty*, a treatise critical of 'all new and late upstart heresies'. All four of Favour's lecturers at Halifax Parish Church were Puritans, as were most of the curates in the restored parochial chapelries. In all, thirteen Puritan ministers served as lecturers or curates at Halifax Parish Church during the period 1603–40. Favour's influential allies included Sir John Savile of Howley, Sir Arthur Ingram of Temple Newsam, and Archbishop Tobias Mathew (1606–28). When nationally the Marprelate tracts satirising leading churchmen provided the pretext for an anti-Presbyterian reaction, Favour succeeded in protecting the Puritan cause at Halifax.[40]

Favour's successors, Robert Clay (1624–28), Hugh Ramsden (1628–29) and Henry Ramsden (1629–38) all had local Protestant roots, and it was not until the appointment of Richard Marsh in 1638 that vicarage was occupied by a Laudian. However, during the primary visitations of the Laudian Archbishop Richard Neile in 1632, 1633 and 1635 the churchwardens in the parochial chapelries were ordered 'to provide surplices and all the other necessary ornaments'. Puritanism was again proscribed and several local Puritans, including Matthew Mitchell, 'a pious and wealthy' Halifax layman, and Richard Denton, curate of Coley, emigrated to New England to escape the Laudian persecution during the period 1635–38. The strength of Protestant feeling within the parish was evidenced by the 1,127 signatures from Halifax appended to the 1641 Protestation oath 'to maintain and defend … the true Reformed Protestant Religion expressed in the doctrine of the Church of England, against all popery and popish innovations', and by the support for the Parliamentarian cause during the English Civil War, despite the fact that Sir William Savile, the largest landowner in the parish, was a commander in the Royalist army (1642–8).[41]

Clarendon, the contemporary royalist historian of the Great Rebellion, noted that Halifax, Leeds and Bradford, three 'very populous and rich' clothmaking towns, which 'naturally maligned the gentry', were wholly at the disposition of the parliamentarian forces in the English Civil War. Captain John Hodgson of Coley Hall helped to repel the royalist attack on

Bradford in December 1642, while Jonathan Scholefield, minister of Cross Stone, led the parliamentarian assault on Leeds in January 1643, with mainly 'inexperienced fresh water men taken up about Bradford and Halifax but upon the Saturday before'. These successes enabled the parliamentary army to garrison Leeds and Bradford and occupy Halifax. According to the official dispatch to the Speaker of the House of Commons, which was sent from Halifax on the day following the battle, no fewer than 500 men from the parish of Halifax fought with the parliamentarian armies under the Fairfaxes at the battle of Adwalton Moor on 30 June 1643. Their defeat by a greatly superior royalist army forced many of them, including the Halifax apothecary and antiquary, John Brearcliffe, to seek refuge across the Pennines.

By 8 July 1643, a royalist army under Major General Sir Francis Mackworth had occupied the town of Halifax after a skirmish with the rearguard of Sir Thomas Fairfax's departing forces on Old Bank. It comprised four regiments of infantry and one regiment of cavalry, the latter stationed at King Cross, with an outpost at Sowerby Bridge to guard the strategically important route to the Lancashire border. A parliamentarian counter-offensive through Heptonstall in October 1643 harassed the royalist outposts and subsequently repelled a royalist assault on the craggy hilltop village on 1 November, inflicting heavy casualties. Another daring counter-offensive

Figure 3.7 The Waterhouse windows, Halifax Parish Church. These distinctive, plain-glazed windows were donated to Halifax Parish Church in 1652 by Dorothy Waterhouse (1589–1652), widow of Nathaniel Waterhouse (1586–1645), in memory of her husband, a local merchant, salter and benefactor of the poor. They were considered more appropriate than stained-glass windows during the Puritan ascendancy in the Commonwealth period. Waterhouse had provided property in Halifax for use as a workhouse and house of correction. He had also endowed almshouses for the elderly poor and a Blue Coat School for the education of twenty orphans. (Photograph courtesy of J. G. Washington)

Figure 3.8   High Sunderland, drawn by John Horner, 1835. Situated on the hillside above Horley Green, this house with its striking frontage and distinctive embattled cornice, was a rebuilding of an earlier timber-framed gabled house. Langdale Sunderland of High Sunderland, the brother-in-law of Sir Marmaduke Langdale, one of the king's generals, commanded a troop of royalist horse during the Civil War. He subsequently suffered a heavy fine for taking up arms against Parliament and was obliged to sell the family estates at High Sunderland and Coley Hall. Some of the features of High Sunderland are believed to have been incorporated into the novel *Wuthering Heights* by Emily Brontë, who taught at a neighbouring private school at Southowram in 1838–39. The house was finally demolished in the 1930s. (Photograph courtesy of Calderdale Museums Service, Bankfield)

in December pursued the retreating royalists to within musket shot of Halifax. After securing reinforcements from Keighley, Mackworth marched upon Heptonstall on 9 January, but the parliamentarians had discreetly evacuated the village before he arrived. The raising of the siege of Nantwich by Sir Thomas Fairfax on 25 January 1644, and the threat from Parliament's Scottish allies, resulted in Mackworth finally withdrawing from Halifax on 28 January 1644, falling back on Bradford and Leeds en route to York. The subsequent royalist defeat at the battle of Marston Moor on 2 July 1644 secured the north for Cromwell for the rest of the war. Scottish troops were quartered in Halifax from April 1645 to June 1646.

On balance, more local residents probably died from the outbreak of bubonic plague in Halifax in 1645, which claimed 529 lives, than from the fighting. Some also died of natural causes as refugees in Lancashire. In July 1643, Phoebe Lister hurriedly buried the deeds of Shibden Hall then fled for Manchester, dying there seven months later. Anne Tattersall of Warley was one of several local refugees, buried in Burnley in the summer of 1643.

The home of Joseph Priestley, a Puritan clothier of Goodgreave whose son Samuel had enlisted in Fairfax's army, was ransacked and plundered by royalist troops after other members of the family fled to Lancashire. Some local residents with royalist sympathies also suffered, including Richard Gledhill of Barkisland Hall, who was killed at Marston Moor, and Langdale Sunderland of High Sunderland, who, at the end of the war, was obliged to sell his family estates in Calderdale to pay the heavy fine of £878 imposed by Parliament. Tobias Law, who held land in Halifax, Northowram and Southowram, was also fined £350. Moreover, during the royalist occupation of Halifax, two royalist soldiers were hanged as deserters on a gallows erected near the gibbet. Nor were soldiers the only royalist casualties of the war. The wife of Richard Marsh, the royalist vicar of Halifax, went into premature labour and died in childbirth, when Parliamentarian soldiers arrived at the vicarage in 1643 to arrest her husband, who had already fled.[42]

During the parliamentarian occupation and the Commonwealth and Protectorate (1649–60) the royal arms were removed from the parish church, together with the baptismal font with its exquisitely carved decorative wooden cover, and geometrically patterned, clear-leaded glass windows were installed in 1652 by the widow of Nathaniel Waterhouse. Among the Presbyterian ministers appointed to the sequestered living at Halifax during this period was John Lake (1624–89), a native of Halifax. He subsequently became Dean of York and Bishop of Chichester and, as one of the seven bishops who opposed the extension of the royal prerogative, was imprisoned in the Tower by James II in 1688. The parish of Halifax, a Commonwealth fiscal area, was represented in Oliver Cromwell's Parliaments of 1654 and 1656 by Jeremy Bentley of Elland, but a bid to secure a municipal charter for Halifax in August 1654 failed. Halifax suffered considerably from the military occupation and the disruption of the woollen trade during the Civil War, but at least one local clothier continued to make regular journeys with packhorse trains full of cloth pieces for sale in London throughout the period. Others, however, must have experienced severe deprivation, and for many the Restoration would have signalled a welcome return to normality. The churchwardens' accounts record payments to bell ringers to celebrate the end of the Commonwealth in 1659.[43]

With the restoration of Charles II (1660–85) and the imposition of the Clarendon Code by the Cavalier Parliament, Puritanism was effectively outlawed. Dr Richard Marsh, the royalist Vicar of Halifax who had fled for his life in 1642, returned to Halifax in 1660 to 'administer the sacrament with surplice and red tippet', ousting the Puritan incumbent, Eli Bentley. Among several other local ministers ejected for their refusal to conform was Oliver Heywood, at Coley, whose inspired and determined leadership was crucial to the survival of Yorkshire Dissent during the period 1660–88. Following his ejection from Coley he went to reside at Northowram where

Figure 3.9 John Tillotson (1630–1694) was the son of Robert Tillotson, a Dissenting clothier of Haugh End in Sowerby. He was educated at local grammar schools and Clare Hall, Cambridge. He preached the thanksgiving sermon for 'the deliverance by the Prince of Orange' in January 1688 and became an influential ecclesiastical figure during the reign of William and Mary. He was appointed Archbishop of Canterbury in 1691. Despite his Puritan upbringing and early reputation as a Puritan preacher, his primacy was characterised by a liberal Latitudinarianism. (Photograph courtesy of Chetham's Library)

he exercised both a powerful local and wider itinerant ministry, often travelling 1,400 miles in a year strengthening the morale of the many small congregations of artisans, craftsmen and farmers who continued to meet in cottage and barn in the small Pennine hamlets. Repeatedly excommunicated and fined, and imprisoned for a whole year at York in 1685, he wrote in his diary during the year 1683:

> I am so fully satisfied in my conscience with my Nonconformity as a minister, that it is the way of God, and I have so much peace in my spirit, that what I do is for the main, according to the word, that if I knew of all the troubles beforehand, and were to begin again, I would persist in this course to my dying day.

Protestant triumphs were used as the occasions for popular celebration in the late seventeenth and early eighteenth centuries, and the Halifax churchwardens' accounts reveal that the parish church bells rang out on the proclamation of William and Mary in February 1689; the Protestant victories of William III in Ireland 1690–91; and on the 'day of rejoicing' for the act of union with Scotland in 1707. Moreover, John Tillotson (1630–94), son of the Puritan Robert Tillotson of Haugh End in Sowerby and subsequently Archbishop of Canterbury, preached the sermon at the national thanksgiving for 'the deliverance by the Prince of Orange' on 31

January 1688. Large sums of money were collected locally in 1689–90 for the relief of the Irish Protestants, reflecting the intensity of popular support for the Revolution Settlement. A degree of toleration had been granted to Nonconformists initially through Declarations of Indulgence in 1672 and 1687 and more permanently when Dissent became legalised under the Toleration Act of 1689. By 1689 there were seven Dissenting congregations in the parish of Halifax, including one at a newly licensed meeting house at Northowram, built by Oliver Heywood in 1688, which had a membership of fifty-one in 1703, the majority of whom were women. By the end of the century the first Nonconformist meeting house had been opened by Presbyterians at Northgate End in Halifax.[44]

By 1715, when the Hanoverian succession secured the Protestant ascendancy, the Northgate End meeting had no fewer than 600 adherents, and Dissenters in the parish, including Quakers and Baptists, as well as Presbyterians and Independents, numbered over 2,000. Daniel Defoe recorded no fewer than sixteen Dissenting meeting houses during his visit to the parish ten years later. But some congregations had evidently declined in numbers by 1743 when Dr George Legh, Vicar of Halifax, reported to Archbishop Herring a mere '300 Presbyterian families; scarce any Baptists or Independents; sixty Quaker families and very few Papists' resident in the parish. However, he also observed that there was 'one unlicensed meeting house where the people called Methodists assemble' at Lightcliffe, with 'several hundreds' attending the Sunday morning services which were conducted by teachers 'various and unsettled'.

During the 1740s Methodists were accused of being Jacobite emissaries and attempts were made to suppress itinerant preaching. In May 1744, John Nelson, the Birstall stonemason, who had preached the first Methodist sermon in the parochial out-township of Skircoat in 1741 was impressed for army service at Halifax. John Wesley, who had preached initially in out-townships at Lightcliffe and Skircoat during the period 1742–47, first preached in the centre of the town in the open air at the market cross on 22 August 1748. His preaching aroused an intensity of opposition reminiscent of Heywood's, when a 'most uproarious disturbance', initiated by a gentleman throwing money into the crowd, forced him to withdraw, mud-bespattered and bleeding, to a field at Salterhebble. Undeterred, however, he returned to the market place at dawn the following morning and shortly afterwards a Methodist society appears to have been formed, meeting in former Quaker premises in Cow Green.[45]

Religion therefore remained a contentious issue in Halifax and its hinterland throughout the early modern period. Moreover, Halifax also remained the focal point of religious controversy throughout the period from the English Reformation to the Evangelical Revival. But after the excitement and upheaval of the Civil War years, when political divisions had been largely fuelled by religion, parliamentary politics appeared humdrum by comparison in the period from 1660 to 1750. Halifax lost its short-lived status as a parliamentary borough at the end of the Interregnum, and freeholders had to travel to York to vote in the Yorkshire constituency elections, on one occasion in the middle of winter. Moreover, elections were rarely contested in Yorkshire, the largest English county constituency. Between 1708 and 1750 there were only three contests: in 1727, 1734 and 1741. The poll books for 1734 and 1741 show that a majority of Halifax freeholders supported the Tories, suggesting the emergence during the early eighteenth century of a Tory urban elite. In the 1741 contest, 109 Halifax township electors voted for the unsuccessful Tory candidate, George Fox, and 31 for the victorious Whig candidate, Cholmley Turner. Most of the leading Anglicans voted Tory, while most of the leading Dissenters supported the Whigs. Dr George Legh, the Vicar of Halifax, however, supported Walpole's Whig administration, perhaps because his appointment was in the gift of the crown. Indeed, Legh had been specially chosen by Walpole as the incumbent for what the Archbishop of York described as 'a most disaffected corner of my diocese'.[46]

Local government

Dr Alan Betteridge has concluded that in 1585 Halifax was 'still firmly rooted in manorialism and many aspects of local social and economic life were regulated by manorial officialdom'. During the seventeenth century this situation was to change with the development of parochial and township government in Halifax and its hinterland and the growing responsibilities of the West Riding justices of the peace for the regulation of important aspects of the life of the local community. However, manorial administration played a key role in the development of the infrastructure of the emerging urban centre of Halifax in the sixteenth and seventeenth centuries; although manorial control was weakening by the mid-seventeenth century as a result of the enfranchisement of large numbers of copyholders, the vestiges of manorialism survived beyond 1750.

The manor of Halifax-cum-Heptonstall, a sub-manor of the manor of Wakefield, had been a rectory manor owned by the Priory of Lewes until the dissolution of the monasteries, after which it passed first to the Waterhouse family of Halifax in 1545 and then to the Ingram family of Leeds in 1609, who sold Heptonstall in 1626. The parent manor of Wakefield had reverted to the crown in 1461 and was administered by the Duchy of Lancaster from 1554 until 1629, when it was given by Charles I to the Earl of Holland as part of a debt settlement. He had granted it to his son-in-law, who had promptly sold it to Sir Christopher Clapham, in whose family estates it remained until the beginning of the eighteenth century, when it passed to the Duke of Leeds. Both the parent manor and sub-manor had jurisdiction in Halifax. Although the Halifax court was legally subordinate

Figure 3.10 Sir Arthur Ingram (1565–1642). A financier who amassed a considerable fortune as Controller of Customs for the port of London, Ingham became one of the wealthiest landowners in Yorkshire. Acquiring the lordship of the sub-manor of Halifax-cum-Heptonstall in 1609, he sold Heptonstall in 1626. He also encouraged the enfranchisement of copyholders in Halifax, which enhanced the legal and social status of many of the town's inhabitants during the early seventeenth century. This portrait by George Geldorp, the only surviving contemporary image of Ingram, hangs at Temple Newsam, which Ingram purchased from the Duke of Lennox for £12,000 in 1622. (Photograph courtesy of the Department of Leisure Services, Leeds City Council)

to the manor of Wakefield, there was a history of conflicting jurisdiction and of encroachment of judicial powers from the Wakefield court. But in practice there was little differentiation at local level between the administrative and judicial business of the manor and sub-manor transacted at the Halifax Moot Hall.[47]

The provision of an adequate water supply, the regulation of housing and the suppression of street nuisances were the most common administrative duties of the Halifax and Wakefield manorial courts, and in all these respects the business of the courts foreshadowed that of the town trustees in the 1760s. The source of the main town water supply was a spring at Well Head, and there were frequent presentments for pollution of the watercourse, particularly against butchers but also against others for allowing the water to be contaminated by geese and ducks, the disposal of garbage and the washing of wool and dirty clothes. In 1625 the Halifax court imposed a penalty on keepers of dyehouses for excessive use of water, and there were many presentments for the diversion of the watercourse for private use. In 1587 a local by-law, which anticipated national legislation of 1589, attempted to regulate the number of persons occupying property, since housing accommodation was clearly not keeping pace with population growth in the town. From the 1690s the court also attempted to check such nuisances as the riddling of ashes, the making of dunghills and the foraging of swine in the streets. In 1706 an order was issued prohibiting animal slaughter in the street, and fines were imposed on those who did not clean their market standings at the close of business on Saturdays.

Both manorial courts also heard and determined civil suits between tenants and dealt with problems of law and order which arose from manorial administration, but the Wakefield manorial court retained jurisdiction over criminal matters. Tenants had to be supervised to ensure that manorial property such as walls and stiles were kept in good repair. All manorial tenants, including freeholders and leaseholders, were obliged to do suit at the lord's corn and fulling mills, and attempts were also made from the late sixteenth century by the lord of the manor and his agents to gain revenue from local trade by control of the cloth halls. The custom of holding markets and fairs in the town may have been established during the fifteenth century, but rights cannot have been clearly defined, for the lord attempted to secure, and in 1607 was granted, a charter allowing him to hold markets at Halifax on Thursdays and Saturdays, fairs on the feast days of St John the Baptist and St Martin, and a court of pie-powder to deal with disputes involving itinerants. There was opposition from the inhabitants, however, and, under the lordship of Henry Farrer and Dr Favour, the townspeople resisted the manorial control of the market and were eventually granted the right to hold markets in Halifax free of toll.

From the late sixteenth century until the 1630s the Halifax manorial court dealt with a wide range of local administrative matters, and its officials contributed greatly during this period to the maintenance of the social order and the regulation of economic life in the town. By the 1630s, however, it is apparent that the Halifax court was past its prime, and was falling into decay as an instrument of town government. The gradual disappearance of common rights and copyhold tenure, the emergence of the freeholder, and the tenants' constant opposition to obligatory suit at the manorial mills resulted in the decline of local manorialism. However, many of the functions of the court had not been superseded by 1750 and the court continued to play a vital role in regulating some aspects of the life of the urban community into the second half of the eighteenth century.

The evolution of parochial and civil township administration during the early modern period also profoundly influenced the future development of local government within the urban community and its hinterland. The Tudor governments gave new responsibilities, for example for poor relief and highway maintenance, to civil parishes, which, in large parishes like Halifax, eventually became devolved upon civil townships in both Halifax itself and the parochial out-townships. But the ecclesiastical parish authorities retained responsibility for the collection of the small tithes, the incumbent's main source of income which had been commuted into a complicated system of payments in kind and money in the 1530s, and the church rates for the maintenance of the fabric of the parish church. From the late seventeenth century there was a growing conflict between the historic centre of parochial power in Halifax, represented by the parochial vestry, and the parochial out-townships with their developing civil administration. For example, fixing the church rate, which appears to have been an annual assessment from 1620, was a frequent source of dispute, as in 1748 when the town and parish entered a costly litigation about moneys disbursed by the Halifax wardens on the church fabric without the consent of the out-township churchwardens or the vote of the parish vestry. Such tensions generally weakened the administrative cohesion of the area and resulted in a devolution and decentralisation of power which was not fully reversed until local government re-organisation in 1974.

The appointment of a parish clerk as the paid officer of the parish who served under the churchwardens and the incumbent is recorded from the 1570s. From at least 1634 he occupied a special seat in the parish church near the pulpit, and during the eighteenth century he was provided with a gown and desk, outward symbols of his official status within the local hierarchy. Two churchwardens nominated annually met at monthly intervals with their colleagues from the parochial out-townships to deal with a wide range of ecclesiastical and secular business. Just as township business from the late seventeenth century was directed by the town vestry, the key questions of parochial administration were dealt with by substantial inhabitants from the whole parish. From 1677 parochial accounts had to be submitted annually to the vestry for inspection and approval, and from 1685 consent was required before more expensive repairs could be carried out on the church fabric. During the late seventeenth century the vestry seems to have emerged as a parochial oligarchy with more official status and regular functions and to have assumed a greater measure of control over parochial business, probably at the expense of the incumbent and churchwardens who in the early seventeenth century had dominated parochial administration.

The gentry, yeomanry and professional classes were always well-represented in manorial, parochial and township administration during this period, but there is also evidence of participation in local government across the social spectrum. Between 1661 and 1692 the manorial office of steward was held by a Halifax scrivener and subsequently by members of the gentry. By the eighteenth century the jury of the manorial court was also composed exclusively of gentry, and members of the vestry were drawn predominantly from the upper ranks of the local community – merchants and professional men linked by ties of blood, marriage and administrative office. However, during the late sixteenth and early seventeenth centuries members of the gentry rarely held the office of overseer, which was occupied more frequently by tanners, woolmen, butchers, badgers, mercers, clothiers, chandlers and grocers, and in the 1730s the average value of property owned by overseers was approximately half that of the value of property belonging to churchwardens. So the day-to-day administration of early modern Halifax was undertaken increasingly not so much by the neighbouring local gentry but by an urban professional elite and those even lower in the social hierarchy.[48]

Members of the neighbouring local gentry, however, maintained a regulatory role over important aspects of local government as justices of the peace, meeting at the Quarter Sessions, which rotated among the principal towns of the West Riding. Their responsibilities were extended under the Tudors to include not only the enforcement of law and order but the implementation of religious conformity, the regulation of commerce and employment, the operation of the Elizabethan Poor Laws of 1598 and 1601 and the maintenance of roads and bridges. Their role in the maintenance of public order included regulating the liquor trade, since alehouses were regarded with some suspicion possibly as agencies of social disorder. In 1635 a report by the West Riding justices of the peace revealed no fewer than fifty-one illegal alehouses in the town of Halifax and 134 in the parish, more than in any other township or parish in the West Riding. Occasionally, the responses of the county justices to local crises were regarded as inadequate by those most directly involved at local level. John Waite, the Vicar of Halifax, complained during the bubonic plague epidemic of 1645 that he 'was much wearied in labouring to rule the poor from rising to infect the town', but the county justices were 'backward to assist the town' to keep them in quarantine.[49]

A. G. Dickens has argued that the state of public order in mid-Tudor Yorkshire was lower than in most parts of England, citing the murder of Robert Holdsworth, Vicar of Halifax, 1526−56, during a robbery at the vicarage in May 1556, as one of the most shocking crimes of the era. Affrays were certainly commonplace in Halifax during the sixteenth century, involving both sexes and often also members of the local elite. In 1574, for example, John Waterhouse of Shibden, lord of the manor of Halifax, was fined ten shillings for his involvement in an affray on John Watmough, and in 1576 Sybil Wilson was fined five shillings after she 'made an affray and drew blood' from the wife of William Dickenson. Several assaults on the greave, the manorial officer responsible for the collection of rents, are also recorded in the manorial rolls between 1585 and 1600.[50]

Moreover, Dr John Addy's study of the consistory court records at York has led him to conclude that the parish of Halifax was 'uncontrollable and ungovernable' by the ecclesiastical authorities during the seventeenth century. Cases brought before the courts in 1635 and 1679 illustrate the problem. In 1635, during morning service at Halifax Parish Church, Richard Nicholson, churchwarden at Warley, and Abraham Parkinson, of Halifax, became involved in an unseemly brawl, during which Parkinson called Nicolson a lying rascal and 'bade a turd in his teeth'. In 1679, the parish clerk, John Wilson was presented to the archdeacon for 'defiling the church wall by pissing against it and very irreverently and contumaciously speaking of Richard Hook', the vicar.[51]

Between 1500 and 1750 the development of local government in Halifax involved the gradual reshaping of manorial and parochial responsibilities by an increasingly powerful local oligarchy and the evolution of the civil township in order to meet the growing demands of an expanding urban population for improved public services. In the process the urban community partially freed itself from manorial control while its links with its out-townships within the parish were weakened. By 1750, Halifax town had come to be run much more as an independent secular entity, managed by resident property owners, but the responsibilities of local government were largely confined to providing economic services, notably markets, basic amenities such as water and drainage, and maintaining law and order, within the wider framework of law enforcement in early modern Yorkshire. Other services which later devolved upon local government were largely provided initially by the voluntary sector, only supplemented later by ratepayer support.

Social welfare, education and culture

During the sixteenth and seventeenth centuries the yeomanry and gentry of Halifax and its hinterland assumed growing responsibility for social welfare, motivated by Puritan piety, humanitarian concern and a desire to maintain social stability. Their philanthropic activity, much of it inspired by the energetic incumbency of Dr John Favour as Vicar of Halifax between 1593 and 1623, supplemented the limited statutory provision for the poor and needy during this period. The Revd John Barlow, Favour's lecturer at Halifax Parish Church, calling on the local gentry to develop more of a social conscience, observed:

> Gentility consists not only in the cutting of a card, casting of a die, throwing of a bowl, watching of a cock, manning of a hawk, or in following after a deep-mouthed cry of hounds: but in good hospitality, virtuous actions and generous deeds.[52]

Such charitable deeds in Halifax were channelled mainly through perpetual trusts, established under isolated benefactions and bequests, and the cities of York and Hull excepted, Halifax gave more money for charitable purposes than any other place in Yorkshire between 1480 and 1640, most of it being donated in the years following Favour's arrival.[53]

The Brian Crowther Charity, which provided for the annual distribution of outdoor relief amongst the poor of the town under the terms of his will of 1606, was one of the town's earliest social welfare institutions. The account book of the charity, which was reconstituted following the Pious Uses Commission of 1651, provides fascinating insights into the condition

Figure 3.11   Effigy of Old Tristram, Halifax Parish Church. Old Tristram was a licensed beggar, who operated within the precincts of Halifax Parish Church in the late seventeenth century. He is depicted wearing the typical apparel of a pauper during this period, clutching an alms box and bearing upon his chest a scroll with the legend 'Pray Remember the Poor'. The effigy, which stands at the west end of Halifax Parish Church was carved by John Aked, who also painted the royal arms of Queen Anne for the parish church in 1704. (Photograph courtesy of J. G. Washington)

of the poor. Much of the relief took the form of small money doles, ranging from one penny to eighteen pence, presumably to be spent on food, but emphasis was also placed on the provision of clothing. The specification in the accounts of such individual items of clothing as shoes, clogs, shirts, jumpcoats, smocks, stockings, hose, doublets, breeches, petticoats, gowns, waistcoats and vests, provides a vivid picture of the appearance of the poorer sort in late seventeenth-century Halifax. This complements the eloquent surviving testimony of Old Tristram, the effigy of a licensed beggar who operated within the precincts of Halifax Parish Church during this period, which depicts a bearded, gaunt, drably attired figure, clutching an alms box and bearing upon his chest a scroll with the legend; 'Pray Remember the Poor'. The principal reasons for destitution, as revealed in the charity account book, appear to have been old age, sickness, disability, confinement and dependent children, whose maintenance was also financed on occasions from charity funds.

In 1610 Jane Crowther and Ellen Hopkinson, the widows of two Halifax clothiers, built almshouses for eighteen poor widows of the town, a particularly vulnerable sector within the local community. Each woman inmate was required to accommodate one pauper child to be taught by a specially appointed master in two adjoining rooms. In 1614, under Jane Crowther's will, the endowment was augmented by a small annuity which was to be paid towards the maintenance of the school and schoolmaster. In 1748 the almshouses and school were rebuilt at the expense of the town and allowances and clothing provided out of the rates. By the mid-eighteenth century, widows over sixty occupied the almshouses and children aged between

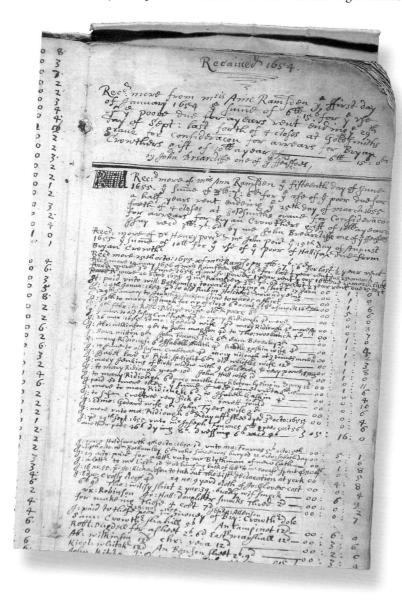

Figure 3.12 Bryan Crowther Charity, 1654–55. In September 1606 Brian Crowther devised by will to Dr John Favour and others a yearly rent of ten pounds out of land and property to be distributed annually amongst the poor of Halifax. After the death of Favour the charity appears to have been neglected and did not become fully operative again until 1654, as a result of the 1651 Pious Uses Commission. The dole account book, 1654–1692, records in minute detail the allocation of poor relief, providing valuable information about the structure of social welfare in the town, the nature of disease and disability and the condition of the poor. (Photograph courtesy of West Yorkshire Archive Service, Calderdale)

Figure 3.13   Heath Grammar School. This unfinished early nineteenth-century sketch by an unknown artist shows groups of boys playing games in the foreground. A royal charter was obtained for the foundation of a grammar school in 1585, but the school did not open in Free School Lane until 1600. The fundraising activities of Dr John Favour after his appointment as Vicar of Halifax enabled the school to be built and provided an endowment fund to pay the schoolmaster. Public subscription provided £200 to enlarge and rebuild the school and house in 1777 and the school was further remodelled in 1879. (Photograph courtesy of Calderdale Museums Service, Bankfield)

three and ten years attended the school. In the 1640s further almshouses were established under the Waterhouse trust, the aims of which were to provide shelter, maintenance and clothing for twelve elderly poor. The provision seems to have been so carefully planned and generously endowed that, in spite of periods of mismanagement, the institution continues to provide sheltered accommodation for the elderly in the twentieth century.

In response to the widespread poverty and escalating poor rates, a royal charter was granted to Nathaniel Waterhouse (1586–1645), a wealthy local merchant, for the establishment of a workhouse and house of correction. His frequent business visits to London had aroused his interest in the Bridewell, founded in 1552 to provide work for the poor within a disciplined environment. The workhouse was administered by a body of thirteen of the 'ablest and most discreet persons of the town and parish', headed by a master and prime governor, who were elected annually from within their ranks and who also served as justices of the peace within the town. During the period from 1635 to 1639, when the workhouse was apparently dissolved, the workhouse corporation was responsible both for the preservation of law and order in the town by the suppression of begging and vagrancy and for the provision of indoor relief and work for the poor. The inmates worked long hours from dawn till dusk with only short meal breaks, and discipline was severe, with some seventy workhouse inmates, men and women, whipped, several repeatedly, between 1635 and 1638. When the workhouse was reconstituted in 1682 during a period of acute economic hardship, a greater emphasis was placed on social welfare. In 1684 paupers capable of working were admitted into the workhouse, while those unable to work were badged and authorised to beg in the town. In 1687 a survey of the poor was conducted, following which cash allowances were provided for thirty-seven families suffering particular hardship. After the 1680s the workhouse appears to have declined and despite moving to new accommodation in 1700 was again inactive by 1710. In the 1740s it was again reconstituted largely at the town's expense, with accommodation for thirty residents.[54]

The growing concern for social welfare was also reflected in attempts to improve educational provision within the town. There are sporadic references in sixteenth-century manorial court rolls to schoolmasters and a grammar school in Halifax, but little evidence of institutional continuity before 1600, despite the granting of a royal charter for the establishment of Heath Grammar School in 1585. The fundraising activities of Dr John Favour ultimately ensured the financial viability of the school, which opened in 1600. Donations were secured from all the principal office-holders in the parish and from Halifax men who had achieved success elsewhere, such as Sir Richard Saltonstall, Lord Mayor of London, Sir Henry Savile, provost of Eton, and Joseph Lister, an alderman of Hull, and by the time of Favour's death over £800 had been raised as an endowment from gifts and bequests. Hipperholme Grammar School, which probably originated in the chantry chapel at nearby Coley, also secured a generous endowment from Matthew Broadley in 1648 and a permanent site by 1660. The curriculum of the grammar schools was classical and discipline severe. The novelist Laurence Sterne (1713–68), author of *Tristram Shandy*, who was educated at a local grammar school until his father's sudden death in Jamaica in 1731 left him penniless, recalled being 'severely whipped' by the master for inscribing his name on the newly whitewashed ceiling of the schoolroom.

The grammar schools enabled the sons of the upper and middling ranks to proceed to the universities and into the growing professions of medicine and the law. By the Civil War more Halifax students were being sent to the universities than in the reign of Elizabeth, but the number was still relatively small.[55]

The main function of the charity schools established under the Crowther-Hopkinson, Waterhouse and Smith trusts was to provide religious instruction, social conditioning and industrial training for those without private means. The Crowther-Hopkinson charity accounts indicate that children at the charity school linked with the almshouse foundation were taught to read, but there is no reference to their being taught to write.

The Blue Coat Hospital established under the will of Nathaniel Waterhouse, was modelled on Christ's Hospital in London. It provided accommodation and education for twenty poor orphans of the parish, from six to fourteen years, in preparation for later apprenticeships. Dr Betteridge has concluded that notwithstanding the lack of emphasis on the teaching of writing, there is some evidence in local parish registers of improving standards of literacy by the 1750s, particularly amongst shoemakers, clothdressers, butchers and woolcombers, whose signatures demonstrate higher than average levels of literacy. However, husbandmen, labourers and clothiers displayed lower than average literacy levels.[56]

In 1626, the Vicar of Halifax, Robert Clay, converted the charnel house at the parish church into a parochial library. Records reveal how the collection grew by means of bequests and gifts, particularly from the Puritan clergy and laity, and indicate its careful maintenance during the Interregnum when many parochial libraries fell into decay. But its use was probably restricted to the local clergy and a narrow circle within the local laity for whom reading was a leisure activity. The Yorkshire diarist Adam Eyre recorded purchasing in Halifax a recently published theological treatise, John Saltmarsh's *Divine Right of Presbyterie Asserted*, for a shilling in 1647, and a growing proportion of the parish inhabitants mentioned the possession of books in their wills during this period.[57]

Some urban historians have detected considerable cultural polarisation during the Tudor and early Stuart period. Others, notably Dr Peter Borsay, have concluded that the English urban renaissance in the century after 1660 'opened up a cultural gap' between the higher echelons of society and 'the populace as a whole'.[58] The evidence from the developing urban centre of Halifax for the nature, timing and extent of such cultural differentiation is ambiguous. There is some evidence of an emerging cultural polarisation in Halifax from as early as the 1590s when Puritan moralists, led by Dr John Favour, condemned sexual immorality, drunkenness, sabbath breaking and the many excesses associated with popular recreation and leisure activities. William and Sarah Sheils have concluded that Dr John Favour 'seems to have won over the principal inhabitants of the parish to his reforming policy, and consistent and thorough presentments against sexual offenders, drunkards and profaners of the sabbath were made by churchwardens at successive visitations throughout the thirty years of his ministry'.[59] In 1596 two Halifax men were presented before the archdeacon at York by Dr Favour for playing shoolnige (shove-halfpenny) during evening prayers. In his meticulous annotation of the moral lapses of his parishioners in the parish registers, Dr Favour recorded that Widow Foster of Halifax had been 'an infamous prostitute'; William King of Skircoat Moor 'a common swearer, drinker and most filthy adulterer'; Richard Theaker of Sowerby 'a drunkard drowned in his own drunkenness'; and that Richard Bridge of Southowram had 'lived an incestuous life and died excommunicate'.

He also established that bastardy had recurred in some Halifax families across four generations.[60]

The extent and the effectiveness of Favour's moral crusade is difficult to assess. Dr Betteridge has concluded that the Halifax illegitimacy ratio, ranging from approximately two per cent to approximately six per cent in the 1590s, although extremely high by national standards, was probably no higher than that of many other northern parishes and lower than in some, for example the neighbouring parish of Rochdale, with an exceptionally high illegitimacy ratio for the same decade of ten per cent. However, Dr Addy has calculated from visitation returns that some 226 Halifax couples were presented to the archdeacon for ante-nuptial fornication during the seventeenth century. One woman, Sara Fielden, was recorded as having 'committed fornication on a dark night in the open field with whom she knows not', and a young man, John Hardcastle, was reputed to have 'slept so long and so often with Ann Mitchell that she had made him so weak he could scarce eat fried eggs'. When Oliver Heywood commenced his ministry at Coley Chapel, he remarked: 'Oh what rioting, rebelling, gluttony, drunkenness, abominable beastly luxury, lechery scarce heard of among the heathen'. He later recorded instances of incest and adultery and reckoned that illegitimacy had been commoner in Halifax parish in the years following the Restoration than at any time in living memory. He reported that the vicar had prepared a list of over thirty cases currently under consideration. He wrote in his diary in 1691: 'I have seldom heard of so many young women with child by fornication as lately and some of them to cover their shame do marry – great wickedness.'[61]

Oliver Heywood also recorded in his diary a recurrence of sabbath breaking in Halifax on Easter Sunday in 1681, when 'there were hundreds of people … in the churchyard and on the green, and all along the town playing stool-ball and other recreations, without any control'. He also condemned midsummer and May Day revelling in Halifax. On 24 June 1679 Heywood found 'a great tumult in the town', during the midsummer fair week, with 'young men all in a heap striking and laying about each other'. He recorded that when the constables were sent for 'one was sorely wounded in the struggle'. On Saturday, 1 May, in the following year, he observed:

> a great number of persons of the poor and baser sort began early in the morning, even while it was yet dark, to bring in May. There were men, women and big youths, and all had white waistcoats or sheets about them; they carried garlands, flowers or branches of trees. They were accompanied by pipers and fiddlers; some had drums, and some carried white banners with red crosses. They rambled about most of the day. Towards night many of them were drunk and mad.[62]

Puritan preachers from Favour to Heywood also endeavoured to discourage popular beliefs in magic and superstition. Dr John Favour recorded cases of heretical practices involving the alleged use of magical powers. Oliver Heywood later recorded in his diary that he was called to Wakefield in October 1665 to see a young man judged to be possessed or bewitched, and in February 1672 he attended the funeral of another young man who had been taken away by strange diseases attributed to witchcraft. His own scepticism, however, is evident in an entry in his diary in May 1683, where he criticised a local physician, Dr Thornton, for his treatment of 'a strange illness that had fallen upon one of his flock' at Northowram. The doctor had evidently taken the view that his patient 'hath some hurt by an evil tongue' and had refused to prescribe any medicine for him until a mixture of his urine, hair, wheatmeal and horse-shoe stumps had been baked in a fire. Heywood ultimately convinced the patient that spiritual healing through prayer and fasting was preferable.[63]

Cockfighting and horse racing also attracted Heywood's censure, though his denunciations evidently failed to suppress these popular recreational activities. Moreover, their continuing appeal to participants from both the gentry and 'the poorer sort of Halifax', emphasises the very limited development of cultural differentiation in the town by the late seventeenth century. Nevertheless, Heywood's denunciation of the unseemly brawl which developed at a cock fight in a purpose built cocking house at the rear of the Cross Inn in May 1680 – where 'they all fought desperately a long while', 'an abundance of money was lost and won', and 'they drank all night and were so high in swearing and ranting that they were heard far in the town' – constitutes a vigorous assertion of alternative cultural values. When horse racing was held in Halifax in 1678, Heywood observed that the sporting event was a pretext 'to gather the country to drink their ale, for it was hoped it would be as profitable to the town as a fair'. A similar occasion at Northowram in 1681, hosted by John Mitchell of Scout Hall, attracted crowds of between 400 and 500, including 'many idle persons' from Halifax, Boothtown, Ovenden and Holdsworth.

Horse racing appears to have been resumed in Halifax in 1736, when the principal innkeepers of Halifax, joined by the vicar, a couple of gentlemen, and several prominent manufacturers, entered into an agreement to finance a regular race meeting on Skircoat Moor in an effort to improve the tone of such events. An advertisement in the *Leeds Mercury* for a three-day race meeting on Skircoat Moor in June 1738 revealed that spectators were expected from a wide area. Moreover, additional attractions included 'in the forenoons, cock fightings betwixt the gentlemen of Yorkshire and the gentlemen of Lancashire', and in the evenings 'for the amusement of the ladies there were assemblies, for social intercourse and dancing at the Assembly Rooms', suggesting that the appeal of these events crossed social barriers.[64]

Puritan values made a considerable impact on Halifax and its hinterland from the late sixteenth century, particularly in the sphere of social welfare and educational provision, where considerable charitable activity was stimulated. However, Puritan moralists appear to have been less successful in promoting sexual morality and sabbath observance, in discouraging beliefs in magic and superstition, and in suppressing a range of popular recreational activities. Dr John Smail has characterised the Puritanism of seventeenth-century Halifax as basically egalitarian, concerned more with orthodoxy of belief than with social status, arguing that this was typical of upland or urban communities which lacked 'a strong local gentleman and where

Figure 3.14   John Mitchell (1659–96) and Scout Hall, Northowram. A naive painting by an unknown artist of this local nouveau riche gentleman, with his home at Scout Hall in the distance. The grandson of Samuel Mitchell (1597–1645), a Halifax cloth merchant, John Mitchell was frequently castigated by Oliver Heywood, the Northowram Nonconformist preacher for dissipating his energies and inherited wealth on horse racing, gambling and drinking and went to an early grave at the age of thirty-seven in 1696. (Photograph courtesy of Calderdale Museums Service, Bankfield)

Figure 3.15   Scout Hall, Northowram. A conjectural drawing by John Horner published in 1835. The imposing three-storeyed rectangular Caroline mansion built in 1681 for John Mitchell exhibits tall cross-mullioned windows combined with asymmetrically placed oval windows and a stylish hipped roof, which the artist has modified in this representation. It is one of the earliest examples in the county of a formally designed double-pile, lesser gentry residence with a near-symmetrical facade. The hall was flanked by heated parlours, with a kitchen and cellars to the rear. (Photograph courtesy of Calderdale Museums Service, Bankfield)

Figure 3.16   The house at the Maypole during demolition in the summer of 1890. The house formerly stood at the junction of Crown Street and Corn Market in Halifax and was one of the finest examples of a wealthy northern merchant's house outside York. Dated between 1480 and 1510, the house frontage was adorned with lavish wood carvings, including the arms of the Merchant Adventurers of York. (Photograph courtesy of Halifax Antiquarian Society)

economic and social conditions allowed immigration and economic independence'. Consequently, Smail has argued, the society which emerged in Halifax after the demise of Puritan ideology 'was dominated by a large and relatively undifferentiated social middle'. It is also apparent that as Halifax developed as a leisure centre for its hinterland during the early modern period, some activities, for example cockfighting and horseracing, brought together people from different social classes, thereby contributing in some degree to social cohesion.[65]

'A pretty well built town of stone'

Population growth, economic development, changes in social structure, alterations in local government and the work of the voluntary sector affected the size of the town and the number, distribution and appearance of buildings and streets during the early modern period. Although Halifax was emerging as a busy market town by the late sixteenth century, a contemporary visitor described it baldly as a town 'of no great account'. In contrast, John Aston, the first diarist to visit the town, commended it

Figure 3.17   The house at the Maypole after its re-erection at Shibden. Recognising the importance of this former merchant's residence, the antiquary, John Lister of Shibden Hall arranged for its reconstruction on the Shibden estate, where it was re-named Daisybank. The elevation of the building consists of three bays indicated by the projecting chamber windows, supported by richly carved corbels. The building originally had a through passage with access to a courtyard at the rear of the property. (Photograph courtesy of Halifax Antiquarian Society)

in 1639 more enthusiastically as 'a pretty well built town of stone', populated mainly by clothiers. By the early seventeenth century, Halifax was beginning to display many of the characteristics of an urban centre. Contemporary quarter sessions records refer to Halifax as a market town, and its cloth halls served as commercial centres for the buying of wool and cloth. Moreover, its open market, corn and cattle markets and proliferating shops supplied a growing range of provisions for the voracious population of its rural hinterland, which the late sixteenth-century visitor who had been singularly unimpressed by the town had described as 'wonderful populous and strong' and which, as we have seen, did not suffer depopulation as the town expanded during the early modern period. The township also abounded in alehouses and inns, including the Turk's Head, the Swan, the Talbot, the Crown, the Star and the Cross, where John Aston found accommodation for the night and which he described as 'one of the fairest inns in England'.[66]

No early maps of the town have survived, but a reconstructed town plan for the mid-seventeenth century based upon documentary evidence, and the later survey of the town by the energetic and enterprising excise officer John Warburton in 1719, identifies the medieval route from Wakefield across Clark Bridge leading to a street of Woolshops connecting the old and new markets. Continuing westwards, the High Street merged with Gibbet Lane, ascending to Halifax Green and over Halifax Moor to High-road Well and Lancashire. From the market place, Northgate and Southgate branched north and south and not far from the market place were Cow and Bull Greens and Swine Market. The most prominent local public building remained the medieval parish church, extended in the sixteenth century with the addition of the Rokeby and Holdsworth chapels in 1533 and 1544.[67]

Buildings constructed after 1500 included the woollen Cloth Hall at Hall End, founded in the late sixteenth century and one of the earliest cloth halls to be built in the county and the Linen Hall, erected nearby in 1629. The market cross, referred to by John Aston, and the maypole were both located in the market place in the seventeenth century. Nathaniel Water-house's workhouse of 1635 was situated to the west of the parish church near to the medieval Moot Hall which was located to the north-west of the church. In 1696–97, a Presbyterian meeting house, the town's first Nonconformist chapel, was erected at Northgate End on the northern perimeter of the town and remained the only purpose-built chapel in the town until the construction of a new Quaker meeting house in Clare Road in the 1740s.[68]

But Halifax, with its unpaved streets and largely uncovered water supply, still displayed some features of an overgrown village by the mid-seventeenth century, and was less well-developed as an urban centre than Leeds. By the early seventeenth century much of Halifax's common wasteland had

3.18 Woolshops, half-timbered building 1670, photographed in 1971. The sole surviving timber-framed building in the modern town centre, subsequently restored and incorporated into the re-developed shopping precinct, which was completed in 1984. (Photograph: J. A. Hargreaves Collection)

been enclosed, though unenclosed moorland west of the town was still considered 'so barren and unfruitful' that it was 'not worth 2*d*. the acre by the year'.[69] However, by the mid-eighteenth century most of the township had been enclosed and the land parcellation of the town during the early modern period through piecemeal enclosure is now regarded as an important factor in the patterning of the spatial structure of the nineteenth-century industrial town. But despite widespread enclosure beyond the urban perimeter, there is no evidence of extensive dispersed settlement within the township. The expanding town, which doubled in size between 1500 and 1750, remained quite firmly nucleated and its focal centre did not experience a major locational shift.

Stone-cladding, however, had radically altered the external appearance of many of its older timber-framed buildings, and brick was beginning to appear in the construction of town houses from about 1700. The appropriately named Red Hall in Old Market, a three-storeyed house with stone surrounds, string courses and quoins, referred to in a deed of 1714, built around 1700 and demolished in 1866, was probably the first brick building to be built in the town. Nevertheless, a 1735 valuation records a score of barns within a stone's throw of the market cross, and the Revd Thomas Wright's bird's-eye description of the town from Beacon Hill accentuates its compact development and rural character:

So compact is now the town and so contrived by art, that from the hill which leads to and from Wakefield, it represents a cross, or rather two large beams laid cross one upon another with the left arm rather declining; the whole consisting chiefly of four streets in the midst whereof stands the market cross with a large and plentiful shambles. To the town thus described are annexed many regular and well-walled closes variously chequered with the different beauties of corn and grass, that from the aforesaid heights the most curious traveller hath not seen a more delightful landscape, if such prospects are viewed in their proper seasons.[70]

Over the next century the appearance of the town, and much else about its people, would be transformed.

CHAPTER FOUR

'An astonishing trading town': Halifax in the age of industrial expansion, 1750–1850

Commercial and industrial expansion

Although the town of Halifax was already by 1750 a place of significance within its parish, it hardly as yet rated as a substantial town nationally or even, in truth, regionally. However, economic development was to draw into the urban centre considerable numbers of people, and changes of production were to alter dramatically over the next century the social structure, living standards, politics and appearance of the town.

During the age of industrial expansion from 1750 to 1850 the population of the town of Halifax quintupled, rising from around 5,000 in 1743 to 25,159 in 1851, while the population of the parish as a whole rose at almost the same rate from around 31,000 to 149,257. As Table 4.1 shows, the town's share of the parish population, averaging around fifteen per cent during this period, therefore remained remarkably stable, arresting the downward trend of the period 1550–1750, though failing to reverse the trend until after 1851.

Table 4.1. *Population of the township and parish of Halifax 1743–1851*

Date	Halifax township population	% change	Halifax parish population	% change	township % share of parish population
1743	5000		31000		16.1
1764	6360	[+27.2]	41220	[33.0]	15.4
1801	8886	[+16.1]	63434	[53.9]	14.0
1811	9159	[+ 3.1]	73415	[15.7]	12.5
1821	12628	[+37.9]	93050	[26.7]	13.6
1831	15382	[+21.8]	109899	[18.1]	14.0
1841	19881	[+29.2]	130743	[19.07]	15.2
1851	25159	[+26.5]	149257	[14.2]	16.9

Sources: Herring and Drummond Visitation Returns, 1743 and 1764; Census Returns, 1801–51

It is readily apparent how this demographic growth occurred. High mortality rates, particularly of infants, were offset by a growing migration into

Halifax from the outlying townships as former domestic workers were absorbed into the new urban factory workforce, and by large numbers of extra-parochial immigrants, many of them Irish. During this period Halifax not only remained the commercial hub of the parish but also emerged as a major manufacturing centre, acquiring spacious new factory and warehouse accommodation, progressive banking and insurance facilities and increasing access to turnpike, waterway and railway networks.[1]

Economic growth was evident particularly within the established woollen and worsted industries. Dr Richard Pococke, the well-travelled Irish bishop, visiting Halifax in 1750, commented on its 'very plentiful market' and observed that the residents of the town were 'all people of business' engaged in 'a great manufacture in serges and cloths'.[2] In 1758 the Revd John Watson recorded no fewer than thirty-nine fulling mills in operation in the parish, over a fifth of them in the immediate vicinity of Halifax. He commented that by 1775 there was 'scarcely a single instance in the whole parish of a man's living entirely by farming'.[3] Besides supplying a growing domestic market and clothing British armies in the colonial conflicts of the late eighteenth century, export markets developed with Spain, Portugal, the Levant and Guinea where, Thomas Pennant observed in 1770, the cloths were 'wrapped in an oilcloth painted with negroes and elephants to captivate the natives'.[4] The Revd Thomas Twining, a Colchester cleric, visiting Halifax in 1781 remarked that 'the appearance of trade, population and advancement of every kind there is striking', with 'a perpetual stream … of men carrying bundles of cloth' to and from the magnificent new Manufacturers' Piece Hall constructed in 1779.[5] In 1788, Charles Dibdin, the popular composer, pronounced Halifax 'an astonishing trading town for its size' and compared the cloth hall with its 'prodigious number or cells' to a bee-hive humming with activity on market day.[6]

However, by the second decade of the nineteenth century, if not earlier, Halifax had lost its ascendancy in West Riding worsted production, which it had enjoyed since 1750, to neighbouring Bradford. Bradford's population was increasing at an even faster rate than that of Halifax after 1801 and receiving substantially higher rebates on the tax on soap used in the processing of wool for worsted manufacture during the period 1810–30, suggesting higher levels of worsted production. Paradoxically, because Halifax had a superior supply of water power, Bradford was compelled to make the transition to steam power earlier, exploiting its richer coal supplies. Halifax, on the periphery of the West Yorkshire coalfield, had fewer local reserves, and it proved costly to transport coal into the town until the opening of a direct canal link from the Calder and Hebble Navigation in 1828. Dr John Simpson of Bradford, comparing the fortunes of the two towns in 1825, concluded rather too forcefully that Halifax 'can scarce be called a manufacturing town, yet it is a place of considerable trade, but that trade is considerably on the decline and has been ever since Bradford began to rise into notice'.[7]

In truth, worsted manufacture continued to grow in Halifax and its neighbouring townships. No fewer than 50 per cent of the textile labour force was engaged in worsted production by 1835. Moreover, new textile industries were also successfully established in the parish, notably cotton and silk. Cotton manufacture had grown to predominance in the western townships of the parish bordering on Lancashire after 1780, and by the 1790s no fewer than one-third of the 140 cotton mills in the county of Yorkshire were located in the parish of Halifax. As shown in Table 4.2, by 1835 the number of cotton mills in the parish had risen to fifty-seven, though only two of these were situated in the township of Halifax. There were also four silk factories in the parish, where it was considered that local conditions were 'peculiarly adapted for the preservation of its colour', including two in the township of Halifax. By 1835, 16 per cent of textile workers in the parish were employed in textile mills in the township of Halifax. In 1837, the diarist Anne Lister, who only six years earlier had contrasted 'the fine clean air of Halifax' with the smoky atmosphere of Bradford and Leeds, observed that 'Halifax is now brightening into the polish of a large smoke-canopied commercial town'.[8]

Figure 4.1   Contemporary engraving of Halifax Piece Hall by William Burgess, 1788. This massive rectangular structure, enclosing a spacious courtyard, was built at a cost of over £12,000 as a market for woollen cloth between 1775 and 1778. It was opened on New Year's Day 1779 and was unusual because the clothiers made their sales from individual rooms accessed from the galleries. Although the hall flourished for three-and-a-half decades, buyers subsequently made their purchases directly from factory warehouses and by the early 1830s fewer than 200 of its 315 rooms were occupied. (Photograph: J. A. Hargreaves Collection)

Table 4.2.   *Textile mills and workers in the township and parish of Halifax, 1835*

	township		parish	
	mills	*workers*	*mills*	*workers*
Woollen	4	160	35	2104
Worsted	14	769	45	2551
Cotton	2	351	57	4267
Silk	2	272	4	777
Unoccupied	0		12	
Total	22	1552	153	9699

Source: Returns to Factory inspectors, 1835.

The transition to factory-based production was a gradual process in the parish of Halifax. Technological breakthroughs before 1780 in carding and spinning had stimulated the move towards factory production of cotton yarn during the last two decades of the eighteenth century and cotton power-loom weaving had become widespread by the late 1820s. But the mechanisation of the woollen and worsted industries was more gradual, extending over a period of at least sixty years. While woollen scribbling and worsted spinning had been mechanised by 1800, woollen spinning and worsted weaving were not mechanised until the 1820s. Woollen weaving and worsted combing remained predominantly cottage-based hand processes until the late 1840s and 1850s respectively. Indeed, until the 1840s there were no fewer than eleven gig mills engaged in the finishing process of woollen cloth, and these were still dependent on human or horse power. Water power was extensively used within the parish until the 1870s. Steam power was used initially only to supplement water power, and by 1806 only twelve steam engines can be identified in use in mills around Halifax. At least forty-seven were installed between 1807 and 1833 and a further seventy-three between 1834 and 1851, the majority in cotton and worsted mills.[9]

By 1851 the number of textile mills in the parish had risen to 254, including eighteen new spinning mills in the municipal borough of Halifax. During this period there were shifts in industrial location as new mills sprang up along the lines of the new railways into Halifax and other growing urban centres in the valley bottoms outside the town. By the time of the 1851 census 22 per cent of adult males in the Halifax registration district were employed in worsted manufacture, compared with 9 per cent in woollen and nearly 4 per cent in cotton manufacture. A sample study of 10 per cent of the working population of the Halifax and Skircoat Green registration districts shows that almost half of the total textile workforce was employed in the worsted industry.[10]

Although the economy of the town therefore depended primarily on textiles, it was the diversity of its manufactures by the second quarter of the nineteenth century that particularly impressed contemporary observers. Comparing Halifax and Bradford as centres of worsted manufacture in 1849, the journalist Angus Bethune Reach of the *Morning Chronicle* concluded that Halifax possessed a greater industrial diversity:

> The mayor, Mr. Crossley, for instance, is the chief partner in an immense carpet manufacturing establishment, employing about 1,500 hands, principally adult males, and paying about £1,000 weekly in wages. Besides this and other establishments of different kinds, the worsted manufacturers of Halifax prepare so great a variety of the staple production that periods of distress fall in general lighter upon them than on their Bradford neighbours.[11]

Besides textiles, carpet manufacture, trades allied to textiles such as dyeing, an embryonic machine-tool industry, and card-making (all businesses located principally in Halifax itself) there was also substantial pottery manufacture in the adjoining townships of Northowram and Southowram and fairly extensive coal mining and stone quarrying in the south east of

Figure 4.2   Dean Clough Mills, Halifax, c.1803. In 1802, John Crossley (c.1772–1837) and his business partners Thomas Crossley and James Travis took out a twenty-year lease of the premises at Dean Clough illustrated in this contemporary sketch. When the lease expired in 1822, the partnership was dissolved. John Crossley then renewed the lease for £340 and set up his own business. In 1824 he moved with his wife, Martha, and family to the house alongside the mill. By the time of his death in 1837, the firm, with 150 looms and some 300 employers, ranked as the fourth largest in the country. He left a personal estate of around £18,000 and was 'deeply lamented by his family and numerous circle of friends'. Three of his sons, John, Joseph and Francis, continued their father's business after his death, trading under the name of John Crossley and Sons. (Photograph courtesy of the West Yorkshire Archive Service, Calderdale)

Figure 4.3 Martha Crossley (1775–1854). Following her marriage to the carpet manufacturer John Crossley in 1801, Martha Crossley became 'the backbone of the family', taking 'a full share in the labours and responsibilities of her husband', in the view of the Victorian prophet of honest toil, Samuel Smiles. She later recalled that 'in addition to carpet making we carried on the manufacture of shalloons and plainbacks, the whole of which I managed myself'. She also 'made and stitched, with assistance, all the carpets that we sold retail', rising regularly before dawn. The oil portrait commissioned by her youngest son, Sir Francis Crossley, shows her plainly attired in silk bonnet, white shawl and dark dress, with an open Bible on her lap. Her earnest evangelical Nonconformity and celebrated vow that, 'if the Lord does bless us at this place, the poor shall taste of it', inspired a lavish philanthropy in her sons. (Photograph courtesy of Lord Somerleyton)

the parish, employing at least 1,200 men by 1831. In the Upper Calder Valley, at the time of the 1851 census, about one in eight families had some involvement with farming, many households still practising a dual economy, although by 1851 this often took the form of one or more members of the household working in textile factories. The topographer William White declared that Halifax by the middle of the nineteenth century ranked 'next to Leeds, Bradford, and Huddersfield as one of the principal seats and emporiums of the woollen and worsted manufactures' and that

> the scenery, viewed from the surrounding heights, exhibits a tract of country, which perhaps more than any other in the kingdom, serves to show how completely the wealth and industry of man can triumph over the most stubborn indispositions of nature.[12]

However, 'stubborn indispositions of nature' continued to hinder the development of transport systems. The rough, hilly terrain of the parish presented early road builders and later waterway and railway engineers with formidable problems. Some remoter parts of the parish continued to depend on the pack-horse until at least 1850. Elsewhere, increasing use was made of horse-drawn waggons. Details of regular services offered by carriers, no fewer than fifty of whom were operating in the town by 1845, were advertised in local newspapers and directories. Further turnpike roads were constructed, including routes to Keighley in 1753, to Burnley and Little-borough in 1760, to Huddersfield in 1777, and to Leeds in 1814 and 1826, but some of the major difficulties of approach to Halifax were only overcome

Figure 4.4
Pack-horses, 1814.
West Riding
clothiers
transporting their
cloth to market on
galloway ponies as
illustrated by the
Leeds artist George
Walker. The rough,
hilly terrain of the
parish of Halifax
presented road
builders with
considerable
problems and
some remoter parts
of the parish
continued to
depend on the
pack-horse until at
least 1850.
(Photograph;
J. A. Hargreaves
Collection)

1 Halifax and Keighley, 1753
2 Halifax, Burnley
   and Littleborough, 1760
3 Halifax and Huddersfield, 1777
4 Oldham and Ripponden, 1795
5 Leeds and Hebden Bridge, 1814

6 Mytholmroyd and Blackstone Edge, 1815
7 Huddersfield and Low Moor, 1824
8 Godley Lane Head and Northowram, 1825
9 Brighouse and Denholme Gate, 1826
10 Leeds and Whitehall, 1826

Figure 4.5
Turnpike roads,
1750–1850.

by major feats of civil engineering during the nineteenth century. The
Godley cutting and the Shibden embankment were constructed under a
Turnpike Act of 1824, amended in 1827 and completed in 1830. Hailed by
the diarist Anne Lister as 'a stupendous feat', the project involved cutting
through 731 metres of rocky hillside and building a high embankment to

take the road across the Shibden valley to Stump Cross. On the Halifax side of the cutting, Old Bank gave way to New Bank in 1837, leading towards the high-level six-arched North Bridge, which had been re-constructed in stone and opened for traffic in 1774.[13]

An Act of Parliament had been passed in 1700 for the construction of the Aire and Calder Navigation, the first project of its kind in England. However, its extension, the Calder and Hebble Navigation, surveyed by John Smeaton in 1757–65, and designed to bring the navigation into the

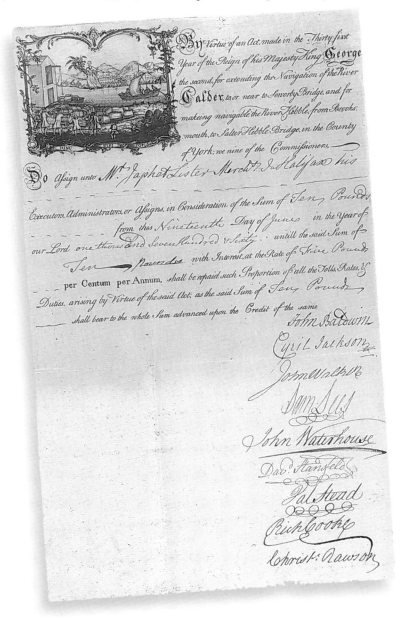

Figure 4.6 Share certificate of Japhet Lister, a Halifax merchant, in the Calder and Hebble Navigation, 1760. A meeting at the Talbot Inn, Halifax, on 2 September 1756 had decided to seek an Act of parliament to make navigable the Calder from Wakefield 'to Elland, and so on to Halifax' with the purpose of improving raw wool and corn supplies to the town. An Act of 1758 authorised the extension of the navigation and the whole works were surveyed and superintended by the builder of the Eddystone lighthouse, John Smeaton. In October 1767, however, a torrential storm so severely damaged the navigation that a further Act of Parliament was necessary before the ruined locks and sluices could be restored. (Photograph courtesy of West Yorkshire Archive Service, Calderdale)

parish of Halifax, was beset with problems, and the whole length of the navigation to Sowerby Bridge did not open until September 1770. Moreover, the critical trans-Pennine link with the Rochdale Canal was not made until 1802, and the Halifax Branch Canal from Salterhebble to Bailey Hall, linking Halifax directly with the new trans-Pennine route and the Calder and

Figure 4.7   Advertisement for the fast-sailing sloop, Altisidora, for the transhipment of cargo from the Three Cranes Wharf at Cheapside 'in the very heart of the City' of London to Salterhebble. The advertisement was printed in Halifax in the 1820s by T. Walker of Silver Street for James Boyne, the Halifax agent of the Union Contract Vessels. The handwritten note on the poster suggests that the cargo included flax destined for local mills. Goods would be transported from the Navigation Yard at Salterhebble by wagon into the town until the opening of the Halifax Branch Canal in 1828. (Photograph courtesy of West Yorkshire Archive Service, Calderdale)

Figure 4.8   Canals and railways, 1750–1850.

Hebble Navigation system, was not opened until 1828. The ascending gradient, rising thirty and a half metres in one-and-a-quarter miles, required the construction of no fewer than fourteen locks between Salterhebble and Bailey Hall and a pumping station at Siddal to augment the supply of water at Bailey Hall. The extension of the canal facilities to Halifax in 1828 enabled coal to be transported more easily into the heart of the town for use in manufacturing. Indeed, Anne Lister, who was keen to exploit the coal reserves on her own estates at Shibden, recorded ruefully in 1828 that local coal carted from Swale Moor to Halifax was considerably more expensive than coal fetched by canal from Kirklees to Salterhebble.[14]

There were similar delays in bringing the railway to Halifax; both Bradford and Huddersfield had the commercial advantage of earlier direct rail links. While the Calder Valley was along the route of the first trans-Pennine railway route, the Manchester and Leeds Railway, completed in 1841, a branch line to Halifax was not completed until 1844. Moreover, owing to a combination of difficult terrain and financial stringency, only a single line to Shaw Syke was constructed initially. Before 1844, passengers for Halifax had to alight at Sowerby Bridge and finish their journey by road. By 1850, the line had progressed as far as Low Moor but Halifax was only served by a temporary wooden station at the bottom of Horton Street, and this was not replaced by a more permanent stone structure until June 1855.[15]

It is evident, therefore, that the location of the town of Halifax gave rise to problems, but that its demographic and economic growth had not been thwarted by them. Halifax had become and remained by 1850 a principal manufacturing as well as retailing centre, one among several such new industrial towns in the West Riding of Yorkshire. But this transformation was more than economic. It carried implications for social structure and living standards.

Social structure, occupations and living standards

Few landowning gentry families continued to reside in the parish of Halifax during the period of its industrial transformation in the late eighteenth and early nineteenth centuries following the departure of the largest landowning family, the Saviles, in the early modern period. An assessment list of thirty-eight gentry from the parish who paid the male servants' tax in 1780 revealed only seven property owners with more than one male servant. Only two, John Rhodes and Samuel Smith, each with two servants, resided in the urban township of Halifax. Joshua Horton (1720–93) of Howroyd, Barkisland, who headed the list with five servants, was exceptional, serving as a county magistrate and initiating hare hunting in the parish in 1754. The only other property owner assessed for more than two servants in 1780 was John Caygill, a wealthy merchant who lived at the Shay and

Figure 4.9   Howroyd, Barkisland, drawn by John Horner in 1835, was the seat of the Horton family, the most prominent local landed gentry family in the late eighteenth and early nineteenth centuries. The hall-and-cross-wings house with hearth-passage was constructed in 1642. A 1655 inventory reveals a dining parlour, little parlour and maids' parlour in the east wing, a lower parlour and timber store in the west wing, a kitchen and buttery to the rear. The hall, open through two storeys, served as an impressive reception area with its decorated fireplace, plaster overmantel and ceiling, gallery and painted glass windows. (Photographed courtesy of Calderdale Museums Service, Bankfield)

Figure 4.10   Anne Lister (1791–1840). Although born in Halifax on 3 April 1791, Anne Lister spent her childhood years in the East Riding and was educated at Ripon and York. She moved to Halifax in 1806 and to Shibden Hall in 1815 to live with her uncle and aunt, inheriting the 400-acre Shibden estate in 1826, in the death of her uncle. She subsequently embarked on a Lesbian affair with Ann Walker of Crow Nest, a neighbouring heiress. They ultimately contracted a clandestine dynastic marriage, developing the coal deposits on their estates with entrepreneurial flair and energy. Her journal, partly written in a secret code, commenced 1806 and runs to almost four million words. (Photograph courtesy of Calderdale Museums Service, Shibden Hall)

Figure 4.11 The Russian passport of Anne Lister of Shibden Hall, Halifax, 1839. Anne Lister was already an accomplished European traveller when she left Shibden in June 1839 to embark on her final journey to Russia, the Caucasus and the Middle East, where she hoped to ascend Mount Ararat. She had been the first amateur mountaineer to reach the summit of Vignemale in the French Pyrenees in August 1838, beating the Prince of Moscow by several days. Her travels, described vividly in her journals, were brought abruptly to an end when she was bitten by a fever-carrying tick on 8 August and died in Georgia on 22 September 1840. Her body was brought back to England for burial in Halifax Parish Church and her obituary in the *Halifax Guardian* in October 1840 compared her exploits to those of such distinguished contemporaries as Lady Mary Wortley Montagu and Lady Hester Stanhope. (Photograph courtesy of West Yorkshire Archive Service, Calderdale)

contributed generously to the building of the Halifax Manufacturers' Piece Hall in 1779.[16]

Increasingly, by the early nineteenth century, socially aspiring families such as the Rawsons, the Edwards, the Priestleys and the Listers combined land or property ownership with manufacturing or trade. Anne Lister (1791–1840), who inherited the Shibden estate from her uncle, James Lister (1748–1826), was by far the most remarkable. Astutely managing her rental incomes and exploiting the limited mineral resources on her estate sufficiently to sustain extensive European travel, she bequeathed to posterity, when she finally succumbed to a fatal fever-carrying tick in the Caucasus in 1840, a candid four-million word diary. It revealed her business acumen, clandestine lesbian lifestyle and disdain for *nouveaux riches* worsted manufacturers, whose Liberal politics and nonconformist roots she despised.[17]

The opulence of many local merchants and manufacturers is evident from the fine Georgian mansions they commissioned in the late eighteenth century on the southern edge of the town. They impressed contemporary visitors to the town such as Thomas Twining, who in 1781 commented on 'the many magnificent houses lately built, and now daily building', in and about the town 'by the manufacturers chiefly'.[18] They included Shay House, Stoney Royd, Hope Hall, Clare Hall, Well Head, Savile Hall, Pye Nest and, close to the centre of the town, Somerset House. This last was built in 1766 by the celebrated York architect, John Carr, for John Royds, a prosperous woollen merchant, who provided overnight accommodation in his new mansion for King Christian VII of Denmark on his northern tour in 1768. Dorothy Wordsworth (1771–1855), sister of the poet, on her return to Westmorland in 1817, recalled the hospitality and domestic comforts of the Rawsons in their 'large house' at Savile Green in Halifax with 'servants to perform the work as by magic'.[19] Dr John Simpson of Bradford remarked,

Figure 4.12   A view of Stoney Royd from the grounds of Hope Hall by John Horner in 1835. Stoney Royd, built for Christopher Rawson 'a little before 1764' was an early example of fashionable brick construction in Halifax. Christopher Rawson (1712–80), the third son of John Rawson of Bolton, who married Grace, the daughter of John Rawson of Beckfoot, was succeeded in the possession of Stoney Royd by his elder son, John (1744–1815), who married Nelly, the daughter of David Stansfeld of Hope Hall. Stoney Royd as depicted by Horner was of square design with slightly projecting pedimented central boys on two visible sides and a hipped roof. The house was demolished after the grounds were purchased by the borough for a public cemetery and hospital in 1860. (Photograph courtesy of Calderdale Museums Service, Bankfield)

Figure 4.13   A view of Hope Hall by John Horner from the grounds of Stoney Royd in 1835. Hope House, as it was then known, was erected in 1765 for David Stansfeld, a cloth merchant from Leeds, by James Green. It replaced an earlier building on the site and is one of the few remaining examples of find Georgian mansions built for local merchants and manufacturers on the southern edge of the town in the late eighteenth century. However, the unusual winged two-way stone stairway at its east front entrance and its extensive landscaped grounds have not survived. The house became the home of Christopher Rawson, the eldest son of John and Nelly Rawson, a leading Halifax banker, after his marriage to Mary Anne Brooks of Westminster in 1808. It was acquired by the Albany Club in 1906. (Photograph courtesy of Calderdale Museums Service, Bankfield)

in an entry in his journal for 1825, that 'the neighbourhood of Halifax is much better filled with families of respectability than most provincial towns'. He concluded that 'Halifax is a much genteeler place than Bradford'.[20]

Indeed, Halifax even gained some recognition as a fashionable Regency spa following the opening of a suite of hot and cold baths and extensive pleasure gardens by Thomas Rawlinson, an enterprising Halifax plumber, on a site adjoining Lilly Lane, which he acquired in 1784. Early patrons included Charles Howard (1746–1815), eleventh Duke of Norfolk, who in July 1806 pronounced the buildings 'elegant and commodious' and 'highly creditable to the town of Halifax'. An advertisement in the *Halifax Journal* in 1803 maintained that the baths at Lilly Lane were as 'completely fitted up' as those of Bath, Buxton and Matlock, while Walker's *Directory* of 1846 boasted that Halifax possessed 'one of the most extensive suites of baths

Figure 4.14 Britannia, Somerset House, George Street, Halifax. The York architect John Carr built a magnificent town house for the prosperous Halifax woollen merchant John Royds in 1766, with ornate rococo plasterwork by Giuseppe Cortese. In the saloon, the coved ceiling represented Royds as Neptune surrounded by his four daughters, while above the fireplace his wife was depicted as Britannia. The couple provided overnight accommodation for the young King Christian VII of Denmark on his tour of northern England in 1768 and for the Marquis of Rockingham's enquiry into counterfeiting in 1769. (Photograph courtesy of Ian Beesley)

to be found in Yorkshire, consisting of hot, cold, tepid, swimming, shower, vapour and sulphur baths, with suitable and convenient dressing rooms'.[21]

During the first half of the nineteenth century yet more manufacturers who had risen from obscure beginnings established their town houses and

Figure 4.15   Lilly Lane Baths, Halifax. Extensive bathing and recreational facilities were developed by Thomas Rawlinson, an enterprising Halifax plumber, on a site at Coldwell Ing leased from the trustees of the Waterhouse Charities in 1784. Of fashionable brick construction, the baths ultimately comprised the long oval-shaped open-air pool, illustrated in this contemporary lithograph by N. Whittock, an entire suite of indoor baths, dining and dressing rooms, extensive pleasure gardens, a quoits ground and bowling green. An early patron, Charles Howard, eleventh Duke of Norfolk, pronounced the buildings 'elegant and commodious' and 'highly creditable to the town of Halifax'. (Photograph courtesy of Calderdale Museums Service, Bankfield)

Figure 4.16   Bankfield. Edward Akroyd, the Halifax worsted manufacturer, purchased Bankfield following his marriage in 1838 and defended it against an attack by a Chartist mob in 1842. It was extended and redesigned in the Regency style in 1857. In 1867 the Atkinson brothers of York transformed it into a grand Italianate mansion with 100 rooms, at a cost of £80,000. Shortly before it was sold in 1886, the *Halifax Courier* compared the house with the residences of Sir Titus Salt at Crow Nest and John Crossley at Manor Heath: 'They were not just so many spacious buildings: they were the homes of men who were dear to their fellows by reason of the love they bore to them and the good they did, true living philanthropists with souls far above the huge businesses which each had to conduct'. Appropriately, it soon re-opened as a museum and public library. (Photograph: J. A. Hargreaves Collection)

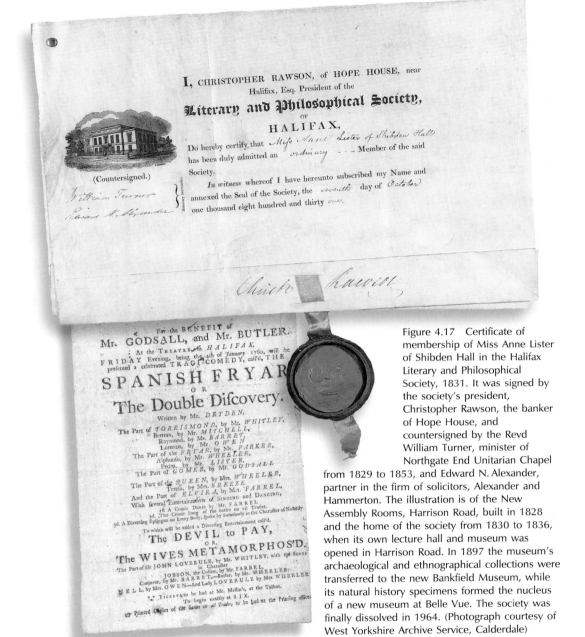

Figure 4.17 Certificate of membership of Miss Anne Lister of Shibden Hall in the Halifax Literary and Philosophical Society, 1831. It was signed by the society's president, Christopher Rawson, the banker of Hope House, and countersigned by the Revd William Turner, minister of Northgate End Unitarian Chapel from 1829 to 1853, and Edward N. Alexander, partner in the firm of solicitors, Alexander and Hammerton. The illustration is of the New Assembly Rooms, Harrison Road, built in 1828 and the home of the society from 1830 to 1836, when its own lecture hall and museum was opened in Harrison Road. In 1897 the museum's archaeological and ethnographical collections were transferred to the new Bankfield Museum, while its natural history specimens formed the nucleus of a new museum at Belle Vue. The society was finally dissolved in 1964. (Photograph courtesy of West Yorkshire Archive Service, Calderdale)

Figure 4.18 Theatre bill for 1760. Before the opening of the first purpose-built Halifax theatre in 1789, plays were performed in the inn yards of the Old Cock and the White Lion and the Assembly Rooms at the Talbot. Indeed, surviving play-bills exist from as early as 1758 announcing performances at 'The New Theatre at the Talbot' in Woolshops, where the tragi-comedy 'The Spanish Fryar' was to be presented in January 1760. A regular London theatre-goer, writing to the Halifax *Union Journal* in 1759, recalled the pleasure enjoyed 'this night at the performance at the little theatre in the town' and concluded that 'there are performers now here worthy of the attention and applause of the judicious'. (Photograph courtesy of West Yorkshire Archive Service, Calderdale) mansions in Halifax. In 1818 Jonathan Akroyd (1782–1847) moved from the remote hilltop farmstead where his father James Akroyd (1753–1830), a small yeoman clothier specialising in the production of 'little Joans' and figured 'Amens', had founded the family worsted manufacturing enterprise, to a town house in North Parade, Halifax, conveniently situated near the firm's Bowling Dyke Mills, and later to a mansion at Woodside. His son, Edward (1810–1887), who inherited an estate valued at £300,000 and one of the most successful textile firms in the country on his father's sudden death in 1847, set about transforming the small house at Bankfield, which he had purchased on his marriage in 1838, into a more substantial Regency style mansion. John (1772–1837) and Martha (1775–1854) Crossley, founders of the carpet-weaving dynasty at Dean Clough remained close to their Dean Clough mills, but their sons, John, Joseph and Francis, who inherited the family business in 1837, lived in town houses in Halifax until, following their marriages, they moved to more commodious mansions on the outskirts of the town.[22]

The leading property owners, merchants, industrialists and representatives of the professional classes of the town and its environs formed an urban elite which dominated the social and cultural life of the town for most of this period. It is true that the London doctor and author, Dr A. B. Granville, who visited Halifax in 1839, remained singularly unimpressed by the social ambience of the town:

Society affords, perhaps, fewer resources in Halifax than one would be led to expect, considering the large number of opulent families resident in or about the place. There is not much intercourse among the various sections of the community: and although six great public balls are given in the very handsome Musical Hall, few families of distinction are known to attend them.[23]

Figure 4.19   New Halifax Assembly and Concert Rooms. Built by public subscription in the 1820s, the New Assembly Rooms provided commodious rooms for many purposes which the Old Assembly Rooms at the Talbot Inn in Woolshops could no longer accommodate. The circulating library there in 1836 contained 7,000 volumes and in 1881 the first municipal library was housed there. The rooms became the venue for dinners and balls held by the West Yorkshire Yeomanry. The rooms were demolished by 1898, when the site was used for the erection of the Halifax Borough Police Court, which was opened in October 1900. (Photograph courtesy of Calderdale Museums Service, Bankfield)

Nevertheless, socially and culturally, the town was bursting with activity. There were two public circulating subscription libraries, one founded as early as 1769, the other in 1823; a music club formed in 1767 by the musician hired to play the parish church's new organ; a choral society, founded in 1817, for which Mendelssohn in 1842 composed a setting of the 114th Psalm; an orchestral society, founded in 1833; a madrigal society, founded in 1844; a mechanics institute, founded in 1825; a literary and philosophical society, founded in 1830, and a host of other clubs and societies. One of the first provincial theatres was opened at Halifax in 1791, superseding earlier open-air venues in the inn yards of the Old Cock and White Lion and the Assembly Rooms at the Talbot. New Assembly Rooms were opened in Harrison Road in 1825, and the Oddfellows' Hall, described by one contemporary visitor as 'by far the handsomest edifice in the town', was opened in St James's Road in 1840, both buildings providing extensive accommodation for a wide range of social and cultural activities.[24]

Moreover, Edward's bookshop in Old Market had gained a national reputation, as Thomas Twining observed in 1781, as 'one of the best and

Figure 4.20 Old Market, 1800. A prospect taken from the window of Thomas Edward's famous bookshop by John Horner in 1835. Edwards' eldest son Walter Fawkes Edwards and his son-in-law Thomas Adam were subscribers to Horner's collection of prints of buildings in the town and parish of Halifax 'drawn from nature and on stone' and the view of Old Market completed the series. Several open-air stalls are visible displayed a variety of wares and the soldiers in the foreground are wearing the uniform of the Halifax Volunteers. (Photograph courtesy of Calderdale Museums Service, Bankfield)

most elegant binders in England', supplying and binding books for the most discriminating collectors throughout the land. On the other hand, William Milner (1803–50) of Swine Market and later Cheapside, was one of the pioneer publishers of popular cheap editions of literary classics. The *Union Journal*, one of the earliest Yorkshire newspapers, published in 1759–60, was printed by Pressic Darby, a pioneering Halifax printer. A successor, the *Halifax Journal*, published between 1801 and 1811, was also relatively short-lived. However, the *Halifax Guardian*, established in 1832, survived until its amalgamation in 1921 with the *Halifax Courier*, founded in 1853, providing evidence of a growing urban readership and reflecting the increasing interest in local politics following the borough's enfranchisement in 1832.[25]

Rateable values of property in the township of Halifax climbed steadily in the second half of the eighteenth century from £3,117 in 1750 to £5,960 in 1800. However, in 1832, of the 20,000 inhabitants of the townships of Halifax, Northowram and Southowram included within the boundaries of the new parliamentary constituency of Halifax created by the 1832 Reform Act, only 531 adult men qualified for the new £10 householder franchise. Indeed, the proportion of relatively poor households in the township of Halifax appears to have increased in the late eighteenth and early nineteenth centuries as Halifax developed into a manufacturing as well as a commercial centre. In 1760 it was reckoned that over half of the population of the township of Halifax could not be expected to contribute towards water rents, some because they resided outside the supply area but the vast majority because they simply could not afford it. Moreover, Dr John Smail's analysis of the land tax returns of 1782 has revealed that no fewer than 83 per cent of the 1,514 households in the township of Halifax were exempted from payment. This was twice the number exempt from the Hearth Tax in 1664, suggesting that there were double the number of households in late-eighteenth century Halifax living at or below the poverty line than there had been a century earlier. He has therefore concluded that the impact of the development of large-scale manufacturing on Halifax's society was 'an increasingly polarised social structure that no longer corresponded to the social world of the middling sort' of the early modern period.[26]

Technological and structural innovation in the primary textile industries of the parish in the last two decades of the eighteenth century and the first half of the nineteenth century, when Halifax masters strove vainly to halt the area's relative decline as a centre of textile production in the face of growing competition from Leeds, Bradford and Huddersfield, had a devastating effect on some sections of the community and in particular on the domestic outworkers. The transition from an extensive web of relatively small-scale domestic manufacture to an all-embracing system of factory production was a slow, painful and inexorable process for the individuals, families and communities most directly affected. Large numbers of male

Figure 4.21
Waltroyd,
Wheatley,
photographed from
the south in 1938.
The handloom
weaver, Cornelius
Ashworth farmed
at Waltroyd from
c.1780 to 1816
with the assistance
of two or three
men, possibly
relatives. The
property consisted
of three bays each
with low mullioned
windows at ground
floor and first floor
levels and a simple
doorway.
(Photograph
courtesy of Halifax
Antiquarian Society)

handloom weavers and woolcombers, for example, experienced not only a marked decline in their material prosperity and an erosion of their independent artisan status, but also a diminution of their authority within their own families as the demand for female and juvenile factory labour increased.[27]

Returns to the factory inspectorate in 1835 reveal that textile factory workers then represented 10 per cent of the population of the township of Halifax: of these 46 per cent were male, 54 per cent female and 71 per cent under twenty-one. A sample study of the Halifax and Skircoat census returns for 1851 has shown that, sixteen years later, one-third of the total work force of the two townships was under twenty years of age, with a higher ratio of females to males, and one in eight of the workers were under fourteen. Most of the younger children in full employment were employed as spinners, doffers and menders in textile factories, though examples could still be found of very young children working for their fathers at home.[28]

Controversy erupted in October 1830 over the treatment of young factory workers when, following Richard Oastler's famous 'Yorkshire Slavery' letter to the *Leeds Mercury* denouncing the worsted mills in the town and neighbourhood of Bradford as 'magazines of infantile slavery', another correspondent, Richard Webster of Halifax, promptly alleged that conditions in the mills around Halifax were even more miserable. The controversy was fuelled by the issue of a pamphlet at the height of the campaign for a Ten Hours Bill in 1833 which made more specific allegations about long hours, harsh regulations, severe punishments, low wages and inequitable

Figure 4.22 Extract from the diary of Cornelius Ashworth of Waltroyd, Wheatley, 1785. Ashworth appears to have been exceptionally literate and served in 1780 as overseer of the poor for the township of Ovenden. His four diaries covering the period from 1782 to 1816 provide invaluable information about the domestic system of cloth production, farming, the climate and social conditions. In 1785, following an illness, he abandoned his weaving and concentrated on farming his smallholding. The extract records visits to Halifax to attend Sunday worship. (Photograph courtesy of West Yorkshire Archive Service, Calderdale)

Figure 4.23 Halifax General Dispensary. A meeting at the Talbot Inn called by Dr H. W. Coulthurst, the Vicar of Halifax in 1807, resolved to establish the first general dispensary in Halifax, where medical treatment, medicine and advice could be received by the poor 'free from all expenses'. The total number of patients admitted to the dispensary from its opening in Hatters Close in February 1808 to 1831 was 80,346. In 1825 a surgical ward was opened in a nearby cottage property. (Photograph courtesy of Calderdale Museums Service, Bankfield)

truck systems in local mills. These allegations were strongly repudiated at the time by the Halifax masters, but over the next two decades, as a response to the unremitting efforts of the factory reformers, factories became subject to increasing statutory regulation and inspection. Indeed, in 1849, Angus Bethune Reach was most favourably impressed by the congenial working environment at Holdsworth's Shaw Lodge Mills and Akroyd's Bowling Dyke Mills, the two largest worsted factories in Halifax. They contrasted markedly, he judged, with the rapidly deteriorating conditions of the local domestic outworkers he also visited.[29]

The poorer sections of Halifax society were also, of course, more susceptible to sickness and disease, which could have devastating effects. Cornelius Ashworth (1752–1821), who combined handloom weaving with the management of a smallholding at Waltroyd, Wheatley, abandoned his weaving in 1785, following an illness. Three years earlier in his diary he had recorded observing ten open graves in Halifax parish churchyard, 'nine of them for children, and was informed that 110 children had been interred in the above yard in four weeks who had died of smallpox'.[30] In 1807, on the initiative of the Vicar of Halifax, the Revd Dr H. W. Coulthurst (1753–1817), the Halifax General Dispensary was founded, particularly to meet the needs of poor patients residing within the township of Halifax. It opened in 1808 in Hatters Close, moving subsequently to premises in Dispensary Walk owned by the trustees of the Waterhouse Charities. In 1825 a surgical ward was opened in nearby cottage property and by 1830 some 213 patients had been admitted for treatment, of whom 178 were casualties, many of them admitted as a result of industrial accidents caused by 'the general and extensive introduction of machinery'. However, demand continued to grow and in 1838 the magnificent new Halifax Infirmary and Dispensary with its imposing portico, designed by George Townshend Andrews and financed largely by public subscription, was opened on a site in Blackwall adjacent to the New Assembly Rooms.[31]

However, death rates in general and infant mortality in particular remained high, and in 1845 the Health of Towns Commission reported that the average life expectancy at birth within the Halifax Poor Law Union was 26 years 10 months and of those surviving into adulthood 53 years 9 months. The commissioners' report identified the lack of an adequate sewerage system and the industrial pollution from the steam-powered factories along the Hebble as major problems, but reserved its most severe strictures for the poor quality housing. It condemned the 'damp wretched looking dwellings' in the east end of the town and the folds or enclosed spaces in other localities in which 'the lowest grade of working people' were confined in 'very damp and filthy' conditions as 'seats of poverty and disease'. It commented that 'with a low state of finances and morals' they were 'kept in a depressed condition by the outward filth and effluvium which assails them at every step'.[32]

During the period from 1750 to 1850 there was growing concern for the cultural deprivation and moral depravity of the lower classes in Halifax and its hinterland. John Styles has argued that the rise of the yellow trade, a novel combination of counterfeiting and clipping gold currency, in Cragg Vale and other parts of the Calder Valley in the late 1760s, was 'facilitated by the isolation of the locality from those sources of formal and informal authority which sustained eighteenth-century law enforcement'. The activities of the coiners, which by 1769 were believed to be 'so firmly established in the neighbourhood of Halifax' as almost 'to bid defiance to the civil power', sent shock waves through the urban community when William Dighton, supervisor of the excise at Halifax, was assassinated at Savile Close, near to the centre of the town, in 1769. His death prompted a government enquiry conducted by the Marquis of Rockingham and a series of trials which resulted in the executions of David Hartley and James Oldfield in 1770; Robert Thomas in 1774 and Matthew Normanton in 1775. The bodies of Thomas and Normanton were hung in chains on Beacon Hill, Halifax, at the request of magistrates in the hope that 'such a notorious and public example may happily deter any future crimes of so shocking a nature being perpetrated in a neighbourhood that has long been infested with a most dangerous set of villains'.[33]

However, there were further prosecutions for counterfeiting in 1779 and

THE HALIFAX INFIRMARY.

Reports of Superintending Inspectors of the General Board of Health.

VIEW OF OPEN SEWER
ABOVE CORN MARKET, HALIFAX.

Facing: Figure 4.24 Halifax Infirmary. This drawing by John Horner shows the new infirmary, which replaced the old dispensary. Designed by George Townshend Andrews and financed largely by public subscriptions it opened on a site in Blackwall adjacent to the New Assembly Rooms in 1838. In 1845 a member of the commission inquiring into the sanitary conditions of large towns described the new infirmary and dispensary as 'an elegant and commodious house, where good attention is paid to patients', though the housekeeper and her assistants 'much complained' of deficiencies in the sanitation. (Photograph courtesy of Calderdale Museums Service, Bankfield)

Figure 4.25 Open sewer, Corn Market, Halifax. The report of the Health of Towns Commission in 1845 identified the lack of an adequate sewerage system as a major problem in Halifax. The town was only partially sewered and there was a great need for under-sewerage. In April 1845 a branch of the Health of Towns Association chaired by the Vicar of Halifax, Archdeacon Musgrave, was formed, but William Ranger, surveying the sanitary provision in the township of Northowram in 1850 commented on the lack of privies and discovered that in Middle Street, Haley Hill, there was only one privy for the use of 221 persons. (Photograph courtesy of Halifax Antiquarian Society)

WHEREAS the Practice of Clipping the Gold Coin of this Kingdom hath for a considerable Time last past been carried on in the Parish of Halifax, and Towns adjacent, and in divers other Places within the West-Riding of the County of York,

AND WHEREAS there is great Reason to believe, that numbers of Persons have been drawn in to the Commission of the said Offence, not knowing at the Time, that by the Laws of this Realm, the same is declared to be HIGH TREASON, and afterwards having come to the Knowledge of the Consequence of their Offence, have nevertheless continued in the Practice thereof, from an Apprehension that they could not make a Discovery without convicting themselves;

It is therefore thought proper to give this Public
NOTICE,

That by an Act of Parliament past in the Seventh Year of the Reign of his late Majesty King William the Third, any Person guilty of Coining, Clipping or Diminishing the Current Coin of this Realm, who shall afterwards Discover two or more Persons who have committed either of the said Crimes, and give Information thereof to any One of his Majesty's Justices of the Peace, so as Two or more be convicted of the same, is thereby declared intitled to his MAJESTY's PARDON for all his said Crimes which he may have committed before such Discovery, and if such Person be an Apprentice, he is thereby declared to be a Freeman, and hath thereby Liberty to Exercise any lawful Trade, Profession, or Mystery, with all Liberties and Privileges, and in as full and ample Manner as if he had served the full Time of his Apprenticeship, and is moreover by the said Act intitled to the Reward of FORTY POUNDS for every Person convicted.

WM. CHAMBERLAYNE,
Sollicitor to his Majesty's Mint.

WHITE LION, HALIFAX,
14th DECEMBER, 1769.

N. B. The Towns of *Halifax, Leeds*, and *Bradford*, have offered a Reward of TEN GUINEAS for every Person convicted, over and above the Reward allowed by Act of Parliament.

Figure 4.26 Government proclamation issued by the Solicitor to the Royal Mint from the White Lion, Silver Street, Halifax 14 December 1769. The government despatched William Chamberlayne, Solicitor to the Royal Mint, to Halifax in December 1769 following the assassination of William Dighton, supervisor of the excise at Halifax by local coiners. His first action was to issue a proclamation in the form of a handbill and as a newspaper advertisement offering rewards for information leading to the conviction of those engaged in clipping or counterfeiting coin of the realm. (Photograph: J. A. Hargreaves Collection)

With acknowledgments to "The Illustrated London News."

PLUG RIOTERS AT NORTH BRIDGE, 15th August, 1842.

Figure 4.27   Plug rioters at North Bridge, 15 August 1842. Disturbances erupted in Halifax in August 1842, following the rejection of the second Chartist national petition. Rioters converged on the town from both Todmorden and Bradford, determined to halt factory production by removing the plugs from the mill boilers. Large numbers of special constables were sworn in to supplement the two companies of infantry and two troops of cavalry already stationed in the town. The *Halifax Guardian* estimated that at the height of the trouble there was a mob of around 25,000 people on the streets of Halifax, which succeeded in bringing most of the mills in the town to a standstill. On the following day a crowd threatened the Akroyd mills at Haley Hill. Shots were fired, the cavalry made a number of charges, three men were wounded and over thirty prisoners taken. However, by 19 August the riots had subsided and the mills had re-opened. (Photograph courtesy of *The Illustrated London News*)

Figure 4.28 Wesley Chapel, drawn by John Horner, 1836. The years 1827–29 were years of sustained growth in membership for Halifax Wesleyanism. The growing confidence was signalled by the opening of a second Wesleyan chapel for the town in November 1829 in Broad Street to relieve overcrowding at the South Parade Chapel, which had been opened in 1777 and extended in 1812. The new chapel which was praised for its 'general symmetry', 'handsome palisadoes' and 'chaste, comely and pleasing' interior was completed at a cost of £4,000, a quarter of which was raised in collection at the opening services conducted by leading Wesleyans, including Jabez Bunting, a former circuit superintendent minister. The chapel closed in August 1949 and was demolished in September 1968. (Photograph courtesy of Calderdale Museums Service, Bankfield)

1782, when three Halifax coiners originally sentenced to death were later reprieved and transported for life. In 1783 another former coiner, Thomas Spencer, was arrested with a recently discharged young soldier, Mark Satton-stall, for inciting a starving mob to seize supplies of corn from carts and wagons in the centre of the town. The two ringleaders were tried at York 'for being concerned in the late riots in the town and neighbourhood of Halifax', sentenced to death and executed on Beacon Hill, the last public executions to take place in Halifax. Moreover, quarter sessions records reveal a social world built around the workshop and the alehouse often issuing in petty theft and sexual slander. In 1783, Isaac Schofield, a weaver, and some of his mates, who were woolcombers, perpetrated a series of thefts over several months including rabbits, ducks, fleeces, bags of shot and coal, generally selling what they took and spending the money on beer. An earlier defamation case in 1769 depicted the same kind of workshop culture. Elizabeth Hitcheon claimed that Absalom Wilkinson, who had been drinking ale with his shopmates, called her a 'whore and a brimstone whore'.[34]

Later, G. S. Philipps, secretary of the Huddersfield Mechanics' Institute, visiting Cragg Vale in 1848 where counterfeiting had formerly thrived, formed an impression of continuing cultural and moral deprivation:

> there is an aspect of ... barbarism about the people which is very melancholy. The children are ragged and dirty, running about the roadside, as if they belonged to nobody. The men are uncouth, brutal, and cast in the most animal moulds. Their leisure hours are spent in playing at pitch-halfpenny, in eating, drinking, and all manner of debaucheries ... The women, likewise, are unwomanly in their appearance, reminding one of the sexless witches in Macbeth ... I think *missionaries* were never more wanted, not even in the floating islands of Polynesia, than amongst this sad, degraded people.[35]

In 1849 Edward Akroyd, shocked by the rural and urban rioting which accompanied the Plug Plot disturbances in the summer of 1842, commenced his first model industrial community at Copley, near Halifax, where he had purchased mills in 1844. This attempt to raise the living standards of the labouring classes and develop an industrious and loyal factory work-force, was an early manifestation of 'a general movement in the West Riding which saw the introduction of a whole range of paternalistic measures to heal class divisions and indoctrinate working men and women with the middle-class values of respectability, earnestness and self-help'. However, the movement only came to maturity after 1851.[36]

Religion and politics

The cultural deprivation and moral depravation evident within the new industrial society of Halifax and its hinterland in the late eighteenth and early nineteenth centuries also presented a challenge to both the Established Church and Nonconformity during this period. Nowhere did the Church of England's parochial and diocesan structure appear less well-equipped to respond to the impact of social and economic change than in the vast, sprawling upland parish of Halifax, situated on the remote south-western periphery of the huge diocese of York. Covering an area larger than that of the county of Rutland, the parish of Halifax was the largest parish in Yorkshire, and twice as large as the neighbouring parish of Bradford. While the establishment of two medieval parochial chapelries at Elland and Heptonstall had effectively subdivided the parish into three more manageable administrative units, the parochial district of Halifax, the largest of the three units, encompassed no fewer than ten civil townships. The inadequacies of the parochial system were mirrored by the inadequacies of the diocesan structure. Until the creation of the diocese of Ripon in 1836, Halifax occupied a far-flung corner of the huge diocese of York, with its 903 parishes and chapelries.[37]

Where Anglican provision was weak or non-existent, Evangelical Nonconformity tended to be strong. John Crabtree, the first local historian to take account of the industrial transformation of the parish, attributed the 'rapid increase of dissenting meeting houses' within the parish by 1836 to 'the want of church accommodation'. By 1843 Edward Baines's denominational survey identified 110 Nonconformist chapels in the parish with accommodation for almost a third of the parish population, more than double that provided by the 22 Anglican churches. Moreover, Nonconformist Sunday school enrolment of 22,713 scholars had completely outpaced that of the Church of England with its 5,633 scholars. When the Census of Religious Worship was taken in 1851, only 31 of the 126 places of worship included in returns from the Halifax Poor Law Union were Anglican. Total Methodist attendances alone in the incomplete returns for the Halifax Municipal Borough amounted to 73.28 per cent of total Anglican attendances.[38]

Despite a series of damaging secessions in which the Halifax Wesleyans lost nearly half of their membership to the Independents in 1762, over a quarter of their membership to the Methodist New Connexion in 1797, and over a third of their remaining membership to the Wesleyan Reformers in 1851, the Halifax Wesleyans still recorded the largest number of Nonconformist attendances at worship in Halifax on Census Sunday in 1851. Membership growth was steady rather than spectacular in the middle years of the eighteenth century, reaching 1,000 in 1786, but accelerated dramatically during the Great Yorkshire Revival of 1793–94. John Wesley visited the town for the opening of the new South Parade Wesleyan Chapel in 1777. A second, more ornate Wesley Chapel, displaying, John Crabtree acclaimed, 'a degree of taste' unsurpassed 'by any chapels belonging to this denomination of Christians in the West Riding', was opened at Broad Street in

Figure 4.29 Hanover Street Methodist New Connexion Chapel. The Methodist New Connexion chose a location in the expanding western sector of the town for their second chapel at Hanover Street. Laying the foundation stone for the new chapel, the foundation stone for the new chapel, the Revd William Ford proclaimed confidently that the New Connexion Methodists new 'were advancing in a cheering degree, as might be proved by comparing their followers, as to wealth, numbers and station with any other species of seceders'. The new chapel, which opened in 1836, was both 'commodious' and 'entirely free from ornamentation'. After the closure of the chapel, it was acquired by the Halifax Thespians for conversion into the Halifax Playhouse. (Photograph courtesy of Calderdale Museums Service, Bankfield)

Figure 4.30 Square Independent Chapel, drawn by Thomas Bradley, 1789. The design of both the chapel, which opened in 1772, and the adjacent Halifax Piece Hall, which opened in 1779, have been attributed to Thomas Bradley, who subsequently became engineer to the Calder and Hebble Navigation Company and was later buried in the chapel graveyard. The classical red-brick chapel, which was situated in the south-east corner of a field known as Talbot Croft in the Square, was adapted for use as a Sunday School when the adjacent Victorian Gothic Square Congregational Church was opened in 1857. When both buildings closed, after years of neglect, the Square Chapel Trust acquired the chapel building in 1988 for restoration as an arts centre. (Photograph courtesy of Calderdale Museums Service, Bankfield)

Figure 4.31 Sion Independent Chapel, drawn by John Horner, 1836. Occupying a building in Wade Street formerly used by Wesleyan Secessionists and Southcottians, Sion Chapel was an offshoot of Square Chapel in 1816. In 1819 a ashlar-fronted building of classical design was opened with seating for 1,020 and a schoolroom in the basement. Among the first trustees of the chapel was John Baldwin, who became first Mayor of Halifax in 1848. The chapel and school were enlarged and extended between 1846 and 1866, but the church finally closed in 1959. In 1989 the facades of both the church and school buildings were incorporated into the design of the new bus station. (Photograph courtesy of Calderdale Museums Service, Bankfield)

1829. As Halifax had become the centre of ecclesiastical organisation for its hinterland, it also became the focal point for Methodist organisation. Halifax became the head of a new Wesleyan circuit in 1785 and a new Wesleyan district in 1791, when the Halifax superintendent minister, the Revd William Thompson, a conciliatory Ulsterman, succeeded John Wesley as President of Conference.[39]

A Halifax superintendent minister also became first President of the Methodist New Connexion in 1797, when the Revd William Thom, a cultured Aberdonian, amazed his Wesleyan associates by defecting to the Kilhamites in Leeds. By 1801 Halifax was also the head of a large Methodist New Connexion Circuit extending as far as Bingley, Keighley and Burnley by 1819. The first purpose-built Salem Chapel, erected on North Parade in 1798, was reconstructed 'in a plain, robust style' in 1815 and enlarged in 1845, and a second Hanover Chapel, serving the expanding western sector of the town, was opened in 1836. The Primitive Methodists opened their first Ebenezer Chapel on Cabbage Lane in 1822, when the new Halifax Primitive Methodist Circuit became the nucleus of revivalistic preaching in no fewer than twenty-three surrounding localities. The Wesleyan Reformers, whose attendances on Census Sunday in 1851 at their one place of worship in Halifax narrowly exceeded those of the Primitive Methodists, formed their first society in Halifax in 1849.[40]

The Independents or Congregationalists had also established a strong presence in the town by 1851, although this is not apparent from the published returns for the municipal borough of Halifax for the Census on Religious Worship of 1851: this inexplicably not only lacks data for the Independent congregations, but also for the Particular Baptist, Unitarian and Roman Catholic congregations. The Wesleyan secessionists of 1762 under the leadership of Titus Knight, a self-educated collier converted by the preaching of John Wesley, built the new Square Independent Chapel – a magnificent red-brick Palladian building – in 1772, with financial assistance from the Countess of Huntingdon. In 1819 a second, finely proportioned, Sion Chapel was opened in Wade Street, and in 1837 a third, classically styled, chapel opened in Harrison Road.[41]

Both the General and Particular Baptists had places of worship in Halifax by 1851, the former reporting attendances of 298 on Census Sunday. The Presbyterian congregation at Northgate End espoused Unitarianism in 1775, and the chapel, which had been modified in 1762 and 1817, was further enhanced by the addition of an impressive new west front in a bold classical style in 1847. The foundation stone of St Mary's, the first Catholic church to be built in Halifax since the Reformation, was laid in 1836 and the church opened three years later. Almost a century elapsed, however, before the church was completely free from debt and ready for formal consecration in 1934, an indication of the poverty of the Roman Catholic community in Halifax, many of whom were Irish immigrants.[42]

Nonconformity appealed particularly to artisans, shopkeepers and

Figure 4.32 General Baptist Chapel, Haley Hill, by William Burgess, 1788. The chapel sprang from the evangelistic outreach of a General Baptist society at Queensbury during the pastorate of the Revd John Taylor (1742–1818), supported by his brother, the Revd Daniel Taylor (1738–1816). After cottage meetings in 1773 the fledgling society met initially in a rented room in Gaol Lane in 1775, moving to a new chapel on Haley Hill opened in September 1777. In 1782 when the society formally separated from the Queensbury society it had a membership of 30 and in October 1783 Daniel Taylor became its pastor for almost two years before reluctantly responding to pressure for him to move to London in the wider interests of the connexion. In 1854 the congregation moved to a more central site on North Parade. (Photograph courtesy of Calderdale Museums Service, Bankfield)

Figure 4.33   Jonathan Akroyd (1782–1847). The reclining effigy of this prominent Methodist New Connexion worsted manufacturer surmounted his tomb in the Akroyd mausoleum at the All Souls Burial Ground, Haley Hill, Halifax. Akroyd had originally been buried in the graveyard of Salem Methodist New Connexion Chapel, North Parade, Halifax, following his sudden death at a stormy election meeting in 1847. Part of the £300,000 legacy that he bequeathed to his sons Edward and Henry was used by Edward to finance the construction of All Souls Church, Haley Hill and his body was later exhumed and reinterred in the nearby All Souls Burial Ground. The photograph shows the vandalised Akroyd mausoleum in the All Souls graveyard in 1967. Further extensive damage to the mausoleum resulted in the decision by the All Souls Parochial Church Council to demolish the structure. (Photograph courtesy of the *Halifax Courier*)

women during this period. The diaries of Cornelius Ashworth, handloom weaver and smallholder, record his frequent attendance at Baptist and Congregational preaching services, and domestic outworkers figure prominently in the non-parochial registers and trust deeds of Halifax Nonconformist chapels from the late eighteenth century. Some early industrialist entrepreneurs also had Nonconformist backgrounds, for example the carpet manufacturers John and Martha Crossley and the worsted manufacturers J and J Baldwin, who were Congregationalists, and the worsted spinners James and Jonathan Akroyd, who were New Connexion Methodists. Nonconformists were also prominent in the public life of the town during the early nineteenth century. For example, Rawdon Briggs, one of the first Members of Parliament for Halifax, was a Unitarian banker; John Baldwin, the first Mayor of Halifax, was a Congregationalist manufacturer and George Buxton Browne, the first Chairman of the Halifax Poor Law Union Board of Guardians, was a Wesleyan civil engineer. Many others served as township trustees and later as town councillors and aldermen.[43]

Although the demographic, economic and social changes in the parish during the period 1750–1850 imposed an increasing strain on already overstretched Anglican structures and resources, the Church of England was far from moribund in the parish of Halifax during this period. Episcopal visitation returns reveal an impressive level of pastoral concern and devotion to clerical duty at parochial level. Recognising the need for a second church to serve the growing population of Halifax township, the Revd Dr Henry William Coulthurst, Vicar of Halifax from 1790 to 1817, obtained a special

Figure 4.34   St James's Church, drawn by John Horner. The second new
Anglican church to be built to serve the growing population of the town during
this period, it was financed partly by public subscription and partly 'out of the
fund at the disposal of the commissioners appointed by parliament for the
erection of new churches'. Michael Stocks gave the stone for its construction
from his quarries at Shibden Dale. The church was designed in a 'pseudo-Gothic'
style and was opened in St James's Road, formerly Cabbage Lane, on 2 January
1832. It was described in a contemporary directory as 'a very handsome edifice
of stone'. The church was demolished in 1955 and its district, which had been
declared a Consolidated Chapelry in 1842, was combined with that of St Mary's,
Rhodes Street. (Photograph courtesy of Calderdale Museums Service, Bankfield)

act of Parliament to build a second church for the town, Holy Trinity,
which opened in 1798. The Revd Dr Charles Musgrave, Vicar of Halifax
from 1827 to 1875 and first Archdeacon of Craven, who held the incumbency
for almost half a century, initiated an ambitious programme of church
building, supported by Charles Longley, Bishop of Ripon, and assisted by
Robert Peel's ecclesiastical reforms. Two more churches, St James's and St
Paul's, were opened in expanding western sectors of Halifax in 1832 and
1847. By the end of his incumbency no fewer than thirty-eight churches
throughout the ancient parish had been constructed or completely restored.[44]

The churches and chapels also made an invaluable contribution to the
educational and cultural development of the town and parish during this
period, through their Sunday schools, day schools and mutual improvement
societies. The 1833 Education Enquiry reported that there were some 5,567
children under instruction in fifty-seven schools in the township of Halifax,
68 per cent of whom attended Sunday schools and 14 per cent of whom
attended charity schools. The Sunday schools, moreover, made a particular
contribution to the provision of education for girls, for whom there was
a paucity of other educational provision. The 1833 Education Enquiry

Figure 4.35   British School Rules. The non-denominational British and Foreign Schools Society opened the Halifax British School in rented premises in April 1813. The school, which aimed 'to enable the scholars to read the Scriptures', acquired 'large and commodious', purpose-built premises in Albion Street in 1818 and received support from members 'of almost every Christian denomination, including the Church of England'. In 1833 there were some 508 scholars enrolled at the school, vastly more than at any other school in the township. Parents of children at the school were requested to display these printed regulations 'in some conspicuous part of the house'. (Photograph courtesy of West Yorkshire Archive Service, Calderdale)

revealed that while only 42 per cent of the children receiving elementary education at the day schools in the Halifax township were girls, 50 per cent of the Sunday school scholars in the township were girls. However, educational provision failed to keep pace with the rapid rise in population. Literacy rates, measured by the number of bridegrooms able to sign their names in the parish registers, appear to have plummeted in Halifax during the early nineteenth century. In 1845 a Young Men's Society was commenced at Square Chapel, together with a Saturday evening class 'to promote a taste for reading' in the older boys. In 1850 a Young Men's Christian Society was formed at Sion Chapel 'for mutual improvement by means of lectures and discussions'.[45]

Churches and chapels also helped to foster a strong musical tradition. When Charles Dibdin, the popular composer, visited Halifax in 1788, he pronounced the town 'the most musical spot, for its size, in the kingdom', marvelling at 'the facility with which the common people join together … in every species of choral music'. Handel's *Messiah*, composed in 1741, was first performed in Halifax in 1766 to celebrate the opening of the new Snetzler organ at Halifax Parish Church, and such was its popularity by 1788 that Dibdin observed 'cloth makers as they sweat under their loads in the cloth hall roar out "For his yoke is easy and his burden is light"'. However, there was entrenched Nonconformist opposition to the theatre in the town. Thomas Wilson Manly, travelling theatrical impresario, faced such opposition in 1835 that he had to plead that 'the religious and virtuous life is not impaired by an occasional engagement with rational amusements'.[46]

Religious divisions, and their associated social distinctions, inevitably impacted also upon electoral politics, especially with the emergence of sensitive moral and religious issues such as the abolition of the slave trade and Roman Catholic emancipation in the late eighteenth and early nineteenth centuries. However, contested elections in England's largest county remained relatively rare on account of the prohibitive costs involved in providing refreshment for voters attending local election meetings and transport to the poll at York. Dr E. A. Smith has calculated, for example, that the 1807 Yorkshire election left the three candidates with a total bill in excess of £200,000. But when contests were anticipated or held between 1750 and 1832, they generated greater interest from electors than had early eighteenth century elections. This was partly on account of the growing importance of commercial issues after 1750. For example, in December 1758 Sir George Savile, an independent Whig and major landowner in the parish of Halifax, gained almost universal support from Halifax's freeholders, many of whom had voted Tory in 1741, when he canvassed their support for his anticipated candidacy, because the passage of the Calder Navigation Bill through Parliament had forged a commercial consensus in Halifax which transcended party divisions.[47]

The growing political awareness of the Halifax electorate was also a consequence of the development of a provincial parliamentary reform movement against a background of dearth and distress when harvests were poor as in 1783. Although the release from imprisonment of John Wilkes, 'the popular champion of the people's rights', in April 1770 was greeted in Halifax with the 'ringing of bells, fireworks and other demonstrations of joy', it was the political crisis generated by the War of American Independence between 1775 and 1783 that gave birth to the agitation for parliamentary reform in Yorkshire in the late eighteenth century. Moreover, despite the collapse of the Revd Christopher Wyvill's Yorkshire Association movement for parliamentary reform shortly before the general election of 1784, and the loyalty to the government interest of the Vicar of Halifax and other leading parishioners, the Associationist candidates William Wilberforce and Henry Duncombe were supported by some influential merchants and manufacturers in Halifax and most of the leading Dissenters.

The reform movement was sustained during the 1780s by Major John Cartwright's radical constitutional societies and Protestant Dissenters in their unsuccessful campaigns for civil and religious liberty. However, it was not until 1791–92 that an organised popular radical movement developed in the West Riding, stimulated by the outbreak of the French Revolution, the publication of Tom Paine's avowedly republican *Rights of Man*, the foundation of the Sheffield Society for Constitutional Information and the London Corresponding Society. By November 1792, when magistrates at Bingley obliged a Halifax bookseller who had sold copies of a penny paper, *The French Constitution*, to acknowledge the error of his

Figure 4.36   Speech by William Wilberforce, anti-slavery campaigner, at Halifax Piece Hall during the Yorkshire election of 1807. Wilberforce, who had represented the Yorkshire county constituency since 1784, appealed to the freeholder electorate for their support on the basis of his 'unremitting attention' to their 'civil and commercial interests', without making explicit reference to the campaign for the abolition of the slave trade. An appended note confirms that his campaign had 'peculiarly endeared him to the hearts of the freeholders of the county'. Indeed, Wilberforce headed the county poll with 11,806 votes, 95 of which were cast by Halifax freeholders. (Photograph courtesy of West Yorkshire Archive Service, Calderdale)

Figure 4.37   Poster advertising John Hodgson's offer to grind corn at no charge to help the poor of Halifax, 6 May 1812. Corn prices reached their peak for the whole of the nineteenth century in 1812, a year of acute distress throughout Halifax and West Yorkshire. During the first half of the year Luddite disturbances erupted across the textile belt. The death of Samuel Hartley, a Halifax cropper in a Luddite raid on William Cartwright's Rawfolds Mill in the Spen Valley in April had prompted a large display of radical sympathy at his funeral at the South Parade Wesleyan Chapel. (Photograph courtesy of West Yorkshire Archive Service, Calderdale)

ways, a Jacobin society had been established at Halifax, and at a huge open-air meeting in the town on Easter Monday 1794, plans were approved for a National Convention. Such activity stirred Pitt's government into a policy of repression which continued throughout the wars with Revolutionary and Napoleonic France.

A growing popular political awareness resulted in an increasing involvement of non-electors at election meetings. During the elections of 1806–07, a detachment of Inniskillen dragoons had to be dispatched to the town to quell disturbances during the poll. In 1806, both William Wilberforce and Henry Lascelles addressed well-attended election meetings at the Halifax Piece Hall, but Lascelles, weakened by his family's reputation as slave-owners and his own controversial role in the woollen-trade committee of 1806 which had alienated many West Riding clothiers, subsequently withdrew from the contest, allowing Wilberforce and Walter Fawkes to be returned unopposed. When, in the following April, George III dissolved Parliament to prevent the passage of a Roman Catholic Emancipation Bill through Parliament, a public meeting in Halifax supported by the Vicar, Dr Henry Coulthurst, and other leading local landowners and manufacturers, presented a loyal address to the king, expressing gratitude for his 'support and protection of the Protestant religion and his constitutional exercise of the royal prerogative'. During the ensuing election campaign, the three candidates, Wilberforce, Lascelles and Viscount Milton, the son of the Whig lord lieutenant, Earl Fitzwilliam, all visited Halifax. However, despite Milton's provision of nine free barrels of beer for the crowds attending his election meeting at the Piece Hall and the subsequent spectacle of two supporters impersonating Lord and Lady Milton being carried around the town by men with blackened faces caricaturing the slaves on the Lascelles' West Indian plantations, 95 votes of Halifax freeholders went to both Wilberforce and Lascelles and only 74 votes to Milton. Moreover, during the poll, the *Halifax Journal* reported intense excitement in Halifax, with the town being disturbed each evening by 'a riotous and desperate mob' carrying effigies of Lascelles, and concluded that 'nothing since the days of the Revolution has ever presented such a scene as has happened during this fortnight'.[48]

The death of Samuel Hartley, a local cropper, in a Luddite raid in the Spen Valley in 1812 prompted a large display of radical sympathy at his funeral at the South Parade Wesleyan Chapel, and when Major Cartwright renewed his campaign for parliamentary reform, some 17,000 signatures were collected in under two months in 1813 for a petition for parliamentary reform. Reform meetings near Halifax in December 1816 and January 1817, stimulated by post-war distress, were also well-attended, and reaction to the Peterloo Massacre at St Peter's Field in Manchester in 1819 was vociferous and indignant. As the Tory diarist, Anne Lister, commented, Halifax was full of talk 'of the sad work at Manchester', and on Monday, 4 October, an estimated 50,000 'male and female reformers' attended a large open-air meeting in the town. This was followed by a patriotic dinner, during which toasts were proposed to 'The People, the source of all

Figure 4.38 Halifax Borough election poster, 1832. The poster for the first parliamentary election for the new two-member borough constituency was issued only weeks after the Reform Bill reached the statute book in June 1832. By the time the election took place in December, John Whiteley, constable of Sowerby, had been discredited and had withdrawn from the contest. Michael Stocks, a local radical businessman and magistrate, polled 186 votes. Rawdon Briggs, a local Whig Unitarian banker, topped the poll with 242 votes. The other two candidates, the Whig Charles Wood and the Tory James Stuart Wortley, who polled 235 and 174 votes respectively, were 'interloping strangers' from outside the immediate locality. (Photograph courtesy of the West Yorkshire Archive Service, Calderdale)

legitimate power', 'The Saviour of our country, Major Cartwright', and 'Henry Hunt, the Champion of Liberty'. Moreover, in 1820, the ladies of Halifax expressed their radical sympathies by presenting a loyal address to Queen Caroline, the estranged wife of the unpopular George IV. Later, when the Whig lawyer, Henry Brougham, visited Halifax during the general election campaign of 1830, he was given a rapturous reception when he proclaimed:

> We don't live now in the days of barons. We live in the days of Leeds, of Bradford, of Halifax and Huddersfield. We live in the days when men are industrious and desire to be free.[49]

The parliamentary reform movement reached its climax during the struggle for the Reform Bill in 1831–32, particularly following the rejection of the bill by the House of Lords in October 1831 and the resignation of Earl Grey in May 1832. On 17 May, after the Duke of Wellington had failed to form an administration, his effigy was carried through the streets of Halifax and then burned. Anne Lister recorded in her diary that 'the town was like a fair. The people had a bonfire of three carts of coal for rejoicing at the speedy return of Lord Grey'. However, the size of the ten-pound householder electorate of the new two-member borough of Halifax created under the terms of the Great Reform Act of 1832 was scarcely larger than the electorate which had qualified for the county franchise as 40 shilling freeholders before 1832. In 1807 Halifax electors had constituted 6 per cent of the adult male population; in 1832 the proportion had risen to 7.5 per cent and even by 1847, when the size of the borough electorate had almost doubled to 1,022, the electorate still only represented 11.7 per cent of the adult male population.[50]

J. A. Jowitt has characterised the electoral politics of the new two-member parliamentary borough of Halifax during the period 1832–47 as a 'conflict between the Tory oligarchy whose strength lay in the upper crust and professional electors and the Whig-Liberal oligarchy whose power lay in textiles'. He has also emphasised the 'potent and powerful force of religion' in determining election outcomes. Although serious divisions had arisen within the local Tory Anglican elite during an acrimonious dispute over the levying of tithes between 1827 and 1829, Anglican and some Wesleyan voters provided a nucleus of support for the Tories in the electoral politics of the period 1832–47, while other Nonconformist voters tended to support candidates of the Whig-Radical alliance. Religious issues often dominated election campaigns. For example, the Tories fought the 1835 election under the slogan 'the Established Church in danger', and the Radicals fought the 1847 election on the issues of disestablishment and educational volunta-ryism. Indeed, the Radical-Voluntaryist challenge of the Chartist Ernest Jones and the Political Dissenter Edward Miall in 1847 forced the upper crust to close ranks, and only a high incidence of cross-party voting secured

Figure 4.39 (*right*) Sir Charles Wood (1800–85), MP for Halifax from 1832 to 1865. Wood was not a member of the urban industrial elite, but a scion of the county landed aristocracy. The son of Sir Francis Lindley Wood, a former Deputy Lieutenant of the West Riding and son-in-law of the Whig Prime Minister Earl Grey, he was the only leading Whig politician of his generation to enjoy such a long relationship with an urban-industrial constituency. He served in every Whig-Liberal government from 1832 until his retirement in 1874, including a term as Chancellor of the Exchequer from 1846–52. He was created first Viscount Halifax of Monk Bretton in 1866 and was patron of the Halifax Permanent Building Society from its formation until his death in 1885. (Photograph courtesy of Halifax plc)

Figure 4.40 (*left*) Sir Henry Edwards of Pye Nest (1812–86). A prominent local woollen manufacturer and later Captain of the 2nd West York Yeomanry cavalry, which he was instrumental in raising during the Plug Plot disturbances of 1842. At the extraordinary Halifax Borough election of 1847 he topped the poll with 511 votes as a result of tactical voting by upper crust voters determined to prevent the election of both the Chartist, Ernest Jones, and the Political Dissenter, Edward Miall, thereby becoming the first Tory MP for Halifax. Despite his vigorous association with the movement for factory reform, however, he lost his seat at the 1852 election when the Liberal candidates Charles Wood and Francis Crossley headed the poll. (Photograph: J. A. Hargreaves Collection)

the election of the Whig candidate, Charles Wood, and the Tory candidate, Henry Edwards, a prominent Anglican textile manufacturer. Edwards topped the poll and became the first Tory Member of Parliament to be returned for the borough.[51]

All the other candidates returned in the five Halifax borough elections between 1832 and 1847 were either Whigs or Radicals, including Halifax's longest serving Member of Parliament, Sir Charles Wood (1800–85), who represented the borough from 1832 to 1865. Curiously, he was drawn not from the local urban industrial elite, but from the county landed aristocracy. Wood, the son of Sir Francis Lindley Wood, a former Deputy Lord Lieutenant of the West Riding and son-in-law of the Whig prime minister Earl Grey, was the only leading Whig politician of his generation to enjoy such a long relationship with an urban-industrial constituency. He served in every Whig-Liberal government from 1832 until his retirement in 1874, including a term as Chancellor of the Exchequer from 1846–52. He was created first Viscount Halifax in 1866.[52]

Although the electorate remained relatively small throughout the period up to 1850, the turnout was high, averaging 91 per cent for the five borough elections held between 1832 and 1847. There was a wider public interest at the hustings and campaign meetings, reflecting a strong tradition of extra-parliamentary protest in the town. J. A. Jowitt's analysis of the social composition of the Halifax borough electorate from 1832 to 1847, reproduced in Table 4.3, reveals a predominance of craftsmen, textile manufacturers, and other businessmen and tradesmen, averaging 72.48 per cent of the electorate with smaller strata of upper crust and professional voters, averaging 17.26 per cent, and a dearth of working-class voters averaging 2.35 per cent.[53]

Table 4.3. *Social composition of the Halifax borough electorate,
1832–47*

Occupation	1832	1835	1837	1841	1847
craft	16.06	19.97	23.97	20.17	20.48
shopkeeper	14.43	16.64	15.38	15.20	18.74
textile	16.26	19.97	21.19	17.33	15.06
upper class/professional	16.67	20.63	15.38	16.19	17.45
drink	9.35	8.99	6.68	6.82	7.91
business	10.98	11.31	10.09	9.94	9.53
other	1.42	2.16	3.91	2.56	1.73
unclassified	14.83	0.33	3.40	11.79	9.10

Source: J. A. Jowitt, 'Parliamentary Politics in Halifax, 1832–47', *Northern History*, XII, 1976, 174.

The displacement of large and significant groups of domestic outworkers in the woollen and worsted industries had provided the basis for considerable working-class organisation and agitation during the 1830s and 1840s. This ensured that the Halifax working-class movement assumed a political rather than a trade union complexion during the successive social crises between the Reform Bill struggle in 1832 and the last major Chartist demonstration at Kennington Common in 1848. There was strong support in Halifax for the Factory, Anti-Poor Law, Chartist and Anti-Corn Law Movements, and some of the most serious Plug Plot disturbances in the country occurred at Halifax in August 1842, when thousands of rioters converged on the town to try to stop the Halifax mills. Following an abortive attempt to rescue seventeen prisoners being escorted to Elland station by a detachment of the 11th Hussars, the soldiers were ambushed on Salterhebble hill on their return journey to Halifax by a mob of several thousand who hurled boulders down on the cavalrymen.'At no time during the Chartist period', the Chartist historian F. C. Mather concluded, 'had regular troops

Figure 4.41 Attack on the military at Salterhebble, 16 August 1842. Following the Plug Plot disturbances on 15–16 August, rioters attacked a military escort taking seventeen of those arrested in Halifax by horse omnibus to Elland station en route to Wakefield for examination by the magistrates. They failed to rescue the prisoners, but later ambushed the returning troop of cavalrymen of the 11th Hussars at Salterhebble. The soldiers were pelted with stones by the rioters. When three cavalrymen were hurled from their horses they were kicked and beaten by the angry mob. Order was only restored after the troops opened fire on the crowd. 'At no time during the Chartist period', concluded the historian F. C. Mather, 'had regular troops come nearer to being overwhelmed by rioters' (Photograph courtesy of *The Illustrated London News*)

come nearer to being overwhelmed by rioters'. As late as 1848, when the Halifax borough police force was in process of formation, concern about the ability of the magistrates to maintain public order prompted one Halifax magistrate to advise the Home Office of the impracticability of removing the military force from Halifax 'for a very long time, if ever'.[54]

Local government

During the period 1750–1850, the functions of local government within the ancient parish of Halifax were exercised by a diverse and bewildering array of authorities. They included firstly the county magistracy, secondly the lords of the manor of Wakefield and the honor of Pontefract and their sub-manors, thirdly the parochial and township vestries and finally, in Halifax itself, a body of improvement commissioners or town trustees, brought into being by a series of local Acts of Parliament between 1762 and 1823 in response to the needs of a rapidly expanding urban community. Superimposed upon this unwieldy structure of local government in 1837 were the Poor Law Unions of Todmorden and Halifax, and then, at last, in 1848, the municipal borough of Halifax was created.[55]

Before this reorganisation of responsibilities, the county had been concerned with the administration of justice through the West Riding Quarter Sessions, presided over by a group of justices of the peace, and had maintained the county gaol at Wakefield. The county justices also played a key role in local government, for example, monitoring the appointment of township officers such as the overseer of the poor and surveyor of highways, approving local assessments and rates, and resolving thorny poor relief questions relating to migration and settlement. They were also responsible for the maintenance of the majority of the bridges in the county and were empowered to levy a charge for this purpose as part of the county rate. For most people, however, the county authorities were remote, and as a social unit they mattered only to the gentry.[56]

The vestiges of manorialism continued to impinge upon many people's lives throughout the eighteenth century. The manorial court with its quaint medieval nomenclature, though divested of much of its former authority, was still an institution of some importance in the local community. Constables were formally sworn in at the court leet by the steward, who after 1750 was usually an attorney. By the eighteenth century, the manorial court, which continued to meet at the Moot Hall in Halifax, had come to be selected exclusively from the local gentry who controlled parochial and township administration. The provision of an adequate water supply, the suppression of street nuisances and the control of sanitation remained the most common administrative duties of the court until they became the responsibility of the town trustees in the 1760s.[57]

The parochial chapelries remained under the ecclesiastical authority of the Vicar of Halifax, who approved the appointment of their chaplains and paid them an annual stipend, until the sub-division of the parish was authorised under Peel's legislation in 1842 and commenced in 1843. They were allowed to exercise the right of baptism, marriage and burial, free from the jurisdiction of the vicar. Within the parish there were a number of chapels-of-ease, each with its own perpetual curate who was appointed by the vicar but paid by the inhabitants of the local chapelry. The vicar, assisted by a curate, a lecturer and various parochial officers, was thus a key figure in the local administrative hierarchy, providing a link between town, chapelry and parochial district, vicarage and diocese. His main income continued to be derived from the small tithes and vicarial dues until 1829, when they were finally commuted into a vicar's rate, levied on each township. The main sources of parochial revenue were the church rates, burial fees and revenue derived from sales of parish property.[58]

Until 1837 the basic unit for the management of community affairs throughout the parish remained the civil township. The administration of the township was the responsibility of four sets of officers acting under

Figure 4.42   Halifax from the South East, 1775. This view reveals the limited urban expansion and predominant rural character of the townscape at this date. Indeed, a terrier compiled by John Moore of Hipperholme in 1797 reveals almost 600 small closes or enclosed fields within the township. However, Dean Tucker observed in 1774 that 'the towns of Birmingham, Leeds, Halifax and Manchester ... being inhabited by tradesmen and manufacturers are some of the richest and most flourishing in the kingdom'. Evidence of the finishing of woollen cloth in the town is provided by rows of tenterframes in the fields. (Photograph: J. A. Hargreaves Collection)

the direction and control of the vestry, a select group of the township's most influential inhabitants, who met annually to examine the previous year's accounts and appoint the township officers: the constables, surveyors of the highways, overseers of the poor and the churchwardens. By the end of the century poor relief was by far the largest branch of township government and the responsibility of the townships for the administration of poor relief continued until Poor Law Unions were established under the terms of the Poor Law Amendment Act of 1834, which replaced the overseers of the poor by elected Boards of Guardians. Eighteen townships from the parish of Halifax were joined with Hartshead and Clifton to form the Halifax Union. The Halifax Guardians were elected in February 1837, and the Halifax Union Workhouse was opened in 1841.[59]

The rapidly expanding population of the urban township of Halifax during the second half of the eighteenth century and the first half of the nineteenth century imposed a tremendous strain on the machinery of local government. In 1762 statutory powers were obtained from Parliament to establish a body of commissioners or trustees charged with the responsibility of supplying the town with water and empowering them to levy rates on all who made use of the water supply. A further local Act was obtained in 1768 to make the 1762 Act more effective and to extend the range of functions of the town trustees to include 'better paving, cleansing, lighting' and the removal of 'all nuisances, encroachments and obstructions' within the town. A subsequent Act in 1823 included provision for the employment of watchmen. Other local acts provided for the establishment of a new market in 1810 under a separate body of trustees and for the creation of the Halifax Gas, Light and Coke Company in 1822, which later became associated with the trustees in the public lighting of the town.

The trustees appointed under the Act of 1762 were a non-elective body of 224 male property owners, with power to fill any vacancy which arose among their number. The act of 1768 appointed a further 80 trustees, and the act of 1823 allowed tenants as well as owners of property valued annually at £40 to hold office, enabling craftsmen, shopkeepers and tradesmen to take their places as trustees alongside the more wealthy manufacturers, merchants and professional men. An analysis by G. R. Dalby of serving trustees has identified at least 80 manufacturers and merchants; 33 professional men, including doctors, lawyers, bankers and a civil engineer and 105 tradesmen and shopkeepers, including joiners, grocers, drapers, chemists, painters, plasterers, ironmongers, plumbers and plasterers. The

Figure 4.43   New Street, 1788, by William Burgess. The view of most of the west side of New Street, may have included the home of the artist. A handbill published by E. Jacob, the Halifax printer advertising the publication in weekly parts of Jacob's *History of the town and Parish of Halifax* in 1789 announced that William Burgess, and engraver from London, who had taken a house in New Street, Halifax, had been engaged to engrave the plates for the new publication. The houses appear light and spacious with cellar, ground and first floor accommodation and land to the rear. The street also appears to have been neatly paved and setted. (Photograph courtesy of Calderdale Museums Service, Bankfield)

trustees' financial resources consisted of property and water rates, which
yielded an average annual income of £3,507 during the years 1840–49, loans
up to a permitted maximum of £3,000, and public subscriptions. However,
by 1839 the trustees had accumulated a debt of £12,000 and outstanding
rate arrears of £5,000.

A more rigorous financial policy was initiated under the leadership of
Joseph Thorp, a Quaker woolstapler, but financial retrenchment meant
that many improvement schemes had to be postponed. In his evidence to
William Ranger's enquiry into the sanitary condition of Halifax in 1851,
Thorp concluded that 'slovenly methods in the execution of their enacted
duties' by the trustees 'had resulted in affairs being carried out in an
irregular and unbusinesslike manner'. At a meeting convened by the constable on 7 May 1847, Thorp had seconded a motion proposed by another
trustee, John Abbott, a retired carpet manufacturer, calling for a petition
to be sent to Queen Victoria for a charter of incorporation for the town.
This was granted in 1848. Halifax at last became a municipal borough with
the same boundaries as the parliamentary constituency created in 1832
under the terms of the Great Reform Act. The borough council was to
consist of a mayor, ten aldermen and thirty councillors, elected by six
electoral wards. All those who paid the poor rate were entitled to vote.
The final electoral roll contained 1,609 names, almost one-third more
electors than had qualified to vote at the 1847 parliamentary election.[60]

The outcome of the first Halifax municipal election held on 20 May
1848, a year after the defeat of the Radical-Voluntaryist alliance of Ernest
Jones and Edward Miall at the general election of 1847 and only a month
after the rejection of the third national Chartist petition by Parliament,
was sensational. The veteran Chartist Benjamin Wilson hailed it as a
triumph for the 'friends of Jones and Miall', who had 'carried all before
them'. Henry Martin, editor of the *Halifax Reformer*, declared that the
'Whig Tory victory' at the 1847 election had been 'fully and fairly avenged'
with only a handful of Whigs and Tories elected, the remainder being 'all
of the movement party – friends of progress, of retrenchment and of
reform'. It was also acclaimed as a triumph for Nonconformity, since 'only
three or four' councillors 'are churchmen'; while there are

> three members of the Society of Friends, three Baptists, nine or ten
> Independents, one Wesleyan, four or five of the Methodist New Con-
> nexion; and, altogether at least five-sixths of the body are
> Nonconformists.[61]

A large smoke-canopied commercial town

The economic transformation of Halifax from a market town into a manufacturing town during the century from 1750 to 1850, the activities of interest

Figure 4.44 Northgate, 1824, by John Horner. This drawing, published in 1835, shows old houses in Northgate which were demolished in 1824. The view looks south towards Crown Street and Woolshops. The building in the foreground on the left was the Malt Shovel Inn and the inn sign is clearly visible. The street is paved and setted, but four sheep can be seen straggling the street. (Photograph courtesy of Calderdale Museum Service, Bankfield)

groups like churches and chapels and the efforts of those responsible for local government had transformed the physical appearance of the town. In 1774 Dean Tucker observed that 'the towns of Birmingham, Leeds, Halifax and Manchester … being inhabited by tradesmen and manufacturers are some of the richest and most flourishing in the kingdom'. However, a terrier compiled by John Moore of Hipperholme in 1797 reveals almost 600 small closes or enclosed fields within the township, and contemporary prints of the town in the late eighteenth and early nineteenth centuries confirm its strikingly rural setting. Indeed, as late as 1825 the Bradford doctor, John Simpson, was reluctant to designate Halifax as 'a manufacturing town'. But by 1837, the year in which Victoria ascended the throne, astute observers, such as Anne Lister of Shibden Hall, were pronouncing the birth of the new 'smoke-canopied commercial town' of Halifax. For the remaining years of Queen Victoria's long reign observers found themselves hard-pressed to find a kind word to say about the town's appearance.[62]

Contemporary plans reveal that by the mid-eighteenth century the built

Figure 4.45 Lower Kirkgate, 1825, by John Horner. This drawing, published in 1835, also shows old houses prior to their demolition in 1825, heralding a period of urban expansion in the second quarter of the nineteenth century. One of the half-timbered buildings in the foreground bears the sign: 'Bradley, Gingerbread Maker, Wholesale and Retail'. (Photograph courtesy of Calderdale Museums Service, Bankfield)

Figure 4.46 Woolshops, 1833, by John Horner. This drawing, published in 1835, also records old houses scheduled for demolition in the second quarter of the nineteenth century. The columns supporting the building on the right are identical in style to those still visible at the Halifax Piece Hall. The alignment of the buildings on both sides of the relatively narrow street is quite irregular and a cooper is working on the street in the foreground on the left. (Photograph courtesy of Calderdale Museums Service, Bankfield)

Figure 4.47   Crown Street, 1836, by N. Whittock. This busy commercial thoroughfare, formerly called the High Street, carried the pack-horse traffic from Wakefield to Lancashire. The street contained two inns, the Upper George and White Swan, serving the needs of stagecoaches arriving in the town. A commercial directory reveals a variety of commercial premises in Crown Street in 1834 including a booksellers and stationers, a grocers and tea-dealers, two confectioners, a hat dealer, four drapers, a saddler, two braziers and tin plate workers, three ironmongers, two chemists and druggists, a clog and pattern maker and several boot and shoe maker. (Photograph courtesy of Calderdale Museums Service, Bankfield)

environment of the town had expanded westwards beyond Cow Green and Bull Green. In 1750, the township of Halifax contained some 1,200 houses, which had increased to 1,912 by 1801. Robert Brown, conducting a Board of Agriculture survey in 1793, noted that 'the houses, in general, are built of brick though free stone is also used'. Other red-brick buildings were erected in the town in the late eighteenth and early nineteenth centuries, including shops in the High Street, a new chapel in Square Road, the baths in Lilly Lane and a new market building operated by a market company under a local Act of Parliament of 1810. The most outstanding building constructed entirely from stone during this period was the magnificent Georgian Piece Hall of 1779, which replaced the old cloth hall at Hall End. By 1822, according to Baines's *Directory*, the town was 'generally well built, partly of brick but principally of stone, which latter material is very abundant'.

Fine buildings there may have been, but, as Robert Brown noted in 1793, 'little care appears to have been paid to laying out the town at first'. In 1822 the streets remained narrow 'and very irregular' in their layout. An explosion of new building in the second quarter of the nineteenth century merely exacerbated the problem. T. J. Maslen, who offered advice on

Figure 4.48 Halifax from the south east, 1847. The expansion of Halifax by the mid-nineteenth century is evident in this distant view of the town. Edward Akroyd compared the town in 1848 to a 'growing lad, thrusting his arms beyond his sleeves and his legs out of his trousers, putting out an arm at Haley Hill and a leg at Caddy Field'. (Photograph: J. A. Hargreaves Collection)

improvement to a number of northern towns, described Halifax in 1843 as a 'mass of little, miserable, narrow, ill-looking streets, jumbled together in a chaotic confusion, as if they had all been in a sack, and emptied out together upon the ground'. Using a different metaphor, Edward Akroyd likened Halifax at the time of the incorporation of the borough in 1848 to a 'growing lad, thrusting his arms beyond his sleeves and his legs out of his trousers, putting out an arm at Haley Hill and a leg at Caddy Field'. The northern and southern expansion of the town had begun, alongside a continuing expansion westwards.[63]

So, in sum, although Halifax had by 1850 achieved through economic development some regional and indeed national eminence as a manufacturing and commercial centre, and although it now contained both a substantial population and a thriving elite culture, a century of unplanned development had left a legacy of problems for future generations. These included extremes of poverty, extensive educational and cultural deprivation and an ill-shaped, heavily polluted and in places distinctly unsavoury built environment.

N

Ogden

1892

Bradshaw

Mixenden

Wainstalls

Illingworth

1900

Ovenden

1900

Northowram

Boothtown

Luddenden

1865

ORIGINAL BOROUGH

1848

King Cross

1865

Siddal

1899

Skircoat Green

Miles

Copley

0   1

1902

Figure 5.1   The
growth of the
borough of Halifax,
1848–1902.

CHAPTER FIVE

'Town of a hundred trades': Victorian and Edwardian Halifax, 1851–1914

During the mid-Victorian era, the population of the municipal borough of Halifax more than doubled from 25,159 to 65,510. This increased Halifax's share of the total population of its ancient ecclesiastical parish from 16.9 per cent in 1851 to 37.8 per cent in 1871, reversing sharply the trend of the previous 350 years. The scale of the demographic expansion of Halifax during this period becomes most apparent when the age structure of the population of the municipal borough is analysed. By 1871, as a consequence of an exceptionally high birth rate, almost one-third of the borough's population was under fifteen years of age. The relatively high degree of fecundity appears to have resulted from a high marriage rate, which was entirely compatible with the economic organisation of the local textile industry during its period of most rapid expansion up to 1871. This positively encouraged early marriage and extensive family formation amongst adolescent and young adult workers by providing expanding employment opportunities for men, women and children.

Thereafter, as the population began to age, the rate of population growth in the borough was less dramatic, and between 1879 and 1901 the birth rate declined from 31.6 per 1,000 to 22.8 per 1,000. Nevertheless, by 1881, the population of the municipal borough had increased to 73,630 and, by 1891, following Halifax's redesignation as a county borough in 1889, to 89,832. The population of the new county borough continued to rise, peaking at 104,936 in 1901, but subsequently declining to 101,594 by 1911.[1]

However, boundary extensions to the municipal and county boroughs between 1865 and 1901 may have masked a levelling off in the growth of Halifax's urban population in the last quarter of the nineteenth century. Moreover, by 1901 there were also other substantial urban centres in the former ecclesiastical parish. Todmorden and Brighouse, with populations of 25,418 and 21,735, acquired borough status respectively in 1896 and 1893, and there were rapidly expanding urban centres at Sowerby Bridge and Elland, with populations of 11,477 and 10,412 at the turn of the century. In general, industrial development had mushroomed around the waterway and railway networks in the valley bottoms of the Calder and its tributaries in the second half of the nineteenth century, while the remoter upland handcombing and handweaving settlements had steadily declined.[2]

Halifax's population growth was sustained by increasing industrial diversification in the second half of the nineteenth century, when the new municipal borough earned a reputation as 'a town of 100 trades'. At least one local contemporary writer believed the town to be a city in all but name by 1877. However, Halifax failed to achieve the coveted city status acquired by Wakefield in 1888, Leeds in 1893 and Bradford in 1897. Halifax was considered too geographically remote to become the centre of ecclesiastical administration for the new diocese of Wakefield in 1888, and geographical constraints inhibited Halifax's industrial and urban expansion, denying the town the late nineteenth-century industrial and commercial pre-eminence of Leeds or Bradford. Indeed, Halifax reached the peak of its demographic and economic expansion around the turn of the century and both the cotton and worsted industries had begun to contract before the outbreak of the First World War.[3]

This chapter will seek to explain how the economic expansion which sustained Halifax's demographic growth for most of this period was effected, what the consequences were for social structure and living standards, how it might have affected and been affected by political life, how social and economic provision was made, and how these changes were reflected in the cultural activities of the community and the actual appearance of the town.

The economy: industrial diversification and the service sector

Although industrial diversification became a characteristic of Halifax's economy between 1851 and 1914, nevertheless textiles, which accounted for over half of the exhibits from Halifax at the Great Exhibition of 1851, remained vital to the local economy throughout the period up to the outbreak of the First World War. This was notwithstanding the difficulties experienced by the various branches of the local textile industry as a consequence of the Cotton Famine in the 1860s, changes in ladies' fashions, increasing foreign competition from France and Germany from the 1870s, and the imposition of protective tariffs by the United States of America in the 1890s. In 1871, 8,431 adults were employed in textile manufacture in the municipal borough of Halifax, compared with 1,552 in the extractive and metallurgical industries. Almost half of these textile workers were women, who outnumbered men in worsted manufacturing by 2,416 to 1,280, but remained in a minority of 339 to 809 in the heavier woollen manufacturing sector. Increasing numbers of women were employed during the period up to 1891, and also children from as young as ten or eleven years of age, who were allowed to start work early as half-timers after demonstrating relatively modest levels of educational attainment under a Halifax School

Figure 5.2 Weaving shed, John Whiteley and Sons Ltd, card makers, Brunswick Mills, Halifax, 1894. All the looms have female operators. By the 1890s female textile workers in Halifax outnumbered males by nearly two to one. (Photograph courtesy of the West Yorkshire Archive Service, Calderdale)

Figure 5.3 Memorial card to victims of an explosion and fire at Wellington Mills, Halifax, 4 December 1873. The victims, all young girls aged between eight and eighteen, were among 120 employees on the premises of Lister's silk mill when an explosion occurred. Gas escaping from a pipe during the repair of a meter ignited on the lower floor of the mill causing the dev-astating explosion and disastrous fire. Many other workers suffered severe burns and the mill was totally destroyed. (Photograph courtesy of S. Gee)

Board by-law. By 1901, 19,342 adults and children were employed in the various branches of textile manufac-ture in the county borough of Halifax compared with 7,622 in the extractive and metallurgical indus-tries, and women and girls outnumbered male textile workers by 11,668 to 7,674. The Secretary of the Halifax Chamber of Commerce listed no fewer than eighteen var-ieties of textile trades being pursued in Halifax in 1915, the largest single category of commercial activity.[4]

After 1851, there was an enormous expansion in both the number and size of textile factories in the town, exposing the myth that Britain was already a country dominated by huge factories by 1851. Indeed, between 1851 and 1865 the number of factories in Halifax more than doubled from 24 to 56. Moreover, in 1851 fewer than ten local firms employed more than 100 workers; by 1861 the number had trebled. By 1871, following a period of sustained expansion in the West Riding textile trade, over one-third of the local textile labour force was employed in factory units of more than 100 hands and nearly a half in workshops of 50 or more. At the turn of the century, a dozen leading firms accounted for around 40 per cent of textile employees in the town. The

Crossleys had employed only 350 workers in 1837 but had increased their labour force to 5,000 by 1871, and this figure was maintained until 1914.

From mid-century, the use of steam power technology expanded, although water power continued to be used by some local firms until the late nineteenth century. In 1851, for example, the patent rights of George Collier, who had first applied the power loom to linen manufacture in Barnsley, and the American inventor Erasmus Bigelow were vested in trust to John Crossley and Co., harnessing the techniques of power loom weaving and mass production to carpet manufacture, which placed the firm in the forefront of the carpet industry. However, it was not until 1856 that woolcombing machinery was in regular use in the Halifax worsted industry and, during this period of transition, many Halifax woolcombers 'had to endure much privation and had no prospect of employment in future', and some emigrated to the United States.[5]

The role of textiles within the local economy had begun to decline, however, before 1914. In 1897 the *Halifax Guardian* reported that while Halifax

has largely multiplied the number of its industries, its production of textile fabrics has for some years been on the decrease and the fear is entertained that ... its looms will gradually cease to run.[6]

Figure 5.4   Mechanics' shop, John Whiteley and Sons Ltd, card makers, Brunswick Mills, card makers, 1894. John Whiteley and Sons, founded in July 1791, was one of the earliest local manufacturers of wire for card making. The firm moved from Winding Road to Brunswick Mills in the 1840s and by 1891 it employed a total of 300 workpeople. (Photograph courtesy of West Yorkshire Archive Service, Calderdale)

Figure 5.5 William Asquith Ltd, Highroad Well. In 1902, William Asquith Ltd became the first local machine tool firm to design and fix their own trade plate on machinery supplied to merchant distributors for export. Founded in 1865 by William A. Asquith in premises in Raglan Street, the firm moved to larger premises in Highroad Well in 1871, which were gradually extended as the firm expanded and equipped with new offices, fitting and pattern shops in 1899. In January 1903, following William Asquith's death in 1901, the business became a limited company and the firm began to specialise in the manufacture of the world-famous Asquith redial drilling machine, which superseded the practice of punching in constructional engineering. This specialisation was the basis of the firm's rapid expansion in the period up to 1914, when the firm became wholly engaged in war work. (Photograph: J. A. Hargreaves Collection)

The most spectacular casualty was the former Akroyd worsted manufacturing empire which was gradually dismantled during the period from 1893 to 1918, passing into the ownership of smaller textile concerns. The causes of decline were increasing foreign competition and restrictive tariffs imposed by the United States of America in 1890, 1895 and 1897 and by France in 1892, which seriously affected British textile exports. As *The Times* remarked in 1897 within a week of the inauspicious *Halifax Guardian* report:

> Time was when many important continental countries looked to Halifax for clothing their men-of-war but, one after the other, have developed industries of their own.[7]

The decline of Halifax's textile industry was partially offset by the town's growing industrial diversity. It was Halifax's developing cable, confectionery, construction, extractive, engineering and machine tool industries which earned it a reputation as 'the town of 100 trades' during the period between the Great Exhibition and the outbreak of the First World War. In 1915, in addition to its highly variegated textile industries, Halifax boasted sixteen varieties of iron trades; ten varieties of building trades; a total of 899 registered workshops; a large and flourishing firm of manufacturing jewellers (Charles Horner Ltd); the largest carpet and toffee manufacturing firms in the world; and the leading producer of drilling and boring machinery. Indeed, by the early twentieth century, engineering had become the second most important industry in Halifax and, like the textile industry from which it developed, it was inherently diverse.

Most local engineering firms started from very small beginnings, expanding rapidly during the mid-Victorian period while potential competitors in America and Europe were distracted by the American Civil War of 1861–65 and the Franco-German War of 1870–71. It is striking that many

Figure 5.6   John and Violet Mackintosh on their wedding day, 29 September 1890. A few days after their marriage the young couple opened a pastry-cook's shop in King Cross Lane, Halifax, postponing their honeymoon and investing all their modest joint savings in the new business venture. 'From the opening day', John Mackintosh later recalled, 'this shop attracted customers, the aim of the owner being to offer only articles specially good in an establishment that was spotlessly clean'. Their most popular line was a novel blend of traditional English butterscotch toffee and American caramel, and by 1892 the couple had moved into wholesale marketing of their new product. From these small beginnings the business developed into the largest toffee manufacturing company in the world. (Photograph: J. A. Hargreaves Collection)

began by manufacturing accessories for the textile industry and maintaining and repairing mill machinery. James Ryder Butler (1842–1917), a former apprentice engineer and carpet mill foreman for John Crossley and Sons Ltd, started his own loom making business in a small factory in Weymouth Street in 1868. He subsequently acquired premises in Adelaide Street, diversifying into the manufacture of machine tools in 1873. After a succession of business partnerships, his two sons entered the firm in 1892, and by 1910 Butler had become leading specialist manufacturers of planing machines. William A. Asquith (1840–1901), returning to his native Halifax in the wake of the American Civil War after working in the gold fields of Canada and the American West, founded his firm in 1865 in a converted weaving shed in Raglan Street. Initially undertaking general engineering work, the firm expanded rapidly, particularly during the Franco-German War, moving to larger premises in Highroad Well in 1871. In 1902 Asquiths became the first local machine tool firm to supply machinery bearing the firm's own distinctive trade plate to merchant distributors for export. In January 1903, the business became a limited company and the firm began to specialise in the world-famous Asquith radial drilling machine, which superseded the practice of punching in constructional engineering. This specialisation was the basis of the firm's rapid expansion in the period up to 1914.

Other engineering firms that also expanded through increasing specialisation during this period included John Stirk and Sons Ltd, founded in 1866, which initially produced a wide range of machines to order before specialising on the manufacture of the single belt planer, and Frederick Town and Sons Ltd, founded in 1903, which opened a new purpose-built factory for the specialist production of radial drills at Mile Cross in 1914. Gas construction engineering began in Halifax as early as 1847; boiler-making and heating-apparatus engineering after 1858; the manufacture of woodworking machinery from 1875; and the development of automated cash registers in 1886. Wire manufacture, which had been utilised primarily for carding in the first half of the nineteenth century, became more technically advanced after 1851, producing wire in a wide variety of gauges and metals. James Royston's wire drawing firm, founded in 1797, produced hundreds of tonnes of 'charcoal wire' for the first Atlantic telegraph cable in 1856. In 1859, a former employee, Frederick Smith, established his Caledonia Works in Charlestown Road, specialising in the production of high quality steel wires for marine and colliery applications, and the firm patented several types of continuous wire-drawing machines. With the rapid growth of the electrical industry, Frederick Smith and Co. produced high-conductivity copper wire, but later moved to Salford, where proximity to the Manchester Ship Canal eased the supply of raw materials and eliminated the heavy overland freight costs to Halifax.[8]

There were other very different industrial developments by the later nineteenth century, reflecting a sensitivity to market demand. Rising real wages, growing consumerism among the masses, increasing opportunities for leisure and cheaper supplies of raw materials from overseas, such as sugar, stimulated the development of the confectionery industry, which like engineering grew rapidly from very small beginnings. In 1890 John Mackintosh left his employment at Bowmans' cotton mill to open a pastrycook's business with his new wife, Violet, in King Cross Street. Their most popular line was a novel blend of traditional English butter scotch toffee and American caramel, and by 1892 the couple had moved into wholesale marketing of their new product. In 1894 they secured their first warehouse in Bond Street and in 1895 a second larger one in Hope Street, where John set up his 'Steam Confectionery Works'. To finance further expansion he set up a joint-stock limited liability company, John Mackintosh Ltd, and built a new factory in Queen's Road at a cost of £15,000. After a devastating fire at the premises in October 1909, he used his insurance compensation to resume production in the empty Albion Mills, which had the advantage of proximity to both the canal and the railway. By 1912, the works comprised a general office staffed by at least twenty clerks and typists; a huge manufacturing plant where toffee was boiled and produced; a five-storey mill where hundreds of girls wrapped toffee; and a four-storey mill where tinned toffees were packed for transport by rail. His flair for publicity earned Mackintosh the soubriquet of 'toffee king' and Halifax that of 'toffee town'. Other confectionery firms established in the town during this period included Riley Bros, toffee manufacturers, and

John Whittaker, the first large-scale biscuit manufacturers in the town, established c.1900.[9]

Halifax's extensive and diversified manufacturing economy and expanding population also stimulated a highly sophisticated local retail trade. Halifax was to become, indeed, the region's principal service centre, linked to its periphery by an extensive network of corporation tramway and motor omnibus routes by 1914. A commercial handbook boasted that in 1915 Halifax offered 'handsome and well-equipped business establishments superior to those of many towns of considerably greater population', gaining 'a reputation throughout Yorkshire as a shopping centre hard to beat'. In 1884, for example, Messrs Simpson and Sons Ltd, upholsterers, carpet warehousemen, decorators, painters, complete house furnishers, removal and storage contractors, opened an impressive new store in Silver Street. By 1895 the firm, which had been founded in 1815 in Woolshops, was the largest furnishing establishment in the north of England. Its five-storey showrooms, all linked by elevator, held, it was claimed, one of the largest selections of furniture outside London, embracing 'almost every requisite for the complete furnishing of a mansion or cottage'. They advertised in 1895 that 'a dining room might be furnished from stock at any price from £20 to £250; a dainty drawing room from £25 to £300, and even the cheapest articles may be in good taste, style and quality'. Bedroom suite prices ranged from five guineas to £150, and the firm emphasized that they 'guaranteed the absolute purity as well as the undeniable comfort of their bedding' which was made on the premises. They also carried comprehensive stocks of office furniture and a vast range of carpets, linoleum, drapery, curtains, decorating materials and timber.'Prices', the firm maintained, 'were fixed on the basis of the barest working margin of profit and adhered to'.[10]

Alongside the private retail establishments were the new borough markets and central co-operative stores. Developed on the site of the Georgian red-brick market in Market Street, the magnificent, turreted, Victorian Borough Markets, designed in a French Renaissance style by the Halifax architects Joseph and John Leeming, were completed at a cost of £130,000 and officially opened by the Duke and Duchess of York in 1896. The market complex, hailed by contemporaries as 'amongst the very finest in the country', accommodated nineteen shops and one public house on its outer perimeter and forty-three shops and over 100 stalls under its domed interior of glass and iron construction. In addition, the fish market, originally a separate enclosure under the same roof, contained sixteen lock-up shops inside the building and six outside. The vast central co-operative stores in Northgate were opened at a cost of £23,400 in October 1861, ten years after the foundation of the Halifax Industrial Society. They included drapery, boot and shoe, jewellery, ironmongery, crockery, furniture, grocery, and hosiery departments, plus a large butcher's shop, fruit and fish store, coal

Figure 5.7 The opening of the Halifax Borough Market, 1896. The new Halifax Borough Market, constructed on the site of the former red brick market, was opened by the Duke and Duchess of York, later King George V and Queen Mary, on their return to Halifax station, after they had performed the opening ceremony for the Royal Halifax Infirmary on Saturday 25 July 1896. From 1810 to 1853 the market had been run by a private company, when Halifax corporation took control by compulsory purchase. The decision to redevelop the market was taken in 1890 and plans exhibited in the Mechanics Institute. The design contract west to two Halifax brothers, Joseph and John Leeming, currently working as architects in London. (Photograph: J. A. Hargreaves Collection)

office, clogger's shop, confectioner's shop and cafe. The society also boasted the 'most modern and convenient stables in town' in Culver Street, tenanted by 'some of the finest draught horses in the country'; a slaughterhouse at North Dean; and a bakery in Queen's Road. By January 1901, when the Halifax Industrial Society celebrated its jubilee, it had no fewer than thirty-four branches and a turnover in the last year of the century approaching half-a-million pounds and profits in excess of £50,000. All these develop-ments within the retail sector reflected an increase in consumer spending in the late-Victorian era which helped to establish Halifax as a regional service centre.[11]

This was reflected also in the remarkable development of financial ser-vices in Halifax, which was sustained by industrial and retail expansion during the period between 1851 and 1914. The Halifax Joint Stock Bank, which had moved to new premises in Crossley Street in 1858, was registered as a limited liability company in 1880, and acquired the Midland Banking Co. of Huddersfield in 1881. In 1898 it amalgamated with the Halifax and Huddersfield Union Banking Co., which had opened imposing new premises in Commercial Street that year, and became the West Yorkshire Bank Ltd in 1910, with a capital of one million pounds. In 1852 Edward Akroyd, seeking to encourage thrift by his employers, had started the Woodside Penny Savings Bank at Boothtown, and this became the Yorkshire Penny Savings Bank in 1856 and the Yorkshire Penny Bank in 1871. It acquired new branch premises in Halifax in 1876, and by 1892 there were no fewer than seventy-one district branches in the parish of Halifax. Other banks in Halifax in 1914 included the Halifax and District Permanent Banking Co. in Princess Street, the London City and Midland Bank Ltd in Waterhouse Street, and the Halifax Equitable Bank Ltd in Silver Street, founded by the Halifax Equitable Building Society in 1899.[12]

However, in the financial sector, Halifax became in this period principally associated with the growth of the building society movement. The earliest known building society had been established in Birmingham in 1775 and in the following half-century some 250 societies were formed in the North and Midlands. In Halifax the movement grew out of the friendly societies. For example, the Loyal Georgean Society, which was founded in 1779 and which met at the Old Cock Inn, soon developed the practice of lending money to its members for building houses, including a terrace in St James's Road. During the nineteenth century, so-called terminating building societies, which wound up once the properties whose construction they had financed had been completed, mushroomed throughout the town. They included the Halifax Union or 'Go-Ahead' Building Society, established in 1845, with Edward Akroyd and Francis Crossley among its trustees. This had the ulterior motive of seeking to increase the number of 40 shilling freehold voters at a crucial stage in the campaign for the repeal of the Corn Laws. There was also the West Mount Building Society, which erected fourteen back-to-back houses in Lincoln Street and Penn Street in 1870, and the idealistically named Halifax and District Perfect Thrift Building Society with offices in Ferguson Street in 1894. Indeed, until the last quarter of the nineteenth century the majority of building societies nationwide

Figure 5.8   Jonas Dearnley Taylor (1829–1902). A Halifax solicitor's clerk who became a founder and the secretary of the Halifax Permanent Building Society from its formation in 1853 until his death in September 1902 and senior partner in the firm of J. D. Taylor and Co. Chartered Accountants. A prominent Nonconformist associated with both the Sion and Park Congregational Churches, his integrity and organisational ability contributed to the success of the society, which he served for almost half a century. He declared at the society's 49th annual meeting in March 1902 that 'the success of the society had always been the great aim of his life and that his foremost thought had been that everyone who brought money to the society should receive it back again'. (Photograph courtesy of Halifax plc)

Figure 5.9 Halifax Permanent Building Society Head Office, Princess Street, 1873. In 1869 the Halifax Permanent Building Society acquired a site for a head office opposite the new Town Hall with frontages on Princess Street and Crossley Street, adjoining the Mechanics' Hall and the White Swan Hotel. Competitive designs for the building were received from numerous architects and the design of Samuel Jackson, architect and surveyor of Bradford, was ultimately accepted. The foundation stone was laid on 5 April 1871. The new office, which cost £8,579, opened on 30 May 1873 and reflected the society's growing prosperity. In 1874 the society became incorporated under the Building Societies Act of 1874 and from 1874 to 1880 the profit divided among investing members was 1½ per cent per annum. (Photograph: J. A. Hargreaves Collection)

were terminating societies. Moreover, until 1914 the private mortgage market remained the major source of funding for the finance of house purchase.

More significant for the future development of the building society movement, however, were the permanent benefit building societies which were established in the period 1846–51 at Wakefield, Leeds, Otley, Bingley and Bradford. Then, in 1853, several members of the Loyal Georgean Society took the initiative in founding the Halifax Permanent Building Society. It therefore formed part of a wider Yorkshire movement, with a broader social appeal than the traditional banking institutions. John Fisher, manager of the Halifax Joint Stock Banking Co. and the first president of the Halifax Permanent, maintained that working men believed that banks were only for the rich and that building societies were the bankers of the poor. Jonas D. Taylor assumed the role of secretary from the initial meeting in the Old Cock, holding the office for almost half a century until his death in 1902. Indeed, his personal commitment, integrity, organisational ability, and long tenure of office was a major contributory factor to the success of the newly formed society. The society opened for business in February 1853 in a room over a shop in Old Market, rented for £10 p.a., and by the end of the year had assets totalling £12,074. During the first three years of its operation it advanced more than £40,000 mainly for multi-house purchase by rentiers, with only about one-fifth of advances for individual owner-occupation purchasers. Branch offices were opened at Sowerby Bridge, Thornton and Queenshead in 1853; Brighouse in 1854; Hebden Bridge and Stainland in 1855; Luddenden in 1859; Cornholme in 1860; and even in Huddersfield in 1862, two years before the establishment of the Huddersfield Building

Society. In 1854 the head office of the Halifax Permanent moved to Water-house Street 'over the offices of the County Fire and Life Assurance Company', where a single room housed J. D. Taylor and his staff of just six clerks and an office boy until the society opened its first purpose-built head office in Princess Street in 1873.

The society grew steadily during the 1860s and 1870s. The first 34 balance sheets of the society record an annual increase in aggregate assets, with the single exception of 1865, and by 1885, the Halifax Permanent had the largest reserves of all the Yorkshire building societies. Progress in the 1880s and 1890s, however, was slow and the society's assets which had reached £1 million in 1881 were still only just over a million in 1896. When Jonas D. Taylor died in September 1902, the Halifax Permanent Building Society had some fifty branches, mostly in the villages and small towns around Halifax, but also including major branches further afield at Hull, Leeds and Bradford, a tribute to Taylor's insistence on the need for a policy of expanding branch and agency provision. Nevertheless, all the branches except one at Darlington were in Yorkshire and nearly all were in the West Riding. The society remained in 1902, in the view of O. R. Hobson, who wrote the centenary history of the society in 1953, 'a local building society and no more', still with a relatively small head office staff often working overtime. By 1905, however, the society had more accounts than any other building society and by 1913 had assets exceeding £3 million, more than any other society.

Moreover, in 1913, the second largest building society was also situated in Halifax, namely the Halifax Equitable Building Society, started in 1887. The success of the building society movement in Halifax before 1914 owed much to the development of a culture of nonconformity and thrift in the town. Joseph Harger Mitchell, secretary of the Halifax Equitable Building Society from 1897 until 1927, claimed in a paper presented to the Building Societies' Association, meeting in Halifax in 1908, that the amount invested in building societies in the Halifax district was forty times as great in proportion to population as the average for the whole country. The success of the movement was also related to rises in living standards, the increase in savings to be invested, and the increase in incomes for the purchase or especially renting of houses. Analysis of rate books has revealed that a mere 13.8 per cent of property in the County Borough of Halifax was owner occupied in 1901. Despite their early concern to appeal to the working classes, both societies tended to favour the upper end of the property market before 1900. The average house price in Halifax in the second half of the nineteenth century was £109.20. However, during the 1850s the Halifax Permanent had an average mortgage of about £430, with only 4 per cent of mortgages granted for sums below £100 and a further 25 per cent for sums below £200. In 1896, a quarter of all advances from the Halifax Equitable were above £500 and 17 per cent above £1,000. Nevertheless, in his 1901 report the chairman stated that the society had 248 mortgages where the debt did not exceed £500 'showing that they did a very large business with small borrowers, and this was the business they decidedly wished to cultivate'.[13]

As Halifax centred upon itself increasingly diverse manufacturing and service sector operations, the development of improved internal and external communication helped the town to overcome some of the constraints of its geographical location. In the early 1850s railway links were constructed between Halifax, Bradford, Leeds and Wakefield via the Beacon Hill tunnel, and in 1855 a magnificent new Italianate baroque station, designed by Thomas Butterworth of Manchester, was opened for the Lancashire and Yorkshire and Great Northern railway companies. An extension to Holmfield for goods traffic was completed in 1874, with provision for passengers from 1879. A new station at North Bridge was opened in 1880 and new access to Halifax Station from Horton Street was provided in 1886, by which time there were seven platforms for passengers. Although a high level railway linking King Cross and Pellon with the Halifax–Bradford line of the Great Northern Railway was constructed in 1890, repeated efforts to extend the main line of the Midland Railway from Huddersfield to Halifax in 1864, 1874, 1897, 1899 and 1902 all proved abortive and as late as 1918 a commercial directory concluded ruefully that Halifax might have been 'more advantageously placed from a railway point of view'. Nevertheless, by 1910 there were some 163 train departures every day, and Halifax even had its own boat train which connected with the night steamer to Belfast.[14]

The Halifax Chamber of Commerce, formed in 1862 with 155 subscribing members drawn from the banking, manufacturing and business communities, was very much aware of the problem and strongly supported schemes to improve transport and communications, including rail, water, telegraph and postal links with the town. The Halifax Exchange was founded in 1863 for local businessmen and the Halifax Chamber of Trade in 1903. A new General Post Office, designed by Henry Tanner, was opened in Commercial Street in 1887. It was the first purpose-built accommodation in the town for the post office, which had changed premises three times in the preceding half century. Its scale of business is evident from White's *Directory* of 1887, which listed its opening hours from 7.30 a. m. until 10.00 p. m. on weekdays and 7.30 a. m. until 10.00 a. m. Sundays. The Halifax Chamber of Commerce also established with Halifax Corporation a joint advisory committee on telegraphs and telephones. It secured concessions to telephone users in the town and urged the government to constitute the woollen districts of the West Riding into a single telephone area with regional charge rates, recognising the importance to the development of the local economy of telecommunications: these were ultimately to be the saviour of regional businesses in the future.[15]

Figure 5.10 General Post Office, Commercial Street. Opened on 23 June 1887, the new General Post Office building on Commercial Street was designed by Henry Tanner, architect to the local board of works and constructed in Yorkshire stone at a cost of around £13,000. It was the first purpose-built accommodation for the Post Office, which had changed premises three times in the preceding half century. Its scale of business by 1887 is evident from White's *Directory* of that year, which listed its opening hours from 7.30 a.m. until 10.00 p.m. weekdays and from 7.30 a.m. until 10.00 a.m. on Sundays. A popular innovation in 1902 was the provision of tramcar letter boxes. The new premises were enlarged in 1926–27 to provide accommodation for the first local automatic telephone exchange. (Photograph: J. A. Hargreaves Collection)

There was also a growing recognition of the need to improve local internal lines of communication. One witness told the Ranger inquiry in 1850 that the roads within the town were 'steep and not yet paved, and in a wretched condition', lying in large pools of foul water in which 'carts sink up to the nave', while another witness complained about 'the badly constructed and hilly suburban roads'. Some improvements were undertaken by the new municipal council, but, because of the nature of its terrain, Halifax remained largely a pedestrian town for the majority of its inhabitants until the turn of the century. Early proposals to develop steam or cable tramways in 1882 appeared likely to prove costly given the nature of the local terrain, and consequently failed to secure council backing. A horse omnibus service operated by John Marsh and Co. offered some relief from 1886 until 1898, when an electric tramway system, operated by Halifax Corporation, commenced operation, forcing Marsh and Co. into liquidation in 1900. Only Blackpool, Dover and Leeds had corporation electric tramways before Halifax, and the Halifax system, which was completed by 1905, had a number of distinctive features. A narrow gauge track and small, light tramcars proved necessary to cope with the town's steep gradients and narrow streets. Even so, there were serious accidents in 1906 and 1907 when tramcars were derailed on North Bridge and at Pye Nest. However, travelling by the new 'gondolas of the people' became increasingly popular. In 1914 some 20,276,000 passengers were carried safely on the Halifax tramway system, plus additional passengers by motorised omnibuses, also operated by the corporation from Halifax to the remote upland village of Mount Tabor from 1912.[16]

During the Victorian and Edwardian eras Halifax absorbed more of the population of its periphery and centred upon itself increasingly diverse manufacturing and service sector operations, reaching the limits of its demographic and urban expansion around 1900, when geographical constraints placed limits on the town's spatial development. Moreover, there were also signs of decline by 1900 in some branches of textiles as a result of external factors, especially increasing foreign competition during the 1890s. After 1851 both the local business community and the Halifax Corporation became increasingly aware of the need to improve internal and external communication links if Halifax were to counteract some of the constraints which its geographical location placed upon its economic and urban expansion. However, although improvements in transport and communications were evident by 1914, Halifax's hilly terrain continued to present problems for its pioneering electric tramway system and the town remained relatively inaccessible by rail in comparison with other neighbouring West Riding towns and cities, notably Bradford and Leeds, which continued to grow after 1900.

Social geography

The economic changes of the period 1851–1914 had a profound effect upon the social structure of the locality. The late-Victorian period witnessed a further decline in the influence of the older absentee aristocratic landed

View in People's Park,   HALIFAX.

Figure 5.11   People's Park. Following a visit to the United States of America in 1855, where he had marvelled at the natural beauty of the White Mountains, Francis Crossley resolved 'to arrange art and nature that they shall be within the walk of every working man in Halifax; that he shall go to take his stroll there after he has done his hard day's toil, and be able to get home without being tired'. Sir Joseph Paxton of Crystal Palace fame was engaged to design and landscape a park from 'five flat fields, bounded on three sides by public roads, containing an area of twelve acres and a half, destitute alike of prospect, of water, of wood'. The site was excavated, large quantities of topsoil introduced, trees and shrubs planted, and flower beds, rockeries and ornamental lakes constructed at a cost of £50,000. The park was officially opened on 14 August 1857, amidst scenes of popular rejoicing. (Photograph: J. A. Hargreaves Collection) elite and the rise of a new entrepreneurial elite, whose wealth was derived from the Industrial Revolution. This new *haute bourgeoisie* colonised the exclusive residential suburb of Skircoat on the southern perimeter of the town, and the fashionable area around People's Park, with a profusion of spacious, though predominantly unostentatious, villa mansions. Beneath them in the social hierarchy was a more modest business and professional middle class residing on the manor house estates in and around Skircoat and parts of Northowram and in the superior terraced housing in the vicinity of People's Park. Then there were the struggling lower middle classes, occupying more basic terraced housing at King Cross, along Queen's Road, on Lee Bank, Lee Mount and Claremount. Finally came the manual workers, inhabiting the numerous back-to-back houses, often situated close to the factories where they worked, or the slum ghettos, which by the end of the nineteenth century were concentrated around the parish church, at Cross Fields, Chapeltown, on Foundry Street and at the junction of West Parade and King Street.[17]

During the late-Victorian period a number of symbolic vestigial links with Halifax's long-departed rentier landed aristocracy were loosened when Skircoat Moor, Shroggs Park and Highroad Well Moor were acquired from the Savile family by the Halifax Corporation, now dominated by the new business elite. Skircoat Moor, a vast estate on the south-eastern perimeter of the town, valued at £40,000, was re-named Savile Park and sold to the corporation for a nominal fee of £100 in 1866 by Captain Henry Savile, who also surrendered all his manorial rights on condition that the corporation undertook to abate the pervasive smoke nuisance. Shroggs Park, an area of 24 acres of woodland to the north of the town, was leased to the

Figure 5.12 Crossley and Porter Orphanage. John, Joseph and Francis Crossley jointly contributed over £56,000 towards the erection and endowment of the orphan home and school, which was designed by John Hogg of Halifax and built in 1864. In 1887, Thomas Porter, a Manchester yarn merchant, augmented the endowment fund by a donation of £50,000. By 1895, according to a contemporary directory, 'the orphanage and school liberally feeds, clothes and educates from 200 to 300 children'. Children of both sexes were admitted from the age of seven years from all parts of Britain, boys remaining until the age of fifteen, girls until the age of seventeen. In 1919 the governors were granted the royal assent to change the orphanage into a secondary school, which merged in 1985 with Heath School. (Photograph: J. A. Hargreaves Collection)

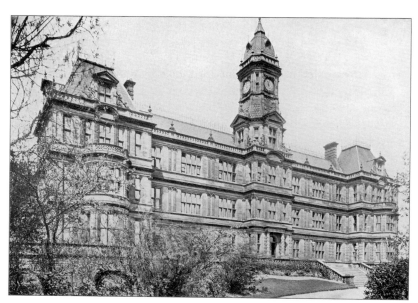

corporation by Henry Savile for 999 years at an annual rent of one pound in 1881, after Edward Akroyd had realised its potential as an amenity for the residents of his model housing development at Akroydon. Finally, Highroad Well Moor was given by Lord Savile in 1899 for development by two local manufacturers, Henry McCrea (1810–1901) and Enoch Robinson (1835–1926), into West View Park.[18]

The Revd Francis Pigou, Vicar of Halifax from 1875 to 1889, maintained that few English parishes could compare with Halifax for its concentration of wealthy manufacturers and merchant princes by the late-Victorian era, including

> Akroyd, Crossley, Baldwin, Foster, Edwards, Watkinson, Hall, Huntriss, Rawson, Appleyard and many more who … living quietly and unostentatiously, are men of large fortunes … and by intermarriages fortunes are kept in families … there are several handsome family mansions … and a recent noble effort to build a new Infirmary at a cost of some £100,000 amongst the evidences of wealth.[19]

George Sheeran's study of the wealth of the West Yorkshire industrial elite during this period as revealed in their domestic architecture, business investments, philanthropic benefactions and probate records confirms the validity of Pigou's impressions. The Crossley family of carpet manufacturers, whose mansions, almshouses, orphanage, hotels and offices featured prominently in the local townscape 'made two or three fortunes in magnitude of half a million to one million pounds'. H. C. McCrea, an Irish entrepreneur who had settled in Halifax in 1834, not only channelled his surplus profits from damask production into the landscaping of West View Park and Albert Promenade in Halifax, but also into the development of the seaside resort of Blackpool, leaving an estate valued at £294,000 at his death in 1901.

Others who had acquired vast fortunes from industrial expansion, however, had dissipated most of their wealth by the time of their deaths. Edward Akroyd, joint heir of an estate valued at £300,000 in 1847, promptly spent £100,000 of it on the building of All Souls Church and subsequently donated substantial sums for its upkeep, including nearly £400,000 between 1869–72. In addition, he spent large sums of money on charities, political campaigns, his two model housing developments at Copley and Akroydon and his Italianate villa at Bankfield, leaving an estate valued at £1,234 when he died in straitened circumstances at St Leonard's-on-Sea in Sussex in 1887. Similarly, the second generation John Crossley's immense fortune was whittled away through a combination of lavish philanthropy and ill-judged investments, leaving an estate valued at under £8,000 when he died in 1879, in marked contrast to the legacies of £800,000 and £900,000 of his brothers Francis and Joseph.[20]

Moreover, long before the period had ended some local industrial magnates had made the transition from entrepreneur to leisured gentleman,

Figure 5.13   All Souls Church, Haley Hill and statue of Colonel Edward Akroyd (1810–87). Completed in 1859, All Souls Church was commissioned by Colonel Akroyd as the crowning feature of his model housing development at Akroydon. The spire, almost 73 metres in height, was the second tallest church spire in Yorkshire. Designed by Sir George Gilbert Scott, the new church won immediate acclaim. The *Building News* concluded that it was 'one of the most elegant specimens he has produced', while the architect himself pronounced it 'on the whole, my best church'. The statue of Colonel Akroyd by J. Birnie Philips, originally located at the southern end of North Bridge, was moved to Haley Hill in 1901 to allow the development of the tramway network. (Photograph courtesy of Ian Beesley)

and like the landed gentry of an earlier age had withdrawn to country retreats some distance from the town. Following the death of Sir Francis Crossley at Belle Vue in 1872, his widow had closed up the family mansion and moved permanently to the family's large country estate at Somerleyton in Suffolk, which Crossley had purchased in 1861. His son, Sir Savile Brinton Crossley, became a member of the Tory landed elite. Other members of the third generation of the Crossley family, however, continued to live locally until the last decade of the nineteenth century, in elegant mansions designed to accommodate their developing scientific interests. Edward Crossley (1840–1905), the eldest son of Joseph Crossley, lived at Bermerside, in Skircoat, where he constructed a well-equipped observatory in the grounds, only to find that the smoke-filled atmosphere impaired the use of his giant reflecting telescope. He therefore withdrew to his summer residence on the Isle of Wight in the 1890s, returning to Halifax only to chair the annual meeting of shareholders at Dean Clough. His cousin, Louis John Crossley (1842–91), the only son of John Crossley, remained a director of the firm until his death at the age of forty-nine, but made frequent visits to his property in Windermere, where he enjoyed sailing on the lake. At Moorside, his home in Skircoat, he had installed a fully equipped electrical laboratory and workshop in the house and an electric tramway system in the grounds. The drawing room was furnished in ebonised wood and gold and contained a huge electric organ in a carved case set in a carved alabaster screen 'somewhat similar to the great organ in the Royal Albert Hall'. His final years were dogged with ill-health and he died after undertaking a round-the-world voyage in search of recovery.[21]

Manufacturers who remained economically active continued to reside close to their workplaces. Harold Mackintosh, the future first Viscount Mackintosh, son of John Mackintosh, 'the toffee king', recalled that he had spent the first twenty-five years of his life at 8 Park Terrace, one of eight houses sharing a communal garden 'within a square mile' of which were 'to be found the first shop, the first warehouse, the first factory, our home, our chapel and our day schools'. His father later moved to Greystones, a very comfortable but unostentatious house, which was not even detached, on the edge of Savile Park. However, while the first and second generations of the Holdsworth family had all lived virtually within a stone's throw of Shaw Lodge Mills, Clement Holdsworth, who succeeded to the sole owner-ship of Shaw Lodge Mills in 1887, purchased the Scargill estate at Kettlewell in 1900. He finally moved from Shaw Lodge to Netherside Hall, a country mansion near Grassington, in 1912, drawing an average of £4,500 a year from the business between 1885 and 1913 and an annual salary of between £1,000 and £1,750 until 1913 to sustain a lifestyle of fishing and shooting in Wharfedale.[22]

Beneath these wealthy entrepreneurs in the social hierarchy were the professional classes and upwardly mobile shopkeepers, merchants and small businessmen. Contemporary directories suggest that the numbers within some professional groups remained remarkably stable throughout the period. For example, the number of auctioneers remained at 10 between 1853 and 1874 and the number of chemists and lawyers rose only slightly from 19 to 21 and 21 to 25 respectively during the same period. Moreover, the number of architects and surveyors and physicians and surgeons actually declined slightly from 18 to 12 and 27 to 22 between 1853 and 1874. However, the number of accountants and agents more than doubled from 17 to 38 between 1853 and 1874. Moreover, the number of professionals enumerated in the censuses more than quadrupled from 368 to 1,525 between 1881 and 1901. The directories and censuses also reveal a sharp rise in the number of shopkeepers and specialist wholesalers and retailers. The number of jewellers and watchmakers, for example, rose from 16 in 1853 to 20 in 1874 and by 1901 there were no fewer than 423 men and 86 women employed in these establishments. Managers, designers and commercial travellers at John Crossley and Sons Ltd earned salaries ranging from £300 and £600 between 1875 and 1882. Many professionals and retailers were therefore able to afford properties on the new manor house estates around Savile Park with their superior terraced housing and imposing villas. Restrictive covenants were incorporated into their sales agreements to ensure the preservation of the exclusive character of this Victorian residential suburb. The *Halifax Courier* of June 1877 revealed that the land adjacent to Savile Park was rapidly being covered:

> a large villa for Mr Shoesmith the auctioneer; lower down a terrace of ten houses for Councillor Denham; the Manor Royd for Mr Patchett, who has also commissioned four large semi-detached villas. Below Heath Villas a new mansion for Councillor Longbottom and one adjacent to it for Mr George Webster, the grocer.[23]

Next in the social hierarchy came the struggling lower middle classes, comprising the multitude of small masters, agents, brokers and dealers who were particularly numerous in Halifax, and the growing army of 'white-collar' clerks and shop assistants staffing the profusion of banks, offices, commercial establishments and more specialist retail outlets in and around the town. In 1881, there were no fewer than 776 small masters, 60 agents, 52 brokers, 273 dealers, 747 clerks and 507 shop assistants. However, the number of skilled craftsmen and artisans, such as smiths, masons, tailors, coopers and other independent, *petit-bourgeois* producers and distributors, was declining during this period. Alderman J. H. Waddington, surveying the changes which had taken place in Halifax during the Victorian and Edwardian eras, observed that:

> some trades have become smaller and smaller, while some have entirely gone out. We think of ... cloggers, button makers, cloth cap makers, straw hat makers, coopers, curriers, saddlers, stay makers, carvers and guilders, blacksmiths, oat cake makers, and makers of clay pipes for smokers.[24]

But new wealth and increasing sophistication had generated a new range of small businesses. For example, a newer breed of restaurant owners, eating-house keepers and beer sellers was undermining the earlier predominance of innkeepers, lodging-house keepers and general publicans.[25]

Finally, at the base of the social pyramid came the manual workers and domestic servants, varying in their status and incomes according to their gender, occupation and the fluctuating demands for their labour. In 1901, by far the largest proportion of manual workers of both sexes, some 8,811 men and 13,624 women, were employed in textile and clothing manufacture. A further 6,281 men were employed in engineering, 3,333 in the building and construction industry and 2,746 in the transport and haulage industry. The largest form of employment for women outside the textile and clothing industries was domestic service, which accounted for 2,771 women and 458 men in 1901. Within domestic service there was some status differentiation related to the type of tasks performed and the status of the employer. Butlers and housekeepers were considered of superior status to general servants, who regarded themselves as superior to washerwomen and char-women. Within industry, a 'labour aristocracy' of exclusively male mechanics and engineers enjoyed higher wages than the bulk of semi-skilled and unskilled labourers. For example, mechanics in the machine tool trade in Halifax were paid around 31s. (£1.55) a week in 1870.[26]

The vast majority of textile workers earned considerably less. A wage census of 1886 confirmed that worsteds was one of the poorest paying of the major textile industries and that wage rates in neighbouring Bradford were as much as five shillings a week higher than in Halifax for the same jobs. Moreover, women, who performed the lighter, intermediate textile processes of spinning, doubling, hanking and warping, were paid between one-third and one-half the wages of men, who dominated the heavier preparatory and finishing processes of sorting, winnowing, felting, scouring, milling, shearing, pressing and packing. In 1870, before the West Riding textile industry suffered a depression as it struggled to compete with in-creasing foreign competition, Halifax male wool sorters could earn up to 28s. (£1.40), engine tenters and mechanics around 30s. (£1.50) for a 72-hour week, but for females employed in spinning, twisting and reeling the rates were from 8s. (40p) to 14s. (70p). Piece work weavers might earn up to 18s. (90p), but were generally hired by the piece and in periods of depression were often kept waiting for the next piece to arrive, losing income through

Figure 5.14 Cottage in Back Foundry Street, Halifax, 1901. In 1851 the small, two-storeyed, stone-built cottage was the home of Richard Horsfall, a Scottish weaver, and in September 1850 it became the original store of Halifax Working Men's Co-operative and Provident Society. Its small size, however, restricted the development of the business and in January 1851 the society moved to larger premises in Cow Green. (Photograph: J. A. Hargreaves Collection)

broken time. Woolcombers similarly were rarely paid a full week's wages and juvenile textile workers working part-time were paid an average of 3s. 8d. (18p) in the late 1880s. Their meagre earnings nevertheless provided a welcome supplement to working-class family incomes.[27]

Most working-class housing, located predominantly around the industrial complexes of western and central Halifax, remained relatively poor in quality. The building of cellar dwellings continued to be permitted until 1869, but national legislation and local by-laws increasingly inhibited the building of sub-standard housing and made provision for better drainage and ventilation in the second half of the nineteenth century. However, most building was speculative and cheap and confined to back-to-back construction of two and three rooms, which was estimated to make up 65 per cent of all housing provision in Halifax in 1888. Wilfred Pickles, the son of a building construction worker, remembered Conway Street, where he was born in 1904, as 'a drab thoroughfare, paved with stone setts, its tiny back-to-back houses sheltering so many people that I now wonder how they could find space to move'. The *Halifax Guardian* ran a series of articles on the slums of Halifax in 1889 which focused on houses near the Halifax Parish Church which were 'squalid beyond description', many of which were demolished following a local government enquiry in 1893, and no more back-to-back houses were built in Halifax after 1900. By contrast, the emergence of 'improving' lower-middle and working-class residential districts on the western and north-western fringes of the town, especially between 1860 and 1890, were expressions of lower-middle and working-class respectability, physically removed from the vice and depravity of the slum ghettos.[28]

The economic changes in Halifax between 1851 and 1914 therefore supported a shifting social hierarchy. The influence of the old landed elite continued to decline and the town became dominated socially and economically by industrial wealth. The growing importance of Halifax as a service centre stimulated the development of the town's professional and business classes, but the vast majority of the town's adult workforce supported themselves and their families through relatively low paid manual labour or domestic service. The widening income gap between those at the top and those at the bottom of the social pyramid, the increasing social segregation of housing and the conspicuous inequalities of living standards contained the potential for social conflict within Halifax which found expression in the growth of class politics in the late nineteenth century.

Politics: Chartism, Liberalism and the rise of Labour

Although four Chartists were elected to the new municipal council in Halifax in 1848 and Chartist organisation was maintained in the town until 1858, Kate Tiller has concluded that after 1848 Halifax Chartism as elsewhere 'undoubtedly lost its momentum'. Despite collections for the imprisoned Chartist leader, Ernest Jones, the Chartists had to abandon their meeting hall and increasingly channelled their energies into co-operation, mutual improvement and temperance. John Snowden (1822–84), for example, a woolcomber and Chartist since 1838, who had 'worked for the Charter with might and main while Chartism was a possible force to be reckoned with', after 1848,

> sensibly espoused the cause of gradual reform, working steadfastly at the task nearest hand, training his brain the while with home study of history and of political principles.[29]

The triumphant return of Ernest Jones in a carriage drawn by four greys to an enthusiastic reception in Halifax, following his release from prison

Figure 5.15   Halifax Borough Election, 1857. Political sketch by Humphrey Thwackem the younger showing the three 'horses' running in the 1857 general election, namely Sir Charles Wood and Mr Francis Crossley, the successful Liberal candidates, and Major Henry Edwards, the unsuccessful Conservative candidate. Francis Crossley topped the poll with 830 votes, followed by Sir Charles Wood with 714 votes. The veteran Charles Wood, who had been re-elected without opposition on 3 March 1855 on becoming First Lord of the Admiralty, congratulated Crossley on heading the poll. Major Henry Edwards, who obtained 651 votes, had now suffered defeat in three successive Halifax contests and subsequently secured election for Beverley. (Photograph courtesy of the West Yorkshire Archive Service, Calderdale)

in July 1850, stimulated a short-lived Chartist revival, particularly amongst local woolcombers, who were suffering wage reductions and unemployment. The main focus of Chartist energies was Jones's second parliamentary candidature in Halifax in 1852, although the very limited franchise did not offer them much prospect of electoral success. Moreover, middle-class radicals had found themselves a strong candidate in the carpet manufacturer, Francis Crossley, who promised his support for a household, ratepaying suffrage and secret ballot. By 1852 Sir Charles Wood had severed his electoral pact with the Tory, Henry Edwards, and now stood with his fellow Liberal, Crossley. This partnership could attract almost every shade of elector in the Whig-Liberal spectrum, but left the Tories and the Chartists electorally vulnerable.

At the poll, Wood and Crossley were returned with 596 and 573 votes, while Edwards and Jones were defeated, polling 521 and 38 votes respectively. Moreover, the pattern of Liberal voting displayed in 1852 was not significantly disturbed again until after the Reform Act of 1867, and neither the Tories nor the Chartists seriously challenged the dominance of the Liberal-Radical alliance in Halifax during this period. In June 1853 the secular funeral of the Ovenden handloom weaver and veteran Chartist Ben Rushton, witnessed by an estimated crowd of 15,000, proved to be 'the last great Chartist occasion in Halifax'. While the absence of trade union organisation deprived Halifax Chartism of a whole dimension of potential growth, Halifax Chartists maintained their organisation longer than in most other provincial centres. The leaders of working-class politics in the town continued to be drawn from the Chartists for almost twenty years after the demise of the movement.[30]

At the general election in 1857 Wood and Crossley were again re-elected but, on this occasion, Crossley topped the poll with 830 votes, with Wood and Edwards polling 714 and 651 votes respectively. When Crossley opted to seek election for the West Riding constituency in 1859, Wood and James Stansfeld, another Liberal, the barrister son of a local county court judge, were returned unopposed. However, in 1865, Wood reluctantly resigned, anticipating a strong challenge from the Halifax worsted manufacturer, Edward Akroyd, who had lost his seat as Whig Member of Parliament for Huddersfield, and Stansfeld and Akroyd were returned unopposed, Akroyd holding the seat until his retirement in 1874, by which time he was regularly entering the division lobbies with the Conservatives. The 1867 Reform Act extended the borough franchise to householders and lodgers who had occupied lodgings worth ten pounds a year for at least one year. This increased the local electorate from 1,900 to 9,328 in 1871 and 11,998 in 1884, thereby enfranchising about 70 per cent of all adult males within the constituency, a higher proportion of voters than in other West Riding urban industrial constituencies.[31]

Nevertheless, most of these male householders were evidently content to vote for Liberals and Whigs and therefore for candidates from higher social classes. In 1868 Liberalism again split into two wings represented by Edward Akroyd, Whig, Anglican and National Reform Unionist, and the radical James Stansfeld, Unitarian and Reform Leaguer. A working man's candidate, E. O. Greening, co-operator, Dissenter, temperance campaigner and Reform Leaguer was adopted in opposition to Stansfeld and Akroyd, with no Tory standing. After a lively campaign Stansfeld and Akroyd were returned with 6,278 and 5,141 votes respectively, while Greening, whose supporters had included five of the ten leading Chartists of the 1850s, came bottom of the poll with 2,802 votes. After the election the radicals set up the Liberal Electoral Association as a rival to the official Liberal Registration Association, but an uneasy *rapprochement* was effected following a shock Tory victory in a by-election in the neighbouring West Riding constituency in 1872. However, only the first School Board elections of January 1874 finally reunited the various strands of Halifax Liberalism, when the former Chartist lecturer, John Snowden, headed the poll.

In the ensuing general election of 1874 John Crossley, elder brother of the late Francis, and James Stansfeld were returned with 5,563 and 5,473 votes respectively, with McCrea, the Conservative candidate, in third place with 3,927 votes. Crossley's sudden retirement in February 1877 as a result of ill-health and financial embarrassment, arising from imprudent speculative investment, evinced much popular sympathy, and at the ensuing by-election J. D. Hutchinson, the Liberal candidate achieved a comfortable victory over the Conservative, Gamble, by 5,750 votes to 3,624. At the 1880 general election Stansfeld and Hutchinson again defeated the Conservative candidate, Barber, the three candidates polling 6,392, 6,364 and 3,452 votes respectively. When ill-health forced Hutchinson to resign in 1882, his Liberal successor, Thomas Shaw, was elected without opposition. Thereafter, Shaw and Stansfeld were returned with comfortable majorities over the Tory candidate, Morris, in both the general election of 1885 and the by-election of 1886, which followed Stansfeld's appointment for a further term as President of the Local Government Board. In 1885, Ben Wilson organised a social evening for twenty-two former Chartists, all now enthusiastic Gladstonian Liberals, at Maude's Temperance Hotel, Broad Street, Halifax to celebrate 'the incorporation in the law of the land of the principal portion of the charter' with the passing of the Third Reform Bill in 1885. The *Halifax Courier* commented: 'at the time of the Chartist agitation they were all poor working men', now

> the majority ... have become men of business and in some cases employers of labour, and a few by economy, industry and temperance have secured a competency for their old age.[32]

The increasing segregation of middle- and working-class housing, which became more pronounced after the revision of ward boundaries in 1892, together with the polarisation of middle- and working-class interests over education, were underlying factors in the emergence of class politics in Halifax in the late nineteenth century. However, the immediate stimulus was provided by the deterioration of industrial relations in the late 1880s and early 1890s, the rise of 'new unionism' and the foundation of the Halifax Trades and Labour Council in 1889 by delegates from eighteen craft unions, including iron moulders, carpenters and joiners, wiredrawers and silk dressers. Trade union organisation in Halifax, pronounced 'hopeless' by Ben Turner in his autobiography, had been traditionally weak in the West Riding textile industry, where the majority of workers were women and young people. However, it was the much stronger craft unions within the expanding, male-dominated, engineering industry that provided the initiative for the founding of the Halifax Trades Council, whose membership fluctuated between around 3,000 and 4,000 members in the 1890s.

Though it drew its support from across the whole spectrum of trade union political opinion, the Halifax Trades Council very quickly gravitated towards Labour politics after Socialism arrived in Halifax in 1891, infused through a middle-class Fabian ideology and organisation. In July 1892 the Halifax Fabian Society joined with the Halifax Trades Council to form the Halifax Labour Union, the forerunner of the Halifax Independent Labour Party, established in the following year. Membership of the Halifax Independent Labour Party fluctuated between 500 and 700 members between 1893 and 1899, and during the 1890s Halifax had the second largest ILP organisation in the country after Bradford. The growing electoral support for the ILP in Halifax in the period up to the outbreak of the First World War is evidenced by its increasing success in municipal elections, rising from 10 electoral successes in the period up to 1900 to 34 in the period from 1900 to 1906 and 63 in the period from 1906 to 1914. Moreover, John Lister obtained 3,024 votes as ILP candidate in the parliamentary by-election of 1893, and 3,818 votes in the general election of 1895, notwithstanding a bitter division within the local party which had erupted in 1894.

Liberalism had remained the dominant political creed of the textile Nonconformist millocracy until the late 1890s, when some prominent local Liberals, including members of the Crossley family, espoused Liberal Unionism. Liberalism had also found widespread support amongst the working-class voters of Halifax until the rise of a trade-union dominated Labour movement in 1892 'whose emergence', Dr P. Dawson has concluded, 'shook the foundations of the political system in Halifax'. It eroded Liberal support and enabled 'a strengthened, business-directed Conservative Party' to benefit from the split-vote system, most notably in the general elections of 1895 and 1900, when they made electoral gains at Liberal expense. Conservative support was drawn predominantly from professionals, gentlemen, land and property owners and their tenants, some manufacturers and their working-class employees, and the drink interest, which felt threatened by the temperance element within municipal Liberalism. In June 1895, James Stansfeld's distinguished 36-year representation of Halifax as Liberal Member of Parliament concluded when he retired with a knighthood from Queen Victoria and the honorary freedom of the county borough. In the general election of 1895, the Liberal vote was split between W. Rawson-Shaw and James Booth, who polled 5,085 and 4,283 votes respectively, allowing the Conservative wire manufacturer Alfred Arnold to top the poll with 5,475 votes.

Sir Savile Brinton Crossley (1857–1935), the only son of Sir Francis Crossley, who had been defeated as a Liberal Unionist candidate in the 1897 Halifax by-election by the Liberal Alfred Billson, stood for election as Conservative candidate for Halifax in the khaki election of 1900, while on active service in South Africa. He topped the poll with 5,931 votes, losing the seat as decisively in the Liberal landslide of 1906, when he came bottom of the poll with 5,041 votes. John Henry Whitley (1866–1935), a partner in the family cotton spinning firm of S. Whitley and Co. and a Halifax Liberal councillor from 1892 to 1900, came second in the poll at the general election of 1900 to Crossley with 5,543 votes and was returned as Liberal member for Halifax. At Westminster, he campaigned vigorously against the Education Act of 1902 and the Licensing Act of 1904 and at the general election of 1906 topped the poll with 9,354 votes. In 1907, when he was appointed a junior treasury minister, he was returned unopposed, and in the two general elections of 1910 again topped the poll in Halifax with 9,504 and 8,779 votes respectively.

This Liberal revival, which benefited from the growing unpopularity of Tory domestic and foreign policies, was perhaps not so remarkable as the advance of Labour. James Parker (1863–1948), coming second in the poll to Whitley, was elected as the first Labour MP for Halifax in 1906, on a progressive alliance with the Liberals to defend free trade. Parker, who had worked for a local electrical engineering company until becoming full-time secretary of Halifax ILP, had come to Halifax as a navvy at age of nineteen from Louth, where his parents were farm labourers. He was re-elected in the Halifax general elections of 1910, obtaining 9,093 and 8,511 votes. Moreover, although the Liberals did well in parliamentary elections between 1906 and 1910, municipal elections show the erosion of their local power base, as allegiances shifted to the Conservatives and to Labour. During the period from 1903 to 1913, the number of Liberal councillors and aldermen serving on Halifax Corporation declined from 44 to 25, whereas the number of Conservative and Labour councillors and aldermen rose from 10 to 24 and 6 to 9 respectively. The Labour movement was also making a cultural as well as a political impact in Halifax in the period up to 1914. By 1898 the Halifax Labour Church was meeting regularly twice on Sundays with its primary objective 'the emancipation of Labour and the re-construction of society upon the basis of justice and brotherhood', and by 1900 the

Halifax Socialist Sunday School had attracted 159 members. The Clarion Movement, founded by Robert Blatchford in the early 1890s, with its numerous cycling, field, scout, glee and vocal unions, also became well-established in Halifax during this period.[33]

Table 5.1. *Municipal seats in Halifax, 1896–1913*

Year	Conservative	Labour	Liberal	Others
1896	21		24	3
1897	20	1	26	1
1898	15	1	32	
1899	18	2	32	
1900	19	2	37	2
1901	17	4	38	1
1902	14	5	40	1
1903	10	6	44	
1904	10	6	43	
1905	15	4	40	1
1906	15	4	40	1
1907	17	6	36	1
1908	16	7	36	1
1909	16	8	35	1
1910	17	7	35	1
1911	17	8	34	1
1912	19	8	31	2
1913	24	9	25	2

Source: P. A. Dawson, 'The Halifax Independent Labour Movement' in K. Laybourn and D. James (ed.), *The Rising Sun of Socialism* (West Yorkshire Archive Service, Wakefield: 1991), p. 52.

Electoral politics, however, were still dominated by men. The campaign for the extension of the franchise to women gathered momentum in Halifax following an open-air meeting on Savile Park addressed by the militant suffragette Annie Kenney, soon after her release from prison in August 1906. A Halifax branch of the Women's Social and Political Union was formed in January 1907, and Emmeline Pankhurst visited the town shortly afterwards to address a meeting at the Halifax Trades and Friendly Club. On 14 February, Halifax women travelled to London to join the 700-strong crowd which marched on the House of Commons, and Mary Alice Taylor, wife of Councillor Arthur Taylor, a Skircoat Green blacksmith, was arrested following clashes with the police. The 63-year-old grandmother was charged with disorderly behaviour and detained at Holloway Prison until 27 February. On her return to Halifax Station she was greeted as a heroine by hundreds of supporters. Other Halifax women also suffered imprisonment, including Mrs Dinah Connelly, mother of Mrs Laura Mitchell, a later Mayor of Halifax, who spent her twenty-eighth birthday in Holloway, and Mrs Laura Willson of Ovenden, the secretary of the Halifax WSPU branch and wife of the Halifax engineer, George Willson, who spent two weeks at Armley Prison in February 1907. The *Halifax Courier* sympathised with the cause but condemned the aggressive tactics adopted by some of the women, arguing that since women in Australia and New Zealand already had the vote 'there is nothing to cause alarm in the prospect of the franchise being extended to women' in Britain.[34]

For most of the period from 1851 to 1914, politics in Halifax therefore remained largely hierarchical, reflecting the local social structure, and was dominated by the business elite because of the restricted franchise following the defeat of Chartism. A mid-Victorian Liberal consensus emerged, absorbing radicalism and binding together middle-class entrepreneurs like Crossley and Stansfeld, many of whom were Nonconformists, and working-class ex-Chartists like Snowden. They shared broadly similar radical-liberal individualist values, and in spite of some friction maintained a coalition which excluded the Tories from success in parliamentary elections until the late nineteenth century, when greater class conflict developed. This was consequent upon a widening franchise, increasing urban segregation and economic stresses which stimulated the development of trade unionism and the rise of Labour. From 1897, Labour began to make gains first in municipal elections and then, from 1906, in parliamentary elections, thereby presenting a challenge to the Liberal hegemony and creating opportunities for a revival of Conservative fortunes as the defenders of property.

The provision of local services

Economic change and the emergence of social and political elites stimulated the provision of a growing range of local services by the Halifax Municipal and County Borough Councils, the Halifax Board of Guardians and the Halifax School Board during its 33-year existence from 1870 to 1903. Moreover, this plurality of provision was supplemented by a remarkable variety of philanthropic activity which provided almshouses, business loans, model housing, a new infirmary, an orphanage, parks and promenades for the expanding town. But the nature and scale of some of the problems created by the rapid industrial and urban expansion of Halifax during the nineteenth century and the constraints of the town's geographical location meant that Halifax lagged behind many other towns in the provision of some services, for example, public transport networks and systems for the water carriage of sewage.

Edmund Minson Wavell, town clerk of Halifax from 1849 to 1864, later recalled that the new municipal corporation, which included seventeen radicals, four Chartists, six Whigs and three Tories, had been 'cradled in strife'. It had failed to set a borough rate in its first year of office on account of a legal technicality and consequently was distracted by acrimonious litigation until June 1851. The by-elections which took place following the election of aldermen had strengthened the representation of the Whigs, the Nonconformists and the manufacturing and commercial interests. The final composition of the council thus included nine retailers, seven merchants, seven manufacturers, six gentlemen, three corn and fodder dealers, two farmers, two agents, two dyers, an inn keeper, a plumber and a joiner. Having resolved its initial difficulties, the council proclaimed its intention 'to confer upon Halifax all the advantages possessed by any other municipal borough, and to keep the local rates low, so as to afford inducement for manufacturing and commercial enterprise and to offer residential advantages'.[35]

The publication of William Ranger's highly critical reports on the sanitary condition of the new borough in 1850 and 1851 ensured that municipal endeavour after 1851 would be focused primarily upon environmental improvement, and, in particular, the urgent need to provide a better water supply for both industrial and domestic consumers. The town clerk told the Ranger enquiry that 'the entire district' lacked an adequate water supply. Ranger commented particularly on the acute lack of provision for the labouring classes who were 'subjected to privations, not only of water for the purpose of ablution and house cleaning, but of wholesome water for drinking and culinary purposes'. The council was advised by a leading civil engineer who had been responsible for the construction of the Manchester and Glasgow waterworks to establish an extensive gathering-shed for water, and a series of new reservoirs were constructed, including the new Victoria, Albert and Ogden reservoirs between 1851 and 1864; Fly Flatts, Dean Head, Castle Carr, Mixenden and Widdop between 1864 and 1878; Roils Head in 1884; Ogden Kirk in 1894–95 and Walshaw Dean in 1915. By 1892, the corporation was able to supply water for the county borough 'unsurpassed in purity' at the rate of 5.5 million gallons per day, realising a clear annual profit of over £9,500.[36]

The provision of a comprehensive sewerage system took longer to develop in Halifax, however, than in most other towns. In 1853 William Ranger planned a network of drains and sewers for the borough divided into five districts with the main outlet emptying into the Hebble Brook below Water Lane bridge. Yet despite expenditure of some £145,924, nearly half a century elapsed before a sewage treatment works was opened at the confluence of the Hebble and Calder at Salterhebble, and most houses within the county borough remained without water closets until the inter-war years. Indeed, a survey by the Local Government Board revealed that Halifax was one of only 15 out of 95 English towns with populations exceeding 50,000 where the conservancy system, rather than the water carriage of sewage, prevailed in 1911. Indeed, only Rochdale, Gateshead, South Shields and Warrington had a higher proportion of houses without water closets in 1911 than Halifax, where barely a quarter of houses had them.[37]

The 1853 Halifax Improvement Act empowered the council to construct the new Victoria cattle market in order to remove cattle sales from the streets and to undertake much needed drainage and street-widening schemes, some of which were undertaken in conjunction with manufacturers such as the Crossleys anxious to improve access to their factories. The Act also transferred to council management the new markets, which had been operated by a private company since 1811. Subsequently the Halifax Corporation also became responsible for supplying the town with gas from 1855; maintaining parks from 1857; providing public baths from 1859; cemeteries from 1861; isolation hospitals from 1872; libraries from 1881; electricity from 1894; an electric tramway service from 1898; and a limited bus service from 1912. The corporation gained valuable revenue from the ownership of many of these public utilities during this period. For example, revenue from the markets between 1853 and 1863 amounted to £5,571. In 1914 profits from gas yielded £83,200; electricity, £10,637; and tramways and omnibuses, £13,643.

The council's main source of revenue however throughout the period was derived from the rates. Indeed, the rateable value of the Halifax township alone quadrupled from £50,884 in 1848 to £201,133 in 1893, while the rateable value of the county borough increased from £358,189 in 1893 to £503,571 in 1914. The boundaries of the municipal borough were extended in 1865, and in 1889 Halifax was redesignated a county borough. Its boundaries were further extended in 1889, 1892, 1899, 1900 and 1902, absorbing less successful communities around its periphery, increasing the number of contributing ratepayers but also requiring an extension of service provision to a larger population over a wider geographical area. Hence, Halifax, like other expanding Pennine towns such as Bradford, appeared below the national average in 1914 in the provision of some services, for example the supply of consumers with gas slot meters and gas cookers.[38]

In 1863, after considerable political controversy and growing ratepayer concern about the cost of the project, Halifax acquired a magnificent new town hall to replace the converted warehouse building in Union Street which had previously been used for council meetings. Designed in a free North Italian cinquecento style by the architect of the Houses of Parliament, Sir Charles Barry, it was completed by his son Edward Middleton Barry, who added the mansard roof with its decorative ironwork cresting and soaring tower and spire. Alternative designs and sites had been been canvassed by rival manufacturers Edward Akroyd and John Crossley. Akroyd had commissioned Sir George Gilbert Scott to design a Gothic town hall at Wards End on the southern edge of the town, while Crossley had produced a classical design by the Bradford firm of Lockwood and Mawson

Figure 5.16   Halifax Town Hall, 1863. The magnificent new town hall was opened by the Prince of Wales during the mayoralty of John Crossley, on whose initiative the project was conceived. It was one of the last buildings designed by Sir Charles Barry, architect of the Houses of Parliament. After his death in 1860, his son Edward Middleton Barry saw the work through to completion, adding the mansard roof with its ironwork cresting. The exquisite stone carving and sculpture was the work of John Thomas, who had worked with Barry on the Houses of Parliament. Colonel Akroyd and his supporters had favoured an alternative site at Ward's End for a building designed by Sir George Gilbert Scott. (Photograph: J. A. Hargreaves Collection)

for a site which he was engaged in clearing and developing near the northern perimeter of the town. Following an acrimonious press campaign, in the event neither design was adopted, but Crossley who was currently both a town councillor and member of the building committee succeeded in securing his preferred site. In a memorandum, Barry argued that the town hall should be 'the exponent of the life and soul of the city and should therefore be as much as possible in the heart of it' but that it should be entirely devoted to the serious business of municipal politics and should not include 'lavish expenditure' on a concert hall.

The final cost of the building, however, which the borough surveyor had originally estimated at £17,000, ran to around £50,000. This sum included £2,592 for the prestigious opening ceremony by the Prince of Wales in August 1863, the first visit to Halifax by a member of the British Royal Family and the first official visit by the heir to the throne to a provincial urban centre following his marriage in March. A triumphal arch was erected in Princess Street, new civic robes ordered and the town hall illuminated with thousands of batswing gas burners. The only disappoint-ments were the sudden withdrawal from the visit at the last moment by the Princess of Wales, who appears to have been suffering from morning sickness, and the torrential downpour which dampened the spirits of the vast crowds, many of whom had travelled to Halifax on 164 special trains to witness the spectacle. The mayor, John Crossley, for whom the visit represented a huge personal triumph, emphasised in his speech at the opening ceremony that the cost and furnishing of the building 'will not entail any serious burden on the inhabitants of the borough, being met mainly by funds accruing by judicious management of the local revenues and resources'. This proved to be an over-optimistic appraisal of the situation. While £13,000 was raised from profits from gas and markets, the remaining debt of £37,000 was not paid off until 1933–4.[39]

A survey of educational provision in Halifax undertaken, for practical reasons, by the borough police force on behalf of the newly formed Halifax

Figure 5.17   The arrival of the Prince of Wales at Halifax Railway Station, 1863. The arrival of the royal train at Halifax Station was signalled by the firing of a royal salute from two 32-pounders of the Heckmondwike Volunteer Artillery Corps on Beacon Hill and the raising of the Royal Standard above the station. The Prince, the first member of the British royal family to visit the town, was met by the mayor, John Crossley, and the councillors in their new corporate robes. A guard of honour was mounted by 300 Halifax Volunteer Riflemen under Colonel Edward Akroyd. The royal party travelled to Manor Heath for lunch and then toured the factories of John Crossley and Sons, James Akroyd and Son and John Whiteley and Sons. Further visits were made to People's Park, All Souls Church and the Piece Hall on the following day before the climax of the visit, the official opening of the new town hall. Some 85,000 people travelled to Halifax by rail to witness the royal visit. (Photograph courtesy of *The Illustrated London News*)

School Board in 1871 revealed a deficiency of elementary school accommodation within the borough for 9,942 children. Moreover, only twenty schools were regarded as efficient, the majority of which were administered by the Church of England. This presented a formidable challenge to the eleven members of the first Halifax School Board, elected without a contest in 1871. The new board embraced a cross-section of representatives from both the Established Church and Nonconformity, including three industrialists, two tradesmen, two gentlemen, a solicitor, an architect, a banker's clerk and a Roman Catholic priest. From the outset it pursued a series of controversial and boldly innovative policies, erecting an ornately designed new board school, with a lofty portico and belfry, at Queen's Road, which exceeded official space and staffing ratio regulations; opening a Higher Board School in Prescott Street in 1882; inaugurating school medical inspections in 1898 before they became a statutory requirement; and installing

Figure 5.18   The reading of the loyal address at the opening of Halifax Town Hall, 4 August 1863. The town clerk of Halifax, E. M. Wavell, in the centre of the picture, prepares to read the loyal address to the Prince of Wales, watched by the Bishop of Ripon, the Mayor of Halifax and other invited guests. The address thanked the Prince for honouring the borough with his first 'special visit' to a 'provincial municipality' and declared that 'the consideration which the town of Halifax enjoys, alike from its antiquity, from the fact that it is the commercial centre of an important manufacturing district, and from other causes, will henceforth be greatly enhanced by the distinction which it receives this day, in the dedication to public service of the edifice in which we are now assembled'. In his reply, the Prince alluded to 'the general prosperity' of the industries of the town which he had witnessed during his visit 'aided by the most ingenious machinery'. (Photograph courtesy of The Illustrated London News)

Figure 5.19
Woodwork class,
Queen's Road
Board School,
1906. Queen's
Road Board School
was one of the first
purpose-built board
schools to be
established in
Halifax following
the 1870 Education
Act. When it
opened in July
1874, there were
1,074 children on
roll, including
half-timers. The
ornate architecture
of the building,
with its lofty
portico and belfry,
aroused criticism
from those who
had favoured a
more functional
and less expensive
style of
construction.
(Photograph:
J. A. Hargreaves
Collection)

a swimming bath at Warley Road School in 1897. When the Halifax Education Committee took over from the School Board under the terms of the Balfour Education Act of 1902 there were twenty-three schools administered by the board with over 12,875 scholars and nine voluntary schools. Four years earlier the Halifax Corporation had also assumed full responsibility for the technical school erected in Hopwood Lane in 1895 from the proceeds of a 'whisky money' windfall grant provided by the Inland

Figure 5.20   St Luke's Hospital, Salterhebble. The new purpose-built Poor Law hospital at Salterhebble was erected in 1901 at a cost of £98,000 by the Halifax Board of Guardians, who had previously cared for the sick in the union workhouse premises in Gibbet Street. Designed by W. Clement Williams, the hospital was opened by the chairman of the building committee, J. W. Tillotson, on 9 April 1901. Its 400 beds were acquired for military use in December 1915 and additional accommodation for 302 provided in marquees in the grounds. Altogether no fewer than 1,300 beds were provided for military use in central Halifax during the wartime emergency. (Photograph: J. A. Hargreaves Collection)

Revenue. From 1904 the Halifax Education Committee offered ten annual scholarships to boys whose parents earned under £200 per year to attend Heath Grammar School, one of several struggling local endowed schools, which had 125 pupils on roll in 1907, but was criticised for failing to make similar provision for girls. In 1914 the Misses Whitley, descendants of Nathan Whitley, a member of the first Halifax School Board, donated their refurbished West House mansion to the Corporation for use as Education Offices.[40]

The Halifax Board of Guardians, elected by ballot after 1894, remained responsible for the relief of poverty in the Halifax Poor Law Union throughout the period up to 1914, under the central direction of the Local Government Board from 1871, whose first president, the Liberal Member of Parliament for Halifax, James Stansfeld (1820–98), sought to curb the extent of outdoor relief. The Halifax Union Workhouse had 291 inmates in 1851, including 60 sick patients. In 1871 it provided for 510, of whom 298 were accommodated in adjacent new three-storey infirmary buildings.

Figure 5.21   Joseph, Sir Francis and John Crossley. The three youngest sons of John and Martha Crossley, photographed in the 1860s, continued the family carpet manufacturing business after their father's death in 1837, trading under the name of John Crossley and Sons. By the time of John's death in 1879 it had become the largest carpet manufacturing firm in the world. Joseph, who unlike his brothers played no prominent role in public life, is often characterised as the partner most closely involved in the day-to-day management of the firm, while Francis has been portrayed as the most enterprising and innovative, taking the initiative in the development of steam-powered tapestry carpet production, which provided the springboard for the firm's mid-century expansion. However, John's association with the firm, extending over half a century, was the longest and on his retirement he expressed particular satisfaction that for nearly forty years 'no dispute or misunderstanding has occurred but such as was there and then, by mutual compromise, adjusted'. All three brothers contributed munificently to a variety of philanthropic schemes within the town. (Photograph courtesy of the West Yorkshire Archive Service, Calderdale)

By 1901, because the Halifax Union Workhouse was constantly full, the Halifax Union was spending £11,820 on outdoor relief, more than any other union in the West Riding except Leeds. After Leeds and Bradford, Halifax also had the largest number of lunatics in asylums in West Yorkshire at a annual cost to the union of over £10,000. In 1901 a new hospital designed by W. Clement Williams, was erected by the Halifax Board of Guardians at Salterhebble at a cost of £98,000. The largest public building in the town, it relieved pressure on the workhouse premises in Gibbet Street, which, with 656 inmates in accommodation designed for 466 in 1900, were extended in 1905.[41]

Philanthropy, inspired by a combination of altruism, evangelicalism and industrial paternalism, also made a significant contribution to health, housing and social welfare provision in Halifax in the period up to 1914. During the 1850s and 1860s model industrial communities were developed by Edward Akroyd at Copley and Akroydon and by John Crossley at West Hill Park. They provided superior housing, gardens and allotments and a range of other self-help institutions such as savings banks, cultural, educational and religious institutions. Collectively they served as 'powerful agencies for ushering in a period of much closer social harmony between millowners and employers'. A succession of generous benefactions commencing with Francis Crossley's trail-blazing People's Park, designed by Sir Joseph Paxton and opened in 1857, provided the town with an abundance of public parks and promenades, including Savile (1866), Shroggs (1881), Akroyd (1887) and West View (1904–5) Parks and Albert Promenade (1861). Almshouses, an orphanage and temporary business loans for men and single women or widows of good character were also provided by the Crossley brothers during the period 1855–68, honouring their mother Martha's vow that 'if the Lord does bless us in this place, the poor shall taste of it'. Francis Crossley, writing to his brother Joseph in May 1857 about their plans to open an orphanage, concluded: 'every loom and every wheel will work all the more merrily and joyfully when their profits are consecrated to such worthy objects'.[42]

However, perhaps the most remarkable local example of community provision through philanthropy, self-help and mutual co-operation in the history of the locality was the voluntary hospital movement which financed the building of the Royal Halifax Infirmary in Free School Lane, opened by the Duke and Duchess of York in 1896. Some £60,000 was raised through numerous voluntary contributions from ordinary men, women and children as well as more substantial donations from wealthy local families such as the Appleyards, Baldwins, Crossleys, McCreas, Porters and Whitworths, whose names designated the wards which they helped to finance.[43]

By the early twentieth century a new middle-class philanthropy had emerged in the Guild of Help movement, which had originated in Bradford in 1904 in response to the rising unemployment of the Edwardian era. It offered a more community-based solution to the problem of poverty, emphasising the moral responsibility of the middle classes to help the poor and the moral discipline required by the recipient, in an attempt to ward off the threat of state socialism. A Halifax Citizens Guild was formed in 1905, which participated in arrangements to provide free school meals to children during the severe economic depressions which occurred in the winters of 1905 and 1908; supported attempts to find work for the unemployed through 'distress committees'; encouraged the local authority to appoint health visitors; and worked closely with the probation service. The Halifax guild expressed its concern at the hunger marches 'in this well-to-do borough' in 1909 and hoped that the new Labour Exchange opened in 1910 would resolve the problem. However, as Professor Keith Laybourn has demonstrated, it was the revival of trade and Liberal social legislation immediately before the First World War, rather than the well-intentioned actions of the Halifax guild, that reduced the problem of unemployment and offered longer term strategies for dealing with the problem of poverty.[44]

Culture: religion and recreation

Institutional Christianity, reflecting to some extent the local social hierarchy, shaped cultural forms as well as religious expression in Victorian and Edwardian Halifax, but during this period there was also a shift from organised religion to more commercialised recreation. Although the Census of Religious Worship revealed that over half of the population of the municipal borough apparently failed to attend worship on Census Sunday in 1851, many inhabitants of the town during the period up to the First World War lived their lives from the cradle to the grave in close association with church, chapel and Sunday school. In 1851, it has been calculated that

Figure 5.22 Royal Halifax Infirmary. In 1896 a new infirmary in Free School Lane was formally opened by the Duke and Duchess of York. During the opening ceremony the Duke announced that the infirmary was to be named the Royal Halifax Infirmary, by command of Queen Victoria. An 1895 directory described the building of the new infirmary as 'one of the most important and public spirited enterprises ever undertaken by the Halifax public'. Designed by Messrs Worthington and Son of Manchester, the hospital was built upon 'the very latest principle approved by the leading hygienic scientists of the day' with 'the wards built separate from the main administration building', each named after an individual or family benefactor – Crossley, Porter, McCrea, Baldwin, Appleyard and Rawson. (Photograph: J. A. Hargreaves Collection)

Halifax ranked fourth out of fifty-five urban centres in the strength of its Sunday school enrolment, but forty-third in church attendance. However, indices of church attendance derived from the 1851 Census of Religious Worship have to be treated with caution, since the published returns omit statistics for the Congregationalists, Particular Baptists, Roman Catholics, Quakers and Unitarians, all of whom had congregations in the municipal borough by 1851. Nevertheless, the revelations of the Census, the rapid increase in the urban population after 1851, a growing rivalry between religious denominations and a shared concern for social cohesion stimulated both the churches and chapels into renewed efforts to reach the unchurched masses, resulting in an upsurge of church building. Dr S. J. D. Green has calculated that probably two-thirds of all those churches, chapels and mission churches ever built in Halifax were constructed between the passing of the second Reform Bill in 1867 and the death of Queen Victoria in 1901. Whereas in 1851 there were some twenty-five churches and chapels serving the recently incorporated municipal borough, by 1900 there were probably around ninety-nine churches and chapels scattered about the new county borough.[45]

An attempt in 1875 to make Halifax the nucleus of a new diocese for the industrial West Riding, however, proved abortive and Halifax remained a remote outpost of the diocese of Ripon until the creation of the new diocese of Wakefield in 1888. Although Halifax became one of two new archdeaconries within the new diocese, the new diocesan structures lacked the resources to make a significant impact on parish life for most of the period up to 1914. Many of the urgent recommendations of the first bishop's diocesan commission of 1889, for example, had still not been implemented when the second bishop's diocesan commission reported in 1909, and it was not until 1914 that the large Rural Deanery of Halifax was sub-divided. It is not therefore surprising that the Revd Francis Pigou, one of the most dynamic vicars of Halifax during this period, should have acknowledged in 1898 that his parish remained a Nonconformist stronghold 'supported by the influence and purses of wealthy capitalists' and that 'the Church of England does not do much more than hold her own'.[46]

Although there was no late-Victorian census of attendance at religious worship in Halifax, an indication of the continuing vitality of the religious institutions within the parish can be gauged from the number of participants at the last Sunday School Jubilee Sing to be held in the Halifax Piece Hall in 1890. The *Halifax Courier* reported that there were no fewer than 30,985 participants from 93 Nonconformist Sunday schools within the ancient parish. Collectively the Methodists accounted for 9,882 scholars, comprising 5,923 Wesleyan, 3,678 United Methodist Free Church, 3,366 Methodist New Connexion, and 2,245 Primitive Methodist scholars. The Congregationalists and Baptists accounted for 6,472 and 2,593 scholars respectively and other Sunday schools 1,010, including 320 from Northgate End Unitarian Sunday school. No Anglicans were present, but diocesan records reveal that there were a further 17,498 scholars enrolled at Anglican Sunday schools within the Halifax Deanery in 1889. When both figures are aggregated it becomes apparent that there were at least 48,483 children within the boundaries of the ancient parish associated with Sunday schools in 1890. Given that the population of the County Borough of Halifax in 1891 was 89,832, this figure must have included an exceptionally high proportion of children from within the local community.

This evidence also confirms the impression that religious institutions within the parish, which collectively represented the largest form of voluntary association within the life of the local community during this period, displayed a continuing vitality in the late-Victorian period. Indeed, their

Figure 5.23 Park Congregational Church. Designed by Roger Ives in the early geometric Gothic style, it was erected in 1869 at a cost of £11,200, including the purchase of the site from Sir Francis Crossley, who laid the foundation stone. It was constructed from Northowram stone and lay close to the West Hill Park model housing estate built by John Crossley between 1863 and 1868. The principal entrance was in the south front, beneath a large five-light traceried window. The tower at the south-west corner was surmounted by a spirelet rising over 36 metres in height. The building provided accommodation for a congregation of 932. In 1875, new Sunday School buildings were erected behind the church, which, since the closure of the church in 1980, are new also used for worship. (Photograph: J. A. Hargreaves Collection)

success was remarkable when compared with the success of other voluntary associations. For example, membership of the Halifax Trade Societies fluctuated between 3,000 and 4,000 and that of the Halifax ILP between 500 and 600 during the 1890s, while membership of registered Liberal, Conservative and Working Men's Clubs in the borough of Halifax in 1903 amounted to 1,122, 1,067 and 1,072 respectively, whilst the maximum attendances of over 15,000 at the Halifax Rugby Club's newly opened Thrum Hall stadium barely exceeded half the number of participants in the Halifax Piece Hall Sings. However, by the outbreak of the First World War the number of confirmation candidates was declining at Halifax Parish Church, and the tractarian Vicar of Illingworth, the Revd G. R. Oakley, discerned an ebb in church attendance and religious observance in the period before the First World War which he attributed to 'the materialism of the prosperity of the pre-war years'. Moreover, by the end of the first decade of the twentieth century, virtually all the available indicators reveal that Nonconformity had already reached its peak and was experiencing a declining rate of growth before the outbreak of the First World War. Roman Catholic baptisms and Easter mass attendances at Halifax also show a pronounced downward trend after 1901. Baptist and Congregational membership in Halifax peaked in 1905 and 1907 respectively. Even the underlying trend in Wesleyan membership recruitment was downward after 1890, and United Methodist recruitment after 1907.

The reasons for this pattern of decline experienced by all the major religious denominations in Halifax before 1914 are complex, but declining membership appears to have followed declining population trends and evidence of contraction within some sections of the local economy. Other reasons included the growth of religious pluralism and the emergence of new denominations such as the Salvation Army in the late nineteenth century; declining levels of Sunday school recruitment; the suburbanisation of middle- and lower middle-class housing; the advance of the Labour movement and a growth in religious scepticism; the rise of state educational and welfare provision; the growth in company size and the decline of the family firm; improving living standards and the growth of organised leisure.[47]

Better communications, wider education, rising real incomes and shorter working hours for those in employment, following the institution of the Saturday half holiday in 1873 and half day closing for shops in 1912, brought increased opportunities for leisure in late Victorian and Edwardian Halifax. Where social life was not centred upon the church or chapel, it was likely, at least for working men, to revolve around the ubiquitous public houses or working men's clubs. There were some 543 outlets of the liquor trade in Halifax Poor Law Union in 1895 and 179 in Halifax itself. The last quarter of the nineteenth century was a period of considerable prosperity for the six main Halifax brewing companies. However, by 1900, with the growing

Figure 5.24 Theatre Royal. The Theatre Royal, opened on 7 August 1905 with a performance by the Halifax Amateur Operatic Society of Gilbert and Sullivan's 'The Mikado'. The new theatre occupied the site of an earlier theatre established in 1790 and demolished in March 1904 and land in Ward's End previously occupied by the old Shakespeare Tavern, a shop that adjoined and four cottages in Shakespeare Street. The Theatre Royal was one of two recently opened theatres in Ward's End. The Palace Theatre had opened on 30 July 1903. Moreover, there was also the Grand Theatre and Opera House, situated at North Bridge, which had opened in 1889. A contemporary directory boasted that 'there are few towns in which a clearer appreciation of real histrionic talent find expression than in the town of Halifax'. (Photograph courtesy of H. Armitage)

diversification of consumer spending into expanding alternative outlets, the demand for beer had begun to fall and the breweries found themselves in a situation where there was not enough trade to support the large number of houses, profit margins were reduced, and many of the smaller local breweries did not survive.[48]

Outside the public houses, music (especially choral singing and brass bands), amateur and professional theatre – organised sport and commercialised popular entertainment came to play an increasing part in many people's lives before 1914. By 1914, Halifax had a new concert hall, the Victoria Hall, opened shortly after the death of Queen Victoria in 1901. The town also boasted three theatres, the Grand Theatre at North Bridge, opened in 1889, the Palace Theatre, opened in 1903, and the Theatre Royal, rebuilt in 1904 – and a growing number of cinemas, following the opening in 1910 of the Electric Theatre in the former Riding School building in Wards End, the first theatre to be opened in Halifax solely for showing

Figure 5.25 Halifax Zoo and Amusement Park. Advertised as 'the most up to date amusement park in the country', Halifax Zoo opened at Chevinedge, Exley, for the Whit weekend in 1909, when it attracted no fewer than 41,000 visitors. The zoo was well-stocked. Its aviaries were filled with gaily plumaged birds from South America and Australia, an eagle and a vulture. There were two African lions, two bears, hyenas, jackals, wolves, zebras, an Arabian camel, and Indian elephant, a yak and a monkey house. There was also a refreshment conservatory, an ornamental bandstand and a lake under construction, soon to be graced by black and white swans, ducks from China and India and a fountain. (Photograph: J. A. Hargreaves Collection)

the new silent pictures. There were also pleasure gardens, a museum, a zoo, and spectacular surrounding countryside for the rambler, cyclist and motorist to explore. Local league matches in both cricket and football were legion, and large crowds of spectators regularly converged on Thrum Hall from 1886 and Sandhall Lane from 1911 and later Exley to watch rugby league and association football in Halifax. Older surviving pastimes such as knur and spell attracted considerable popular interest at Skircoat Moor and West Hill Park in the mid-Victorian period, and when golf courses were opened at Lightcliffe in 1895, Ogden in 1901 and West End in 1906, early golfers were referred to as 'knur and spell players in knickerbockers and spats'. Public baths were opened at Park Road in 1859 and Woodside in 1893, and the Halifax Swimming Club was founded 1864. The Halifax and Calder Vale Hunt probably initiated the Halifax and Calder Vale Steeplechase in 1877, which had acquired a race course and grandstand at West End by 1878. However, the racing seasons lasted only until 1884, and by the 1890s the former race course was being used for shooting matches before its development as a golf course in 1906. A profusion of cultural and debating societies mushroomed in the town in the late-Victorian era including the Halifax Geologists Field Club and Scientific Association (1874), the Halifax Art Society (1879), the Halifax Photographic Society (1885), and the Halifax Antiquarian Society (1900).[49]

Both religion and recreation, though clearly reflecting the local social hierarchy in some respects, also demonstrated a capacity to transcend social class in other respects and during this period there is evidence of an emerging, popular, cross-class culture. The period also saw the abandonment of some older forms of leisure activity and the rise of more ordered, rule-bound, often commercialised or municipalised leisure activities, and a shift from religion to more commercialised recreation.

'Restless Renaissance city'

Following the incorporation of Halifax as a municipal borough in 1848 and the publication of the highly critical Ranger Report on its sanitary condition in 1851, the physical appearance of the town was considerably enhanced by two major phases of redevelopment in the second half of the nineteenth century. The first phase in the 1850s and 1860s saw the development of Crossley and Princess Streets, the construction of Barry's magnificent town hall, opened by the Prince of Wales in 1863, and improvements to Crown Street and Old Market. They gave Halifax an enhanced civic identity and, in the view of Dr Clyde Binfield, the character of a Florentine 'restless Renaissance city'.[50] The second phase in the 1880s and 1890s included the major Commercial Street development and the reconstruction of the borough markets under the direction of Joseph and John Leeming, which were opened by the Duke and Duchess of York in 1898.

In addition, during the second half of the nineteenth century, there was a profusion of church, chapel, commercial, public and residential building in the town and its suburbs. The most striking examples ranged from Sir George Gilbert Scott's magnificent All Soul's Church, Haley Hill (1859), which the architect himself considered 'on the whole, my best church' and which the *Building News* averred was 'one of the most elegant specimens he has produced', to its adjacent model housing development, and to the proliferation of Dissenting Gothic chapels such as Square Congregational

Figure 5.26   Built between 1871 and 1875, Wainhouse Tower was originally designed as a chimney for the Washer Lane Dye Works, situated in the valley below on the estate of John Edward Wainhouse. Wainhouse's primary motive appears to have been to relieve the valley of the smoke pollution from his dyeworks. His architect, Isaac Booth, designed a conventional brick mill chimney with an outer octagonal stone casing containing a spiral staircase leading to four pedimented balcony features. Towards the end of 1873, following a bitter feud with his neighbour, Sir Henry Edwards of Pye Nest, Wainhouse disposed of the dye works, but was unable to sell the unfinished chimney. When the original architect who had also worked for Edwards felt obliged to relinquish his commission, his successor, R. S. Dugdale, brilliantly re-designed the top of the tower as an observatory. (Photograph: J. A. Hargreaves Collection)

Figure 5.27 North Bridge and Bowling Dyke. This sketch of Halifax from the Mount, Haley Hill, was drawn by the architect J. R. Smith in the 1860s and printed by Stott Brothers in 1893. It depicts the modified stone bridge of 1774, prior to its replacement by the modern cast-iron structure in 1868, and the concentration of industrial development in the Hebble Valley. There is an extensive view of Northgate as far as Northgate End Chapel and the tower of Halifax Parish Church and the spire of Square Congregational Church are visible in the distance. James Akroyd and Sons' warehouse is also conspicuous at Cross Hills. (Photograph: J. A. Hargreaves Collection)

(1857) and St John's Wesleyan (1880); the ornate Crossley and Porter Orphanage (1864), technical and board Schools; imposing almshouses, hospitals, banks, building societies, shops, markets and theatres; a plethora of mansions, villas, terraces and mills and warehouses and extravagantly designed buildings which defy easy categorisation such as Wainhouse's tower, an ambitious Victorian folly, erected in 1876. The town also acquired its only equestrian statue during this period, a bronze memorial erected to Prince Albert in Wards End in 1864, but later removed to Albert Park in 1902 to make way for the trams.[51]

On the other hand, the density of the built environment, the inadequate sanitation and the pervasive industrial pollution prompted the sanitary inspector and artist J. R. Smith to describe Halifax at the beginning of the period as 'a veritable muck-midden' and the novelist Charles Dickens to pronounce the town 'as horrible a place as I ever saw' in 1858.[52] The author J. S. Fletcher, writing in 1912, recalled the 'great canopy of dun-coloured smoke which seemed to hang night and day above the grey old town from Beacon Hill to the edge of Skircoat Moor' during his childhood, while the abiding impression created by the town on Holroyd Jackson in 1910 was of a bleak urban landscape where:

> lines and lines of streets and mills stretched and turned away in every direction ... before falling away ... like walls of rugged chasms into the greyness of the world.[53]

However, Montague Blatchford, while acknowledging that no one could have seriously described Halifax in 1901 as pretty, maintained that:

there are times – as on a sunny day, when the atmosphere has been washed by heavy rain, or on a clear dark night, when a thousand lamps are twinkling on the hillsides – when Halifax has a picturesque charm, compared with which, most of the manufacturing towns of Lancashire, and even Yorkshire, look dismal beyond description.[54]

Indeed, despite the dramatic expansion of the urban built environment during the late Victorian and Edwardian eras, there remained vast stretches of uninhabited or sparsely populated countryside within easy reach of the town centre. When Samson Clark, a London businessman visited the town in 1915 'with the aid of a swift car driven by one who was familiar with every inch of the town and country for miles around' it was the rural aspect of Halifax's setting which particularly impressed him:

As we sped through and around the town, up steep hills and down through the dales, along the crests of the high country and out across the moors, the impression obtained was that of a delightful variety within the reach of all. The unavoidable discomforts of factory life are here minimised by the close proximity of God's own country, where the sun and the breeze, the hills and moorland delight the eye and fill one with the joy of life.[55]

Figure 5.28   Halifax from Beacon Hill, 1909. This photograph of Halifax from the south taken on a relatively clear day reveals a profusion of mill chimneys. The viaduct carrying the Sowerby Bridge, Halifax and Bradford line of the Lancashire and Yorkshire Railway is clearly visible left of centre. The author J. S. Fletcher, writing in 1912, recalled the 'great canopy of dun-coloured smoke which seemed to hang night and day above the grey old town from Beacon Hill to the edge of Skircoat Moor' during his childhood. (Photograph courtesy of H. Armitage)

CHAPTER SIX

Halifax at War and Peace, 1914–45

The period 1914 to 1945 opened with one world war and closed with another. Both wars resulted in larger numbers of local casualties than had been sustained in any previous international conflict. They also witnessed greater involvement by civilians on the home front in supporting the war effort. Consequently both wars made a greater impact on the lives of local communities than previous wars. Between the wars it is also easy to identify signs of difficulties and decay in a period often characterised as one of economic depression, mass unemployment, dole queues and hunger marches. But there may be paradoxical components in times of war and recession: evidence of economic restructuring, of new roles for local government, of new political alignments, of new cultural practices, and even of tentative urban re-development also needs to be assessed.[1]

Wars

There are few memorials in Halifax and its surrounding communities to the local soldiers who died in international conflict before 1914. The Stoodley Pike obelisk commemorates the conclusion of the Napoleonic and Crimean Wars, but provides no record of local casualties, only ten of whom are commemorated elsewhere in Calderdale. Two casualties of the Second Afghan War (1878–81) lie in the Halifax General Cemetery and the Soldier's Memorial in West View Park commemorates 73 of the 91 local casualties of the South African War (1899–1902), most of whom died of disease. By contrast, no fewer than 243 war memorials in the modern metropolitan district of Calderdale testify to the appalling slaughter of the two global conflicts between 1914 and 1945. They record the names of some 5,174 dead from the First World War, of whom 2,226 were from Halifax, and 1,317 from the Second World War of whom 588 were from Halifax.

The vast majority of the casualties from the First World War, some 93 per cent of the Calderdale total, were from the army. Out of Halifax's 1,610 dead infantrymen, no fewer than 46 per cent belonged to the Duke of Wellington's Regiment, whose regimental headquarters and barracks were situated at Highroad Well, Halifax. Its 4th battalion territorial unit, a battalion of 'Pals' formed in 1908, endured the first major gas attack of the

Figure 6.1   Soldiers' Memorial, West View Park. In the reconstruction of the British army in 1881 the 33rd and 76th Regiments of Foot were joined to form the Duke of Wellington's Regiment with their headquarters at Halifax. There was no great enthusiasm in the town for the new regiment until the formation of the 1st Volunteer Battalion of the regiment in the town prior to the second South African War. During the war a strong detachment of the battalion formed part of the force under Lord Roberts which compensated for the disasters of the early part of the campaign. The memorial to 73 men who lost their lives in the war, many of them local volunteers, was unveiled by Major Sir Leslie Rundle, K.C.B. on 7 November 1904. (Photograph: J. A. Hargreaves Collection)

Figure 6.2   Halifax territorials, 5 August 1914. On the day following the British declaration of war on Germany on 4 August 1914, Halifax volunteers enlist for service in the armed forces. Watched by large crowds, some 500 territorials marched from the Drill Hall at Prescott Street to board a special train at Halifax Station bound for a secret destination. During the first week, nearly 2,000 men left the Halifax district for some form of war service. In November, a Red Cross corridor train arrived in Halifax with 100 wounded soldiers from Ypres 'all showing the unmistakeable signs of having been among the shrapnel'. They were taken for treatment to the Royal Halifax Infirmary and St Luke's Hospital, Salterhebble. (Photograph courtesy of S. Gee)

war in trench warfare in the Ypres Salient in December 1915. The battalion was subsequently decimated in the abortive attack on Thiepval on 3 September 1916 during the Somme offensive, when a mere 80 survived the attack upon the barbed-wire entanglements and machine-gun emplacements of the Schwaben Redoubt. Another battalion, experiencing its first action in the trenches around Beaumont Hamel early in 1917, later suffered numerous fatalities in the unsuccessful attack on Bullecourt. Huge losses were also sustained in the German Spring offensive of 1918. At sea, local servicemen were involved in most of the major naval actions of the war from Coronel in 1914 to Zeebrugge in 1918, and Calderdale seamen perished with virtually every ship that went down at Jutland. Apart from continuing deaths from war wounds many of the casualties of 1918–19 were victims of the Spanish flu pandemic, which swept across Europe at the end of the war.

Table 6.1. *Halifax casualties in the First World War*

1914:	66
1915:	237
1916:	437
1917:	665
1918:	654
1919:	167
Total:	2226

Source: T. R. Hornshaw, 'Calderdale and the wars of the twentieth century', *Transactions of the Halifax Antiquarian Society* 6 (1998), p. 124.

There were some 75 per cent fewer Halifax fatalities in the Second World War. As in the First World War, the majority of local casualties were men serving in the army (61 per cent), including Hanson Victor Turner, a 33-year-old Halifax Corporation bus conductor, the sole local recipient of a posthumous Victoria Cross, killed in action with the West Yorkshire Regiment in Burma on 6 June 1944. Others served with the 4th battalion of the Duke of Wellington's Regiment (redesignated the 58th Anti-Tank Regiment in 1938) in Norway, France and North Africa, landing at Salerno on D-Day and continuing in action until the end of the war in Europe or with the 68th Anti-Tank Regiment in the war in Singapore, many of whom suffered prolonged imprisonment by the Japanese. Losses were also sustained at sea in both the royal and merchant navies (13 per cent), and in the air (23 per cent), and women were amongst the Auxiliary Territorial Service and civilian casualties. Although Halifax escaped relatively unscathed from the German bombing offensive, eleven civilians were killed and ten injured when a 100kg bomb fell on Hanson Lane on 22 November 1940. The ten other local bombing incidents between June 1940 and December 1944 mostly involved the haphazard discarding of bombs and incendiaries after raids on Manchester and claimed no further casualties. Indeed, Halifax was considered sufficiently safe for King George VI and Queen Elizabeth to rest overnight in the royal train at Copley en route to inspect bomb damage in Liverpool in 1943 and for evacuees from Bradford, the Channel Islands, London and the South of England to be billeted in the town.[2]

Table 6.2. *Halifax casualties in the Second World War*

1939:	1
1940:	54
1941:	64
1942:	79
1943:	113
1944:	189
1945:	70
1946:	18
Total:	588

Source: T. R. Hornshaw, 'Calderdale and the wars of the twentieth century', *Transactions of the Halifax Antiquarian Society* 6 (1998), p. 130.

Figure 6.3   Halifax auction during the Second World War. Alderman George Barker, Mayor of Halifax 1939–40, presides at an auction of a variety of plants, china, freehold property and livestock in aid of the allied war effort. The slogan reminds his audience that others have already given their lives for their country. The two world wars of the twentieth century resulted in larger numbers of local casualties than had been sustained in any previous international conflict. They also witnessed greater involvement by civilians on the home front in supporting the war effort. Shortly after this photograph was taken, Alderman Barker collapsed and died at the Crossley and Porter School speech day in July 1940. (Photograph courtesy of S. Gee)

Population

The average age of death of the local casualties of both wars was almost identical at around twenty-six years of age. It is not surprising therefore that the carnage of international conflict accentuated the downward demographic trend in Halifax during the period 1914–45.[3] The population of the County Borough of Halifax declined by 2.4 per cent from 101,594 in 1911 to 99,183 in 1921 and by a further 1.1 per cent to 98,115 by 1931. At the first post-war census in 1921, it was evident that the population of the county borough was ageing, with more than one-third of the population aged 45 or over. This was in marked contrast to the mid-Victorian period, when only one fifth of the population came into this age group in the census of 1871. This changing age profile was a consequence of a decline in both birth and death rates and a net loss by migration from the region of a younger generation in search of more favourable economic opportunities elsewhere as the staple textile industries of the West Riding contracted, leaving Halifax and neighbouring Bradford among those towns with the highest proportion of native-born inhabitants in the 1920s and 1930s.[4] Moreover, a determination to improve family living standards in an uncertain economic climate, coupled with growing employment opportunities for married women and increasing educational opportunities for children, tended to foster smaller sized families with no more than three or four children, particularly amongst textile workers in the inter-war years. Alderman J. H. Waddington, an informed contemporary observer, commented in 1937 that whereas 'in former days', families had been generally large, 'in latter days they are generally small'. He had also been told that:

> young married people today say 'they are not having many children because they cannot afford them'. You never heard married people of 50 years ago talking that language.[5]

There were also continuing risks associated with childbirth. Maternal mortality figures remained high in Halifax until 1938, when the figures reached their lowest for twenty years.[6] The infant mortality rate in Halifax also remained higher than the national average throughout the period 1920–38, peaking at 98 deaths per 1,000 births in 1921, then declining to 62 by 1930, only to rise again to 86 in 1933 before declining sharply during rest of the decade to 57 in 1938.[7]

The economy: boom, bust and restructuring

The outbreak of the First World War resulted in an immediate shortage of raw materials, which brought the Halifax textile industry to an abrupt standstill. Moreover, since Germany had been one of the industry's most important overseas customers for tops and yarn, many exporters found themselves owed substantial debts by German customers. However, government orders for khaki and navy cloth for the armed forces soon created boom conditions for both larger firms like John Holdsworth's of Shaw Lodge Mills and smaller firms like J. E. Bentley and Co. of Dunkirk Mills. At Holdsworth's Shaw Lodge Mills, for example, from December 1914 until November 1915 overtime was being worked throughout the mill. Overtime hours were reduced in 1917–18 because of a government order restricting the consumption of wool, and in October 1917 the army ordnance depot requisitioned four floors of warehouse space for a boot repair depot. Nevertheless, during the period 1914–18 sales had soared from £189,000 to nearly £447,000 and profits from £3,900 to more than £40,000. As 'the largest firm of British moquette manufacturers', Holdsworths congratulated itself in a wartime advertising leaflet on having built up an industry at home 'which for many years was in the hands of the Germans'. Meanwhile, the largest British carpet manufacturing firm, Crossleys of Dean Clough, also utilised their spinning and weaving equipment for the production of millions of yards of webbing, blankets and khaki yarn for government

Figure 6.4   Women in the burling and mending department, Standeven and Co. Ltd, Ladyship Mills, 1926. The company which had originated in Mixenden in the 1880s, subsequently moved to Ladyship Mills, Old Lane, Ovenden. Some 700 employees were engaged in designing, making and marketing worsted cloth in October 1926, when the factory was visited by the Prince of Wales. During the Second World War Standevens produced some 2,500,000 yards of khaki for battledress. However, the firm experienced increasing difficulties in the 1960s and finally closed in 1969. (Photograph courtesy of the *Halifax Courier*)

contracts, while the firm's machine shops were turned over to shell production.[8]

But the stimulus of war was temporary. The inflationary wartime and post-war boom was followed by 'the great commercial depression' of 1920–21, when the Halifax Chamber of Commerce reported that 'the trade of the town and district came practically to a standstill and the textile and engineering trades practically received the death blow'. Adverse exchange rates, unsettled overseas markets, volatile wool prices and rocketing fuel prices brought trouble for many local businesses. Smaller firms such as J. E. Bentley and Co. struggled for survival, while larger firms such as Holdsworths' faced intermittent short-time working throughout 1920–21 and again in 1924, when a further local recession ensured a fall in Holdsworths' annual profits from an average of £43,000 between 1918–20 to an average of £26,500 during the period 1921–24.[9] A return to the gold standard in 1925 at the pre-war parity, cuts in government expenditure, and the tight monetary restriction of a high bank rate created an unfavourable climate for industry. Consequently when the Northern Joint Industrial Council, which had already imposed wage reductions of 5 per cent on woollen and worsted workers in 1921, attempted to secure further reductions in 1925 it provoked the largest strike and lockout in the industry's history. It was supported by nearly 12,000 workers in Halifax and paralysed all but nine local firms from the end of July to mid-August until a court of inquiry settled the dispute, ruling against the proposed reduction.[10] In 1925–26 local cotton firms also faced 'exceptional difficulties' following turmoil in overseas markets in China, Egypt and the Near East.[11]

Although the General Strike in May 1926, which followed a dispute in the coal industry, was blamed by Phyllis Bentley for the stroke which caused the death of her father who 'saw ruin for the mill ahead' and resulted in short-time working at Holdsworths' Shaw Lodge Mills for most of May 1926, it proved less devastating in its impact on Halifax than on other industrial towns. Indeed, the editor of the *Halifax Chamber of Commerce Journal* concluded that Halifax had secured its 'fair share of business' during the year of the strike, which was 'reflected in unemployment figures showing a bare 2,000 in May totally unemployed, the lowest for many years' in Halifax. In October, when the Prince of Wales visited the town, he was impressed by the multi-coloured designs at Standeven's Ladyship Mills, where he observed all the processes of manufacture from raw wool to finished cloth. At Crossley's Dean Clough Mills he toured a factory which had succeeded in installing electric power and lighting despite the difficulties of the early 1920s.[12]

But this easing of economic difficulties was temporary. The complete collapse of world markets between 1929 and 1932, following the Wall Street Crash, produced distressing conditions throughout West Yorkshire. In 1930 the Northern Joint Industrial Council failed to secure agreement with the unions for further wage reductions to prevent 'the bleeding to death of the industry', and in June 1930, following a ten-week strike, a court of inquiry found in favour of wage reductions and the workers were obliged to accept the employers' terms. The employers proceeded to impose reductions of about 9.5 per cent in 1930 and 11.7 per cent in 1931, although a few employers only imposed a proportion of the reduction. Indeed, a handful of local family firms, where union influence remained weak, including Holdsworths, were again unaffected by the strike, 'the operatives turning up in full strength'.[13] However, intermittent short-time working continued at Holdsworths until November 1931, while at Crossley Carpets some workers were laid off and others obliged to work a three-day week during the slump.[14] The suspension of the gold standard in 1931 and the implementation of a cheap money policy with lower interest rates stimulated investment in the 1930s, but orthodox budgetary policy remained a restraint and other government measures had only a marginal impact on stimulating economic growth until rearmament began in the late 1930s.[15]

Following a revival in the railway trade and a return of confidence in the depressed motor coach industry, production at Holdsworths' Shaw Lodge Mills alternated between full-time and overtime working between 1932 and 1936, apart from one month in the autumn of 1934. As the firm developed a wider range of products, Holdsworths' net profits, which had averaged only £4,000 between 1925 and 1931, rose to more than £36,000 between 1932 and 1936.[16] The introduction of the Duravell process at Crossley Carpets under licence from Leas Fabrics of America, formally inaugurated by the Princess Royal in March 1933, enabled the company to manufacture a blend of nylon and viscose rayon and resulted in a sharp increase of trade with the motor industry. Local woolcombers and top-makers also increased their share of world trade during these years by a vigorous exploitation of new markets for semi-manufactured goods in Canada, Finland and China, and the artificial silk trade, which had been established in Halifax by 1928, also continued to thrive despite the recession.[17] By 1937, encouraged by tariffs on cheap foreign imports, there was also a growth in the domestic market. However, towards the end of 1937 the high levels of production in the Halifax textile trade began to slow down, when wool prices suffered from the deteriorating international political climate, bringing intermittent short-time working back to Shaw Lodge between September 1937 and 1939. Indeed the shortage of work was so acute that the mills worked as little as twenty-five hours a week in July 1938 and profits fell from £33,000 in 1936 to £2,000 in 1938.[18]

After the outbreak of the Second World War, Crossleys continued to make carpets for the American market, but became increasingly involved in the production of webbing for military accoutrements such as respirator cases. Meanwhile the firm's machine shops were extended to produce ground equipment for the RAF and torpedo motors for the Royal

Navy.[19] After some short-time working during the first year of the Second World War, Holdsworths' looms kept busy weaving cotton canvas for khaki webbing, camouflaging and blackouts and fabric for hammocks. The company also produced electrically heated linings for flying suits to keep flyers warm at high altitudes. Between 1940 and 1945 average annual sales rose from £268,000 to £378,000, but tightly controlled prices restricted average annual profits to around £30,000. The Ministry of Supply was the firm's most important single customer during the war, followed by the railway companies, furnishing and motoring firms. But by 1944 the firm was becoming increasingly concerned about the restrictive wartime regulations, the loss of normal markets and the future of the industry.[20]

The local economy experienced more than boom and slumps during this period: there was also a chequered history of restructuring, involving losers and winners. In manufacturing, events in the inter-war years ensured that there would be no long-term recovery of the textile industry in West Yorkshire. Overseas markets in the USA and the Far East were contracting, and local firms were operating within a shrinking world market.[21] Unemployment levels in the Yorkshire textile industry peaked at 25 per cent in 1931 and averaged 17 per cent between 1929 and 1936.[22] The inter-war censuses revealed a decline of 18 per cent in the number of textile workers employed in the county borough of Halifax from 15,612 in 1921 to 12,812 in 1931, though there was an increase of 3% in those employed in clothing manufacture. The number of insured textile workers in Halifax also declined during the period 1935 to 1939, when Halifax had fewer textile workers than most of the historic centres of the textile industry in West Yorkshire with just over one-third of the number of textile workers as neighbouring Bradford and under two-thirds the number of Huddersfield.[23]

On the other hand, as early as 1918 the Halifax Chamber of Commerce, while recognising that textiles were still of 'first importance' to the local economy, also emphasised the growing importance of engineering, machine tool construction, boiler making, card-clothing manufacture and building supplies. Such industrial diversity ensured that Halifax never felt 'the pinch of industrial crises' as severely as single industry towns and protected the town from the worst effects of the economic recessions of the inter-war years.[24] A contributor to a publicity brochure published by the Halifax Chamber of Trade in October 1931 commented that while Halifax 'scarcely ever experienced a boom', it never suffered 'from those terrible slumps which affect such towns as are dependent on a single industry'. In 1936 Percy Saunders, the town clerk of Halifax, observed that 'distress has for a considerable time' been less prevalent in Halifax 'than in any other industrial town in the country'. Halifax's buoyant machine tool trade, for example, kept unemployment down to 6 per cent in 1937.[25]

Many local engineering firms had become engaged in intensive munitions manufacture during the First World War, often doubling shifts and

Figure 6.5   First World War munitions workers photographed in West View Park, Halifax. Most local engineering firms became engaged in intensive munitions manufacture during the war, often doubling shifts and employing auxiliary workers, many of them women. Asquith specialised in the manufacture of shells; Butlers produced gun boring lathes and shell cases; Stirks contributed numerous gun and shell lathes; Sagars designed a propeller-shaping machine and Gledhills developed a bomb release mechanism. (Photograph courtesy of S. Gee)

employing auxiliary workers. Asquiths specialised in the manufacture of 9.2mm shells; Butlers produced gun boring lathes and shell cases; Stirks contributed 'thousands of gun and shell lathes'; Sagars designed a propeller-shaping machine to cut the blades for the Flying Corps aircraft; and Gledhills developed a bomb release mechanism. The war stimulated improvements in research and industrial organisation in the machine tool industry. Indeed, Butlers were the prime movers in the formation of the Association of British Machine Tool Manufacturers in 1917, a marketing organisation which promoted specialisation within the industry, with Butlers, for example, concentrating thereafter almost exclusively on the production of planing, shaping and slotting machines.[26]

The local engineering industry, however, also suffered severe disruption during the recessions of 1920–21 and 1924 and was 'the last to show any material recovery from the slump'.[27] Some local firms such as the United Brass Founders and Engineers Ltd, founded in 1910, which had invested heavily in new premises and plant in Spring Hall Lane 1916, were unable to sustain wartime levels of production during the post-war recession and the company was forced into voluntary liquidation in March 1920. Developments at Butlers' Mile Thorn site were also severely restricted by the slump when orders dwindled. Machines were built mainly for stock, and diversifications included toffee-making machines and presses for stuffing church hassocks.[28] As the heavy industries recovered from the coal dispute, however, the 'Halifax machine tool trade began to benefit'. But the total number of workers employed in metal manufacture in the county borough declined by 27 per cent between 1921 and 1931 and several local engineering firms, for example Oldfield and Schofield, were only rescued from impending bankruptcy by rearmament orders filtering through from the mid-1930s.[29]

Some firms secured major orders even during the most depressed years of the 1920s and 1930s. Asquiths obtained a contract from Dorman Long of Middlesbrough in 1924 for 40 drilling machines for the construction of the Sydney Harbour Bridge; Kitchen and Wade secured a very substantial order for drilling and boring machines from New Zealand Railways in 1926; J. and J. Mallinson supplied large numbers of lathes to assist the development of the nascent Indian cotton industry; while Butlers clinched a contract for some 200 planers, shapers and slotters from Stalinist Russia between 1931 and 1934. Cornelius Redman and Sons Ltd, following a management reorganisation and the redesign of their lathes and planers, also prospered despite the generally depressed state of trade, increasing their workforce from around 30 in 1927 to 115 by 1930. As Churchill Redman from 1935, the firm developed a new range of precision lathes and shapers, and in 1937 secured an agreement with Jones and Lamson of Springfield, USA, to build Fay automatic lathes under licence. This enabled the firm to extend their factory and increase their workforce to 200 by 1939.[30]

The Second World War provided another boost to the engineering sector. The machine tool factories worked round-the-clock on their standard lines, with some variations. Churchill Redman adapted their general purpose lathes for the manufacture of bomb cases; Greenwood Standard Gear Cutting Co. Ltd produced turret rings for tanks; Gledhills produced field service levels, scientific sun compasses, booby traps, aircraft components, tanks and torpedoes; while the newly established Ajax Machine Tool Co., taking the name of the cruiser adopted by Halifax during the war, manufactured many small drilling machines for government orders.[31] As a result of aerial bombardment in the Midlands and South East, some firms were relocated in Halifax. Coventry Machine Tools moved into Stirks' premises at Ovenden, and Alfred Grahams, an offshoot of Siemens manufacturing marine electrical and communication equipment, came to Box Trees, Wheatley, after suffering bomb damage at Woolwich.[32]

On the other hand, both world wars adversely affected the process of restructuring. Sugar, butter and milk rationing in the First World War and the added burden of sweet rationing in the Second World War created problems for Halifax's developing confectionery industry. Supplies of confectionery for domestic consumption were severely restricted and the export business entirely lost. However, during the First World War the food value

Figure 6.6   Newspaper advertisement for Mackintosh's toffee, 1914. Enormous quantities of Mackintosh's toffee were despatched to the armed forces during the First World War and wartime newspaper advertisements, many of them based on suggestions from serving soldiers, depicted how Mackintosh's toffee helped along 'the weary hours' in the muddy trenches. For example, in the autumn of 1914 when the Allied troops were resisting the German invasion of Belgium and France, a full-page newspaper advertisement depicted the Kaiser standing astride Belgium and France glaring at a monster tin of Mackintosh's toffee resting on a map of the British Isles under the caption: 'Ah! that's what makes them fight so well'. (Photograph: J. A. Hargreaves Collection)

of Mackintosh's toffee for those serving in the armed forces was recognised by the military authorities. Indeed, government orders accounted for a high proportion of the firm's wartime output. Moreover, one Halifax soldier serving on the western front later recalled that when he first went over the top: 'All he could remember was that he was eating "Mackintosh's toffee"'. Wartime advertisements for the firm, many of them based on suggestions received from serving soldiers, depicted how Mackintosh's toffee helped along 'the weary hours' in the muddy trenches. Nevertheless, during the First World War, there were difficulties since many male employees of the firm left for military service, while hundreds of the girls who had been accustomed only to wrapping toffee learned to handle deadly explosives or heavy shells in munitions factories. Indeed, John Mackintosh wrote: 'It becomes more and more difficult to steer our "toffee de luxe" ship through the troubled seas. We had over 1,000 workpeople before the War, and now we have not quite 250'.[33]

After a period of lean years in the mid-1920s, the firm began to expand. It established production plants overseas and acquired A. J. Caley's chocolate manufacturing business in Norwich, which enabled the development of the celebrated 'Quality Street' chocolate and toffee assortment, one of its most popular products. During the Second World War, the firm's workforce was again depleted by conscription, and Harold Mackintosh, the son of the founder and managing director of the firm, became increasingly involved in the war savings movement. Production was also severely restricted through the rationing not only of the raw materials used in manufacture but also of the confectionery itself, and domestic consumption was halved. However, the destruction of the firm's new £700,000 manufacturing plant in Norwich by the Luftwaffe on 29 April 1942 resulted in the transfer of production and key personnel to Halifax, where the factories remained intact with plenty of spare capacity.[34]

The building industry too, in spite of ups and downs, managed to grow in this period. Although building work was curtailed during both world wars, the inter-war years witnessed a major expansion in the construction industry, which helped to mitigate the effects of the recession and may well have played a crucial role in the 1930s recovery. Indeed the numbers employed in the local building industry rose by 25 per cent between 1921 and 1931, more rapidly than in any other local industry.[35] The expansion also stimulated the growth of the building supply industry. By 1930 Joseph Brooke and Sons of Lightcliffe had become the largest suppliers of roadway and building materials in the world, while other local firms patented Fulcherite reinforced concrete and Marshalite prefabricated stone.[36]

Meanwhile, the growth of the motor trade in the 1930s brought prosperity to another local firm which had pioneered the remarkable catseye reflecting roadstud. Founded in 1935 by Percy Shaw, whose invention was hailed in the House of Commons as 'the most brilliant invention ever produced in the interests of road safety', Reflecting Roadstuds Ltd at Boothtown achieved peak sales during the early wartime blackout, though the Japanese invasion of Malaya later restricted the availability of rubber and despite experiments with synthetic rubber the firm's output dropped dramatically.[37]

The most significant area of expansion for the future of Halifax, however, was the growth in financial services during the inter-war years. It is true that both the Halifax Permanent and the Halifax Equitable Building Societies disposed of the banks which they had sponsored since 1900 and 1910 in 1917 and 1927 respectively, and the demise of Halifax's own independent banking system occurred in 1919 when the town's oldest banks, the West Yorkshire Bank and the Halifax Commercial Bank were swallowed up in mergers (the former with Lloyds and the latter with the Bank of Liverpool and Martins). Nevertheless, the inter-war years also saw a remarkable expansion of the building society movement.[38] This growth owed much to the building boom of the inter-war years and to the vision and commitment of Enoch Hill, managing director of the Halifax Permanent 1917–38 and chairman of the National Association of Building Societies 1921–33, and of Joseph Harger Mitchell, managing director of the Halifax Equitable 1920 to 1927.[39]

Although by 1918 the Halifax Permanent was the largest building society in the country, its branches were mainly based in Yorkshire and Lancashire, with a few agencies in Durham, Lincolnshire, Nottinghamshire and North Wales. Between 1918 and 1928, around 100 new branches and agencies were opened, including the first office in southern England in Shaftesbury, Dorset

Figure 6.7   Sir Enoch Hill (1865–1942). Born in Leek, Staffordshire, the eldest of seven children, he was selected from 300 applicants to succeed J. D. Taylor as secretary of the Halifax Permanent Building Society in 1903. He became Managing Director in 1917 and President from 1928 to 1938 and directed the remarkable expansion of the Halifax Building Society which resulted in it becoming the largest society in the world. He also served as chairman of the National Association of Building Societies from 1921 to 1933 and became a freeman of the City of London in 1924 and was knighted in 1928. He served as chairman of the Halifax Conservative Association and between 1922 and 1929 unsuccessfully contested four parliamentary elections at Leek and Huddersfield. (Photograph courtesy of H. Armitage)

in 1919. It was followed in the early 1920s by agencies in Bournemouth, Plymouth and Worthing. In 1924, the first London office was opened at 124 Charing Cross Road by the Rt Hon. J. H. Whitley, M. P. for Halifax and Speaker of the House of Commons. A patron of the Halifax Permanent, Whitley represented a family of Halifax industrialists, Liberal in politics and Nonconformist in religion, who had been closely associated with the development of the building society movement in Halifax almost from its inception. His father, Nathan Whitley, and uncle, John Whitley, business partners in a firm of card-clothing manufacturers, were trustees of the Halifax Equitable, and his brother, Brigadier-General Sir Edward Nathan Whitley, became a director of the Halifax Permanent in 1919 and later served as President of the amalgamated Halifax Equitable and Halifax Permanent Building Societies from 1938 to 1945. In his address, Whitley reflected that twenty-four years ago Halifax had 'got rid of him to London', but that now 'Halifax came to London itself . . . offering to the less fortunate Londoners great benefits built on Yorkshire thrift'.[40]

The younger Halifax Equitable expanded rapidly in the decade after the First World War advancing from the eleventh largest society in 1911 to second in 1924. In 1928 its assets of £14,044,972 were just under half the £32,936,510 assets of the Halifax Permanent. Both societies had common roots in the culture of nonconformity and thrift of the Pennine town and were led by a cross-section of representatives of the local banking, industrial and municipal communities. In a number of cases different members of the same families, most notably the Crossleys and the Whitleys, served both societies as directors or trustees, and so the announcement of the merger of the two societies on 22 September 1927, although it took the building society movement by surprise, quickly found strong backing from the membership of both societies. Following the merger the Halifax directors proclaimed: 'the society is no longer a parochial institution; it is becoming nation-wide in its scope.' By 1934 the assets of the society had doubled to £92,600,000. Between 1935 and 1939 the rate of increase slowed down, but by 1939 the society's assets had almost trebled since the merger to £128,200,000, and during that period nearly 100 new branches and agencies had been opened.[41]

During the First World War, both Halifax societies made a major contribution to the war effort, facilitating withdrawals by subscribers for investment in war loans, the Halifax Equitable declaring that its main object was 'to turn as much money as possible into government channels'. Moreover, by the end of the war the Halifax Permanent had £1,300,000 and the Halifax Equitable £642,000 invested in government securities. In the Second World War, the society not only encouraged the public to maximise its savings but by 1945 had also invested £30,000,000 of its liquid assets in British government loans. Moreover, the appointment of a Halifax Building Society director, the toffee manufacturer Harold Vincent Mackintosh, as chairman of the National Savings Committee during the Second World War, conferred further national recognition upon the society. Mackintosh readily acknowledged that his early association with the building society movement in Halifax had provided the essential training for his later leadership of the national savings movement, which underpinned Britain's contribution to the Allied victory over Nazi Germany in the Second World War. Some 39,000 properties mortgaged to the Halifax suffered damage involving claims during the war, and Halifax House itself sustained heavy damage during the London Blitz in April 1941, when one employee of the society was killed and another injured.[42]

Halifax also remained an important retail centre during the inter-war years. Walter Brenard, the Mayor of Halifax, opening the fourth Halifax Chamber of Trade Shopping Festival and Exhibition in October 1936, declared that Halifax had 'steadily progressed' into a major West Riding shopping centre.[43] There had, however, been a number of recent changes in retail provision in the town. Alderman Harold Waddington, reviewing retail developments in the fifty years since he had started his apprenticeship in a large town centre store in 1886, observed that the major innovation was 'the change from the one man shopkeeper to the multiple stores'. In his youth there were:

no cash furnishing companies, no hire purchasing shops, no Boots Cash

Chemists, no Fifty Shilling Tailors, no Maypole Dairy Companies, no Woolworth's Stores, no Marks and Spencer's branches.[44]

Many smaller family businesses, such as Mitchell's ladies' and gents' outfitters, where Wilfred Pickles worked as a young shop assistant, benefited from the growing range of retail outlets. Pickles recalled that on Saturdays, in particular, 'the town had all the atmosphere of a big city, with its packed shops, people coming from smaller towns and nearby villages to shop, to watch a football match and go to the pictures at night'.[45]

The economy of Halifax during the inter-war years exhibited elements of both continuity and change. Notwithstanding the difficulties experienced by the textile and engineering industries during the inter-war years, these staple industries remained the two largest employers of labour in the county borough of Halifax in the censuses of 1921 and 1931. Although the numbers employed in both industries declined between 1921 and 1931 by 18 per cent and 27 per cent respectively, textiles still employed 12,812 workers in 1931 and engineering 5,747 workers. Moreover, despite the growing pre-eminence of Mackintosh's in the confectionery industry during the period, the numbers employed in the food and drink industry in Halifax also declined by 6 per cent from 953 to 896, along with the numbers employed in mining and quarrying, woodworking and furniture manufacture and public administration. By contrast, however, the numbers employed in building and construction increased by 25 per cent from 1,221 to 1,530; personal services by 23 per cent from 3,424 to 4,199; commercial and financial services by 22 per cent from 4,203 to 5,127; the professions by 9 per cent from 1,322 to 1,441 and transport by 4 per cent from 2,857 to 2,953, indicating an expanding service sector.[46]

The census figures also reveal that textiles remained the largest employer of female labour during the inter-war years, though the actual number of women employed declined from 9,863 in 1921 to 3,677 in 1931. By contrast, there was a rise in the number of women employed in the commercial, financial, professional and service sectors, some in occupations which had been strongly male preserves before the First World War. The 1918 annual report of the Halifax Permanent Building Society, commenting upon the changes necessitated by the war, assured shareholders that every effort 'will be made to carry on the work of the society efficiently with the help of the patriotic and capable female workers who have joined the staff'. By 1921, no fewer than a third of the Head Office staff of the Halifax Equitable Building Society were women, four of whom had worked for the society since 1915.[47] In 1915, the first woman gas inspector was appointed in Halifax and in the same year the first local female telegraph messengers and tram conductors were employed. This trend was to accelerate in the period after 1945. [48]

Local government

During the first half of the twentieth century, which has been described by Dr John Stevenson as 'the heyday of local government', the functions of municipal government became more extensive in Halifax than at any time previously in the history of the town, although they became increasingly subject to central government direction. In 1903, following the Education Act of 1902, the local authority had taken over responsibility for state education from the school board. In 1930 it became responsible for the relief of poverty following the abolition of the Poor Law Unions. Moreover, despite the recommendation of the Desborough Committee that police forces in boroughs with populations of under 100,000 should be merged with their county forces, Halifax County Borough Council continued to be responsible for policing until 1968, and the enforcement of public order within the county borough was facilitated from 1924 by the inauguration of the Halifax Quarter Sessions, which were replaced by the Crown Courts in 1972. Besides responsibility for education, social welfare and public order, the county borough council also remained responsible during this period for public health; the fire service; highways and transport; housing and planning; markets, baths, parks, libraries and art galleries; and the supply of electricity, gas and water.[49]

However, the rising cost of services brought increasing tensions during the inter-war years between the county boroughs of the West Riding and the West Riding County Council. Halifax and the other four original West Riding county boroughs had extended their boundaries between 1889 and 1912, divesting the West Riding County Council of some 33,000 acres of suburban land with a rateable value of £550,000. Moreover, between 1913 and 1915 the county's ratepaying land had been further reduced by the creation of three new county boroughs. So, when in 1919 and 1920 Halifax and six other county boroughs applied for boundary extensions which would have deprived the county of a further £2.23m in rates amounting to nearly one-quarter of the county's assessable rateable value, there was strong resistance from the county authority. In consequence, following an official enquiry, the Halifax proposal for an extension to its county borough boundaries by 11,264 acres, which would have augmented its population by 52,535 and its assessable rateable value by £242,811, was dropped. A further proposal in the Halifax Extension Bill of 1934 would have extended the boundaries of the county borough to include the urban districts of Sowerby, Luddenden Foot, Midgley and Hipperholme and the parishes of Norwood Green, Coley, Wadsworth and Heptonstall and parts of other adjoining urban districts, an extension of 24,826 acres with a population of 32,232 and rateable value of £148,226. However, this was rejected by a House of Commons Select Committee on 17 July 1935 after fierce opposition from the county.[50]

MAIN BLOCK EAST, THE INSTITUTE, GIBBET ST, HALIFAX.

Figure 6.8 The Institution, Gibbet Street, Halifax, formerly the Halifax Union Workhouse. The Board of Guardians of the Halifax Poor Law Union, which consisted of 22 townships, first met in 1837 and the workhouse, one of the first to be opened in the mid-Pennines under the New Poor Law of 1834, received its first inmates in March 1840. The workhouse was extended in 1856, 1864 and in 1870–71, when new infirmaries, fever wards, lunacy and reception wards, a dining hall and chapel were added at a total cost of over £30,000, providing accommodation for between 400 and 500 inmates, including children. In 1929, Poor Law Unions were abolished and the responsibilities of the Board of Guardians transferred to local authority public assistance committees. The workhouse subsequently became St John's Hospital and was demolished in 1972. (Photograph: J. A. Hargreaves Collection)

Denied the increase in rate revenue which would have accrued from an extension of its boundaries, the Halifax County Borough Council sought to exploit to the full its revenue from the management of municipally owned services such as gas, water, electricity and public transport. By 1939 the Halifax Corporation gas manufacturing plant was producing 900 million cubic feet of gas per annum for domestic and industrial consumption and 100 gallons of benzine. A policy of prudent investment and plant modernisation had reduced the debt on capital expenditure from £700,000 to £333,000 by 1935, and profits had also contributed some £409,000 to the relief of the rates. Halifax Corporation also supplied water to a population of 220,000, more than double that of the resident population of the county borough, in neighbouring authorities as far afield as Batley, Dewsbury and Morley in the east and Todmorden in the west via a mains network of more than 200 miles. Electricity was also supplied in bulk to the neighbouring Hebden Royd Urban District Council. In 1935 additional plant was brought into commission, so that by 1939 the municipal electricity undertaking was declared to be 'in a particularly healthy financial position, affording supplies at the cheapest and most reasonable charges' and offering consumers hire purchase terms for the wiring of their homes and the purchase of electrical appliances such as cookers, wash boilers, vacuum cleaners and refrigerators. Until the late 1920s the Halifax Corporation Tramways earned substantial profits, some of which were used for the relief of the rates. However, during the period 1926 to 1930 increasing competition from motor buses resulted in huge losses and by 1929 the debt on passenger transport, including road reinstatement, amounted to £403,394. Although Alderman Arthur Gledhill, Chairman of the Tramways Committee, instituted an immediate policy of debt reduction, which almost halved the debt within ten years, the committee ultimately decided to abandon its tramway routes in 1939, as it had its less extensive trolley bus routes in 1926, in favour of the more efficient motor bus services which it had operated in conjunction with the London, Midland and Scottish Railway Company since 1929.[51]

The town council faced constant pressure from the local business community for retrenchment in public expenditure throughout the inter-war years. The Halifax Chamber of Commerce, in the wake of the recessions of 1920–21 and 1924, expressed the hope that the 'prominent business men' in municipal politics would secure a reduction in local government expenditure in the interests of both 'industry and ... the whole community' so that local taxation should match 'the capacity of the ratepayer to pay'. Alderman Harold Waddington observed ruefully in 1936 that the proportion of shopkeepers on the Halifax Town Council had declined during the half century from 1886 to 1936 from nine out of a total of forty to eight out of a total of sixty, though half of the eight remaining shopkeeper councillors in 1936 served on the Finance Committee. An article published in the *Local Government Journal* in April 1935, however, confidently entitled 'Halifax:

Tram Smash, Lee Bridge, Halifax, May 22nd 1915

Figure 6.9   Tram Smash, Lee Bridge, Halifax, 22 May 1915. On Saturday 22 May 1915, a Halifax Corporation tramcar ran out of control and overturned below Lee Mount on the Nursery Lane route. No lives were lost in this accident, but twenty passengers were injured. The shortness of the wheelbase and the narrowness of the gauge of the Halifax tramcars can be clearly seen on the upturned vehicle in this photograph. The steep gradients and narrow streets in the Halifax area necessitated a small, light tramcar, so the tracks were laid to a gauge of 3ft 6in, which imposed limitations on the technical development of the system and contributed to the cause of a number of serious accidents over the years. Halifax Corporation ultimately decided to abandon its tramway routes in 1939 in favour of more efficient motor bus services. (Photograph: J. A. Hargreaves Collection)

the outcome of civic initiative', emphasised the integral relationship which
had been forged between civic administration and local industry, since the
Corporation provided the 'essential framework of the industrial structure'
with its facilities for 'the education, training, housing and health requirements of the workers'. It averred unequivocally that public services in the
county borough were 'highly developed', 'well organised and maintained
at a high pitch of efficiency' and concluded enthusiastically that 'thanks to
the steadily pursued and skilfully administered policy of its Corporation'
Halifax was rapidly solving 'the problem of combining intense and successful modern industrialism with a taste for civic beauty and amenities and
a cultivated pursuit of science and the arts'.[52]

In reality, however, the development of secondary education in Halifax
during the period 1914–45 in response to the Fisher and Butler Acts of 1918
and 1944 and the Hadow Reports of 1926–33 proceeded slowly and unspec-
tacularly, suffering from the severe constraints on public expenditure during
the inter-war years. The Fisher Act of 1918 raised the school leaving age to
fourteen and abolished the half-time system, which had been extensively
adopted in Halifax, where no fewer than 1,057 children were employed as
half-timers as late as 1917. The influential Hadow Report on the education
of the adolescent, commissioned by the Labour government of 1924 and
commended to local authorities by Stanley Baldwin's Conservative
government in 1926, paved the way for free compulsory secondary education
for all. However, the Halifax Education Committee was much slower
than Labour-dominated Bradford to reorganise along Hadow lines.
Although its proposals for reorganisation were accepted by the Board of
Education in April 1929, it was March 1931 before the first changes were
implemented. Full implementation was not completed until after the Butler
Act of 1944.[53]

The Halifax Secondary School, absorbing the Junior Commercial School
for girls, had operated at the Halifax Technical College since the war, and
it became the Halifax Modern School in August 1931, providing 'an education of a practical character' for boys and girls aged from eleven to
fifteen, while the Junior Technical School was to provide preparatory
training for boys from thirteen to fifteen proceeding to apprenticeships in
local trades. The voluntary schools and some smaller outlying schools
continued to offer both elementary and secondary education on the same
premises for some time, but pupils at the larger council schools were
transferred at the age of eleven to senior schools at Siddal, Haugh Shaw,
Battinson Road, Akroyd Place, Sunnyside, Lee Mount and Moorside. However, the reorganisation was not completed until 1949, and only one new
purpose-built non-selective secondary school was constructed in Halifax
in the whole of the period from 1902 to 1945, namely Ovenden School.
Opened in 1937 by Kenneth Lindsay, parliamentary secretary at the Board
of Education, it was built to serve an extensive neighbouring council

Figure 6.10 Sunnyside Infants School, Range Lane, Halifax, 1939. Sunnyside Infants School was one of 28 elementary schools provided by the Halifax Education Committee in 1935. It had 306 children on roll. This photograph of a nursery class in the 'Sun Room' taken in 1939 shows the early development of a purpose-built nursery unit. This self-contained, light and airy wooden structure in the school playground was equipped with a large sand pit, paddling pool, indoor and outdoor play areas, and camp beds, which folded out each afternoon to enable the children to have an hour's sleep. (Photograph courtesy of D. Baxter)

estate development, and its impressive facilities, including a gymnasium, swimming pool and playing field, prompted James Parker, the town's first Labour MP, to declare that 'children attending Ovenden are better provided for than those attending Eton or Harrow'.

The Crossley orphanage received the Royal Assent to change into a secondary school in 1919, but it was only after 1944 that it was incorporated within the local authority. Meanwhile, in 1925 Heath Grammar School for Boys and in 1931 the Princess Mary High School for Girls had been brought under the control of the Halifax Education Committee. The former provided 'a good general education, fitting boys for a business career', higher education and the professions, while the latter, occupying new purpose-built accommodation at Craven Lodge, provided 'a sound, liberal education, leading up to the universities and preparing girls for home life'. However, it was most unusual for even better off Halifax girls to proceed to university in the inter-war years. Phyllis Bentley was the first girl among her family's acquaintance to take a university degree and as such was regarded as 'quite a rarity'. Betty Hoyle, another local millowner's daughter, who married in 1939 Paul Bryan, a Cambridge graduate who later became MP for Sowerby, attended a boarding school at Bexhill and a finishing school in Switzerland. Her husband later recalled that the daughters of the Halifax manufacturing elite 'were not burdened with a serious education', while their brothers went to middle rank public schools, such as Sedbergh and Giggleswick in the north and Shrewsbury and Marlborough in the south, though rarely Oxford or Cambridge.

By 1939 there were 6,103 children attending council elementary schools, but only 479 secondary school children registered at the Halifax Modern School. A further 320 boys attended Heath Grammar School; 305 girls

Princess Mary High School and 340 boys and girls Crossley and Porter School. In addition, some 1,787 children were enrolled at Church of England schools, including the Holy Trinity Senior School established at Savile Hall in 1933, and 1,146 at Roman Catholic schools. There was provision for children with special needs at Quarry House and Bermerside. School attendance continued without interruption during the Second World War, augmented at some schools by evacuees, after some initial precautions had been taken including the filling of thousands of sandbags for protection against air-raids. The war years saw a considerable expansion in the school meals service, because of food rationing and the employment of mothers in factories, and the inauguration of the youth service, which had 50 per cent of its expenses funded by the Board of Education from 1940.[54]

During the period 1914–45 increasing concern was expressed about the standard of living of working-class families. Addressing the Halifax Rotary Club in 1929, W. H. Ostler, clerk to the Halifax Education Committee from 1902–33, had sharply criticised the 'foul conditions' in which so many Halifax children lived, emphasising the need for improved facilities in public health and housing. Phyllis Bentley, a volunteer helper in the 1930s at the Halifax Child Welfare Clinic, held in a Sunday school up Range Bank, 'a poor part of the town' consisting of 'rows of small old smoke-blackened houses, with bad ventilation and no modern conveniences', was profoundly affected by the 'extremely poor circumstances' of the mothers attending the clinic. She recalled that 'incipient anaemia showed in their pale gums; their hands were dirty and work-worn, their hair greasy, un-washed, often in curlers beneath their shawls' while their children were 'sometimes thin, sallow, fretful' and 'the orange juice, proprietary children's foods and remedies to counteract the effect of limeless water on growing bones' sold at wholesale prices were 'often beyond the pockets of the mothers'. Halifax Corporation attempted to cope, and by 1939 it provided a maternity and child welfare service, a school medical service, a general hospital with maternity and children's wards, an infectious diseases hospital, a tuberculosis sanatorium and dispensary, an orthopaedic service and a service 'for dealing with mental deficiency'.[55]

However, the question of birth control remained a more sensitive issue during the inter-war years. When a local committee of ladies assembled by Lady Hattie Fisher-Smith (the American born wife of the Halifax wire manufacturer Alderman Sir George Henry Fisher-Smith), following an initiative from the National Birth Control Association, applied to the local Medical Officer of Health for premises to start a family planning clinic, their request was declined. Undaunted, on 10 October 1934 in the TOC H rooms as 32 Clare Road, they opened the Halifax Women's Welfare Clinic, funded entirely by public subscriptions with the first medical officer, Dr Heynemann, and the first nurse, Miss Williamson, acting as unpaid volunteers.[56]

Figure 6.11   Visit of the Princess Royal to Halifax, 1940. The Princess, in her capacity as Commander-in-Chief of the British Red Cross Society, presents first aid, nursing proficiency and service awards to nurses of the Halifax detachment of the British Red Cross Society at the Princess Mary High School on 13 July 1940. She also inspected the headquarters of the Halifax YMCA in Union Street where she met officers and members of the armed forces. This was her second visit to the town in 1940. She was the most frequent royal visitor to the town during this period. (Photograph courtesy of S. Gee)

Other voluntary provision, financed by legacies and public donations, included extensions to the Royal Halifax Infirmary, two of which were opened by HRH the Princess Mary, the most frequent royal visitor to the town, who was created the Princess Royal in 1932. Between 1921 and 1929 new maternity, open-air and X-ray wards, an orthopaedic outpatients' department, new operating theatres, a pathological laboratory, and a nurses' home were constructed. Other new buildings included the Sir Enoch Hill ante-natal clinic opened in 1940, financed partly from a testimonial fund set up to mark Hill's retirement from the Halifax Building Society. In 1937 a new purpose-built Halifax Children's Holiday Home, funded by voluntary donations, was opened on Norland Moor to provide 'a place of joy, where the foundations of true happiness, health and character will be laid'.[57]

Other environmental health improvements by the local authority in-cluded limited smoke abatement measures; slum clearance and road widening schemes in central Halifax; the designation of residential, indus-trial and shopping zones in Ovenden, Bradshaw, Warley and Skircoat; the recycling or incineration of household and domestic refuse at a mechanical refuse disposal plant; new methods of street cleansing utilising mechanical appliances such as sweepers, gulley emptiers and sprinklers; the extension of the water carriage of sewage between 1924 and 1930; and the opening in 1929 of one of the most up-to-date abattoirs in the country by the Rt Hon. Arthur Greenwood, MP, Minister of Health. Further parks, recreation grounds and open spaces were also acquired. The extensive Shibden Hall estate, including the hall and grounds, was purchased in 1923 for the Halifax Corporation by Arthur Selby McCrea, son of the Victorian philanthropist

Figure 6.12 The proposed site for the Halifax Children's Welfare League Children's Holiday Home at Norland. A building appeal fund was launched in September 1935 by Halifax's first woman mayor Alderman Miriam Lightowler. In less than two years almost £4,000 had been donated and the home opened in June 1937. It aimed to provide 'a place of joy, where the foundations of true happiness, health and character will be laid' and enabled poor children from Halifax to take a fortnight's holiday in the open countryside above Sowerby Bridge. (Photograph courtesy of Irene Spencer)

Henry Charles McCrea. The park was officially opened for public use by the Prince of Wales on 15 October 1926 and the hall opened to the public as a period museum in 1934, following the death of its last resident, the antiquarian John Lister in 1933. Finally, Manor Heath, the former residence of the carpet manufacturer, John Crossley, was purchased by Halifax Corporation for £18,500 in 1929, so that by 1936 there were no fewer than twenty-nine parks, open spaces and recreation grounds within the county borough.[58]

However, the evolution of municipal housing policies, within the framework of new government legislation during the inter-war years, had ultimately the greatest impact on working-class living standards. In 1921 there was a higher percentage of families living in overcrowded conditions, that is with more than two persons per room, in Halifax (13.2 per cent) and Huddersfield (13.6 per cent) than in Bradford (10.7 per cent) and Leeds (12.0 per cent). By 1931, the percentage had fallen in Huddersfield to 7.8 per cent, Bradford to 6.9 per cent and Leeds to 8.2 per cent, leaving Halifax with the highest percentage of overcrowding at 10.0 per cent. The Halifax figure had been more than halved to 5.2 per cent by 1935, though this was still a higher percentage than neighbouring Bradford (2.4 per cent) and Huddersfield (4.6 per cent). The first schemes projected under post-war Housing Acts in Halifax were for 36 houses at Spring Hall Lane and 26 houses at Heathy Lane. However, the Ministry of Health declared the tenders too high for acceptance, and the Council proceeded to erect 36 houses at Pellon by direct labour between October 1919 and December 1921 at an average cost per house of £1,183, exclusive of land, streets and sewers, during a period when building costs were exceptionally high. By 1929, when a total of 1,029 houses erected, the average cost of construction had fallen to £345. By 1939, 3,061 council houses had been constructed, with two to five bedrooms, but also including some pioneering old people's bungalows, flats and maisonettes, all vastly superior to previous working-class housing. Moreover, Halifax council rents in the 1930s were considered some of the lowest in the country.[59]

There were also a number of important private housing initiatives inspired by both the philanthropic tradition of Victorian Liberalism and the concern for social welfare issuing from the rise of Labour. Violet Mackintosh, the widow of the founder of the toffee manufacturing firm, built and endowed the John Mackintosh Memorial Homes adjoining the Albert Promenade for couples of at least sixty years of age with low incomes, preferably employees of the firm or members of the Queens Road United Methodist Church, which her husband had attended. Opened in 1925 by J. H. Whitley, accompanied by the Minister of Health, Neville Chamberlain, they consisted of twelve cottages, a matron's cottage and an assembly hall designed by W. B. Walton of Blackpool. Later, in 1929, Laura Willson and her husband George, one of the founders of Willson Lathes Ltd, who had been actively involved in house building schemes since 1922, helped trade union and Labour activists to purchase new houses in Atalanta Terrace, Pye Nest. These had toilets, bathrooms with hot running water, electricity in every room, and a gas fire in the kitchen.[60]

Local politics

In Halifax, as in many other West Yorkshire towns and cities, an anti-socialist alliance operated in municipal politics during the inter-war years, when it was common for a Labour candidate to be opposed by only one of the other party candidates. There was a three-year cycle of elections for the forty-five council seats, one councillor being elected each year for each of the fifteen wards. Fifteen aldermen were also elected for six-year terms of office by the councillors from within their own ranks, bringing the total membership of the council to sixty. In 1921, for example, in the seven seats where there were Labour candidates the contests were all between a socialist and an anti-socialist and in all the other seats except one, where there was a contest between a Liberal and a Conservative, anti-socialist candidates were elected unopposed. Moreover, the anti-socialist alliance was maintained in Halifax throughout the 1920s and 1930s, unlike in Leeds where the decline of Liberalism made it inoperative after 1925.

Remarkably, as in neighbouring Huddersfield, the Liberals remained the largest group on Halifax Council throughout the inter-war years. However, Labour was also doing as well as the Conservatives. The Labour Party's continuing interest in housing, family allowances, unemployment and education enabled the Halifax Labour Party to expand its membership from under 1,000 in 1935 to 1,200 in 1937. Liberal strength was concentrated in both the inner urban and suburban wards, including the Central, Copley, East, Northowram, Ovenden, Skircoat and Warley wards, and also in Kingston, where they vied with the Conservatives for the control of the ward. The Conservatives held sway in the Illingworth and South wards, while Labour dominated the Akroydon, North, Pellon, West and Southowram wards.[61]

Table 6.3. *Municipal seats in Halifax, 1921–1938*

Year	Conservative	Labour	Liberal	Others
1921	16	15	27	2
1922	17	14	27	2
1923	15	15	24	2
1924	18	17	25	
1925	19	17	23	1
1926	18	17	24	1
1927	19	15	25	1
1928	17	17	25	1
1929	17	17	26	
1930	17	17	26	
1931	17	16	27	
1932	16	18	26	
1933	17	19	24	
1934	16	20	23	1
1935	18	18	23	1
1936	21	15	24	
1937	19	18	23	
1938	21	17	22	

Source: J. Reynolds and K. Laybourn, *Labour Heartland* (Bradford University Press, Bradford: 1987), pp. 59, 159.

Although women ratepayers had been allowed to vote in municipal elections since 1869 and stand for election as councillors since 1907, the councillors elected in Halifax during the inter-war years were almost exclusively men. Phyllis Bentley recalled campaigning unsuccessfully for the return of a woman councillor, commenting that it was 'typical of the period' that the attempt failed, and no woman councillor was elected in Halifax until 1924. Indeed, during the inter-war years Halifax had only two women councillors, the Conservative Miriam Lightowler and the Liberal

Jennie Latham. Miriam Lightowler, the first woman to be elected to Halifax Town Council, had by common consent discharged her duties as the last chairman of the Halifax Board of Guardians 'zealously under difficult political conditions': when the Board ceased its operations in 1929 the pauperism rate in the Halifax Poor Law Union of 118 per 10,000 of the population was lower than both the West Riding and national averages. She subsequently became the first woman chairman of the Halifax Council Finance Committee and the first and only woman mayor of Halifax in the inter-war years, in 1934–35. Moreover, Brighouse and Todmorden had to wait until after the war for their first women mayors and a quarter of a century elapsed before Halifax had another woman mayor. However, women had been admitted to the Halifax bench in 1920, and the number of women magistrates had more than doubled if only to eight by 1945.[62]

In parliamentary contests the Liberals worked with the Conservatives to secure the election of the Rt Hon. J. H. Whitley for the Coalition Liberals in 1918 with a majority of 18,100 over the Socialist Labour Party candidate Arthur McManus, a Clydeside trade unionist, who attracted the support of Halifax trade unionists, especially engineers, but lacked the support of other Labour groups and polled only 4,036 votes. The electoral pact and divisions within the local Labour Party ensured that the outcome of the election was never in serious doubt and produced a turnout of only 53 per cent, the lowest for a parliamentary election during the period 1914–45, despite the widening of the franchise in 1918 to include all adult males and women aged thirty and over.

Labour Party divisions in Halifax had arisen during the First World War. James Parker, Halifax's Labour MP from 1906–18, and Alderman Arthur Taylor, a leading local trade unionist, had upset many ILP members by their pro-war stance and active participation in the recruiting campaigns of 1914. Parker had declared that 'if Britain were defeated in the war, the working class would have everything to lose and nothing to gain', whilst Taylor, though professing his hatred of wars, had concluded that 'there were times when it was absolutely necessary that people should recognise war as inevitable'.[63] This created bitter dissension within the Halifax ILP and Trades Council, which had increasingly adopted an anti-war stance after 1916. For almost a decade between 1918 and 1928 this erstwhile Labour stronghold was unable to find a candidate to contest the single Halifax seat left after the introduction of the Representation of the People Act of 1918. The formation of the Halifax Labour Party in 1918 with its new constitution and local organisations also cut across the established links between the ILP and trades councils.

Moreover, the Halifax MP, J. H. Whitley, who became Speaker of the House of Commons in 1921, had gained a national reputation as the initiator of the consultative councils between employers and employees which bore his name in 1917–18 and was held in high esteem locally for his commitment

Figure 6.13
J. H. Whitley and the Halifax Recreative Evening School Boys' Gymnastic Team. John Henry Whitley (1866–1935), second from the left, was a partner in the cotton spinning firm of S. Whitley and Co., Hanson Lane Mills, who determined to engage in social work in the 1880s amongst young people through the Recreative Evening School and the annual Halifax Boys' Camp at Filey. In 1892 J. H. Whitley became a borough magistrate and in the following year was elected a town councillor. He remained a member of the town council until 1900, when he entered Parliament as Liberal member for Halifax. After a distinguished parliamentary career, he served as Speaker of the House of Commons from 1921 to 1928 and subsequently as chairman of the Royal Commission on Labour in India from 1929 to 1931. (Photograph: J. A. Hargreaves Collection)

to education and his work with socially disadvantaged youths. Following his election as Speaker, an office he held with distinction, displaying 'a quiet tact, confident yet tolerant firmness and utter impartiality', J. H. Whitley was unopposed in each of the three elections between 1922 and 1924.[64]

When he resigned in 1928, however, declining the traditional hereditary viscountcy offered to him by King George V, the Labour Party had recovered sufficiently to secure the election of Alderman Arthur W. Longbottom, a former Mayor of Halifax, as his successor as MP for Halifax. In a three-way contest, he was returned for Labour at the by-election with 17,536 votes, a majority of 4,951 over the Liberal and Conservative candidates, who polled 12,585 and 10,804 votes respectively. Although Labour remained a minority group within the Halifax Town Council because of the operation of anti-socialist coalitions at municipal elections, it was able to achieve success at parliamentary elections in an open contest, winning on a minority of votes. In the general election of the following year Longbottom retained the seat for Labour with an increased majority of 7,063 over his Conservative and Liberal opponents, Gilbert Gledhill and Elliot Dodds, who polled 16,713 and 15,823 votes respectively, in the highest turnout of electors during the period 1914–45. The Conservatives had increased their share of the vote to come second, leaving the Liberals in third place. Longbottom's share of the vote dropped slightly and was below the Labour average for West Yorkshire, but in his victory speech in Bull Green, he declared that the result proved 'conclusively that Longbottom for Halifax is as safe as the rock of Gibraltar'.[65]

His confidence, however, proved misplaced when national events resulted in a change of political climate. Following the collapse of Ramsay Macdonald's second Labour government in August 1931 after it attempted to reduce unemployment benefit by 10 per cent, Macdonald further alienated many Labour supporters by his agreement to lead a National Government in coalition with the Conservatives and National Liberals. Consequently, in the general election of October 1931, the Conservative Gilbert Gledhill, youngest son of George H. Gledhill, founder of the local cash register manufacturing firm, topped the poll with 36,731 votes, taking 65.7 per cent of the vote. The National Government won a landslide victory, and the election proved disastrous nationally for the Labour Party, which had been damaged by MacDonald's attempt to reduce unemployment. In Halifax, Longbottom was clearly ousted by Liberal voters supporting the National Government. However, in view of Labour's performance nationally, he did well to poll 16,601 votes and maintain the same percentage share of the vote which he had obtained in 1929 (29.7 per cent), even though this again fell below the West Yorkshire average. F. Sykes, standing as an anti-National

Photo   VISIT OF MR. WINSTON CHURCHILL TO HALIFAX. June 27th/45   Halifax Courier
The Prime Minister waving to the crowd at his departure

Figure 6.14   Visit of Winston Churchill to Halifax, 27 June 1945. Winston Churchill was given 'a rousing reception' when he addressed an estimated 20,000-strong crowd in Bull Green during his post-war election campaign tour of the industrial north. His speech in support of the Halifax Conservative candidate, Gilbert Gledhill, the sitting MP, appealed to the patriotic sentiment which had enabled Britain to achieve victory over Nazi Germany. He declared: 'By our firmness of character, by our moderation of behaviour in every way, by our good and settled state of law, we have raised ourselves in the storm of war to the very van of the conquering nations and by preserving those characteristic qualities of the British, and I may say of the Yorkshire character, we shall continue to march forward at the head of nations'. Nevertheless, Labour was swept to power in the ensuing general election, including Dryden Brook for Halifax.
(Photograph courtesy of S. Gee)

Government candidate after the local Liberal Association had decided not to put forward a candidate, polled 2,578 votes. Gledhill retained the seat for the Conservatives in 1935, but with a considerably reduced majority of 2,632 votes, indicating, perhaps, that at least some Liberals who had voted National in 1931 were now willing to support Labour in order to challenge the Conservative-National candidate. Longbottom, who came second with 21,471 votes to Gledhill's 24,103, increased his share of the vote to 39.5 per cent, a figure above the West Yorkshire average, indicating the strength of Labour's recovery, while A. Mitchell for the Liberals came third with 8,736 votes.[66]

In 1945, Winston Churchill was given a 'rousing reception' when he addressed an estimated 20,000 strong crowd in Bull Green in June, a tribute to his wartime national leadership. He urged his audience to let 'philosophical discussions about the future system of society stand aside until the main practical jobs we have on hand are carried through', such as the provision of housing which would be treated 'as if it were a military operation'. Nevertheless, Labour was swept to power in the ensuing general election, winning 21 of the 23 West Yorkshire seats, including Halifax. Dryden Brook, a wool merchant and Halifax Labour Councillor came top of the poll with 25,605 votes, securing a majority of 10,781. Gilbert Gledhill, the Conservative came in second place with 14,824 and the Liberal candidate Arnold Gelder a close third with 14,631 votes. Labour had secured its highest share of the vote (46.5 per cent) in any parliamentary contest, and the Liberals their highest number of votes and highest share of the vote since 1929 on a turnout of 77.4 per cent. The former Conservative vote appears to have defected to Labour and the Liberals in somewhat equal measure, giving Labour its majority. It remained to be seen whether this Labour triumph would survive the post-war experience.[67]

Table 6.4. *Parliamentary election results in the Halifax constituency, 1918–1945*

Election	Turnout (%)	Candidate	Party	Votes	share (%)
1918	53.4	J. H. Whitley	Lib	22,136	84.6
		A. McManus	SLP	4,036	15.4
1922		J. H. Whitley	Lib	Unopposed	
1923		J. H. Whitley	Lib	Unopposed	
1924		J. H. Whitley	Lib	Unopposed	
1928	78.7	A. Longbottom	Lab	17,536	42.8
		H. Barnes	Lib	12,585	30.8
		F. S. Crossley	Cons	10,804	26.4

Table 6.4 continued

Election	Turnout (%)	Candidate	Party	Votes	share (%)
1929	81.3	*A. Longbottom*	Lab	23,776	42.2
		G. Gledhill	Cons	16,713	29.7
		G. E. Dodds	Lib	15,823	28.1
1931	80.5	*G. Gledhill*	Cons	36,731	65.7
		A. Longbottom	Lab	16,601	29.7
		F. Sykes	Ind Lib	2,578	4.6
1935	76.9	*G. Gledhill*	Cons	24,103	44.4
		A. Longbottom	Lab	21,471	39.5
		A. Mitchell	Lib	8,736	16.1
1945	77.4	*D. Brook*	Lab	25,605	46.5
		G. Gledhill	Cons	14,824	26.9
		A. Gelder	Lib	14,631	26.6

Source: F. W. S. Craig (ed.), *British Parliamentary Election Results, 1918–1949* (Glasgow 1969), p. 140.

What the contests for 1918 to 1945 also indicate is that all parties were largely competing for the middle ground. This is confirmed by the limited appeal in Halifax of parties of the extreme right and left such as the British Union of Fascists and the Communist Party of Great Britain, neither of which fielded candidates in parliamentary elections in Halifax during the inter-war years. Moreover, Edward Kennedy, a Communist candidate, who had suffered four months' imprisonment for his part in a demonstration in Todmorden in 1932, polled only 74 votes in a municipal election in Halifax North Ward in 1933, against Labour's 1,034. However, there was some enduring sympathy locally for Ralph Fox, a talented local author killed in action in the Spanish Civil War in 1937. Born into a middle-class Halifax family in 1900, he was educated at the Heath and Bradford Grammar Schools and Oxford University, where he gained a first class degree in modern languages. A prolific writer and lecturer, he became a founder member of the British Communist Party in 1920. On the outbreak of the Spanish Civil War, he was one of the first volunteers for service with the International Brigade and within six weeks of enlisting he was killed in heroic circumstances in heavy fighting around the town of Lopera near Cordoba in southern Spain.[68]

During the growing international crisis of the later 1930s, the novelist Phyllis Bentley, who had become a crypto-socialist during the 1920s, sensed a growing opposition to European Fascism and the National Government's policy of appeasement both within her own staunchly Conservative, middle-class family and amongst the wider Halifax public. Indeed, in February

Figure 6.15   Phyllis Bentley as an ambulance driver, 1939. Phyllis Bentley confided in her autobiography that as the approach of war became imminent 'with many thousands of other anxious citizens I joined the A.R.P. (air raid precautions) organisation, attended anti-gas classes and qualified myself to drive an ambulance', which was not without its lighter moments. 'The huge ramshackle old vans on which we were given tuition', she continued, 'were most exhausting and difficult to handle – after a prolonged wrestle with one on an afternoon amid the West Riding hills, or worse still on a blackout practice at dead of night, my own car felt like a perambulator'. In the event, however, there were relatively few air attacks on Halifax during the war and she was never required to drive an ambulance in an air raid. (Photograph: J. A. Hargreaves Collection)

1938, she appeared on a public platform in opposition to the government's recognition of the Italian occupation of Abyssinia, and in November 1938 she wrote to the *Yorkshire Post* repudiating Chamberlain's appeasement of Hitler, following which, she later recalled, 'some Halifax shopkeepers … murmured in my ear their thanks'. She subsequently joined the ARP organisation, attended anti-gas classes and qualified to drive an ambulance. On 26 May 1940, following the Nazi occupation of Holland, Belgium and northern France, she recalled that, although an agnostic, she 'was proud to march in ARP uniform in the mayoral procession' to Halifax Parish Church to observe a national day of prayer for the desperate international situation. By 1940 political divisions in Halifax as elsewhere had been subsumed in united opposition to the tyranny of European Fascism.[69]

Culture: religion and recreation

The economy and the politics of Halifax from 1914 to 1945 had experienced discontinuities while retaining strong links with the past. Could that also be said of the cultural life of Halifax during the inter-war years? One indication is that the churches and chapels which had largely blessed the First World War, as they were later to accept the grim necessity of the Second World War, took a prominent role in celebrating the peace. After the armistice in November 1918, a local Congregational minister, the Revd Henry Iremonger, proclaimed in Halifax: 'The men who fought for freedom have commenced a task which is left for us to fulfil. Peace is the end of destruction and the beginning of construction.'

Moreover, a Sunday school celebration at the Thrum Hall Rugby Ground became the focus of the town's peace thanksgiving following Germany's signature of the Treaty of Versailles on 28 June 1919, indicating the continuing influence of religious life in the town, notwithstanding the trauma of the recent conflict. It was a remarkable occasion and 'one of those great scenes which those who saw it will never forget', commented the *Halifax Courier*. The gathering concluded with expressions of jubilation as 'people leapt to their feet, shouted until they were hoarse and waved handkerchiefs and hats', before 'joining in the singing of the National Anthem and the Doxology'.[70]

No fewer than 120 local Sunday schools had taken part in the Thrum Hall celebrations, and one local commentator, the toffee manufacturer John Mackintosh, writing to the *Halifax Courier* in 1919, repudiated any suggestion that the churches were in decline following the experience of war:

> It is not true to say that the churches are empty in England, and whoever says so is wrong ... My own church (Queen's Road United Methodist Church) has 250 members and more adherents. We have 400 scholars and about 50 teachers. There is something taking place nearly every night in connection with one department or another.[71]

While Primitive Methodism and Wesleyanism in Halifax experienced a further spurt of growth in the 1920s, the United Methodist Church, despite Mackintosh's conviction of its continuing vitality, displayed a declining rate of membership recruitment in Halifax virtually throughout the whole of the period from 1908 to Methodist re-union in 1932. Indeed, the Revd D. B. Proudlove, a local United Methodist Church minister, acknowledged in 1929 that while the town was noted for 'its chimney stacks and church

Figure 6.16   United Sunday Schools Peace Commemoration, Thrum Hall, 28 June 1919. Children and teachers from some 120 local Sunday schools gather in an act of thanksgiving for the signing of the Treaty of Versailles, which formally concluded the peace settlement at the end of the First World War. The event, attended by thousands, provides evidence of the continuing influence of religious life in the town, notwithstanding the trauma of the recent conflict. It was a remarkable occasion and 'one of those great scenes which those who saw it will never forget', commented the *Halifax Courier*. (Photograph courtesy of the *Halifax Courier*)

steeples', Halifax with its four Wesleyan Circuits, two Primitive Methodist Circuits and four United Methodist Circuits served by eighteen ministers was 'somewhat overchurched'. Indeed, he questioned the need for so many spacious Methodist churches within such close proximity of each other near the centre of the town.[72]

His concerns about a superabundance of chapel accommodation were echoed later in 1937 by Alderman J. H. Waddington, surveying the changes which had occurred during the previous fifty years:

> The number of churches and places of worship in Halifax today is the same as it was 50 years ago, but what a difference there is in the attendance on the Sabbath Day, while week-night preaching has practically gone out ... Today with a 25% larger population, the attendance at church is not half what it was when I was young. Then, too, the great Sunday School festivals which were held in the Piece Hall are merely items of history today ... In those days what big enjoyable Sunday School treats were held on Whit-Monday and Whit-Tuesday in gardens and fields, sponsored by officers of the Church of England and Nonconformist churches and chapels.[73]

Similarly, the poet, Ted Hughes, also discerned similar changes between the wars in his native Calder Valley: 'throughout my lifetime, since 1930, I have watched the mills of the region and their attendant chapels die'.[74]

Even the achievement of Methodist Re-union by 1932 and increased co-operation between Anglicans and Nonconformists in the town during the vicariate of Bishop George Frodsham from 1920 to 1937 failed to revive spiritual confidence and halt the decline of institutional Christianity as it struggled to compete with the increasing range of alternative secular leisure activities during the inter-war years. As Dr Simon Green concluded in his study of religious organisations in Halifax, Denholme and Keighley, 'some time during the 1920s the local religious classes lost heart. They ceased to believe in their mission to evangelise the nation', which was now capable of making 'increasingly effective decisions about which organisations to devote its loyalty (and its time and money) to'. The 'much-heralded "threat" of the Labour Party, or the Sunday Lecture Society, or even of various bicycle clubs' became a real distraction from religious association for an increasing number of men and women after 1920.[75]

Alternative leisure activities beckoned. There was a further shortening of working hours in the woollen and worsted industries from 55.5 hours to 48 hours in 1919, and by 1945 a standard working week of 45 hours had been secured by national agreement. Employers appeared increasingly sympathetic to the leisure interests of their employees. In March 1937, for example, Shaw Lodge Mills closed half an hour early so that workers could attend the third round Rugby League cup tie between Halifax and Castleford, while in 1939, the engineering firm F. Pratt and Co. Ltd gave their workforce Saturday morning off and paid the return fares for 200 employees to travel to Wembley to watch Halifax play in the Rugby League Challenge Cup Final. Moreover, during the inter-war years, before annual holidays with pay became compulsory, the Halifax Building Society developed a programme of 'co-operative organised holidays' for their staff, granting one-third of the scheduled cost to employees who took part in them. Starting with motor tours of Devon, more exotic destinations were later

Figure 6.18 (*below*) Sunny Vale Pleasure Gardens, Hipperholme, were opened by Joseph Bunce in 1883 and remained in the ownership of the Bunce family until 1945, when they were sold to Fred Thompson of Cleveleys. In their Victorian and Edwardian heyday they annually attracted 100,000 visitors. In the 1920s and 1930s, 'Sunny Bunce's', as they were affectionately known, enjoyed continuing popularity, with regular open-air dancing to local bands. Local author, Eve Chapman, recalled: 'I suppose what both we and the band lacked in elegance we made up for by enthusiasm, as we clumped around in our ordinary shoes, the boys probably in heavy boots, to the steady beat of brass band instruments, showing off our waltzing, our valeta, the newest foxtrot, the military two step or even the intricacies of the lancers'. (Photograph: J. A. Hargreaves Collection)

Figure 6.17   Office staff excursion, John Holdsworth and Co., Shaw Lodge Mills. This photograph, taken in the 1920s, shows the office staff of John Holdsworth and Co., worsted spinners and manufacturers of Shaw Lodge Mills, about to set off on a staff outing by char-a-banc, a popular form of transport during the inter-war years. The majority of the staff are women, well wrapped up for a ride in the open air. In the background can be seen part of the vast industrial complex which, by the end of the nineteenth century, as a late-Victorian directory observed, had 'assumed gigantic proportions' affording 'an example of organised technical industry not surpassed anywhere in the Yorkshire textile trade'. (Photograph: J. A. Hargreaves Collection)

Figure 6.19   The Halifax Rugby League team returns home with the Rugby League Challenge Cup, 1939. The team had beaten Salford by 20 points to 3 against all predictions at Wembley in the Rugby League Challenge Cup Final. Led by the Lee Mount Brass Band, the victorious team's open-topped bus passes through crowds of supporters in Bull Green en route to a civic reception at Halifax Town Hall. Within four months, local sporting fixtures would be disrupted by the outbreak of the Second World War. (Photograph courtesy of S. Gee)

chosen, with cruises to Norway, the Baltic and the Canary Islands. Meanwhile, the annual wakes week holiday established before 1914 continued a more informal tradition of communal holidays at seaside locations during the inter-war years when factories closed and large sections of the local population travelled to such popular resorts as Blackpool, Cleethorpes, Great Yarmouth, Morecambe, Scarborough, Skegness and Southport.[76]

For those who stayed at home, local beauty spots, parks and pleasure gardens enjoyed continuing popularity during the 1920s and 1930s. At Sunny Vale, Hipperholme, managed by the Bunce family until 1945, up to 100,000 visitors each year arrived by tramcar or train to sample the delights on offer. These included trips on the lake by steamer, lakeside rides on the miniature railway, and dancing in the open air. Indeed, the craze for dancing was evident across Halifax society during the inter-war years. Phyllis Bentley recalled attending weekly dancing classes in order to participate in the proliferation of tea dances and private evening dances at local hotels, as well as engaging in other recreational activities including tennis, table-tennis and badminton. There were also good attendances at local hospital charity events and at the Great Yorkshire Show, which attracted record attendances when it was held in Halifax in 1928.[77]

There was a phenomenal growth in spectator sport in Halifax during the inter-war years. The Halifax Rugby Union Club, founded in 1919 and placed on a firm footing with the backing of Sir William Bulmer, moved to Ovenden Park in 1925 and won the Yorkshire Cup three years in succession from 1926 to 1928. The Halifax Rugby League Football Club, making a number of shrewd signings in the 1920s of both former rugby union players and players from more severely depressed areas than Halifax, such as Dai Rees from Wales and Andrew Murdison from Scotland, won the Rugby League Challenge Cup for the first time since 1904 in 1931, with a 22–8 victory over York at Wembley. To mark the victory, twenty-two fog detonators were set off as the train carrying the returning team arrived at Halifax Station to a rapturous reception from a crowd estimated at 100,000. The scenes were repeated in 1939, when Halifax beat Salford 20–3. In 1914, Halifax Town AFC secured its first trophy when it won the Bradford Charity Cup, only three years after the club's foundation. In 1919 the club

Figure 6.20   Halifax Town AFC first league match at the Shay, 1921. Halifax Town A.F.C. was founded in the summer of 1911 after a crowded meeting at the Saddle Hotel on 24 May under the chairmanship of Mr E. H. Braginton, who later became one of the club's first directors, had agreed to the formation of a limited company to fun the club. The first ground was at Sandhall Lane and the opening match against Bradford City Reserves at Valley Parade in the Yorkshire Combination. The first home game the following Saturday, 16 September 1911, against Scarborough attracted a crowd of 2,000. In 1913 the club was defeated in the first round of the F.A. Cup by Queen's Park Rangers. In 1919 the club moved to Exley and on 3 September 1921, ten years after the formation of the club, the first league match was played at the Shay, when more than 10,000 spectators watched Halifax achieve a famous victory of five goals to nil over Darlington. (Photograph: J. A. Hargreaves Collection)

moved from Sandhall Lane to a football ground at Exley and in 1921 to a new stadium at the Shay, where over 10,000 spectators at their first league match on 3 September saw Halifax Town achieve a 5–0 victory over Darlington. Halifax Town reached the fifth round of the FA Cup in 1932–3 and became Division 3 North Runners-up in 1934–5.[78]

The Theatre Royal and the newer Palace Theatre also continued to attract large audiences during the inter-war years. Wilfred Pickles recalled seeing the Theatre Royal packed 'from floor to ceiling' for Shakespeare productions by Henry Baynton's company, and he made his own professional stage début as an extra in a crowd scene from *Julius Caesar*. Phyllis Bentley recalled that attending the theatre in large parties became 'an accepted way of entertaining one's friends'. Even Halifax rugby players visited the theatre as part of their preparation for the Rugby League Challenge Cup final in 1931. Wilfred Pickles and Eric Portman, both later to become stars of stage and screen, developed their early interest in drama through the King Cross Amateur Dramatic Society, one of a host of local societies active during the inter-war years. In 1927 the Halifax Thespians was founded, and after the Second World War they acquired a redundant Methodist chapel for use as a playhouse.[79]

There was also a growing local cinema-going public, especially after the first 'talking' picture, 'The Singing Fool' starring Al Jolson, in was shown in Halifax in September 1929. By 1936 there were no fewer than ten cinemas

Figure 6.21   The Picture House, Commercial Street, Halifax. One of the first purpose-built cinemas in Halifax, it opened on 20 October 1913, showing silent pictures. 'Talkies' were first shown in the town in September 1929. The Picture House was subsequently renamed the Gaumont and later the Astra. It was one of a dozen cinemas which opened in Halifax before 1939. It finally closed as a cinema in May 1982. In the 1990s, under another new name, the Coliseum, with discotheque dancing and four themed bars, became one of the most popular nightclub venues in the region. (Photograph courtesy of S. Gee)

in Halifax, including the Alhambra, occupying the former Oddfellows Hall, the Cosy Corner Picture Palace in Queen's Road, and the Pioneer Picture House at Ovenden, while films were also now shown regularly at the Grand Theatre and the Victoria Hall. Then, in 1938, the new spacious purpose-built Odeon and Regal Cinemas were opened in Broad Street and at Ward's End. However, not everyone welcomed the growing popularity of the cinema in the inter-war years. James Parker bemoaned the fact that 'the cinema has displaced the singing rooms in public houses and little groups of village glee singers'. He claimed that it stifled the 'gaiety that was obvious when, in a less ambitious way, we provided our own amusement to a much greater extent; in school concerts, basket suppers, and bazaar entertainments'.[80]

Parker acknowledged, however, that Halifax remained very much 'a musical town', citing as evidence the popularity of the Halifax Light Opera Society. Similarly, J. B. Priestley remembered Halifax folk delighting 'in singing Handel and Gilbert-and-Sullivan operas'. The town's musical tradition owed much to its Nonconformist heritage. Halifax's most famous musical son, George Dyson (1883–1964), was the son of the organist and choirmaster of North Parade Baptist Church and a pupil of Arthur Collingwood, organist at Rhodes Street Wesleyan Chapel. A Fellow of the Royal College of Organists by the age of seventeen, he served as Director of the Royal College of Music between 1908 and 1937. He was most active as a composer between 1928 and 1949, with ten major compositions to his name, including the cantatas *In Honour of the City* (1928), which he conducted in Halifax in 1935, and *Canterbury Pilgrims* (1931), his best known work. Knighted in 1941, he was a leading campaigner for the development of music in the provinces and became President of the Halifax Chamber Music Society in 1943. The Halifax Choral Society, proud of its tradition as the oldest choral society in the world with an uninterrupted musical programme, continued its concerts throughout the two world wars. However, in 1930 the society's president reluctantly acknowledged that the Huddersfield Choral Society was the only really strong choral society outside London because of its greater success in attracting recording and broadcasting contracts.[81]

In 1930, when the doyen of local cultural societies, the Halifax Literary and Philosophical Society, held its centenary exhibition at Bankfield Museum, there were some 500 local societies, including the fledgling Halifax Author's Circle, founded in 1926. Its most prolific member was Phyllis Bentley, whose novel *Inheritance*, inspired by her own family's experience of recession in the textile industry in 1930–31, established her reputation as a successful regional novelist. Published in 1932, the novel received more than 530 reviews, went into twenty-nine editions in England, sold more than 40,000 hardback copies in the United States and was translated into eight languages. Another local author, Eleanor Gaukroger, writing under the pseudonym of Jenny Wren during the 1920s and 1930s, published popular anthologies of short stories during the 1920s and 1930s, rich in local dialect and recording 'accents of a life that under the pressure of modern education and civilisation is slowly, but surely passing away'.[82]

Several local authors, including Phyllis Bentley, whose novel *Inheritance* was serialised on the BBC North Region, reached larger audiences through the new medium of radio during this period. The Revd G. Bramwell Evens commenced his immensely popular BBC *Children's Hour* Romany radio broadcasts while stationed as a Methodist minister at King Cross Methodist Church in Halifax during the period 1929–39. He found the graveyard adjoining his manse a rich habitat for wildlife and was able through binoculars to observe sparrowhawks and peregrines perched on the nearby Wainhouse Tower. However, no local broadcaster achieved greater success through this medium than Wilfred Pickles (1904–78), who made his début as a contributor to BBC Children's Hour in 1927. He went on to make broadcasting history in December 1941 as the first national newsreader not only to speak with a pronounced northern accent, but also to sign off his final bulletin of the day with an impromptu flourish in the vernacular, wishing his northern listeners 'good-neet'. His invitation to read the news formed part of the wartime security strategy of Brendan Bracken, Minister of Information, to foil Nazi propagandists, who had become adept at imitating BBC Oxford accents. Pickles's debut as a newsreader created a furore at the time. This former Halifax builder featured in every kind of article, from gossip columns to cartoons, where he was invariably depicted with his shirt sleeves rolled up and wearing a muffler and cloth cap. Nevertheless the experience proved the springboard for his future highly successful career as one of the most popular broadcasters in the history of the medium.[83]

Figure 6.22   The broadcaster Wilfred Pickles and his wife Mabel with his elder brother Alderman Arthur Pickles, Mayor of Halifax 1951–52. Wilfred Pickles (1904–78), whose popular radio quiz show 'Have a Go' attracted an audience of 26 million listeners around the world at its peak, was born in Conway Street, Hopwood Lane, Halifax. He became an assistant at Mitchell's gentlemen's outfitters in Crown Street, Halifax before becoming an apprentice with his father's building firm. His interest in amateur dramatics led to a distinguished career in broadcasting, the theatre and cinema and he made broadcasting history in December 1941 as the first national newsreader with a distinctive northern accent. (Photograph: J. A. Hargreaves Collection)

Halifax also produced one of the greatest painters of the inter-war years in Sir Matthew Smith (1879–1959), the son of a Halifax wire manufacturer. His choice of career was facilitated by his family's considerable industrial fortune. After a public school education at Giggleswick, he worked for a Bradford wool company and then his father's wire making firm in Halifax before training first at the Manchester School of Art and then at the Slade in London. He then moved to France, where he developed his bold use of colour under the influence of Henri Matisse and at the artist's colony at Pont Aven in Brittany. Delicate in health, shy and retiring, he became best known for his landscape, nude and still-life paintings, especially his flowerpieces. He was described by Augustus John as 'the most brilliant and individual figure in modern English painting'. From a markedly less privileged background, Herbert Read, educated at the Crossley Orphanage in Halifax, emerged as a leading art critic and art historian during the inter-war years, with acclaimed publications on *The Meaning of Art* (1931), *Art and Industry* (1934) and *Art and Society* (1936). Thus, culturally, the inter-war years in Halifax provide evidence of vitality, and of continuity as well as change.[84]

'Black Halifax boiled in phosphorus'

Meanwhile, economic, social and cultural change, and local government institutions, began to alter Halifax's built environment. During the inter-war years municipal initiatives directed at slum clearance, road widening and retail development brought changes to the physical appearance of the town centre and spawned new green field housing developments around its western and northern peripheries at Pellon, Ovenden, Mixenden and Booth-town. Cross Fields, one of the most squalid areas of the town, became the first slum housing clearance project in 1926, making way for the Odeon cinema and a new bus station. Other road widening schemes resulted from the increase in motor traffic during the inter-war years. When the local master woodcarvers, Jacksons of Coley, chose to depict transport scenes through the ages on an exterior beam over the entrance of the reconstructed Royal Oak public house (completed in 1931), they included a carving of a motor vehicle, signifying the arrival of the motor age in Halifax. In 1936, a brochure for a shopping festival and exhibition in Halifax provided further confirmation, proclaiming that 'horses are vanishing from our streets and taking to the meadows and hills' and that 'electric trams, motor-buses and taxis have taken the place of the omnibus, hansom cab and phaeton'. In the same year, a special feature for the motorist in the *Halifax County Borough Directory* commended the Trinity Garage Co. Ltd of Skircoat Road as 'one of the best-equipped and most up-to-date garages in the provinces', with showrooms housing a 'range of approximately 50 new and used cars', a petrol filling station, and a suite of lock-up garages

Figure 6.23   Cross Fields. This photograph, taken in the mid-1920s from the balcony of Halifax Town Hall, shows one of the poorest and most densely populated areas of the town centre, with parallel streets of back-to-back houses dominating the foreground. In the background, with its tower and double-arched entrance, can be seen the new Ebenezer Primitive Methodist Church in St James's Road, built in 1922 as a replacement for its predecessor chapel of 1822. The church was connected to a large Sunday School at the rear of the building. Further along the road the Friendly and Trades Club, formerly the Oddfellows' Hall, which was opened in 1840 and demolished in 1963, is clearly visible. Cross Fields was the first slum area in the centre of the town to be cleared in 1926. It later provided the site for the first Halifax Bus Station. (Photograph: J. A. Hargreaves Collection)

available for rent at reasonable rates. Indeed, during the inter-war years a proliferation of petrol filling stations, car showrooms and garages appeared throughout the town.[85]

The evolution of Halifax from a cloth producing centre into a financial services centre was symbolised by the acquisition by the Halifax Permanent Building Society in 1919 of the elegant York Buildings in Commercial Street for their new head office. Built in 1904–05 for Alexander Scott, drapers and milliners, the premises were extensively re-furbished between 1919 and 1921. The adjacent Victoria Buildings were acquired and adapted between 1925 and 1927 to provide additional accommodation for the expanding society. They were subsequently retained as the headquarters of the amalgamated Halifax Permanent and Halifax Equitable Building Societies after 1927, releasing the former head office of the Halifax Equitable in Silver Street for use by Martins Bank Limited. The erection of the lofty domed Westminster Bank in 1927 at the northern end of Commercial Street further enhanced Halifax's developing financial services sector. Meanwhile, the Halifax Post Office on Commercial Street was enlarged to provide accommodation for the first local automated telephone exchange, which commenced operations on 18 June 1927. Moreover, in 1929, further land and buildings adjoining the Halifax Building Society head office in Alexandra Street were acquired and a major extension opened in 1931, designed by local architects Clement Williams and Sons to provide extra strong-room accommodation, a large hall with seating for 700 for the society's annual general meetings, several shops and a café.[86]

Former dilapidated cloth warehouses were also demolished for a new retail and office development at Bull Green as part of a municipal improvement scheme first mooted in 1904 to allow widening of the main arterial route from Halifax to the west. Clearance of the site finally began in 1924, and the development, planned by the Halifax borough engineer

Figure 6.24   Bull Green, Halifax, 1940. Former dilapidated cloth warehouses were demolished for a new retail and office development at Bull Green as part of a municipal improvement scheme first mooted in 1904 to allow widening of the main arterial route from Halifax to the west. Clearance of the site finally began in 1924 and the development, planned by the Halifax borough engineer A. C. Tipple and featuring a substantial block of buildings, was completed in 1932. They included five ground-floor shops, extensive upper-floor office accommodation, and an attractive terraced and landscaped frontage. The project had incurred costs of £32,000 for business compensation and land clearance and £26,000 for building and landscaping. (Photograph courtesy of S. Gee)

A. C. Tipple and featuring a substantial block of buildings, was completed in 1932. They included five ground-floor shops, extensive upper-floor office accommodation, and an attractive terraced and landscaped frontage. During the previous year, another new retail development was completed with the opening on 2 June 1931 of the imposing Prince's Arcade with accommodation for twenty-seven shops at the junction of the recently widened Woolshops and Market Street. Designed by the borough architect and constructed at a cost of £55,000, it aimed to attract shoppers to Halifax from other towns. These municipal retail developments were complemented by the establishment of branches of new chain stores in the town such as Boots at the junction of Corn Market with Old Market and Marks and Spencers and Woolworths on Southgate. Perhaps the most impressive development of this type was the demolition of a huddle of small shops in Old Market and the opening of a stylish new store by Burton's the tailors, with a billiard hall and skating rink on its upper floors. Finally, no fewer than seven public houses were reconstructed in and around the town centre, including the New Talbot, the Bull's Head, the Shay Hotel and the Three Pigeons.[87]

However, despite such obvious evidence of private and municipal rede-velopment, little had been done to improve the constricted northern access to the town. Elsewhere the historic Clare Hall had been acquired and demolished, but the scheme to build a new swimming pool on the site

SOUTHGATE AND TOWN HALL, HALIFAX. 3

Figure 6.25 Southgate and Princess Street, 1940. One of the most impressive retail improvements during the inter-war years involved the demolition of a huddle of old shops in Old Market and the opening of a stylish new menswear store by Montague Burton Ltd, with a billiard hall and skating rink on its upper floors. The store is visible in the right foreground, occupying numbers 2–4 Princess Street. Further along the street the sign for Pohlmann and Son can be seen projecting from the building. During the inter-war years this pianoforte supplier had also become a radio dealer. The increase in motor traffic is evident with the provision for street parking and the display of AA and RAC recommendation signs at the White Swan Hotel on the left. (Photograph courtesy of S. Gee) was postponed with the outbreak of war in 1939. There was also continuing criticism of the lack of effective town-planning regulations, with recent instances cited where works had been 'placed cheek by jowl with dwellings' and growing concern about atmospheric pollution which had left buildings 'overlaid and swathed in sooty vestments'. J. B. Priestley, visiting the town in 1933, pronounced Halifax 'more interesting than Leeds as a genuine West Riding product', but he noticed that 'factories and rows of houses seem to be sticking up and out at all mad angles'. He concluded that the town was 'a grim, craggy place'. Ted Hughes (1930–98), who was born and grew up in the 1930s at Mytholmroyd, later described neighbouring Halifax disparagingly as 'Black Halifax boiled in phosphorus'. Later visitors, Ella Pontefract and Marie Hartley, looking down on Halifax from Beacon Hill on a still winter's day in 1939, were appalled by the extent of the atmospheric pollution:

> you see the town in the deep valley below through a curtain of smoke, black smoke from the chimneys and white from the water-cooling towers mingling into a thick grey haze.

Old Halifax was still present, as well as signs of the new. Another twenty years were to elapse before this problem began to be addressed with discernible results.[88]

CHAPTER SEVEN

Halifax since 1945

When Halifax celebrated its centenary as a borough in March 1948, no fewer than eighteen Yorkshire mayors, watched by thousands of Halifax people, processed to Halifax Parish Church for a service of thanksgiving. In his address, the Archbishop of York, the Rt Revd Dr Cyril Garbett, reflected upon how municipal government in the past century had sought to deal with 'the terrible legacy of neglect' of the Industrial Revolution by:

> creating a town which was healthy as well as prosperous, in which the slums were gradually abolished, in which schools were built for its children and its youth, in which open spaces and parks offered recreation, in which museums and libraries were established, and in which provision was made for the aged and needy.

On the following day at a specially convened meeting of the council, the Mayor of Halifax, Alderman Charles Holdsworth, a road haulage contractor and property developer, recorded a message of greeting to his mayoral successor in the year 2048, expressing the hope that local government during the next century would 'secure a new lease of life'.[1] Neither the archbishop nor the mayor, however, could have foreseen that in little over a quarter of a century, at midnight on 31 March 1974, Halifax would have ceased to exist as a county borough, superseded by the Metropolitan Borough of Calderdale. The reorganisation of local government in 1974, however, effectively restored to Halifax its pre-industrial role as the centre of administration for its hinterland, since the boundaries of the new metropolitan borough were almost coterminous with those of the vast medieval parish of Halifax. This chapter will examine the impact of economic and social change on Halifax in the period since the Second World War and assess how successfully the local community responded to the problems of manufacturing decline and an emergent post-industrial society.

Population

Apart from spurts of growth in the late 1940s and 1980s, the population of Halifax and Calderdale, as shown in Table 7.1, continued to decline in the second half of the twentieth century, in contrast to national trends. The first post-war census revealed a slight rise in the population of the county borough from 98,115 in 1931 to 98,404 in 1951, a product of the post-war baby boom and an influx of refugees from the Nazi and Stalinist persecutions in central and eastern Europe. But Halifax had the lowest proportion of residents aged between fifteen and forty-four and the highest proportion of residents aged sixty-five and over of any county borough in the West Riding in 1951, and by 1961 the population of the county borough had declined by 0.23 per cent to 96,120. Moreover, this occurred despite a wave of immigration from the New Commonwealth, mainly of dispossessed Mirpuri migrant workers from Kashmir seeking night-shift employment in local textile mills in the 1950s. Immigrant numbers reached a peak of 3,360 in 1961–62 before the imposition of immigration restrictions by the Macmillan government's Commonwealth Immigrants Act. Thereafter, the pace of net outward migration by indigenous young adults quickened. As a result, between 1961 and 1971 the population of the county borough fell by a further 0.52 per cent to 91,272. By 1981, it had further declined to 87,488. By then, Halifax formed part of the metropolitan borough of Calderdale, which also experienced a decline in population of 1.4 per cent from 192,946 in 1971 to 190,330 by 1981, when the new metropolitan borough had a much higher proportion of elderly residents than other comparable local authorities.[2]

However, after decades of decline, the population of both Halifax and Calderdale began to grow after 1981, reaching 87,675 and 191,585 respectively by 1991. This was partly a result of the increasing appeal of Calderdale's countryside to commuters working in large conurbations on both sides of the Pennines. It was also a consequence of a growth in Calderdale's ethnic minority communities, which were concentrated in West Central Halifax in the St John's and Town Wards.[3] Calderdale's ethnic minorities, with their larger than average family sizes, grew from 6,500 in 1981 to 8,743 in 1991, rising from 3.5 per cent to 4.6 per cent of the total population: the majority had been born in the United Kingdom. Although this represented a lower proportion than in the neighbouring districts of Bradford (15.6 per cent), Kirklees (10.7 per cent) and Leeds (5.8 per cent), Calderdale's ethnic minority communities were generally more homogeneous than in some other parts of West Yorkshire, with fewer families in 1991 with Indian (5.9 per cent), Bangladeshi (3.7 per cent) and Afro-Caribbean (3.1 per cent) than Pakistani origins (71.8 per cent).[4] Population growth was not sustained after 1991, however, and by 1996 the population of Calderdale had fallen by about 1,200 or 0.6 per cent, reversing the growth experienced in the late 1980s. This was mainly a result of more people, particularly young adults, leaving the district than moving into it. Demographically, therefore, Halifax and Calderdale were not merely static communities after 1945. The ethnic composition had changed and the age profile was shifting towards the elderly.[5]

Table 7.1. *Population of Halifax, 1951–1991 and Calderdale, 1971–1991*

	Halifax	Calderdale
1951	98,404	
1961	96,120	
1971	91,272	192,946
1981	87,488	190,330
1991	87,675	191,585

Source: Census, 1961, 1971; *Census Digest* (Calderdale MBC, Halifax: 1983, 1993)

Employment and industry: the decline of manufacturing and the growth of the service sector

These demographic shifts may be largely explained by reference to the economic experience of Halifax in particular and Calderdale in general. Employment statistics for Calderdale for the period 1951–91, as shown in Table 7.2, reveal a decline in the number of jobs in the manufacturing sector and a growth of jobs in the service sector, particularly after 1971. Whereas manufacturing accounted for 70 per cent and the service industries for 24 per cent of employment in Calderdale in 1951, by 1991 manufacturing employed 38 per cent of the workforce and services 57 per cent.

Within the manufacturing sector the decline of those employed in textiles was most dramatic, falling from almost 36 per cent of the total workforce in 1951 to a mere 5 per cent of the total workforce in 1991. The associated clothing industry saw its workforce fall almost 75 per cent over the same period. Engineering jobs also fell by almost 25 per cent, but less dramatically than textiles. However, the decline of manufacturing was a more protracted process in Calderdale than in other parts of West Yorkshire on account of the area's continuing industrial diversification and its profusion of relatively small industrial units, so that by 1961 some 61 per cent of employees in Calderdale worked in establishments employing under 250, compared with a national average of 42 per cent. Consequently, while manufacturing employment declined steadily from 1951 and rapidly from 1971, it only fell below 50 per cent of total employment in Calderdale for the first time after 1981. Manufacturing therefore remained proportionately stronger in the local economy than in both the regional and national economy. In the mid-1960s 65 per cent of all employees in the area were engaged in manufacturing, compared with 43 per cent regionally and 38 per cent nationally; and by 1993, 34 per cent of employees in Calderdale worked in manufacturing industries compared to 24 per cent in West Yorkshire and 19 per cent in Great Britain.[6]

The number of job losses especially in manufacturing accelerated between 1966 and 1971, 1976 and 1981 and 1979 and 1983. Economic recession led to

Figure 7.1 Workers at Crossley Carpets holding their redundancy notices, February 1982. Carpets International announced the planned closure of virtually the whole of the Dean Clough complex with the loss of over 400 jobs on 28 January in a bid to turn losses into profits. The *Halifax Courier* described the announcement of the closure as 'one of the biggest disasters in Halifax's long industrial history'. By 1982 Carpets International had only one member of the Crossley family on its eleven-strong board. Jonathan Crossley was vice-chairman of Carpets International and chairman of Carpets International (Northern). The workforce at Dean Clough was reduced to around 300 and there was speculation about what use might be made of the eight large mills and other buildings on the site. (Photograph courtesy of the *Halifax Courier*)

the contraction and closure of many of Calderdale's traditional industries. Unemployment in Calderdale reached 11,500 (13 per cent) in 1983, and between 1979 and 1983 applications for benefits from those on low incomes increased by 42 per cent. Moreover, job losses had a disproportionate effect on male workers, so that by 1983 Calderdale had the highest proportion of working women in West Yorkshire (67 per cent).[7] It is true that, between 1983 and 1988 Halifax achieved a marked reduction in unemployment figures from 13 per cent to 7 per cent, better than anywhere else in the north. This was as a result of Ernest Hall's remarkable regeneration of Dean Clough and associated Business in the Community initiatives. The achievement resulted in the removal of Halifax from the government's urban aid list. However, its economy remained fragile and its unemployment figure remained above the national average, rising to 10.5 per cent following the recession of 1990–92.[8]

As manufacturing declined, jobs in the service sector increased. Indeed, from the mid-1980s the service sector became the dominant sector within the local economy. A study of Halifax and the Calder Valley in 1968 concluded that the service sector, with the notable exception of the Halifax Building Society, was considerably below national and regional averages and was devoted predominantly 'to the satisfaction of local needs'. The growth in services was slow in the 1950s and 1960s with an increase of 5 per cent between 1959 and 1966, only half the regional and national increase. However, between 1981 and 1991, employment in the service sector increased by an amount greater than that achieved in the 30 years prior to 1981. The service sector in Calderdale increased its share of employment from 44 per cent in 1981 to 57 per cent in 1991. This was mainly as a result of an increase in the number of women obtaining jobs especially in banking, finance and insurance, hotels, catering, personal services and recreation. Moreover, the number of employees in services continued to increase between 1991 and 1993 despite an overall fall in the number of employees in Calderdale.[9]

Table 7.2. *Employment in Calderdale, 1951–1991*

	1951	1961	1971	1981	1991
Agriculture	849	842	586	450	542*
Mining	546	512	87	64	
PRIMARY	1,395	1,354	673	514	542
Food/drink	5,010	5,124	5,709	7,329	4,279
Chemicals	798	767	557	862	929
Metal manufacturing	793	1,637	995	1,088	*
Engineering	11,495	11,421	10,885	9,200	8,640
Vehicles	1,628	487	677	1,308	1,036
Metal goods	4,184	3,586	3,617	3,055	1,400
Textiles	34,519	30,179	19,142	7,856	3,907
Leather	967	565	422	107	*
Clothing	5,202	4,341	2,999	2,159	1,319
Bricks/pottery	1,551	1,410	1,210	1,449	1,458
Timber/furniture	1,215	1,532	1,673	2,121	2,081
Paper/printing	750	978	1,533	1,250	1,353
Other manufacturing	361	572	732	800	1,393
MANUFACTURING	68,473	62,599	50,151	38,584	28,550
CONSTRUCTION	3,556	3,723	2,680	2,420	2,599
Gas/electricity/water	906	1,225	1,033	1,098	532
Transport/communication	3,883	2,892	2,744	2,466	2,648
Distribution	6,865	6,840	4,944	6,808	8,388
Financial services	735	1,093	1,970	4,428	8,572
Professional services	5,037	5,995	8,289	9,441	12,337
Miscellaneous services	3,514	4,358	4,779	4,569	6,103
Public administration	2,637	2,454	3,442	3,337	4,295
SERVICES	23,577	24,857	27,201	32,147	42,875
TOTAL	97,001	92,533	80,705	73,665	74,566

* categories with low numbers combined or disregarded

Sources: Ministry of Labour Census, 1951, 1961; Department of Employment Census, 1971–1991; Calderdale Report, 1994–5, p. 13.

The decline of manufacturing in West Yorkshire after 1945 has been blamed on the failure of government economic policies. Professor Arthur Marwick, writing in 1982, maintained that after 1945 there was 'no real recovery' for the woollen industry and 'West Yorkshire was on the way to becoming more a museum than a hive of industry' since it was there:

that the post-war policies of the Labour Government, aimed at the distribution of industry, were at their most unsuccessful. New industries were excluded, and even established textile firms were encouraged to expand in areas whose need was felt to be greater, for example the North-East.[10]

One major Halifax textile company certainly re-located to the North East during the immediate post-war period. In September 1945 Patons and Baldwins, the Halifax woollen and worsted yarn spinners founded in 1785, which at its peak had employed a workforce of 3,000, announced the closure of its Clark Bridge Mills and its intention to move to a green field site near Darlington in 1947. Moreover, in a later industrial survey undertaken for the Yorkshire and Humberside Economic Planning Council and Board in 1967, many firms commented on the locational disadvantages of Halifax, complaining of unfavourable treatment compared with development areas, where government inducements were provided for industry. There were also difficulties in obtaining conveniently situated land suitable for development and the negative impact of the urban environment on the recruitment of executives. Consequently, during the period 1953–67 more firms transferred production out of the area than into the area. Other explanations of manufacturing decline in textiles have focused upon changes of fashion, the introduction of a range of new synthetic fibres from the 1950s such as nylon and rayon and also on increasing foreign competition, particularly from Asia and the Pacific Rim where labour costs were cheaper. Nevertheless, the 1967 survey confirmed the continuing importance of manufacturing industries and the dominance of textiles in particular in Halifax and the Calder Valley, with woollens and worsteds still the largest component, with carpets the fastest growing element, and with clothing embracing a wide range of garments from overalls and ladies' coats to suits and dresses.[11]

Indeed, one outstanding local textile firm, John Holdsworth and Co. Ltd, became a world leader in its field by the 1990s, providing a remarkable example of the successful modernisation of a family business spanning 175 years and six generations.[12] Holdsworths doubled their sales and profits between 1946 and 1952 with the post-war demand for moquette for railway carriages, buses and ships and the large orders for navy blue and khaki worsted yarns which resulted from the outbreak of the Korean War in 1950. This enabled new worsted spinning plant to be installed and soon exports amounted to 10 per cent of turnover. However, in the decade following the collapse of world markets in 1952 the firm became more reliant on the domestic market, and its trading situation deteriorated to such an extent that by 1963 sales had almost halved. The firm had sustained heavy losses as a result of increasing competition from overseas and from new synthetic fibres, such as dralon. Nevertheless, the firm managed to survive by stringent cost control, streamlining its workforce, investing in new machinery and specialising in weaving moquette for the commercial transport rather than the domestic upholstery market. Between 1969 and 1979 the company increased its exports as a percentage of turnover from 10 per cent to 35 per cent. The acquisition of new Gusken shuttle-less rapier looms in 1979–80, the introduction of computer-aided design technology, the phased refurbishment of Shaw Lodge Mills, the development of new overseas markets in North America, Australasia, South Africa, the Middle and Far East and the continued exploitation of the European market during the 1980s enabled the firm to become a market leader, increasing its turnover from £3 million in 1979 to over £10 million by 1990. During the subsequent world recession, turnover dropped by 1992 to £7.8 million, but the astute acquisition of the rival Irish business of Max Birr Ltd in December 1991 and the bus and coach division of the neighbouring West Yorkshire firm of Firth Fabrics Ltd, enabled turnover to reach £14.5 million by the end of 1994. Capital reinvestment recommenced through the acquisition of twelve computerised looms with piletronic jacquards, and in 1998 work began on

Figure 7.2   The last workers at the Elizabeth Shed with the final roll of carpet to leave the empty warehouse at Dean Clough in January 1987. For many of the employees it marked the end of more than a generation working for John Crossley and Sons Ltd and Carpets International Ltd. The Elizabeth Shed, opened in Shroggs Road in 1963, had been one of the most recent extensions to the vast Dean Clough complex, where carpet manufacture had taken place since 1803. (Photograph courtesy of the *Halifax Courier*)

the construction of a new purpose-built weaving factory on a site adjacent to the mill.[13]

Other textile firms, however, ultimately fared less well. By investing in new technology, pruning its workforce, paying competitive wage rates and maintaining its reputation for high quality and prompt delivery, John Crossley and Sons remained profitable into the early 1970s. Indeed, in 1961 the new Elizabeth Shed was built on largely reclaimed land at Shroggs Road and was extended in 1968. However, in 1969 Crossleys merged with Carpet Trade Holdings and the Carpet Trades Manufacturing Co. of Kidderminster to form Carpets International, and in 1970, on the retirement of Patrick Crossley, the headquarters of the group moved to Kidderminster. By 1975 when a new carpet printing plant was installed at Elizabeth Shed the number of employees had fallen below 2,000, and by 1977 the workforce numbered 1,600. After the closure of the jute spinning and Duravell departments and the transfer of planning, cutting and dispatching to Northallerton and Wilton weaving to Kidderminster, at least one-third of the vast industrial complex stood idle. In January 1982 the decision was taken to close the entire carpet factory, sending shock waves throughout the local community: the Elizabeth Shed produced its last roll of carpet in 1987. Moreover, Calderdale's other established carpet manufacturing firm, Firth Carpets of Bailiff Bridge, also suffered major job losses during the 1979–82 recession.[14]

Nevertheless, despite the systematic destruction of their redundant machinery at Dean Clough by Carpets International in order to prevent its acquisition by potential competitors, the carpet industry did not disappear completely from the town. Avena Carpets, started by seven former employees of Crossleys in January 1976 following the closure of the figured Wilton department at Dean Clough, returned to Haley Hill in 1983, after trading initially from Denholme. It quickly established a reputation for weaving fine Brussels Wilton carpets and secured prestigious contracts for carpeting the throne room at Windsor Castle and the guest room of the White House in Washington. By 1988 the firm's workforce had grown to thirty. Other firms that were founded by former Crossley employees and executives, including members of the Crossley family, were Hebble Rugs, founded by Jonathan Crossley in May 1982 at Bowling Dyke, which subsequently moved to premises in Lewis Street; Halifax Carpets, established by Charles Crossley at Black Dyke Mills, Queensbury; and Silvarea Textiles Ltd, operating from the new Dean Clough Business Park.[15]

By the late 1990s, however, the extent of the decline of textiles within the local economy was starkly apparent. Willey and Pearson closed their Scarborough Mills in Haugh Shaw Road in 1994 and the site was subsequently acquired by Tesco for their second Halifax supermarket. By 1998 Joseph Horsfall and Sons Ltd at Clarence Mill was the sole surviving worsted spinning mill in Calderdale with an annual turnover of just under one million pounds and a workforce of twenty-five. Furthermore, John

Figure 7.3 Joseph Horsfall and Sons, Clarence Mill, Halifax, 1998. The sole remaining worsted spinning firm in Halifax by 1998 had been founded before 1866, moving to Clarence Mill in Pellon Lane in 1894. Three generations of Horsfalls ran the company until the Butlers who had married into the family took over. When the current managing director, Brian Butler, photographed with his cousin Michael Butler, production director, entered the business in the 1950s there were fifty-one spinning firms in the district. The firm's survival has depended upon its flexibility, its ability to meet changing demands and its willingness to supply small orders. In 1998, Brian Butler told the *Halifax Courier*: 'We are a family run firm. Our livelihood depends on Halifax and we have a vested interest in staying in Halifax and employing in Halifax'. (Photograph courtesy of the *Halifax Courier*)

Holdsworth and Co., John Horsfall at West Vale, and Cawthra Brothers at Halifax remained the sole surviving weaving firms.[16]

Engineering, the second largest manufacturing sector in Halifax in 1945, displayed growth rates below regional and national averages during the period up to 1967. Domestic electrical equipment and small tools expanded substantially, but machine tools, the largest group within the sector, increased its employment only marginally. Moreover, increases were offset by the transfer of production to other areas both within and beyond Calderdale. In 1966, for example, the Halifax Rack and Screw Cutting Co. Ltd moved to a new purpose-built factory in Brighouse and in 1996 the Carrington Wire Division of SG Industries moved from Pellon Lane to a more convenient site at the Lowfield Business Park in Elland, while Churchill Redman transferred production to Blaydon in 1971 and Pegler Hattersley to Doncaster in 1987. Moreover, the increasing application from the mid 1960s of computer-aided design and computer-directed machinery led to a reduction of employment opportunities. There was also an increasing number of amalgamations and closures. The acquisition of Asquiths by Staveley Industries and of Butlers by the Elliott Machine Tool Co. was followed by the closure of Lumbys. Drakes at Ovenden closed in 1968 as a result of the changeover from coal to natural gas. Stirks, which had been taken over by A. Wickman of Coventry, was closed in 1980; Farrar Engineering in 1985; and the Automatic Standard Screw Co. in 1993 following the contraction of its UK market.

Some local engineering firms, however, did achieve remarkable success in exports, becoming world leaders in their fields. James H. Heal and Co. Ltd, manufacturers of textile testing equipment, and Crosrol Ltd, manufacturers of carding machinery, both received the Queen's Award for Export in 1995, Crosrol for the fifth time. Crosrol, founded by André Varga (1893–1998), the Hungarian commercial director of a Belgian firm of card makers who had settled in England following the Nazi invasion of Belgium in 1940, exported 99 per cent of the machinery it made in 1995. By 1996, another local firm, Crosslee, had become Europe's largest tumble dryer manufacturer, employing a workforce of nearly 600. Formed as a result of a bold and enterprising management buyout after Philips had announced the closure of their Hipperholme factory in 1986, the firm was a successor of the Ajax Machine Tool Co. which had developed the celebrated Ada washing machine in 1944 and had achieved annual sales of 36,000 in the 1950s.[17]

The confectionery industry, the third largest manufacturing component in Halifax in 1945, increased its employment significantly by the mid-1960s, but subsequently contracted as a result of a series of amalgamations and closures. The biscuit manufacturing firm Meredith and Drew, which had moved to a disused foundry in Ovenden from the East End of London following the Blitz, expanded rapidly in Halifax during the 1950s and 1960s before amalgamating with United Biscuits in December 1966. Unfortunately, the cost of modernising the Ovenden site resulted in the decision to close the Halifax KP Foods Plant at Ovenden in 1988, making 1,000 workers redundant. In 1969 the leading local toffee and chocolate manufacturers, Mackintosh's, merged with Rowntree of York and in 1986 closed their Queen's Road factory with the loss of 380 jobs. However, the merger of Rowntree Mackintosh with Nestlé UK in 1991, when the firm had 2,500 employees in Halifax, was followed by a major redevelopment of the Albion Mills site, demonstrating a commitment to the continued production of key lines in Halifax.[18] By contrast, the local brewing industry after similar post-war expansion, had completely collapsed by the end of the century. Thomas Ramsden's Stone Trough Brewery, which reached the peak of its prosperity in 1954, was closed in 1967 following its amalgamation with the Leeds-based Joshua Tetley in 1964. In 1968 brewing ceased at Richard Whitaker's Corporation Street Brewery following its merger with Samuel Whitbread, and in 1996 Scottish Newcastle announced the closure of Samuel Websters Fountain Head Brewery with the loss of 182 jobs, after 160 years of operation in the Wheatley Valley.[19]

As noted, however, the decline of manufacturing was offset by the growing strength of the services sector. The Halifax Building Society entered its centenary year in 1952 with total assets of £177,212,000 of which £136,759,000 represented loans on mortgage. In half a century its total assets had multiplied by more than a hundred-fold and its financial strength was unchallengeable. During the second half of the twentieth century it made a major contribution to the local economy. By 1994, with 3,134 employees, it was by far the largest private employer in Calderdale, ahead

Figure 7.4 The new administrative headquarters of the Halifax Building Society under construction, June 1972. The new building was designed by the Building Design Partnership and constructed by John Laing Construction Ltd to replace the former head office in Commercial Street, which had been in use since 1921. Work began on the site of the former Ramsden's Stone Trough Brewery in 1969 and the society moved into the new premises in 1973. (Photograph courtesy of Halifax plc)

of Nestlé UK Ltd with 1,400 and Marshalls plc with 961 employees. In 1967 a new computer centre was built on the site of Trinity Road Baptist Church, and the adjacent premises of the former Stone Trough Brewery were acquired for redevelopment as a new head office, opened in 1972 by HM the Queen. In 1986 John Spalding, chief executive of the Halifax Building Society, reaffirmed the society's commitment to Halifax and Calderdale. He argued that with modern telecommunications there was no reason other than tradition for companies to have their headquarters in London. In 1989 a £25 million computerised data centre was opened at Wakefield Road, Copley, employing 600 staff.

Figure 7.5   HM Queen Elizabeth II opens the new administrative headquarters of the Halifax Building Society on 13 November 1974. The Queen, making her first visit to the town since 1949, is photographed chatting to the Earl of Halifax, the patron of the Halifax Building Society. Also pictured, from left to right, are the chairman of the Mayor of Calderdale, the chairman of the Halifax Building Society, Mr Ian Maclean and Mrs Maclean, with some of the thousands of local spectators who witnessed the visit in the background. She was shown the society's first mortgage deed, dated 1853, and the society's computer centre, where a teleprocessing network connects the society's 280 branches directly to the main computer. The building was designed by the Building Design Partnership and constructed by John Laing Construction Ltd. (Photograph courtesy of Halifax plc)

By the early 1990s with building society membership nationally embracing 70 per cent of the population, the potential for future society growth was becoming limited. In November 1994, the Halifax Building Society with 706 branches, assets of £67 billion and profits of £866 million announced its intention to merge with the Leeds Permanent Building Society, with 455 branches, assets of £19.5 billion and profits of £186 million, and subsequently to convert to a public company. The combined assets of the two societies would total £86.5 billion with profits of £1.05 billion and a network of 1,161 branches, some 400 of which overlapped. The merger was approved by 97 per cent of Halifax members and 95 per cent of Leeds members on 22 May 1995 and the conversion by 97 per cent of borrowers and investors of the amalgamated society on 24 February 1997. It was followed by the biggest stock market flotation in history, 7.6 million people sharing no less than £18 billion. The merger and the change of status from a mutual society to that of a public company resulted in certain operations such as financial services and share dealing being headquartered in Leeds, and in 1998 the treasury department moved from Halifax to London. Nevertheless, the new Halifax plc group head office remained at Halifax with information systems and general insurance at Copley. Indeed, the employment base of the Halifax in Calderdale increased to 4,283 in 1998. Moreover, the bonus payments to local investors and employees of the Halifax provided an estimated £25 million windfall for local businesses, with travel agents especially reporting an upturn in holiday bookings.[20]

The Halifax was not the only corporate financial institution to be based in Halifax during the second half of the twentieth century. The decision to site the Bradford Pennine Insurance Group headquarters at North Park in Halifax, following the merger of the Bradford and Pennine insurance companies in 1964, was taken because land and property were competitively priced in Halifax and living costs low. Following a series of mergers with Phoenix Assurance in 1971, Sun Alliance in 1984 and Royal Assurance in 1996, the Royal and Sun Alliance employed a workforce of 750 at the Dean Clough Business Park by 1998. In addition, in 1997 the neighbouring Hebble Brook Business Park at Mixenden became the headquarters of three companies within the Provident Financial Group, namely Provident Insurance, Colonnade Insurance Brokers and Hebble Insurance Management Services. Provident Insurance, employing 280 staff in Calderdale in 1998, had

Figure 7.6   The approval of the merger between the Halifax and Leeds Permanent Building Societies, 22 May 1995. Roger Boyes, chief executive of the Leeds Permanent Building Society, and Mike Blackburn, chief executive of the Halifax Building Society, shake hands outside the Victoria Theatre, Halifax, following the approval by members of both societies for the merger of the two societies. (Photograph courtesy of Halifax plc)

Figure 7.7   Board members of the Halifax Building Society pose for photographs outside the Old Cock Inn, Halifax, immediately after the conversion of the Halifax Building Society to Halifax plc on 16 July 1997. The Halifax Permanent Building Society had been founded in 1853 following a meeting in the oak room of the hotel in December 1852. (Photograph courtesy of Halifax plc) commenced trading as Halifax Insurance in a terraced house in Prescott Street in 1966, moving to the redundant Holy Trinity Church in 1987, and acquiring other buildings around Blackwall in 1989 and 1992. Between 1989 and 1994 the number of its policy holders increased from 160,000 to 850,000, and the firm, which had initially focused on motor cycle insurance, became a major specialist provider of motor insurance for lady drivers. Acquired by the Bradford-based Provident Financial Group in 1978, it had taken the name of the parent group by agreement with the Halifax Building Society after obtaining a high court injunction against the use of its original trading name by the building society giant when the latter entered the motor insurance business in 1993. Colonnade, originally based in Bradford, expanded rapidly in the 1980s and 1990s. By 1998 it had 320,000 policy holders, 720 employees, a nationwide network of branches and a large telephone call-centre at Mixenden, where Hebble Insurance Management Services,

Figure 7.8   Halifax Insurance Co., Holy Trinity Church, Harrison Road, Halifax, 1988. This former Georgian church was designed by Leeds architect, Thomas Johnson, for the Vicar of Halifax, the Revd Dr Henry William Coulthurst in 1798, to provide additional church accommodation as the population of the town expanded westwards. It was declared redundant in 1978, restored with assistance from English Heritage, and re-occupied in 1987 by the Halifax Insurance Co., providing attractive open-plan office accommodation for ninety-five employees. (Photograph courtesy of Ian Beesley)

the centralised management service company for the group, accounted for a further 140 employees.[21]

One of the fastest growing corporate finance groups in Halifax in the late 1990s was Gartland, Whalley and Barker. This company which specialised in taking stakes in industrial groups, nurturing them and then floating them off on the stock market, was founded in 1989 by Tony Gartland, former chairman of the FKI Babcock group, which he had built up from a small privately owned company. The *Financial Times* described him as a Yorkshire entrepreneurial phenomenon with 'a well-conceived strategy'. By 1998, Gartland, Whalley and Barker employed some twenty-four staff at Belle Vue, Sir Francis Crossley's former residence in Hopwood Lane, renamed by the company Crossley House. In 1996–7 Gartland, Whalley and Barker's profits rose 63 per cent with eight astute new acquisitions in Britain and one in America. By 1998 Gartland's stake in Gartland, Whalley and Barker, was valued at £59.4 million, which with other assets in excess of £5 million made him one of the wealthiest businessmen in Yorkshire, enabling him to play a prominent role in the development of the Calderdale Community Foundation, a locally managed charitable endowment fund, launched in 1993.[22]

The growth of the service sector in Calderdale in the 1980s was also stimulated by the development of tourism, which was accelerated by the devastating impact of the 1979–82 recession on the manufacturing sector. It has been estimated that in 1982 Calderdale venues accounted for around 10 per cent of total tourist activity in West Yorkshire, representing around a quarter of a million visits, three-quarters of a million overnight stays and an estimated expenditure of £7.5 million. While the major West Yorkshire attractions with over 100,000 visitors a year, such as the Brontë Parsonage and the Keighley and Worth Valley Railway, were situated outside Calderdale, both Shibden Hall and Bankfield Museum were attracting over 50,000 visitors a year by 1982. The Civic Trust report in 1984 concluded that 'with its combination of unique landscape and largely unspoiled towns and villages steeped in history' and its proximity to major motorway routes and airport connections, Calderdale had environmental assets no less marketable to tourists 'than the products of its formerly bustling factories'. Calderdale, however, with only 2,500 bed spaces, nearly 70 per cent of which were in the self-catering sector, had an acute shortage of quality serviced overnight accommodation and lacked a single major attraction to entice visitors to Calderdale until the opening of the Eureka interactive children's museum in 1992. However, visits to Calderdale Tourist Information Centres showed a steady growth during the 1980s, although the number of visitors to the Tourist Information Centre at the Halifax Piece Hall fluctuated in contrast to the rising spiral of visitors to Hebden Bridge, stimulated by the proximity of Hardcastle Craggs. Nevertheless, by 1998 day-trippers were spending annually an estimated £12 million in Halifax and overnight visitors £3 million.[23]

Retailing remained a vital element within the local economy throughout the second half of the twentieth century. Halifax accounted for over 60 per cent of Calderdale's retail turnover in 1971. Brighouse, the next largest retail centre in Calderdale, accounted for only 13 per cent. This contrast emphasised the continuing role of Halifax as a major retail centre for its periphery. Moreover, the overall retail space in Halifax increased by over 10 per cent between 1988 and 1998, when a survey revealed that half the retail floor space in Calderdale was concentrated in Halifax town centre. However, the development of the retail sector throughout the period was fraught with controversy. Plans for a major new shopping development in Halifax were first mooted in 1951, but over thirty years elapsed before the successful Woolshops centre finally opened in 1983, with provision for thirty-three shops, including premises for Woolworths, Boots, Sainsburys, W. H. Smith and Mothercare.[24] The original scheme had envisaged massive blocks of flats, play areas, a bowling green, health centre, dance hall and parking for 3,750 cars. Even as late as 1977 a large covered Arndale Centre modelled on centres in Bradford and Manchester was being planned. However, members of the Halifax Civic Trust, led by their chairman, the carpet manufacturer Charles Crossley, were concerned at the impact of the scheme on listed buildings in the town centre. They forced the issue to a public inquiry and commissioned a firm of architects to produce plans for an alternative development on a smaller scale. After the inquiry the government rejected the £30 million Arndale Scheme. This was hailed by the *Halifax Courier* as a 'major victory for the conservation movement'. The revised scheme proved so successful that in 1998 approval was given for an expansion of the development, though this dealt the final blow to an imaginative scheme for the re-development of Westgate, which had experienced difficulties in attracting a major anchor store. Plans were also revealed for a new retail development of six stores, a pub-diner and multi-screen cinema complex on the northern edge of the town at Broadway.[25]

By the 1990s, however, there were growing concerns about the impact of out-of-town shopping centres and supermarkets on town centre shopping. An increasing number of town centre retail outlets were being converted into pubs, clubs, wine bars and charity shops. The number of empty shops in Halifax rose from 7 per cent in 1988 to 11 per cent in 1998, although this was still below the national average of 14 per cent. Moreover, council income from the Piece Hall, where there were also untenanted shops and market stalls, declined sharply from £278,542 in 1993–4 to £140,934 in 1997–8. Consequently, the promotion of Halifax as a retail centre became a major priority in the regeneration of the town and led to the establishment of a Halifax Town Centre Forum and the appointment of a town centre manager in February 1996. This initiative was funded principally by the private sector with the aim of making Halifax Town Centre an attractive, lively and successful shopping venue. A new shopping guide, published in

1998, listed over 300 shops in the town centre, including 33 fashion stores, sixteen jewellers, eleven shoe shops, ten furniture stores, six fishmongers, six bookshops, five florists, four supermarkets, two covered markets and two department stores. Between 1996 and 1999 the number of empty shops in the town centre was reduced to eight.[26]

The economic restructuring and regeneration of Halifax and Calderdale in the 1980s owed much to two other inter-related factors. The first was the drive and vision of Ernest Hall, an accomplished concert pianist, industrial entrepreneur and property developer, who transformed Dean Clough from a redundant carpet mill into a major centre for business, education and the arts. Born into a working-class family in Bolton, Hall had developed an early passion for music, but after a promising education at the Royal Manchester College of Music he had embarked upon a successful career in textiles. He came to live in Calderdale and saw the potential of Dean Clough in 1983 for realising his vision, inspired by the Dartington ethic, of 'a practical utopia' by creating a balanced environment in which

Figure 7.9   The official inauguration of the Calderdale Partnership on 6 February 1987. Calderdale was selected by Business in the Community from a short-list of several northern towns to participate in a pioneer partnership scheme between the private and public sectors. HRH the Prince of Wales travelled to Calderdale to launch the partnership at Dean Clough. The meeting was also attended by the Mayor of Calderdale, local councillors, members of Business in the Community's governing council, participants in similar schemes in the USA, and local business and community leaders. (Photograph courtesy of Sir Ernest Hall)

both commerce and culture could interact and thrive. By 1995, Dean Clough provided accommodation for some 200 companies and organisations employing around 3,000 people, together with an enterprise campus providing training for both college students and company employees, a contemporary art gallery, a language laboratory, the Henry Moore Sculpture Trust Studio, two theatre companies, and the first regional centre of the Royal Society for the Encouragement of the Arts, Manufactures and Commerce. Hall's commitment to the arts both regionally and nationally led to honours, including an OBE in 1986 and a knighthood in 1993 and his appointment as Deputy Lieutenant of West Yorkshire and Chancellor of the University of Huddersfield. The success achieved by Hall at Dean Clough impressed visitors, including the then Prime Minister, Margaret Thatcher, who described it in 1987 'as a showcase of small industrialised units, and an example of what can be achieved through innovation and enterprise'.[27]

The second factor was the influence of Business in the Community, an initiative spearheaded by its president, HRH the Prince of Wales, which selected Calderdale as the pilot for an innovatory partnership scheme in 1986, partly on account of Hall's remarkable success and partly because Calderdale, with unemployment below the national average, failed to qualify for either government or European Community assistance. The scheme was Business in the Community's most ambitious project since its foundation by a small group of businessmen in the wake of the inner city disturbances of 1981 in Brixton and Toxteth. When HRH the Prince of Wales personally launched the 'demonstration partnership' on 9 December 1986, designed to regenerate the entire 140-square mile metropolitan district of Calderdale, he expressed the hope that it would become the model for other such schemes in other regions suffering from industrial decline. Calderdale was similar in size to the North American town of Lowell, near Boston, Massachusetts, which had provided the inspiration for the project. The partnership received all-party support from Calderdale Metropolitan Borough Council and the enthusiastic backing of Calderdale's newly appointed chief executive, Michael Ellison, a native of the town who had lived as a child in the socially deprived St John's Ward.[28]

Business in the Community's project team under Richard Wade and Paul Greetham began sponsoring co-operative links between the community, its local politicians and businessmen, and generated plans for a variety of new businesses and attractions, including an interactive children's museum, Eureka, funded by grants from central government, the Clore and Vivien Duffield Foundations, business sponsorship and Calderdale Council. Eureka, the first museum of its kind in the UK, which opened in July 1992 on a previously derelict site next to the railway station, rapidly achieved phenomenal success, attracting its millionth visitor in March 1995, well ahead of target and scooping a host of awards for its imaginative approach to active learning and child development. Business in the Com-

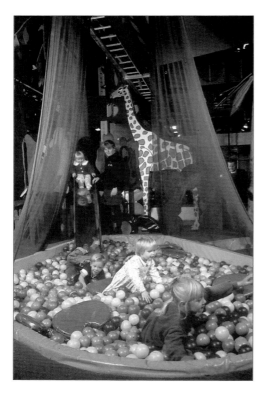

Figure 7.10   The Eureka Museum for Children, Halifax, was opened in July 1992 by HRH the Prince of Wales. It was funded by the Clore and Vivien Duffield Foundations, business sponsorship, government grants and Calderdale Metropolitan Borough Council. It was designed to teach children about themselves and the world around them, using a hands-on, fun approach to learning and development. By August 1997, two million visitors had explored the innovative new museum, with its 400 or more interactive activities, games and challenges. By 1999, the museum had scooped eighteen prestigious awards, including the English Tourist Board Visitor Attraction of the Year award in 1993. (Photograph courtesy of Eureka)

munity also encouraged the development of industrial, retail, leisure and tourist facilities, improved transport links, and environmental improvement programmes. The support of the Prince of Wales was undoubtedly a key factor in the success of the project. Everywhere he went he extolled the virtues of the Calderdale experiment in speeches to business leaders, city financiers and American architects in Pittsburgh, and he made a series of personal visits to Calderdale to monitor the progress of the partnership.[29]

Halifax and Calderdale therefore successfully made the turbulent transition from a predominantly manufacturing economy to an economy increasingly dependent upon services during the second half of the twentieth century, just as previously Halifax had evolved from economic dependence on subsistence agriculture into a thriving commercial and industrial centre. Moreover, this was achieved without a complete abandonment of Calderdale's manufacturing inheritance. Carpet and moquette weaving, precision engineering and confectionery production ensured a continuation of economic diversification within the local economy. The remarkable growth of the service sector in Halifax in the last quarter of the twentieth century was facilitated by a telecommunications revolution, which finally neutralised some of the constraints which geographical factors had imposed upon Halifax's economic and urban development at the beginning of the twentieth century. Indeed, during the late twentieth century there was also a growing realisation that Halifax's remote and rugged Pennine location, which was proving increasingly attractive to both commuters and tourists, had considerable potential for further economic development. This was accompanied by an increasing recognition that economic restructuring depended not merely on market forces but upon a partnership for renewal between private investment and public authorities. Indeed, Halifax was a pioneer in pursuing this form of partnership, which was itself largely learned in the early Thatcher years from the United States. This unusual combination of factors was to provide the springboard from which Halifax would launch itself with confidence into the twenty-first century.

Local government

The period after 1945 witnessed a considerable increase in the role of central government and the public services. To what extent were the county and metropolitan boroughs of Halifax and Calderdale affected by these changes, and how did their roles within the local community change in the second half of the twentieth century?

As a county borough, Halifax after 1945 still retained considerable local responsibilities for education, health, housing, highways, markets, public transport, fire and civil defence. Moreover, post-war requirements led to the development of responsibilities for town planning and social services, in dedicated departments by 1965 and 1971. Borough architects, town planners and engineers worked in close partnership on an increasing variety of related schemes. These included the design and planning of new housing estates, high-rise flats, offices, shops and schools; a new swimming pool on Huddersfield Road opened in 1966; a new central cleansing and transport depot on Battinson Road in 1968; a new fire station at King Cross opened in 1970; a multi-storey car park on Cow Green opened in 1971; and a multi-million pound inner relief road opened in 1973. The new social services department established as a result of the Local Authority Social Services Act 1970 aimed to provide a co-ordinated approach to social work, taking over the functions of the welfare services committee and children's committee and some of the functions of the health committee. The growth of the proportion of elderly people within the local community, a rising divorce rate and changing patterns of family life generated an increasing range of problems for the new department in the last three decades of the twentieth century.[30]

However, local authorities like Halifax also lost some of their roles and also their sources of revenue with the creation of nationalised public utility companies for electricity, gas and water between 1949 and 1961. And some duties were transferred to other public authorities like the Halifax Area Hospitals Management Committee in 1948 and the West Yorkshire Police Authority in 1968. Indeed, the scope and resourcing of local administration became a matter of considerable debate during this period, leading to the Redcliffe-Maud inquiry into the financing of local government in 1968 and local government reorganisation in 1974. Redcliffe-Maud's inquiry ranked Halifax the poorest of seventy-nine English local authorities with a rateable value of only £29.60 per head of population, underlining the relatively limited local resources available to fund services. The case for merging Halifax into a larger unit of local government, covering a wider geographical area, was therefore strong. However, after local government reorganisation, Calderdale was the fifth smallest of the thirty-six new metropolitan districts and the smallest metropolitan borough in West Yorkshire. It commanded only 7.6 per cent of the rateable value of the West Yorkshire Metropolitan County although it comprised 17.6 per cent of the county's land area. Indeed, the West Riding County Council, in its observations on the government White Paper which proposed to modify the Redcliffe-Maud proposals by placing the responsibility for the administration of education

Figure 7.11   Re-development of Cow Green and Broad Street, 1970. This aerial photograph appeared in the *Halifax Courier* with the caption: 'Halifax steadily growing taller'. New high rise flats are visible on the extreme right, while a site for the construction of another tower block is being cleared at the top left of the photograph alongside the new multi-storey car park on Cow Green opened in 1971. Crown House, the first high rise office block to be built in Halifax and the Broad Street retail development, commenced in 1968 at a cost of £250,000, is nearing completion, together with the modification of the adjacent road network. The Broadway supermarket is visible in the left foreground sandwiched between the National Provincial and the Yorkshire banks. The new bus station at Cross Fields occupies a former slum clearance site behind the Odeon cinema. (Photograph courtesy of the *Halifax Courier*)

Figure 7.12   Burdock Way, 1973. The increase in road traffic created growing pressure after 1945 for schemes to relieve town-centre congestion. In 1967 the Ministry of Transport approved the construction of a ring road around the town centre, and in 1970 confirmation of a government grant for 75 per cent of the cost of the project was received. The road network incorporating a massive concrete flyover was completed within two years at a cost of £4.5 million and opened in April 1973. It was named after Alderman John Burdock, a long-serving member of the Halifax County Borough Council. (Photograph courtesy of the *Halifax Courier*)

at district rather than county level, insisted that of the metropolitan districts in West Yorkshire only Leeds and Bradford would have sufficient resources to provide an adequate education service.[31]

Moreover, the abolition of the West Yorkshire Metropolitan County Council in 1986 and the creation of single tier local authorities further depressed Calderdale's financial situation. Calderdale had benefited from the redistributive effect of the provision by the metropolitan county of some services such as road gritting and snow clearing, but now more responsibilities were devolved upon district councils. On the other hand, Conservative government policies in the 1980s and 1990s resulted in the loss by district authorities like Calderdale of some responsibilities because of the sale of council houses, schools opting out of local education authority control, the autonomy of further education colleges, the implementation of care in the community schemes, and the privatisation of some council services: for example, in 1994 Calderdale Council lost its refuse collection contract to an outside contractor. There were also major changes in the way local government was financed, with the changeover in 1990 from rates to the controversial community charge and its subsequent replacement by the council tax in 1993, and the still tighter control of local government spending by central government through charge capping from April 1990, when Calderdale Council was obliged to cut its agreed budget from £132 to £125 million. In spite of these reorganisations and rigorous financial controls, first Halifax and then Calderdale continued to provide a range of services to the community.[32]

Education, in particular, required major resourcing after 1945 to implement the provisions of the 1944 Butler Act, and to accommodate the post-war population bulge and the raising of the school leaving age to fifteen in 1944 and sixteen in 1973. School buildings, which had been neglected in Halifax during the inter-war years, had to be modernised and extended. Although greater progress was made after 1945 than in the preceding period, in some years there were severe constraints on expenditure, as in 1956 when the education budget estimate was cut by £80,000 even though the Ministry of Education identified Halifax as being the fourth most under-staffed education authority in the country. The first of a dozen new primary schools built between 1949 and 1970 was opened in 1949 to serve the new Cousin Lane housing estate at Ovenden. Two new secondary schools were also opened in 1952 on green field sites at Illingworth and Exley, the J. H. Whitley Secondary School and Exley Secondary School. In 1957, the Junior Technical High School, later Highlands, and St Thomas More's Roman Catholic Secondary School were opened at Illingworth, followed by the Holy Trinity Church of England Senior School in 1962.

In 1964 protracted debates began in Halifax about the reorganisation of secondary education. The arguments for selective education although often couched in meritocratic terms, versus notions of social egalitarianism, reflected deeper social and political divisions within the local community. A 1966 report suggested a three-tier system with transfer between tiers at nine and thirteen. This was approved by the education committee and council by the narrowest of margins, prompting a rash speculation from the *Halifax Courier* that the eleven-plus would end in Halifax by 1970. However, the proposed three-tier plan went through a series of revisions, encountering strong opposition from the grammar school lobby, and by 1972 it had failed to secure acceptance by both the council and the Ministry of Education and the issue remained unresolved when Calderdale Metropolitan Borough Council was established in 1974. Calderdale assumed responsibility for schools formerly administered by the West Riding County Council. It inherited a number of successful comprehensive schools such as Calder High School, established in 1953, and Brooksbank School, Elland, established in 1959. However, it also acquired a number of seemingly intractable problems which the county council had been grappling with since 1937, for example the future of the small voluntary-aided grammar schools at Hipperholme and Rastrick. In 1985 Calderdale refused to accommodate Hipperholme Grammar School as a voluntary-aided school, but it became independent, losing its head and two-thirds of its staff who expressed a preference to remain within the state sector. It survived by the astute sale at the top of the market of surplus playing fields and by fundraising efforts which realised over half a million pounds between 1984 and 1998. Rastrick amalgamated with a failing secondary modern in 1984 and was transformed into a highly successful voluntary-controlled comprehensive school, one of several which opted for grant-maintained status in 1993.[33]

In Halifax itself, the Crossley Heath School, an amalgamation of the neighbouring Heath and Crossley and Porter grammar schools, and the North Halifax Grammar School, an amalgamation of the Highlands and Princess Mary high schools in 1985, were consistently placed in the top 150 secondary schools in national examination league tables, and Ofsted reports recognised the quality of educational provision at both schools. However, there was growing concern about the problems faced by the remaining non-selective former secondary modern schools in Halifax, such as Halifax High School, the successor of the Clare Hall and Haugh Shaw secondary schools, where 578 of the 700 pupils on roll in 1995 came from homes where English was not the first language and where many had reading ages below the national average. Moreover, at the Ridings School, another school with a large number of children with special learning needs, which came into being as a result of a merger of the Holmfield and Ovenden secondary schools, there was a major crisis in 1996 following the breakdown of discipline at school.[34] The crisis was defused when the local education authority approached Peter Clark, head of the neighbouring grant maintained school at Rastrick, to manage the Ridings School with Anna White, deputy head of Todmorden High School, as associate head. Their competent leadership rescued the school from direct intervention by the Department for Education, Clark returning to Rastrick with a CBE, a national celebrity, and White securing permanent appointment to the post of head in 1998. The media, whose coverage of the problem became the subject itself of controversy, dubbed the Ridings the worst school in Britain and the problems of the school became a focus for the national debates surrounding education prior to the 1997 general election. A subsequent inspection criticised the leadership of the local education authority's senior management team and the Director of Education, Ian Jennings, ultimately took early retirement in September 1998.[35]

By 1993, a century after its foundation as the Halifax Technical School, Calderdale College was operating independently of local authority control under the supervision of the Department of Education. The Second World War had interrupted local educational authority plans to extend the college, but a new building was finally opened in Francis Street in September 1957.

It was renamed the Percival Whitley College of Further Education in honour of Alderman Percival Whitley (1894–1956), son of J. H. Whitley and chairman of the education committee for thirty years. One of his achievements had been to establish links between Halifax and Aachen after a group of students from the college had travelled to Germany to build a hostel for families returning to the war-ravaged town in 1949. This proved the springboard for the launch of a growing series of cultural exchanges between the two towns in the 1950s. During the 1950s and 1960s most of the college's students were part-time or day-release students, but during the 1970s increasing numbers of students enrolled on full-time courses. In the 1980s many enrolled on courses relevant to careers in the new service industries such as tourism and leisure, hospitality and catering, and business administration, and the college worked closely with the Manpower Services Commission, the Training and Enterprise Councils, and agencies of the European Community to develop retraining programmes as the local economy was restructured. By 1998 with a budget of over £12 million, a staff of over 360 and more than 7,500 students, including more than 25 per cent of young people in post-16 education in Calderdale, Calderdale College also had links with over 240 companies and organisations throughout the area. However, Calderdale remained the only West Yorkshire metropolitan district without a single institution of higher education within its boundaries by the end of the twentieth century.[36]

Advances in medicine and a reorganisation of health service provision resulted in a changing role for the local authority in the post-war improvement of public health. The availability of sulphonamide drugs, antibiotics and mass immunisation programmes through the National Health Service after 1948 gradually reduced high mortality rates from infectious diseases. Although there were 53 deaths from tuberculosis in Halifax in 1947 and 63 beds maintained at Northowram Hospital in 1970 for cases of tuberculosis and other infectious diseases and chest conditions, the number of deaths from infectious diseases and bronchitis was declining after 1945. G. C. F. Roe, Halifax's Medical Officer of Health, who had responsibility for monitoring public health within the county borough, expressed alarm at the harmful effects of atmospheric pollution in 1948: 'Clean air does not exist. Who knows how much damage results to the human body from smoke and chemicals emitted into the air we inhale'.[37] Environmental and socio-economic factors contributed to a rise in the number of deaths from cancer and coronary heart disease and Halifax had the highest death rate of all the West Riding county boroughs in the period 1961–65. Calderdale's mortality rate from heart disease though declining during the period 1974–1987 was still higher than both the regional and national average, and the problem remained particularly acute amongst lower socio-economic groups in Mixenden, St John's, Todmorden and Ryburn Wards, where the exceptionally high incidence of the disease was related to poor diet, smoking, alcohol and lack of exercise. Moreover, while the perinatal mortality rate in Calderdale was more than halved between 1974 and 1987, the infant mortality rate in Calderdale remained slightly above the regional average.[38]

The new Laura Mitchell Clinic, catering for a wide range of local health services including family planning, opened in October 1968 and the Frank Swire Health Centre in May 1970. After 1948 the Halifax Area Hospitals Management Committee assumed responsibility for the management of both the Halifax General Hospital, formerly administered by the local authority, and the Royal Halifax Hospital, a former voluntary hospital, as parts of the National Health Service. An ageing population required new initiatives in the care of the elderly, and a new geriatric unit with provision for 256 patients was opened at Northowram in September 1970. New psychiatric and maternity units were opened at Halifax General Hospital in April and June 1971. The need for a new hospital was under consideration as early as 1968 and after intensive campaigning and a succession of management reorganisations between 1974 and 1996 the Calderdale and Kirklees Health Authority finally obtained government approval for the commencement of work in 1998 on a new hospital on the site of the Halifax General Hospital, scheduled for completion in 2001. Following the incorporation of the Royal Halifax Infirmary into the National Health Service in 1948, the voluntary tradition was kept alive when Halifax became the first town to form a League of Friends of Halifax Hospitals whose stated object was to continue 'that spirit of voluntary help and service in sympathetic assistance and comfort for patients and nurses in Halifax hospitals which was characteristic of Halifax people prior to the passing of the National Health Act, 1946'.[39] There was also strong support for the development of a hospice at Elland, and an appeal for a body scanner for the Royal Halifax Infirmary in September 1988 reached its target of £500,000 by June 1989.[40]

The role of local government in the provision of housing which had developed during the inter-war years underwent further changes during the second half of the twentieth century. In 1954 Halifax had the highest proportion of back-to-back houses in the Calder Valley, but by 1966 the Halifax County Borough had the lowest proportion of houses without a fixed bath and water closet in the Calder Valley and the lowest proportion without hot water apart from Brighouse. By 1970 slum clearance was continuing at a rate of 700–800 houses a year. By 1972 over 6,000 council houses had been built since 1945 on large new estates encompassing the north-east of the town at Mixenden, Illingworth and Ovenden. However, 26 per cent of Calderdale's housing stock was sold between 1971 and 1991, and only 245 new council houses were built between 1980 and 1990. By 1992 waiting lists for council houses were the highest on record, but by 1995 Calderdale Housing Department was responsible for only 13,700 homes. The role of the local authority in the provision of housing had therefore changed dramatically. Between 1990 and 1995, 524 dwellings were under construction by housing associations, 989 by private builders and none by the local authority, which recognised that housing associations had now taken on the role of being the main providers of new social housing.

However, in 1997 there were some 200 empty council houses in North Halifax, mostly concentrated on estates with a poor reputation and high investment needs. They displayed an array of intractable problems poignantly captured in the photographs and prose of Nick Danziger, which were published in 1996. They included drug abuse, graffiti, vandalism and violence, with tension on one estate 'more like Sicily than Yorkshire'. In 1999, the council's economic and community development sub-committee undertook responsibility for co-ordinating a major project of social and environmental improvement on the troubled estates of Mixenden, Illingworth and Ovenden. Significantly, the project was funded by resources provided by a variety of agencies acting in partnership, including more than £4 million from the government's regeneration budget, £2.7 million from Calderdale Council, £1.1 million from the employment service and the rest from businesses, Calderdale College and the Calderdale and Kirklees Training and Enterprise Council. This emphasises the changing role of local government from provider to facilitator.[41]

Alderman Charles Holdsworth, in his address at Halifax's centenary celebrations in 1948, suggested that having spent a century securing material improvements of 'drains, sewers, public health, highways and parks' it was now time for the local authority to concern itself more 'with the cultural aspects of life'. During the following half-century, however, the role of the local authority in this sphere was severely constrained by limited resources. The appointment of Frank Atkinson as director of museums in Halifax in 1951 proved an inspired choice, and when the Shibden Hall Folk Museum was opened by the Duke of Devonshire in 1953 it was the only open air folk museum in England. But the demolition in 1971 of the timbered house, which had been painstakingly moved in the early 1870s by John Lister from the centre of Halifax to the grounds of Shibden Hall, revealed a reluctance to realise the full potential of Lister's and Atkinson's vision.[42]

However, recognition of the potential of Halifax Piece Hall in 1973 proved a major turning point. The future of the Piece Hall, then in use as a wholesale fruit and vegetable market, hung in the balance following the recommendation of the development committee not to submit an application for a grant for its restoration under the 'Operation Eyesore' scheme. It was saved not by the casting vote of the mayor as often asserted but by the development committee chairman Councillor Keith Ambler, a fancy yarn manufacturer and Conservative councillor for Northowram, who spoke passionately against the recommendation of the development committee he had chaired. He was supported by the vice-chairman, Hugh Lawler, a master baker and Labour councillor for Lee Mount. After a lively

Figure 7.13   Cripplegate House, Shibden Park. The late-medieval, timber-framed house, which stood originally in Cripplegate, between King Street and Lower Kirkgate, was rescued from destruction by the antiquary John Lister, who purchased the structure from the railway authorities in the early 1870s. It was later restored and re-erected in the grounds of Shibden Hall, which were officially opened to the public by the Prince of Wales in October 1926. However, following serious neglect, which had aroused considerable controversy, it was finally demolished in 1971. (Photograph courtesy of H. Armitage)

debate in which one councillor had argued that the Piece Hall 'should be pulled down' and another had suggested that 'fruit could disappear from Halifax if the wholesalers were to move', they received the backing of council by 29 votes to 12, with support from representatives of all three parties. Ambler had argued that 'a complete facelift and other use of the valuable Piece Hall would be far more beneficial to the town and rate-payers than its present use which had been under review since 1923'. He concluded: 'We have a unique building steeped in history and very much part of the town's past. It could well be part of the town's future, too'.[43] The restored Piece Hall was re-opened in 1976, with a new market and a variety of smaller retail outlets. In 1985 Calderdale Industrial Museum was opened in an adjacent former engineering works, winning the best industrial museum award in the following year, but financial constraints forced it to close to the public in 1998.

Other cultural projects included municipal provision for music and the performing arts and new leisure and library facilities. In 1960 Halifax Council purchased the Victoria Hall for use as a civic theatre, and Gordon Brooksby (1923–96), under the auspices of the Halifax Arts Council and later Calderdale Leisure Services, arranged an ambitious programme of

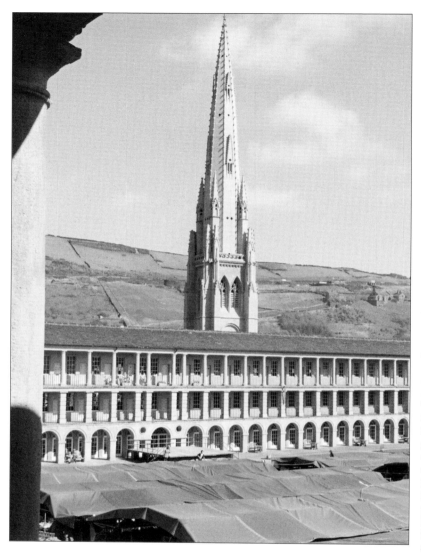

Figure 7.14
Open-air market,
Halifax Piece Hall,
1980. The former
Manufacturers'
Piece Hall was
acquired by Halifax
Corporation in
1868 for use as a
wholesale fish, fruit
and vegetable
market and opened
in 1871. In the
1890s, sheds and
lean-to buildings
were erected in the
courtyard,
remaining there for
eighty years until
the Halifax Council
finally resolved in
1973 to apply for
funding to restore
the building, which
had been
scheduled as an
ancient monument
in 1928. The
building was
re-opened in 1976
with an open-air
market, textile
museum, art
gallery, antique and
craft shops and
other retail outlets.
In 1976, Calderdale
MBC resolved to
promote the Piece
Hall as 'a centre of
tourism, culture
and entertainment'.
(Photograph
courtesy of
J. G. Washington)

over 100 visits by international symphony orchestras between 1972 and
1996. However, an attempt to provide a permanent base in Halifax for the
Northern Ballet Theatre at Spring Hall, which had been presented to the
town for the use of local people by Patons and Baldwins in 1948, proved
more controversial. Though Christopher Gable received critical acclaim
for a series of productions developed there, notably *Romeo and Juliet* and
Swan Lake, the company left Halifax in 1996 to move into purpose-built
accommodation in Leeds. The former army barracks which were also
acquired by the council and renamed Wellesley Park in 1963 were used as
a base for musical and physical education activities for schoolchildren, and
when threatened with closure in 1997 raised storms of protest. The creation

of the metropolitan district of Calderdale facilitated the development of two major cultural and recreational amenities in the early 1980s. The new North Bridge Leisure Centre, opened in 1982, provided facilities for a wide range of sports and in 1988 hosted a major Council of Europe Conference on 'heritage and successful town regeneration'. Finally, after almost four decades of campaigning, the new Calderdale Central Library, with some of the finest archive storage facilities in Europe, opened in 1983 on a site adjacent to imposing new civic buildings in Northgate.[44]

The development of Calderdale Metropolitan Borough's tourist strategy, another new role for the local authority, was partly in response to the re-opening of the Piece Hall in 1976 and a growth of interest in the town's unique built environment following the removal of industrial grime from many local buildings in the early 1970s. It was also stimulated by a growing appreciation of the recreational potential of Calderdale's natural environment following the restoration of the Rochdale Canal and the designation in 1978 of the Calderdale Way, a fifty-mile public footpath around Calderdale's rural periphery. In its 'Tourism Policy for Calderdale', published in February 1980, Calderdale Council saw the encouragement of tourism as a means of 'fostering civic pride, generating commercial confidence and helping to create a new image of Calderdale as a pleasant and interesting place to live'. An annual Calderdale Walking Festival, introduced in 1997, quickly proved its popularity with visitors, attracting 1,600 participants in 1998, when Calderdale Council's Tourism Unit received over 13,000 requests for its accommodation brochure.[45]

There had been strong all-party support for the Calderdale Inheritance Project, which had commenced in 1983. It had a ten-year programme of economic, social and environmental improvement, focusing upon the promotion of the town's heritage. Labour councillors, however, were keen to re-assert housing and social welfare priorities, and in 1989 the Inheritance programme was transformed into the 'Fair Shares Inheritance and Community Development Project'. Subsequently, political differences diminished as private sector investment in the project increased year by year, especially after the half-way stage had been reached in 1988. By 1990, other investment in the project amounted cumulatively to some fourteen times the Council's expenditure. The realisation that urban regeneration and cultural renaissance could be achieved through partnership between local government and the private sector reassured councillors concerned about shrinking public financial resources, particularly following the advent of charge-capping in 1990.[46]

The second half of the twentieth century had therefore witnessed major changes in local government. The County Borough of Halifax had been superseded by a larger administrative unit, the Metropolitan Borough of Calderdale, though the new authority remained relatively small, generating recurring concerns about its viability. Moreover, during the period local government lost some roles in the provision of public services. On the other hand, the development of the notion of partnership between the local authority, central government and the private sector offered new opportunities for the creative involvement of local government in economic, social and environmental improvement.

Local politics

Both nationally and locally in the quarter of a century which followed the end of the Second World War there developed a broad political consensus which recognised the need for improved public services. No party had overall control of Halifax County Borough Council during the period from 1945 to 1969, when a landslide victory gave the Conservatives an overall majority for the first time for half a century. Moreover, despite a swing to Labour in 1971, which enabled Labour to take five seats from the Conservatives and three from the Liberals, the Conservatives still maintained control with a majority of six. In 1972, after Labour gained another eight seats, Labour and the Conservatives both held twenty-six seats and the council became hung, with the Liberals holding the balance with seven seats.

The new metropolitan borough of Calderdale had only fifty-one elected members until the number was increased to 54 after the rationalisation of ward boundaries in 1979, whereas there had been no fewer than 215 elected representatives serving on the predecessor authorities. The first elections

Figure 7.15
Electoral wards, metropolitan borough of Calderdale after 1979.

for the new Calderdale Council in 1973 gave Labour control but with an overall majority of only two. The *Halifax Courier* observed that the 'closeness of the vote in Calderdale repeats the unclear succession of power in Halifax which for years has given neither of the biggest parties a sizeable majority'. The turnout, which was regarded as 'the single biggest problem facing the new council', was far higher outside the former Halifax County Borough than in the borough where electors were not used to casting votes in both county and district elections and where the periphery appeared determined to assert itself in the first elections to the new authority.[47]

A resounding Conservative win in 1975 swept the ruling Labour group out of power, with the Conservatives gaining eleven seats from their Labour opponents and returning five of their own candidates, giving them a total of twenty-eight seats, whereas Labour seats on the council were reduced from twenty-seven to eighteen and the Liberal representation remained unchanged at five. By 1979, however, the number of Conservative seats had fallen to twenty-three, only one more than Labour and the Liberal representation had increased to nine, once more giving no single party overall control. For a decade parties took turns in chairing committees. For example in 1985–6 the Conservatives and Liberals each took chairs of committees for six months. At one time chairmanship of council and its committees passed from party to party on a six-weekly basis, scarcely a formula, critics observed, for decisive political action.[48]

A by-election in April 1989 gave the Labour group a majority using the mayor's casting vote, and Labour retained control until the municipal elections in May 1992, when the council again became hung. During the following three years there were no fewer than fourteen different political leaders. In the elections of May 1995, however, six Conservative seats were lost to Labour, including the Conservative strongholds of Ryburn, Warley, Hipperholme and Lightcliffe. Labour regained political control, and under the leadership of Councillor Pam Warhurst began to implement a distinctly New Labour vision of social justice for all the people of Calderdale, partnership with key stakeholders including the private sector to enhance the value of council services, and sustainable development to ensure better provision for the future within the constraints of government policies.[49]

Despite the boldness of the vision and the energy of Warhurst in forging ahead with its implementation in difficult circumstances, the party suffered a rebuff by the electorate. Subsequent elections focused on educational issues: problems at the Ridings School, the threatened closure of the Queen's Road Junior and Infant School and the music and physical education centre. Moreover, the dismissal of Michael Ellison, the authority's widely respected chief executive, for reasons which were never fully explained had also provoked controversy. Labour's share of the vote, which had been 48 per cent in the 1996 local elections and 50 per cent in the 1997 general election plummeted to 29 per cent in the 1998 local elections on a low turnout. The main beneficiaries were the Conservatives who increased their share of the vote from 29 per cent in the 1996 elections to 42 per cent in the 1998 elections, though the Liberal Democrats also increased their share from 22 per cent in 1996 to 26 per cent in 1998.

An editorial in the *Halifax Courier*, commenting on the results of the 1998 local elections, which deprived Labour of its majority and made it dependent on the casting vote of the Labour mayor, concluded that:

> The diverse economic, social and political nature of our district means that it was never destined to become the fiefdom of any one party. Calderdale is neither a leafy Tory suburb nor urban Labour stronghold. It is both of those things and much more besides, with a fairly strong tradition of Liberalism thrown in for good measure.[50]

As a result of the 1999 local elections Labour lost six seats to the Conservatives and one to the Liberal Democrats, but increased its share of the vote to 35 per cent despite another low turnout. Although losing overall control of the council, Labour remained the largest political group with twenty seats, followed by the Conservatives with nineteen seats, and the Liberal Democrats holding the balance with fourteen seats. The legacy of Labour control included an innovatory system of Cabinet government with a representative group of seven councillors responsible for major decisions, scrutinised by council committees and implemented by streamlined directorates with redesignated responsibilities for schools and children's services, community services, regeneration and development, central services and social care.[51]

Although Halifax remained the centre of administration for the new metropolitan district of Calderdale, Halifax councillors were in a minority on Calderdale Council after 1973 and leadership roles were often filled by councillors from other parts of the district. Indeed the first leader of Calderdale Council was Harry Wilson, a retired headteacher and former Labour Leader of Todmorden Council and Mayor of Todmorden, who had served on the former Todmorden Council since 1947. John Bradley, a former further education lecturer, who served as leader of the Conservatives on Calderdale Council from 1974 until 1991 and leader of the Council from 1976 to 1979, was a member of the former Queensbury and Shelf Urban District Council and chairman in 1973–4. Prominent Liberals, notably David Fox, David Shutt, Stephen Pearson and Margaret Riley, had their power bases in Elland, Greetland and Stainland. Some long-serving councillors served on both the Halifax and the Calderdale councils, for example, John Ford and Eric Whitehead, Conservative councillors for Skircoat, and Joe Tolan, Labour councillor for Ovenden. Among the newer members were the first two representatives of the Asian community, Mohammed Najib, elected for Labour at a by-election in 1986, and Shakar Saghir, the successful Conservative candidate for the St John's Ward at the 1998 election, which ended the 46-year political career of Liberal Democrat, Albert Berry, fishmonger and Labour mayor of Halifax in 1970 and of Calderdale in 1988.[52]

Calderdale Council included a much higher proportion of women members in 1998 than had Halifax in 1945. In 1945 Jennie Latham and Miriam Lightowler were the only women councillors, and when the veteran Mrs Lightowler retired in 1952, there were only four other women councillors. However, by 1998 a third of the members of Calderdale Council were women. Women had served as the leaders of both the Liberal Democrat and Labour groups on the council. Pam Warhurst, a former animal rights activist, served as the first woman leader of the council from 1995 to 1999, when she left the council to become the first woman chairman of the Calderdale Healthcare NHS Trust and vice-chairman of the new Countryside Agency established to implement the Labour Government's right to roam policy.

During the period from 1945 to 1998 the occupational composition of the council had also changed. In 1945 there was only a handful of representatives from the professions on Halifax Council, including a solitary architect, chemist and a former schoolmaster, but a stronger representation of manufacturers, quarry owners, engineers, retailers and tradesmen. In 1998, the professions were more strongly represented on the Calderdale Council, especially lecturers, teachers, educational administrators and social workers. A number of councillors also had industrial and commercial backgrounds, several in engineering though none in textiles (with the exception of a solitary self-employed tailoress) and there were relatively fewer representatives from the retail sector. Local politicians by the end of the twentieth century had become, by occupation at least, less representative of dominant local economic interests.

The economic and social complexity of Halifax in the second half of the twentieth century was reflected in the electoral politics of the Halifax parliamentary constituency, where an oscillation in allegiances made Halifax a marginal constituency for much of the period. In the 1950 general election the Halifax Conservative and Liberal Associations failed to agree on a joint anti-socialist candidate, and Dryden Brook was re-elected for Labour with a majority of 8,344. However, the Liberals decided not to contest the next general election, and so when Clement Attlee went to the country to strengthen his narrow House of Commons majority in October 1951 Brook's majority was slashed to 763. Moreover, at the 1955 election when Maurice Macmillan was returned for the Conservatives with a majority of 1,535, again no Liberal stood. The son of the future Conservative Prime Minister, Macmillan, conquered a serious alcohol problem during the late 1950s. He held the seat in 1959 with an increased majority of 2,515, when he defeated Peter Shore, the future Labour minister, again without Liberal opposition. However, Macmillan lost the 1964 election to Dr Shirley Summerskill, the daughter of Baroness Edith Summerskill, a former Labour minister and party chairman, who obtained a majority of 1,058. Labour clearly benefited from the entry of a Liberal into the contest, which split the Conservative vote. Macmillan later renewed his association with Halifax by taking the title of Viscount Ovenden, when his father was created Earl of Stockton in 1984.[53]

Table 7.3. *Parliamentary election results in the Halifax constituency, 1950–1997*

Election	Turnout (%)	Candidate	Party	Votes	share (%)
1950	85.1	D. Brook	Lab	28,800	47.6
		C. H. Lucas	Cons	20,456	33.9
		A. Pickles	Lib	9,573	15.9
		R. H. Blackburn	Ind	1,551	2.6
1951	84.2	D. Brook	Lab	30,433	50.6
		C. H. Lucas	Cons	29,670	49.4
1955	80.2	M. V. Macmillan	Cons	28,306	51.4
		D. Brook	Lab	26,771	48.6
1959	83.3	M. V. Macmillan	Cons	29,212	52.2
		P. D. Shore	Lab	26,697	47.8
1964	82.1	S. Summerskill	Lab	23,143	43.7
		M. V. Macmillan	Cons	22,085	41.8
		J. F. Crossley	Lib	7,664	14.5
1966	80.4	S. Summerskill	Lab	25,391	50.3
		G. A. Turner	Cons	19,687	39.0
		D. A. Carlin	Lib	5,423	10.7
1970	73.5	S. Summerskill	Lab	24,026	49.4
		G. A. Turner	Cons	23,828	48.9
		A. J. W. Graham	Ind	847	1.7
1974 (Feb.)	81.2	S. Summerskill	Lab	20,970	40.9
		S. R. Lyons	Cons	17,967	35.1
		A. Clegg	Lib	12,300	24.0
1974 (Oct.)	74.6	S. Summerskill	Lab	20,976	44.3
		S. R. Lyons	Cons	16,798	35.5
		A. Clegg	Lib	8,693	18.3
		R. S. Pearson	Ind	919	1.9
1979	76.7	S. Summerskill	Lab	21,416	43.8
		J. Ford	Cons	20,182	41.3
		A. Clegg	Lib	6,853	14.0
		B. Wadsworth	Nat Fr	455	0.9

Table 7.3 continued

Election	Turnout (%)	Candidate	Party	Votes	share (%)
1983	75.1	R. Galley	Cons	22,321	40.9
		S. Summerskill	Lab	20,452	37.4
		F. Cockroft	SDP	11,868	21.7
1987	77.7	A. Mahon	Lab	25,115	43.4
		R. Galley	Cons	23,529	41.3
		L. Cockroft	Alliance	8,758	15.3
1992	78.7	A. Mahon	Lab	25,115	43.5
		T. R. Martin	Cons	24,637	42.6
		I. R. Howell	Lib Dem	7,364	12.8
		R. Pearson	Nat	649	1.1
1997	70.5	A. Mahon	Lab	27,465	54.3
		R. Light	Cons	16,253	32.2
		E. Waller	Lib Dem	6,059	12.0
		C. Whitaker	UKIP	779	1.5

Sources: F. W. S. Craig, *British Parliamentary Election Results, 1950–73* (Parliamentary Research Services: 1983), *British Parliamentary Election Results, 1974–83* (Parliamentary Research Services: 1984); F. W. S. Craig (ed.), *Britain Votes 4* (Parliamentary Research Services: 1988); C. Rallings and M. Thrasher, *Britain Votes 5* (Parliamentary Research Services: 1993).

Shirley Summerskill, one of only five new women elected to the House of Commons in 1964, increased her majority to 5,702 in 1966, a margin which exceeded the number of votes obtained by the Liberal candidate in that election. However, in 1970, when Heath's Conservative government was swept into office, the Conservative candidate, G. A. Turner, obtained an increased share of the vote, and her majority was reduced to 198. The situation was reversed after the confrontation between Heath and the miners and the three-day week in February 1974, when Summerskill was re-elected with a majority of 3,003. This increased to 4,178 in the election of October 1974, at the end of the shortest parliament of the twentieth century. For the first time at this election immigration became an issue, when R. S. Pearson stood as a Powellite, obtaining 919 votes. At the 1979 election, following the defeat of Callaghan's Labour government on a vote of confidence, Shirley Summerskill was still returned but with a majority reduced to 1,234 over local Conservative councillor, John Ford, with a National Front candidate trailing the Liberal candidate in fourth place, and obtaining a mere 0.9 per cent of the votes.

In June 1983 with a commanding lead in the opinion polls following the Falklands conflict, Margaret Thatcher called a snap election, and Roy Galley, a local councillor, was returned for Halifax for the Conservatives with a majority of 1,869. However, he failed to retain the seat in 1987, losing to another local councillor, Alice Mahon, a lecturer in trade union studies and former nursing auxiliary, who obtained a majority for Labour of 1,212. Although Alice Mahon held on to her seat in 1992, with a swing of 0.6 per cent from Labour to the Conservatives, her majority was cut to 478 and the seat became the most marginal Labour seat in Yorkshire. And then, in 1997, with a swing of 10.7 per cent to Labour, she increased her majority to 11,212, the largest majority obtained by any Halifax Member of Parliament since 1931. With a reputation for her hardline, left-wing views, she developed a strong interest in health and welfare issues and proved no less outspoken in opposing Labour policies with which she disagreed than she had been in attacking those of the Thatcher and Major governments. In a dispute over female quotas in the Shadow Cabinet elections in 1993, for example, she had claimed that 'some of the men in the Parliamentary Labour Party would be more at home in Jurassic Park'.

During the period 1945–98 Labour had succeeded in winning Halifax in most elections, losing only in disastrous years like 1955, 1959 and 1983, but until 1997 the contests were invariably close-run, especially when fought by three or more candidates. Moreover, during a period when relatively few constituencies were represented by women, Halifax was represented by a woman member for almost half of the period from 1945 to 1999.[54]

Religious, social and cultural life

It would be a mistake to assume that life in Halifax was determined solely by politics and public authorities. While these might facilitate or mould social behaviour, much also depended on the personal energies and inclinations of local people. For example, during the second half of the twentieth century there was increasing evidence of the decline of religious observance and the growing secularisation of leisure. The first poll taken at a public meeting in the Victoria Hall in January 1947 produced a resounding victory for the Halifax Citizen's Sunday Defence Committee: 1,039 votes to 673 against the opening of cinemas on Sundays. However, in February 1947, a poll of electors, 25.1 per cent of whom recorded their votes, reversed the decision by 9,935 votes to 8,458, a majority of 1,477. Total attendances at the first Sunday cinema performances in March reached 7,000. Moreover, the second half of the twentieth century witnessed the closure of a considerable number of churches and chapels of all denominations, including the Anglican churches of Holy Trinity, St James's and St Mary's; the Methodist churches of Wesley Broad Street, Brunswick, Hanover and St John's in Prescott Street; Square and Sion Congregational Churches; Trinity Road Baptist Church; Clare Road Quaker Meeting House; and Northgate End Unitarian Church. Attendance and membership at many other places of worship were also declining. Between 1959 and 1983, for example, Halifax Methodist circuit membership declined rapidly from 2,896 to 1,574. Though the rate of decline subsequently slowed down there had been a further reduction to 1,132 by 1998. The number of ministers had also been reduced from twelve to six during the period 1959 to 1998.[55]

As a consequence of the inner relief road development, however, there were also new churches built in the centre of the town for the congregations of Salem Methodist, Elim Pentecostal and the Salvation Army, and others were built to serve new community needs in other parts of the town such as the Anglican Church of the Holy Nativity at Mixenden, the Roman Catholic Churches of St Malachy's and St Alban's, and the Methodist churches of St Andrew's and Highgate. Although ministering within an incredibly small parish with a tiny resident population reduced considerably by ecclesiastical subdivision and demographic change, the Vicar of Halifax retained the patronage of no fewer than twenty-six benefices in Calderdale. An energetic incumbent like Eric Treacy, who served as Vicar and Arch-deacon of Halifax from 1950 to 1961, and was adept at using the media, was still able to exercise considerable influence within the local community to such an extent that he was dubbed 'the ecclesiastical mayor of Halifax'.[56]

Mary Morris conducted a detailed independent survey into voluntary organisations in the County Borough of Halifax in 1962 and reported that there were some seventy-one churches and places of worship in the town including fourteen Church of England, two Baptist, seven Congregational, four Methodist circuits embracing thirty-three churches (not all of which were within the county borough), three Pentecostal, four Roman Catholic and eight other denominations. She concluded that while congregations were considerably smaller than fifty years ago, worshippers were more likely to attend 'from real conviction'. She also revealed that many of the 193 voluntary organisations in her survey 'were founded by active members of religious bodies and are still dependent on such people for their voluntary workers'. Furthermore, although some churches were experiencing a decline in attendance and membership in the late twentieth century, others were growing, especially the evangelical churches such as St George's at Lee Mount, All Saints in Dudwell Lane, Christ Church at Pellon, and the Calderdale Community Church, which bought the redundant Park Road Baths for conversion into a 400-seat worship and community centre in 1997.

There were also other examples of imaginative attempts by the churches to serve the needs of the local community. For example, youth clubs were operated by local Methodist churches at Boothtown, King Cross and St Andrew's in partnership with the local authority. Similarly, the Bembridge Community Centre was developed at Park United Reform Church; a Chris-tian Contact Centre, financed initially by contributions from thirty-eight churches of different denominations, operated from empty shops in the town centre during the summers of 1996 and 1997; and an Afro-Caribbean Community Centre linked with the New Testament Church of God in

Figure 7.16   Muslim procession, July 1996 to mark the anniversary of the birth of the prophet Muhammad. Hundreds of Sunni Muslim men and boys after joining together for prayers at the Madni Mosque walked through the St John's area of Halifax, carrying banners, as part of the Eid Milad Un Nabi festival. The procession was led by Abdul Sattar Knazi, a member of the Pakistan Senate and a former religious leader. The recording artist, Mohammed Rafiq Chishiti, from Lahore, Pakistan, also took part in the celebrations. (Photograph courtesy of the *Halifax Courier*)

Akeds Road was opened. Joint prayers were also offered by Christians and Muslims during the Gulf War, and a Christian–Muslim dialogue was initiated in 1995 'to break down barriers and bring a clearer understanding between the two faiths'. For during the late twentieth century, Halifax had become a multi-cultural society, symbolised by the opening of a new mosque in 1984 in the heart of the West Hill Park suburb which had been colonised by Victorian Nonconformist manufacturers in the late nineteenth century.[57]

But there were alternatives to religion as forms of cultural expression. The immediate post-war years saw an increase in spectators at sports fixtures at Thrum Hall and the Shay, at least until the advent of television and the growth of supermarket shopping in the late 1950s. In 1950 Halifax reached the Rugby League Cup Final from the lowest league position ever recorded by a finalist, but became the first team not to score in the final. Four years later they reached Wembley again, and when the match against Warrington went to a replay at Odsal Stadium it attracted record crowds of 102,575: Halifax lost after a try by wing Arthur Daniels was disallowed in the closing minutes. The club also reached Wembley in 1956, losing to St Helen's, but finished runners-up to Warrington in the League. The 1960 season saw Halifax heading the League table by December, but they did not achieve similar success again for over a quarter of a century. In 1986, with the backing of the club president David Brook, the Halifax-born chairman of Modern Maintenance Products, and the coaching skills of Chris Anderson, they won the League championship and in 1987 the Rugby League Challenge Cup, returning home to an enthusiastic public reception from 70,000 fans, lining the streets of the town. In 1996, the club entered the new Super League as Halifax Blue Sox and played their final game at Thrum Hall on 21 March 1998 before moving to the Shay to share the stadium with Halifax Town AFC.[58]

Halifax was also a football town, but in a more modest way. In 1953 a record attendance of 36,885 spectators at the Shay watched the match between Halifax Town and Tottenham Hotspur in the fifth round of the FA Cup, but the club only narrowly survived a major financial crisis in 1987 with help from Calderdale Council. After facing relegation to the Vauxhall Conference in 1993, however, the club won promotion to the Football League in 1998 attracting a crowd of 6,357 to their final match of

Figure 7.17   Community Relations Partnership Cup match at the Shay in May 1996 between Queen's Road Football Club and the Halifax Police. The police won the match, which was organised by community PC Lisa White, by 6 goals to 4. The event was designed to forge links between the police and the local Asian community and subsequently became an annual sporting fixture. In 1998 the match, which was again won by the police, was followed by a presentation of medals by the Deputy Mayor of Calderdale, Councillor Leslie Smith, at a reception hosted by Superintendent Jawaid Akhtar, the first Asian divisional commander of the Halifax Police. Halifax avoided the more serious racial disturbances which erupted in neighbouring Bradford in 1995 and 1998. When confrontations occurred between Asian youths and the police in Halifax in November 1998, they were quickly defused with the assistance of community leaders. (Photograph courtesy of the *Halifax Courier*)

the season at the Shay. Moreover, amateur soccer achieved growing popularity in Halifax in the second half of the twentieth century. When the Halifax and District Association Football League, which had started with eight clubs in 1898, celebrated its centenary in 1998, it had fifty-eight teams playing in five divisions. Sport was not only a major leisure pursuit for many of the town's residents, it was also central to the town's identity. Halifax also produced some larger-than-life sports personalities during the second half of the twentieth century, including the England Rugby Union player Brian Moore, the heavyweight wrestler Shirley Crabtree, alias 'Big Daddy', and the speedway ace, Kenny Carter. Meanwhile, one of the most colourful figures of the English turf, Phil Bull, made Halifax (somewhat incongruously) the headquarters of his Timeform Organisation, which from 1948 published a series of definitive directories of horse-racing performances.[59]

Halifax was a town, like all others, with plural cultural activities in the second half of the twentieth century, many of which operated under considerable difficulties. The problems of the Halifax Choral Society of rising costs, lack of male recruits, and the lure of professionalism were highlighted

Figure 7.18   Halifax in 1951. This painting of Halifax viewed from Beacon Hill by Charles Cundall, RA, on a relatively clear day, shows a profusion of mill chimneys still dominating a congested built environment. Vegetation on the lower slopes of Beacon Hill in the foreground remains sparse and the atmosphere clouded by the emissions from the cooling towers and chimneys right of centre. (Photograph courtesy of Halifax plc)

7.19 Halifax in 1995. Mill chimneys no longer dominate the Halifax townscape in this 1995 view of Halifax from Beacon Hill, with the solitary exception of J. E. Wainhouse's tower on the distant skyline, which was conceived as a chimney for a dyeworks but then embellished and transformed into a Victorian folly of monumental proportions. The Halifax townscape is now dominated by the administrative headquarters of Halifax plc in the centre of the photograph. However, evidence of the town's medieval inheritance is also visible in the still smoke-encrusted, towered form of the Halifax Parish Church in the foreground. Beyond to the left, the red-bricked, gabled Square Chapel and the magnificent rectangular Manufacturers' Piece Hall, extending horizontally across the centre of the photograph, testify to the town's rich Georgian heritage. And finally, the soaring, crotcheted spire of the later Square Congregational Church provides a glimpse of the delights of the town's Victorian legacy. (Photograph courtesy of Halifax plc)

in a report in the *Yorkshire Post* in 1949. Moreover, many of the problems had not eased significantly by 1991, when it cost the society nearly £15,000 to stage their annual performance of the *Messiah* at the Halifax Civic Theatre. The concert made a loss of £6,800, despite performing to a full house. Even the new popular culture experienced problems. The Plebeian Jazz Club founded in April 1961 attracted such a large cult following that it was soon evicted from the third floor of Martins Mill and had to seek alternative accommodation in the Upper George Yard. In February 1962, the *Halifax Courier* reported sell-out concerts for a rock concert at the Odeon cinema. Sadly, the 3,000 fans who attended the two performances were disappointed when laryngitis obliged top-of-the-bill crooner Billy

Fury to cut his act. Furthermore, a Halifax Pop and Blues Festival held at Thrum Hall to raise much needed funds for Halifax Rugby League Club in April 1970 left the club with a deficit of £11,000 after only 2,750 turned up on a freezing cold night.[60]

Although amateur drama flourished following the opening by the Halifax Thespians of the Halifax Playhouse in a redundant Methodist chapel in 1949, the lure of television and an increasingly home-centred culture resulted in a decline of support for the performing arts and even the cinema. Many homes acquired television sets for the coronation of Queen Elizabeth II in 1953: the number of television licences in the Halifax postal area had reached 15,113 in 1955. The Grand Theatre finally closed in 1956, and the Palace Theatre was demolished in 1959. Mary Morris reported in 1962 that some of the town's cultural societies were experiencing difficulties, and in 1964 the doyen of local cultural societies, the Halifax Literary and Philosophical Society, was finally dissolved. But Halifax was still considered 'a bookish town with probably more established writers than any other Yorkshire town'. The novelist Phyllis Bentley's autobiography was published in 1961 and other celebrities with local roots of birth or residence followed her into print, including the controversial judge James Pickles and the journalist Sir Bernard Ingham. Maurice Procter, a Halifax police constable, achieved success on both sides of the Atlantic as a thriller writer; likewise John Marsh, as a writer of biography and romantic fiction, under a variety of pseudonyms, Glyn Hughes as a novelist and poet, and Juliet Barker for her acclaimed biography of the Brontes. In many respects, however, the most outstanding book to be written in Halifax since the war was *The Making of the English Working Class* by the historian E. P. Thompson (1926–93). Published in 1963, it has been hailed as 'probably the most imaginative post-war work of English social history' and, interestingly, as essentially a study of 'the Halifax working class ... a tribute to the small manufacturing communities of the Calder Valley whose spirit is the heart and meaning of the book'.[61]

'A town full of character and hidden beauty'

Halifax since 1945 has experienced demographic changes, economic restructuring, a transformation in local government, and has shared in cultural transformations affecting the rest of Britain. How have these forces affected Halifax's built environment? Halifax unlike Manchester and Sheffield escaped relatively unscathed from the Luftwaffe in the Second World War, but its congested townscape was ripe for renewal after 1945. The town also continued to suffer severely from the effects of industrial pollution. Photographs of the town through the haze of smoke from Beacon Hill in the 1940s and 1950s were often censoriously captioned 'Hell's cauldron'. Hundreds of saplings planted by Charles Holdsworth to mark his mayoralty in 1948 succumbed to industrial pollution. It was not until the clean air legislation of 1956 began to be implemented locally that vegetation started to return to Beacon Hill. Although the architectural historian Nikolaus Pevsner found the situation of the town spectacular in the 1950s, he deplored the ubiquitous slum housing, the evident lack of planning in the post-war townscape and the impact on the natural environment of pollution from the multitude of mills of various sizes 'encroaching on its boundaries on all sides'. The recently created open spaces which he observed within the town centre owed more, he opined, to 'traffic than to aesthetic considerations'. The site of the town hall was too congested, and 'as for building in the town centre there is nothing of a high order' except for the Piece Hall which he regarded as 'the most noteworthy architectural monument of Halifax'.[62] In 1966 an official report concluded that in comparison with other parts of the Calder Valley, Halifax had a larger share of derelict land 'so damaged by industrial, or other development that it is an eyesore'.[63]

However, by 1973 some £560,000 had been allocated to Halifax through grant-aided 'Operation Eyesore' schemes. It qualified 'as one of the most clean-up-conscious towns in Britain'. Indeed, the increasing use of electricity for motive power, the impact of clean air legislation, stone-cleaning and new pedestrianisation schemes soon began to change the way in which the town was perceived by visitors. Ian Nairn in a television documentary in 1975 found Halifax more expressive and architecturally interesting than neighbouring Huddersfield, and he concluded that Halifax viewed from Beacon Hill occupied 'one of the most dramatic town sites anywhere in Britain'.[64] Sir John Betjeman discerned the town's future potential when he wrote in 1979:

> Halifax is full of character and hidden beauty. The Piece Hall is symbolic of its hidden and great worth. The skyline of Halifax, its churches, chapels, mills and warehouses, is something never to be forgotten, and gives Halifax its identity.[65]

Pevsner's criticism in 1959 that there had been few notable twentieth-century contributions to the townscape was subsequently remedied by the spectacular flyover spanning North Bridge and the new headquarters of the Halifax Building Society. Nairn viewed the latter as the twentieth-century equivalent of the Piece Hall, the 'grand gesture' of the eighteenth century. Civic Trust reports on Halifax in 1984 and Calderdale in 1986, while critical of the continuing evidence of industrial dereliction, extolled the town's outstanding architectural merit. By 1984 there were no fewer than fourteen conservation areas in Calderdale including most of Halifax Town Centre. Moreover, Calderdale contained the greatest density of pre-industrial vernacular architecture in northern England with no fewer than 3,655 listed buildings in 1988, the highest ratio of listed buildings to population in West Yorkshire. In 1989 Glasgow University placed Halifax second only to Exeter and above York, Wakefield and Huddersfield in a national survey of the quality of life in medium-sized towns based upon such criteria as cost of living, cost of housing, access to scenic countryside and sports facilities. By then, it was clear that local residents had recovered their self-esteem.[66]

The unique built environment of Halifax reveals its fascinating urban history. As the seminal Civic Trust report of 1984 recognised, in the surviving built environment of Halifax are 'several towns overlayed'. Major features of the late medieval and early modern town have survived, including one of the finest medieval parish churches in West Yorkshire. The line of the medieval track to the town, from Wakefield into Woolshops, passes the rare inner urban survival of a restored seventeenth-century half-timbered building. Also evident are outstanding features of the Georgian market town with its fine town houses, neo-classical Square Chapel and Holy Trinity Church. The magnificent manufacturers' Piece Hall is recognised as 'one of the most remarkable buildings of its kind in the whole of Europe'. And then there are the mills and warehouses of the Victorian industrial town 'with one of the most consistently homogeneous town centres in the United Kingdom'. It boasts one of the finest provincial town halls in England, and nearby are the model industrial communities at Akroydon, Copley and West Hill Park. The town is overlooked by the soaring Gothic masterpiece of All Souls Church at Haley Hill, which Scott considered his finest church building. Finally, the rich historical tapestry is completed by a twentieth-century financial quarter, with the diamond-shaped fortress of the only headquarters of a major UK financial institution outside London, and an array of banks, building societies and insurance companies extending along Commercial Street and around Blackwall and Ward's End. There is also the largest privately financed mill regeneration scheme in Europe at Dean Clough, and the exposed steel, stone and glass structure of the first interactive children's museum in the UK close to the town's Victorian railway station.

The vested interests of market traders and town centre retailers in the post-war years and the timely development of a strong conservationist lobby in Halifax from the 1970s succeeded in preventing the wholesale redevelopment of the town along the lines experienced by other neighbouring West Yorkshire towns and cities. So Halifax retained its Piece Hall and Victorian Borough Markets, unlike neighbouring Huddersfield where the eighteenth-century Cloth Hall was demolished to make way for a cinema in 1935 and the Victorian Market Hall was swept away in an ill-conceived redevelopment scheme in 1970, and unlike Bradford where the Swan Arcade and Kirkgate Market fell victim to an orgy of destruction between 1955 and 1965. Moreover, the curtailment of atmospheric pollution after 1956 and the removal of the accretions of industrial grime from town centre buildings have revealed both the spectacular beauty of the Halifax's urban location and the splendour of its built environment. Imaginative new uses have been found for some of the town's redundant churches, chapels, mills and warehouses and the magnificent manufacturers' Piece Hall.

Halifax's built environment remains therefore perhaps the most complete surviving testimony to the pre- and post-industrial economic and social history of a northern urban community over the last millennium. Moreover, the geographical factors which inhibited Halifax's continuing industrial development at the beginning of the twentieth century, most notably problems of accessibility and a shortage of flat land for further industrial development, proved to be of less significance to the town's economic vitality in the telecommunications age at the end of the twentieth century. Indeed, the formidable shield of hills encompassing the town not only provides a spectacular backdrop to Halifax's urban location but also enhances both the sense of community and individuality which have been the town's twin strengths throughout its fascinating history.[67]

Notes

Notes to Chapter 1

1. P. Bentley, 'The romance of Halifax' in J. J. Mulroy (ed.), *The Story of the Town that Bred Us* (J. J. Mulroy, Halifax: 1948).

2. J. Ogden, 'The shaping of Calderdale' in *The Calderdale Way* (Calderdale Way Association, Calderdale: 1978), p. 11.

3. Ibid., pp. 9–11.

4. D. James, *Bradford* (Ryburn, Halifax: 1990), p. 18; G. Firth, *A History of Bradford* (Phillimore, Chichester: 1997), p. 48.

5. J. B. Priestley, *English Journey* (Folio Society reprint, London: 1997), p. 162.

6. For a development of this theme see A. Dingsdale, 'Yorkshire mill town: a study of the spatial patterns and processes of urban industrial growth and the evolution of the spatial structure of Halifax, 1801–1901', unpublished Ph.D. thesis, University of Leeds, 1974.

Notes to Chapter 2

1. M. L. Faull and S. A. Morehouse (eds), *West Yorkshire: an Archaeological Survey to AD 1500* 1 (West Yorkshire Metropolitan County Council, Wakefield: 1981), pp. 82–88; J. A. Gilks, 'The mesolithic in and around Halifax', *Transactions of the Halifax Antiquarian Society* [hereinafter *THAS*] (1991), pp. 1–25.

2. B. Jennings, *Pennine Valley* (Smith Settle, Otley: 1992), pp. 5, 16–17; Faull and Morehouse, *West Yorkshire Archaeological Survey* 1, pp. 90–91, 93, 107–9, 118; 4, Maps 5, 6; J. A. Gilks, 'An early bronze age flat axe from Norland town, near Halifax', *THAS* 1 (1993), pp. 12–14; N. Lunn, 'Bronze age man in the Pennines', *Huddersfield and District Archaeological Society Bulletin* 18 (1966). I am grateful to Jenny Marriot of the West Yorkshire Archaeological Service for information on the dating of the prehistoric finds.

3. Faull and Morehouse, *West Yorkshire Archaeological Survey* 1, pp. 124, 126–7, 132, 154–67; J. Watson, *The History and Antiquities of the Parish of Halifax* (T. Lowndes, London: 1775), p. 32; H. P. Kendall, 'Roman evidences in the parish of Halifax', *THAS* (1912), p. 79; D. Haigh, 'Blue Ball and Baitings, Soyland: a tall story explained', *THAS* 2 (1994), pp. 15–27; "At Gretland in the toppe of an hill"; four hundred years of the Greetland Roman altar, 1597–1997', *THAS* 5 (1997), pp. 13–35.

4. Faull and Morehouse, *West Yorkshire Archaeological Survey* 1, pp. 179, 182, 187.

5. T. W. Hanson, *The Story of Old Halifax* (F. King and Sons, Halifax: 1920), p. 111; H. P. Kendall, 'Domesday Book and after', *THAS* (1935), pp. 29–31; A. H. Smith, 'Place names of the ancient parish of Halifax', *THAS* (1936), pp. 219, 229–30.

6. Faull and Morehouse, *West Yorkshire Archaeological Survey* 1, pp. 216–18.

7. A. H. Smith, *The Place Names of the West Riding of Yorkshire*, III (Cambridge University Press, Cambridge: 1961), pp. 104–06; Faull and Morehouse, *West Yorkshire Archaeological Survey* 1, pp. 175, 177, 204–07; Jennings, *Pennine Valley*, pp. 16–17. I am grateful to Dr George Redmonds for discussing with me the place-name evidence.

8. Hanson, *Old Halifax*, p. 111; Kendall, *THAS* (1935), pp. 29–31; Smith, *THAS* (1936), pp. 219, 229–30.

9. J. Lister and J. H. Ogden (eds), *Poll Tax (Lay Subsidy) 1379* (Halifax Antiquarian Society, Halifax: 1906), p. 48; M. Wood, *Domesday. A*

Search for the Roots of England (BBC Publications, London: 1986), p. 18; M. L. Faull and M. Stinson (eds), *Domesday Book. Yorkshire* (Phillimore, Chichester: 1986), pp. 299 c, d, IY15; Hanson, *Old Halifax*, p. 21; Jennings, *Pennine Valley*, pp. 13–14; W. E. Wightman, 'The significance of "waste" in the Yorkshire Domesday', *Northern History* X (1975), p. 67; D. R. Roffe, 'Domesday Book and northern society: a reassessment', *English Historical Review* CV (1990), pp. 310–36 and 'The Yorkshire summary: a Domesday satellite', *Northern History* XXVII (1991), pp. 242–60; D. M. Palliser, 'Domesday Book and the "harrying of the north"', *Northern History* XXIX (1993), pp. 1–23; B. Jennings, 'The study of local history in the Pennines: the comparative dimension', *THAS* 3 (1995), pp. 13–30.

10. Jennings, *Pennine Valley*, pp. 28–38; Jennings, *THAS* 3 (1995), pp. 13–30.

11. Jennings, *Pennine Valley*, pp. 40–41. I am grateful to Mr Peter Ryder for discussing his interpretation of the tombstone evidence with me.

12. Table 2.1; Jennings, *Pennine Valley*, pp. 41–42.

13. J. Lister, 'The making of Halifax' in H. Ling Roth (ed.), *The Yorkshire Coiners, 1767–83* (F. King and Sons, Halifax: 1906), pp. 130–1, 136, 143; Jennings, *Pennine Valley*, p. 37; M. Habberjam, M. O'Regan and B. Hale (eds), *Court Rolls of the Manor of Wakefield, 1350–52* (Yorkshire Archaeological Society, Leeds: 1987), pp. xv, xvi; D. Hey, *Yorkshire from AD 1000* (Longman, London: 1986), p. 89.

14. Lister in *Yorkshire Coiners*, pp. 135, 138, 143–44; ; Hanson, *Old Halifax*, pp. 57, 66; Hey, *Yorkshire*, pp. 109–110.

15. J. A. Gilks, 'Yorkshire Archaeological Register', *Yorkshire Archaeological Journal* [hereinafter *YAJ*] 43 (1971), pp. 196–7; 44 (1972), p. 223; 45 (1973), p. 204; 46 (1974), p. 147; C. Platt, *Medieval England* (Routledge and Kegan Paul, London: 1978), pp. 202–3.

16. E. Crossley, *The Monumental Inscriptions of Halifax Parish Church* (John Whitehead and Son, Leeds: 1909), p. 147; C. Giles, *Rural Houses of West Yorkshire, 1400–1830* (HMSO, London: 1986), pp. 213, 219; Jennings, *Pennine Valley*, p. 5; H. Heaton, *The Yorkshire Woollen and Worsted Industries* (Oxford University Press, Oxford: 1965), pp. 68–76; M. Bonney, 'The English medieval wool and cloth trade: new approaches for the local historian', *Local Historian* 22 (1992), pp. 24–5, 37.

17. Faull and Morehouse, *West Yorkshire Archaeological Survey* 3, pp. 781–2, 786, 810; J. A. Gilks, 'Boothtown Hall: a fifteenth-century house in the parish of Halifax', *YAJ* 46 (1974), pp. 80–1; J. A. Heginbottom, 'Fences and fields: the evolution of the Calderdale rural landscape from prehistoric times to the present day', *THAS* 1 (1993), p. 31; H. M. Jewell (ed.), *Court Rolls of the Manor of Wakefield, 1348–50* (Yorkshire Archaeological Society, Leeds: 1981), p. xxi.

18. Jennings, *Pennine Valley*, p. 42; M. J. Ellis, 'A study in the manorial history of Halifax parish in the sixteenth and early seventeenth centuries', II, *YAJ* XL (1961), p. 431; Lister in *Yorkshire Coiners*, pp. 143, 149–51.

19. Faull and Morehouse, *West Yorkshire Archaeological Survey* 1, pp. 241, 385–6, 399–400, 726–7, 746; M. J. Ellis, 'A study in the manorial history of Halifax parish in the sixteenth and early seventeenth centuries', II, *YAJ* XL (1960), pp. 250–64; Lister in *Yorkshire Coiners*, pp. 126–30.

20. M. E. Francois, 'The social and economic development of Halifax, 1558–1640', *Proceedings of the Leeds Philosophical and Literary Society* [hereinafter *PLPLS*], xl (1966), p. 220; Faull and Morehouse, *West Yorkshire Archaeological Survey* 1, p. 216; Hey, *Yorkshire*, p. 59; A. Goodwin, 'How the ancient parish of Halifax was divided', *THAS* (1961), pp. 23–36; A. Betteridge, 'Halifax before the Industrial Revolution', I, *THAS* (1978), pp. 17–41.

21. Faull and Morehouse, *West Yorkshire Archaeological Survey* 3, pp. 626–7, 631, 652; S. Moorhouse, 'Documentary evidence for the landscape of the manor of Wakefield during the Middle Ages', *Landscape History* 1 (1979).

22. Francois, *PLPLS* (1966), p. 220; Gilks, *YAJ* 43 (1971), pp. 196–7; 44 (1972), p. 223; 45 (1973), p. 204; 46 (1974), p. 147; Heginbottom, *THAS* (1993), pp. 18–21; Lister in *Yorkshire Coiners*, pp. 142–4, 182–3; Hanson, *Old Halifax*, pp. 76–8; P. Ryder, *Medieval Churches of West Yorkshire* (West Yorkshire Archaeological Service, Wakefield: 1993), pp. 36, 52, 56, 63, 75–7, 155.

Notes to Chapter 3

1. M. E. Francois, 'The social and economic development of Halifax, 1558–1640', *PLPLS* ll (1966), pp. 225–6; W. Camden, *Britannia* (George Bishop, London: 1586), p. 692; H. Holroyde, 'Protestantism and Dissent in the parish of Halifax, 1509–1640', *THAS* (1988), p. 20; A. Betteridge, 'Halifax before the Industrial Revolution', I, *THAS* (1978), pp. 31–2, 38; J. A. Hargreaves, 'Religion and Society in the Parish of Halifax c.1740–1914', unpublished PhD thesis, Huddersfield, 1991, p. 27; J. Smail, *The Origins of Middle-Class Culture* (Cornell University Press, Ithaca and London: 1994), p. 35.

2. Camden, *Britannia*, p. 692; D. Defoe, *A Tour Through the Whole Island of Britain* (Yale University Press, New Haven and London: 1991), p. 258.

3. P. Clark and D. Souden, *Migration and Society in Early Modern England* (Hutchinson, London: 1987), p. 236.

4. D. Hey, *Yorkshire from AD 1000* (Longman, London: 1986), pp. 7, 96.

5. H. Heaton, *The Yorkshire Woollen and Worsted Industries* (Oxford University Press, Oxford: 1965), pp. 54–5.

6. D. M. Palliser, *The Age of Elizabeth* (Longman, London: 1992), p. 289; R. N. Thornes, *West Yorkshire: 'A Noble Scene of Industry'* (West Yorkshire Metropolitan County Council, Wakefield: 1981), pp. 7–12.

7. J. Thirsk, 'Industries in the countryside' in F. J. Fisher (ed.), *Essays in the Economic and Social History of Tudor England in honour of R. H. Tawney* (Cambridge University Press, Cambridge: 1961), pp. 70–88; B. Jennings, 'The study of local history in the Pennines: the comparative dimension', *THAS* 3 (1995), pp. 22–8; Heaton, *Yorkshire Woollen and Worsted Industries*, p. 77.

8. B. Jennings, *Pennine Valley* (Smith Settle, Otley: 1992), p. 43; T. W. Hanson, *The Story of Old Halifax* (F. King, Halifax: 1920), pp. 84–6; C. Giles, *Rural Houses of West Yorkshire, 1400–1830* (HMSO, London: 1986), pp. 26–47; Heaton, *Yorkshire Woollen and Worsted Industries*, p. 76.

9. Hey, *Yorkshire*, p. 96; G. Parker, *Cambridge Illustrated History of Warfare* (Cambridge University Press, Cambridge: 1995), pp. 151–2;

Francois, *PLPLS* (1966), p. 217; Hanson, *Old Halifax*, p. 112; Heaton, *Yorkshire Woollen and Worsted Industries*, pp. 19, 81–4.

10. 2 and 3 Philip and Mary c. 13, 1555.

11. Hey, *Yorkshire*, p. 110; Heaton, *Yorkshire Woollen and Worsted Industries*, p. 94; Hanson, *Old Halifax*, pp. 112–13, 184–5; Palliser, *Age of Elizabeth*, pp. 205, 289–90,267; J. Addy, *The Textile Revolution* (Longman, London: 1976), pp. 67–68.

12. Heaton, *Yorkshire Woollen and Worsted Industries*, pp. 268–71; Hanson, *Old Halifax*, pp. 179–83; Smail, *Origins of Middle-Class Culture*, p. 75.

13. Defoe, *Tour*, pp. 257, 259.

14. Francois, *PLPLS* (1966), pp. 252–55; H. P. Kendall, 'Gleanings from local Elizabethan wills', *THAS* (1915), pp. 119, 126, 128; J. A. Heginbottom, 'Fences and fields: the evolution of the Calderdale rural landscape from prehistoric times to the present day', *THAS*, 1 (1993), p. 15.

15. M. J. Ellis, 'A study in the manorial history of Halifax parish in the sixteenth and early seventeenth centuries', II, *YAJ*, xl (1961), 420–22; Thornes, *West Yorkshire*, pp. 34–6; Betteridge, *THAS* (1978), p. 27; Hanson, *Old Halifax*, p. 185; C. M. Fraser (ed.), *The Court Rolls of the Manor of Wakefield for 1608–09* (Yorkshire Archaeological Society, Leeds: 1996), pp. 118, 175.

16. Giles, *Rural Houses of West Yorkshire*, pp. 107–12; C. Platt, *The Great Rebuildings of Tudor and Stuart England* (UCL Press, London: 1994); T. W. Hanson, 'Halifax builders in Oxford', *THAS* (1928) pp. 253–317; J. W. Houseman, 'Notes and comments on the Halifax churchwardens' accounts, 1620–1714' *THAS* (1925); Hanson, *Old Halifax*, pp. 129–33.

17. J. A. Heginbottom, 'Halifax is made of wax', *THAS* (1990) 2; H. Ling Roth, *The Yorkshire Coiners* (F. King, Halifax: 1906), p. 239.

18. J. A. Heginbottom, 'Iron and wool: ironworking and the woollen textile industry in Calderdale from the Middle Ages to the Industrial Revolution', *THAS* 5 (1997), pp. 54–65; Thornes, *West Yorkshire*, pp. 28–31; H. P. Kendall, *THAS* (1915), pp. 118–19; Smail, *Origins of Middle-Class Culture*, p. 95.

19. West Yorkshire Archive Service, Leeds District Archives, Lease of greater and lesser Blackwell Hall, Halifax by John Waterhouse of Shibden and his heir Robert Waterhouse to Robert Waterhouse of Halifax, 7 Jan 1562, TN/HX/A55; British Museum, Letter of James Ryder to Lord Burghley, 3 January 1589, Lansdowne MSS, v. 119, f. 118. I am grateful to Dr Alan Betteridge for supplying me with copies of these documents.

20. S. Hughes, 'Church and Society in the Seventeenth Century Parish of Halifax', unpublished dissertation, St John's College, York, 1974, pp. 12–13.

21. C. Morris (ed.), *The Illustrated Journeys of Celia Fiennes, 1685-c.1712* (Alan Sutton, Stroud: 1995), p. 182; Defoe, *Tour*, p. 261.

22. Hey, *Yorkshire*, p. 183.

23. Defoe, *Tour*, p. 259.

24. Thornes, *West Yorkshire*, pp. 42–5; W. B. Crump, 'Halifax visitors' book', I, *THAS* (1937), pp. 35, 41; J. H. Priestley, 'The Rochdale to Halifax and Elland turnpike', *THAS* (1952), pp. 95–114; (1953), pp. 31–53.

25. Francois, *PLPLS* (1966), pp. 217–38, 246; Smail, *Origins of Middle-Class Culture*, pp. 29–30; Holroyde, *THAS* (1988), pp. 23–4; 'Halifax landowners in 1630–32', *Halifax Guardian Almanack* (1902); W. and S. Sheils, 'Textiles and reform: Halifax and its hinterland' in P. Collinson and J. Craig (eds), *The Reformation in English Towns, 1500–1640* (Macmillan, London: 1998), p. 133 Hanson, *Old Halifax*, pp. 94–102, A. F. Upton, *Sir Arthur Ingram* (Oxford University Press: 1961), pp. 45–51.

26. A. Betteridge, 'Halifax before the Industrial Revolution', I, *THAS* (1978), pp. 22, 27.

27. Betteridge, *THAS* (1978), pp. 27–8; Smail, *Origins of Middle-Class Culture*, pp. 94–95.

28. Smail, *Origins of Middle-Class Culture*, pp. 21, 26–7, 93–5.

29. Betteridge, *THAS* (1978), pp. 19, 22, 25–8; 2 (1979), pp. 89–90; Smail, *Origins of Middle-Class Culture*, pp. 25, 37; Holroyde, *THAS* (1988), p. 30; Betteridge, *THAS* (1978), pp. 27–8; A. L. Beier, *Masterless Men* (Methuen, London: 1985), p. 45; YAS, Wakefield Court Rolls, 15 October 1537, MD 225/1/263A/5/80B; Defoe, *Tour*, p. 256.

30. Francois, *PLPLS* (1966), pp. 243, 247; Thornes, *West Yorkshire*, p. 51; West Yorkshire Archive Service, Calderdale District Archives, Letter from John Waite to Nicholas Denman, Mayor of Hull, 24 August 1645, MISC: 331/1; Smail, *Origins of Middle-Class Culture*, p. 24.

31. Smail, *Origins of Middle-Class Culture*, pp. 24, 37–8.

32. P. N. Farrar, 'John Waite and the plague of 1645', *THAS* (1978); Betteridge, *THAS* (1978), pp. 31–2; T. Wright, *The Antiquities of Halifax* (Leeds: 1738), p. 15.

33. Sheils, in Collinson and Craig, *The Reformation in English Towns*, pp. 140, 143.

34. Hanson, *Old Halifax* (1920) pp. 89–94.

35. C. Haigh, *English Reformations: Religion Politics and Society under the Tudors* (Oxford University Press, Oxford: 1993), p. 201; A. G. Dickens, *Lollards and Protestants in the Diocese of York* (Oxford University Press, Oxford: 1959), pp. 149, 172; Holroyde, *THAS* (1988), p. 20.

36. E. Duffy, *The Stripping of the Altars, Traditional Religion in England 1400–1580* (Yale University Press, New Haven and London: 1992), p. 479; J. Youings, *Sixteenth Century England* (Allen Lane, London: 1984); Holroyde, *THAS* (1988), p. 26; Dickens, *Lollards and Protestants*, pp. 198, 217; Sheils in Collinson and Craig *Reformation in English Towns*, pp. 138–9.

37. Dickens, *Lollards and Protestants*, p. 181; Holroyde, *THAS* (1988), p. 26; Sheils in Collinson and Craig *Reformation in English Towns*, pp. 140, 142–3.

38. Dickens, *Lollards and Protestants*, pp. 225–6; J. M. Turner and J. A. Hargreaves, *Thunderclaps from Heaven* (Calderdale Metropolitan Borough Council, Halifax: 1984), pp. 8–9; Haigh, *English Reformations*, p. 219.

39. R. Whiting, *The Blind Devotion of the People* (Cambridge University Press, Cambridge: 1989), p. 266; Turner and Hargreaves, *Thunderclaps from Heaven*, p. 9.

40. C. Hill, *Society and Puritanism in Pre-Revolutionary England* (Secker and Warburg, London: 1964), pp. 137–8; J. Horsfall Turner, *Halifax Books and Authors* (Idle: 1906), pp. 46–7; Holroyde, *THAS* (1988), pp. 29–32.

41. J. Addy, 'The uncontrollable and ungovernable parish of Halifax in the seventeenth century', *THAS* 1 (1993), p. 37; C. T. Clay, 'The protestation of 1641 – Halifax signatories', *THAS* (1919), pp. 105–115.

42. Jennings, *Pennine Valley*, pp. 70–72;
H. P. Kendall, 'The Civil War in Halifax
parish, 1639–50', *THAS* (1909–11); Smail,
Origins of Middle-Class Culture, p. 31; Hanson,
Old Halifax, pp. 137–63.

43. J. W. Houseman, 'Notes and comments on
the Halifax churchwardens' accounts,
1620–1714', *THAS* (1925), pp. 137–67.

44. Houseman, *THAS* (1925–26); Turner, *Halifax
Books and Authors*, pp. 11–17; G. V. Bennett,
'John Tillotson: portrait of a liberal' in
G. Powell (ed.), *To the Church of England*
(Churchman Publishing, Worthing: 1988),
pp. 75–86; W. J. Sheils, 'Oliver Heywood and
his Congregation' in W. J. Sheils and D. Wood
(eds), *Voluntary Religion* (Basil Blackwell,
London: 1986).

45. Hargreaves, Ph.D. thesis, pp. 131–3; C. Stell,
'Calderdale Chapels', *THAS* (1984), 16–22;
E. V. Chapman, *John Wesley and Co* (Halifax:
1952), pp. 5–13.

46. *The Yorkshire Poll Book, 1741* (S. A. and
M. J. Raymond, Exeter: 1997); J. F. Quinn,
'Yorkshiremen go to the polls: county
contests in the early eighteenth century',
Northern History XXI (1985), pp. 137–74;
Smail, *Origins of Middle-Class Culture*,
pp. 160–61.

47. Betteridge, *THAS* (1978), pp. 18–19; M. J. Ellis,
'A study in the manorial history of Halifax
parish in the sixteenth and early seventeenth
centuries', I, *YAJ* xl (1960), pp. 252–4.

48. Betteridge, *THAS* (1978), pp. 19–26.

49. Hughes, dissertation, p. 18; Farrar, *THAS*
(1978).

50. Dickens, *Lollards and Protestants in the
Diocese of York*, p. 2, n. 3; J. Lister, 'Halifax in
the time of Queen Elizabeth', *THAS* (1921),
p. 55; Betteridge, *THAS* (1978), p. 19.

51. Addy, *THAS* (1993); Holroyde, *THAS* (1988),
p. 20; Hanson, *Old Halifax*, p. 134.

52. J. Barlow, *An Exposition of the Second Epistle
of the Apostle Paul to Timothy* (John Bellamie,
London: 1625).

53. Sheils, in Collinson and Craig, *Reformation in
English Towns*, p. 142.

54. Betteridge, *THAS* (1979), pp. 82–88;

55. Holroyde, *THAS* (1988), pp. 19–20;
A. Thirlwell, *Folio Anthology of Autobiography*
(Folio Society, London: 1994), p. 40; Francois,
PLPLS (1966), pp. 275–7; Sheils, in Collinson
and Craig, *Reformation in English Towns*,

p. 142; A. J. Petford, 'Matthew Broadley's
benefactions of 1648 and the origins of the
grammar school at Hipperholme', *THAS* 6
(1998), pp. 30–35.

56. Betteridge, *THAS* (1978), p. 31; (1979), p. 83;
M. W. Garside, 'Halifax schools prior to 1700',
THAS (1924).

57. Betteridge, *THAS* (1978), pp. 30–31; (1979),
p. 98; Kendall, *THAS* (1915), p. 145;
K. Wrightson, *English Society, 1580–1680*
(Routledge, London: 1982), pp. 198–9. I
am grateful to Dr K. Wrightson for this
reference.

58. P. Borsay, *The English Urban Renaissance*
(Clarendon Press, Oxford: 1989), p. 285.

59. Sheils, in Collinson and Craig *Reformation in
English Towns*, p. 142.

60. Addy, *THAS* (1993), pp. 37–8, 40.

61. Betteridge, *THAS* (1978), p. 29; Holroyde,
THAS (1988), p. 20; J. Addy, *Sin and Society in
the Seventeenth Century* (Routledge, London:
1989), pp. 116, 157–8; *THAS* (1993).

62. M. W. Garside, 'The social history of Halifax
in the seventeenth century', *THAS* (1923),
p. 74.

63. Betteridge, *THAS* (1978), p. 33; J. Lister,
'Halifax in the time of Queen Elizabeth',
THAS (1921), p. 38; Garside, *THAS* (1923),
pp. 79–81; Keith Thomas, *Religion and the
Decline of Magic* (Weidenfeld and Nicolson,
London: 1971), p. 592.

64. Addy, *THAS* (1993), pp. 38–9; Garside, *THAS*
(1923), pp. 68–9; Borsay, *English Urban
Renaissance*, p. 366; Smail, *Origins of
Middle-Class Culture*, pp. 185–6; WYAS, CDA,
Horse racing agreement, MISC: 325.

65. Smail, *Origins of Middle-Class Culture*,
pp. 35–7.

66. W. B. Crump, 'Halifax visitors' book', I,
THAS (1937), pp. 26–8; Ellis, *YAJ* (1961),
p. 422; Francois, *PLPLS* (1966) pp. 217–24.

67. W. B. Crump, 'Ancient highways of the parish
of Halifax', V, *THAS* (1926); P. Ryder,
Medieval Churches of West Yorkshire (West
Yorkshire Archaeology Service, Wakefield,
1993), p. 155.

68. Hanson, *Old Halifax*, pp. 177–8; J. Lister, 'The
genesis of the Halifax Manufacturers' Hall' in
H. Ling Roth, *Yorkshire Coiners*, pp. 207;
Betteridge, *THAS* (1979), pp. 85–6;
Hargreaves, Ph.D. thesis, p. 122.

69. A. McInnes, *The English Town, 1660–1760*

(Historical Association, London: 1980), pp. 5–6; Francois, *PLPLS* (1966), pp. 217–24; Ellis, *YAJ* (1961), p. 425.

Notes to Chapter 4

1. S. L. Ollard and P. C. Walker (eds), *Archbishop Herring's Visitation Returns, 1743*, Yorkshire Archaeological Society, Record Series (1928–29); University of York, Borthwick Institute of Historical Research. Archbishop Drummond's Visitation Returns, 1764; Census Returns, 1801–51.
2. J. J. Cartwright (ed.), *The Travels through England of Dr Richard Pococke* (Camden Society, London: 1888), p. 50. Serges were originally fabrics with a worsted warp and woollen weft, though the term later came to be used for worsted warp and worsted weft cloth.
3. J. Watson, *History and Antiquities of the Parish of Halifax* (T. Lowndes, London: 1775), pp. 8, 69–70.
4. T. Pennant, *Tour in Scotland*, 1770, cited in H. Heaton, *The Yorkshire Woollen and Worsted Industries* (Oxford University Press, 2nd edition, Oxford: 1965), p. 271.
5. T. Twining, *Recreations and Studies of a country clergyman of the eighteenth century* (London: 1882), pp. 98–9.
6. C. Dibdin, *The musical tour of Mr Dibdin* (Sheffield: 1788), pp. 276 and 279.
7. E. Sigsworth, *Black Dyke Mills* (Liverpool University Press, Liverpool: 1958), pp. 18–25; *The Journal of Dr John Simpson of Bradford* (Local Studies Department, City of Bradford Metropolitan Council, Bradford: 1981), p. 41.
8. Table 4.2; D. T. Jenkins, 'The cotton industry in Yorkshire, 1780–1900', *Textile History* 10 (1979), pp. 78–82; T. W. Hanson, *The Story of Old Halifax* (F. King and Sons, Halifax: 1920), pp. 239–40; G. Ingle, *Yorkshire Cotton* (Carnegie Publishing, Preston: 1997), pp. 130–60.
9. H. Holroyde, 'Power technology in the Halifax textile industry, 1770–1850', *THAS* (1980).
10. H. Holroyde,'Textile mills, masters and men in the Halifax district, 1770–1851', *THAS* (1979); N. Rycroft et al., '1851 census returns for Halifax and Skircoat townships', I, *THAS* (1979), p. 118.
11. C. Aspin, (ed.), *The Yorkshire Textile Districts in 1849* (Helmshore Local History Society, Helmshore: 1974), p. 13.
12. J. Crabtree, *Concise History of the Parish and Vicarage of Halifax* (Halifax: 1836), pp. 296, 312; W. White, *Directory of the Clothing Districts of the West Riding of Yorkshire* (David and Charles reprint, Newton Abbot: 1969), p. 546.
13. R. C. N. Thornes, *West Yorkshire: 'A Noble Scene of Industry'* (West Yorkshire Metropolitan County Council, Wakefield: 1981), pp. 42–4; D. Taylor, 'Annals of the parish of Halifax', *THAS* (1972), p. 116.
14. Thornes, *West Yorkshire*, pp. 44–6; Sigsworth, *Black Dyke Mills*, p. 25.
15. H. W. Harwood, *Centenary Story* (Halifax: 1948), p. 19.
16. H. P. Kendall, 'Halifax hunts and huntsmen', *THAS* (1928), pp. 63–5; Hanson, *Old Halifax*, p. 199.
17. J. Liddington, *Family Fortune. Land, gender and authority* (Rivers Oram Press, London: 1997); D. M. Lang, 'Georgia in 1840: the Lister diaries', *THAS* (1989). I am grateful to Jill Liddington for sharing with me her insights on Anne Lister.
18. Twining, *Recreations and Studies*, pp. 98–9.
19. A. G. Hill, (ed.), *The Letters of Dorothy Wordsworth* (Oxford University Press, Oxford: 1981), pp. 141–2.
20. Simpson, *Journal*, p. 41.
21. P. W. Robinson, 'Lilly Lane baths and Albion mill', *THAS* (1991).
22. R. Bretton, 'Colonel Edward Akroyd', *THAS* (1948), pp. 67, 69; E. Webster, 'Edward Akroyd', *THAS* (1987), pp. 19–20, 36; E. Webster, *Dean Clough and the Crossley Inheritance* (Halifax: 1988), pp. 4–9.
23. A. B. Granville, *Spas of England*, 1 (Adams and Dart reprint, Bath: 1971), pp. 400–401.
24. A. Porritt, 'Eighteenth and nineteenth century clubs and societies in Halifax', *THAS* (1964); Idem, 'The old Halifax theatre, 1789–1904', *THAS* (1956); J. Smail, *The Origins of Middle-Class Culture* (Cornell University Press, Ithaca and London: 1994), p. 183.

25. W. B. Crump, 'Halifax visitors' book', II, *THAS* (1938), pp. 93, 110–11; D. Bridge, 'William Milner: printer and bookseller', *THAS* (1969); D. Taylor, 'Annals of Halifax', *THAS* (1972), pp. 114, 117.

26. Smail, *Origins of Middle-Class Culture*, pp. 101–2.

27. A. Betteridge, 'Halifax before the Industrial Revolution', I, *THAS* (1978), pp. 27–8; II, *THAS* (1979), p. 101.

28. P. Hudson, 'Proto-industrialisation: the case of the West Riding wool textile industry in the eighteenth and early nineteenth centuries', *History Workshop Journal* 12 (1981), pp. 12, 51, 61; Crabtree, *Concise History of Halifax*, pp. 307, 309; N. Rycroft et al., *THAS* (1979), pp. 112, 122.

29. J. T. Ward, *The Factory Movement, 1830–55* (Macmillan, London: 1962), pp. 35, 107; Aspin (ed.), *Yorkshire Textile Districts*, pp. 14–16.

30. E. Webster, 'Cornelius Ashworth of Waltroyd', *THAS* (1985).

31. J. G. Washington, 'The origins and development of the Royal Halifax Infirmary, 1807–1995', *THAS* 4 (1996), pp. 66–72.

32. G. R. Dalby, 'Halifax town trustees', *THAS* (1957); J. Smith, *Second report of the commissioners for enquiring into the state of the large towns and populous districts* (London: 1845), pp. 158–60.

33. J. Styles, '"Our traitorous money makers": the Yorkshire coiners and the law, 1760–83' in J. Brewer and J. Styles, (eds), *An Ungovernable People* (London: 1980), pp. 207, 214; J. Marsh, *Clip a Bright Guinea* (Robert Hale, London: 1971), pp. 162–3.

34. Hargreaves, Ph.D. thesis, p. 243; Marsh, *Clip a Bright Guinea*, pp. 172–6; Smail, *Origins of Middle-Class Culture*, p. 194.

35. G. S. Phillips, *Walks Around Huddersfield* (Bond and Hardy, Huddersfield: 1848), pp. 51–2.

36. D. G. Wright, 'The West Riding textile districts in the mid-nineteenth century' in J. A. Jowitt (ed.), *Model Industrial Communities in mid-nineteenth century Yorkshire* (University of Bradford, Bradford: 1986), pp. 5, 8, 12, 73.

37. J. A. Hargreaves, 'The Georgian and early Victorian church in the parish of Halifax, 1740–1851', *THAS* (1991); J. M. Turner and J. A. Hargreaves, *Thunderclaps from Heaven: Calderdale's Heritage of Nonconformity* (Metropolitan Borough of Calderdale, Halifax: 1984), pp. 11–12.

38. Hargreaves, Ph.D. thesis, pp. 88–91, 96–7.

39. Ibid., pp. 131–42.

40. Ibid., pp. 142–48.

41. Ibid., pp. 114–121.

42. Ibid., pp. 98–114; J. A. Hargreaves, 'Catholic communities in Calderdale in the eighteenth and nineteenth centuries', *THAS* 3 (1995), pp. 57–70.

43. Hargreaves, Ph.D. thesis, pp. 154–76, 227–40.

44. J. A. Hargreaves, *THAS* (1991), pp. 44–82.

45. Hargreaves, Ph.D. thesis, p. 199.

46. Ibid., pp. 176–200; W. B. Crump, 'Halifax visitors' book', II, *THAS* (1938), pp. 98–9; J. Golland, 'A dramatic discovery or a manly enterprise', *Local History Magazine* 42 (1994).

47. Smail, *Origins of Middle-Class Culture*, pp. 160–62; E. A. Smith, 'The Yorkshire elections of 1806 and 1807: a study in electoral management', *Northern History*, II (1967), pp. 62–90.

48. Ibid., pp. 62–90; E. Webster, 'Parliamentary elections in the parish of Halifax 1806–1837', *THAS* 1 (1993), pp. 43–5.

49. J. A. Hargreaves, 'Methodism and Luddism in Yorkshire, 1812–1813', *Northern History* XXVI (1990), pp. 160–85; Idem, '"Evangelical piety and Gallic flippancy": religion and popular protest in the parish of Halifax in the age of revolution, 1775–1848' in K. Dockray and K. Laybourn (eds), *The Representation and Reality of War: The British Experience: Essays in Honour of David Wright* (Sutton Publishing, Stroud: 1999); Idem, *Factory Kings and Slaves: South Pennine Social Movements, 1780–1840* (Pennine Heritage, Hebden Bridge: 1982), pp. 4–5.

50. Webster, *THAS* (1993), pp. 44, 46–7; J. A. Jowitt, 'Parliamentary politics in Halifax, 1832–47', *Northern History* XII (1976), pp. 172–201.

51. J. A. Hargreaves, 'Methodism and electoral politics in Halifax, 1832–1848' *Northern History* XXXV (1999), pp. 139–60.

52. J. A. Jowitt, 'From Whiggery to Liberalism: Sir Charles Wood and Halifax, 1832–65', *THAS* 2 (1994).

53. C. Hall, 'Domestic harmony, public virtue' in L. M. Smith, (ed.), *The Age of Revolution* (Macmillan, London: 1987), p. 79.

54. F. C. Mather, *Public Order in the Age of the Chartists* (Manchester University Press, Manchester: 1959), pp. 174–5, 116–17.

55. B. Jennings, *Pennine Independency* (Pennine Heritage, Hebden Bridge: 1982), pp. 14–16; A. Betteridge, 'Halifax before the industrial revolution, 1585–1762', I and II, *THAS* (1978–9); J. W. Houseman, 'The development of local government in the parish of Halifax, 1760–1848', *THAS* (1929); G. R. Dalby, 'The Halifax town trustees', *THAS* (1957); White, *Clothing Districts of the West Riding, 1853*, pp. 547–8.

56. Jennings, *Pennine Independency*, p. 14; Houseman, 'The development of local government in the parish of Halifax, 1760–1848', *THAS* (1929), p. 121.

57. Betteridge, *THAS* (1978), pp. 18–22.

58. Ibid., pp. 22–34.

59. Jennings, *Pennine Independency*, pp. 14–16; Betteridge, *THAS* (1979), pp. 88–95; C. Spencer, 'Township workhouses', *THAS* (1983), pp. 42–7.

60. G. R. Dalby, 'The Halifax town trustees', *THAS* (1957); Houseman, *THAS* (1929), pp. 173–9.

61. Hargreaves, Ph.D. thesis, p. 239.

62. P. J. Corfield, *The Impact of English Towns, 1700–1800* (Oxford University Press, Oxford: 1982), p. 23; A. Betteridge and D. Bridge (eds), *Maps and Views of Old Halifax* (Ryburn, Halifax: 1991).

63. Watson, *History and Antiquities of the Parish of Halifax*, p. 201; H. Ling Roth, *The Yorkshire Coiners, 1767–1783* (S. R. Publishers reprint, Wakefield: 1971), p. 112; Hanson, *Old Halifax*, pp. 260–61.

Notes to Chapter 5

1. Census of England and Wales, 1871; S. J. D. Green, *Religion in the Age of Decline* (Cambridge University Press, Cambridge: 1996), pp. 54–5.

2. Census of England and Wales, 1901.

3. Anon, *The Restoration of Halifax Parish Church*, Halifax, 1877, p. 21, cited in Green, *Religion in the Age of Decline*, p. 26; Asa Briggs, *Victorian Cities* (Odhams Press, London: 1963), p. 149.

4. T. Baines, *Yorkshire Past and Present*, 2 (London: 1875), pp. 403–404; G. P. Wadsworth, (ed.), *Halifax. A Commercial and Industrial Centre* (Sells Ltd, London: 1915), p. 30.

5. A. Dingsdale, 'Yorkshire mill town: a study of the spatial patterns and processes of urban industrial growth and the evolution of the spatial structure of Halifax, 1801–1901' (unpub. Ph.D. thesis, University of Leeds, 1961), p. 33; Green, *Religion in the Age of Decline*, p. 39; A. Miller, 'What were the factors that enabled John Crossley and Sons Ltd to become the largest manufacturer of carpets in the world between 1840 and 1914?' (unpub. dissertation, University of Durham, 1995), pp. 14, 44; J. A. Jowitt, 'Parliamentary politics in Halifax, 1832–47', *Northern History*, XII (1976), pp. 172, 199; Baines, *Yorkshire Past and Present*, 2, p. 415; E. Webster, *Textiles and Tools* (Halifax: n.d.), p. 36; *Halifax Courier*, 7 January 1854.

6. *Halifax Guardian*, 21 August 1897.

7. E. Webster, *Halifax the Town We Live In* (Halifax: 1965), p. 32; *The Times*, 24 August 1897.

8. H. W. Harwood, *Centenary Story* (Halifax Courier, Halifax: 1948), pp. 39–40; J. M. Brendan in J. J. Mulroy (ed.), *The Story of the Town that bred us* (Halifax: 1948), pp. 38–9, 56–9, 91–2, 96–9; E. Webster, *From rule of thumb to CNC. Two hundred years of engineering and machine tools in Calderdale* (Halifax: n.d.), p. 44; Anon, *Butler, 1868–1968* (Halifax: 1968); J. A. Hargreaves, *Halifax in Old Picture Postcards* (European Library, Zaltbommel: 1989), p. 52.

9. Harwood, *Centenary Story*, p. 39; D. Jeremy, 'John Mackintosh, Halifax Methodist and toffee manufacturer, 1868–1920: a typical Victorian entrepreneur?', *THAS* 5 (1997), pp. 116–31.

10. Wadsworth, *Halifax. A Commercial and Industrial Centre*, p. 18; Hargreaves, *Halifax in Old Picture Postcards*, pp. 12–13.

11. E. Webster, *Under the Clock* (Calderdale Amenities and Recreation Department, Halifax: 1985); Hargreaves, *Halifax in Old Picture Postcards*, pp. 33–5; M. Blatchford, *The History of the Halifax Industrial Society* (Halifax: 1901), pp. 21, 54, 210–16.

12. Wadsworth, *Halifax. A Commercial and Industrial Centre*, pp. 92–4, 107; W. C. E. Hartley, *Banking in Yorkshire* (Dalesman, Clapham: 1975), pp. 120–22; H. B. Sellers, *Memoranda from a note book on the Yorkshire Penny Bank* (Leeds: 1899), pp. 3–40; E. M. Wavell, *Growth of our Borough* Halifax Guardian, Halifax: 1898), pp. 13–14.

13. M. H. Yeadell, 'Building societies in the West Riding of Yorkshire and their contribution to housing provision in the nineteenth century' in M. Doughty (ed.), *Building the Industrial City* (Leicester University Press, Leicester: 1986), pp. 59–60, 72, 76–8, 96–9; E. Webster, 'Nineteenth century housing in Halifax and the growth of the town', *THAS* (1986), pp. 80–82; O. R. Hobson, *A Hundred Years of the Halifax* (Batsford, London: 1953), pp. 60, 62, 90; R. Rodger, *Housing in Urban Britain, 1780–1914* (Macmillan, London: 1989), pp. 23–4; M. J. Daunton, *House and Home in the Victorian City* (Edward Arnold, London: 1983), pp. 97–8; P. Pugh, *The Strength to Change* (Penguin, London: 1998), pp. 46–8.

14. Harwood, *Centenary Story*, pp. 19–22; G. Sheeran, *Railway Buildings of West Yorkshire* (Keele University Press, Keele: 1994), p. 17; *Halifax Courier*, 17 March 1998.

15. Wadsworth, *Halifax. A Commercial and Industrial Centre*, pp. 19–22, 27.

16. Wavell, *Growth of our Borough*, pp. 7, 9; H. B. Priestley, *Halifax in the Tramway Era* (Turntable Publications, Sheffield: 1977); J. R. Moore, 'Halifax Corporation Tramways', I *THAS* (1974).

17. Dingsdale, thesis, pp. 340–49, 373–4.

18. Hargreaves, *Halifax in Old Picture Postcards*, pp. 9, 85.

19. F. Pigou, *Phases of My Life* (London: 1898), pp. 83–6.

20. G. Sheeran, *Brass Castles* (Ryburn, Halifax: 1993), pp. 8, 13; J. Wild, 'Some local people of note', *THAS* (1976), pp. 29–30; Green, *Religion in the Age of Decline*, pp. 102, 142, 144.

21. E. Webster, *THAS* (1986), 83–6; Sheeran, *Brass Castles*, pp. 83, 106.

22. A. A. Thomson (ed.), *By Faith and Work* (Hutchinson, London: 1966), pp. 28–29; Jeremy, *THAS* (1997), 125; Watson, *Holdsworths*, p. 25.

23. W. White, *Directory of Leeds and the Clothing Districts of Yorkshire* (David and Charles

reprint, Newton Abbot: 1969); F. Smith, *Directory of Halifax* (Halifax: 1874); J. N. Bartlett, *Carpeting the Millions* (John Donald, Edinburgh: 1978), pp. 142–3; E. Webster, 'Nineteenth century housing and the growth of the town', *THAS* (1986), pp. 83–6.

24. J. H. Waddington, *Essays and Addresses* (Halifax: 1939), p. 56.

25. Census of England, 1881; Green, *Religion in the Age of Decline*, pp. 61–2.

26. N. Rycroft et al., '1851 census returns for Halifax and Skircoat townships', I, *THAS* (1979), pp. 113–14.

27. Green, *Religion in the Age of Decline*, pp. 46–9; Webster, *From Rule of Thumb to CNC*, p. 49; M. J. Daunton, *House and Home in the Victorian City* (Edward Arnold, London: 1983), p. 81.

28. Green, *Religion in the Age of Decline*, pp. 80–84; Webster, *THAS* (1986), 85–6; Sheeran, *Brass Castles*, p. 11; W. Pickles, *Have Another Go* (David and Charles, Newton Abbot: 1978), p. 15.

29. K. Tiller, 'Late Chartism: Halifax 1847–58' in J. Epstein and D. Thompson (eds), *The Chartist Experience* (Macmillan, London: 1982), p. 318; E. Royle, *Chartism* (Longman, London: 1996), p. 127.

30. Tiller, 'Late Chartism: Halifax 1847–58' in Epstein and Thompson, *The Chartist Experience*, pp. 311–44.

31. J. A. Jowitt, 'From Whiggery to Liberalism: Sir Charles Wood and Halifax, 1832–65', *THAS* 2 (1994), pp. 43–54; A. Porritt, 'The Rt Hon. Sir James Stansfeld', *THAS* (1971), pp. 87–100.

32. B. Wilson, 'The Struggles of an Old Chartist', in D. Vincent, *Testaments of Radicalism* (Europa, London: 1977), pp. 211–42; Tiller in Epstein and Thompson, *The Chartist Experience*, pp. 318–44.

33. P. A. Dawson, 'The Halifax Independent Labour Movement: Labour and Liberalism 1890–1914' in K. Laybourn and D. James (eds), *The Rising Sun of Socialism* (West Yorkshire Archive Service, Wakefield: 1991), pp. 45–74; K. Laybourn and J. Reynolds, *Liberalism and the Rise of Labour, 1890–1918* (Croom Helm, London: 1984), pp. 21, 24–5, 35, 42, 44, 51–2, 58–9, 62, 65, 69, 79, 93, 106, 109, 116–18, 120, 130–33, 149, 167.

34. *Halifax Courier*, 24 February 1998; E. Webster, *From Rule of Thumb to CNC*, p. 89.

35. Wavell, *Growth of our Borough*, pp. 4–6; J. A. Hargreaves, 'Religion and Society in the Parish of Halifax, c. 1740–1914' (unpub. Ph.D. thesis, Huddersfield Polytechnic, 1991), pp. 238–40.

36. Wavell, *Growth of our Borough*, pp. 8, 10–11.

37. Daunton, *House and Home in the Victorian City*, pp. 256–60; E. Webster, 'William Ranger's reports on the sanitary condition of Halifax, 1850–51', *THAS* 6 (1998), p. 77.

38. Harwood, *Centenary Story*, pp. 15–17; 'The making of our municipality' in J. J. Mulroy, *The Story of the Town that Bred Us*, pp. 16–35; Daunton, *House and Home in the Victorian City*, pp. 256–60; Wavell, *Growth of our Borough*, pp. 10–11.

39. M. Girouard, *The English Town* (Yale University Press, Yale: 1990), pp. 209–10; R. de Z. Hall, *Halifax Town Hall* (County Borough of Halifax, Halifax: 1963), pp. 26–48, 73.

40. E. Webster, 'Halifax Schools, 1870–1970', *THAS* (1972), pp. 10–36; Harwood, *Centenary Story*, pp. 23–6; W. A. Davies, 'Local educational history' in Mulroy, *The Story of the Town that Bred Us*, pp. 81–4.

41. J. G. Washington, 'Poverty, health and social welfare: the history of the Halifax Union Workhouse and St John's Hospital, 1834–1972', *THAS* 5 (1997), 89–94; Harwood, *Centenary Story*, pp. 27–9.

42. Wadsworth, *Halifax. A Commercial and Industrial Centre*, pp. 65–6; Wavell, *Growth of our Borough*, pp. 12–13, 16.

43. J. G. Washington, 'The origins and development of the Royal Halifax Infirmary, 1807–1995', *THAS* 4 (1996), 68–85; J. A. Jowitt, (ed.), *Model Industrial Communities in Mid-Nineteenth Century Yorkshire* (University of Bradford, Bradford: 1986).

44. K. Laybourn, *The Evolution of British Social Policy and the Welfare State* (Keele University Press, Keele: 1995), pp. 153–7; K. Laybourn (ed.), *Social Conditions, Status and Community 1860–c.1920* (Sutton Publishing, Stroud: 1997), pp. 9–26.

45. Hargreaves, Ph.D. thesis, pp. 88–92, 191–2; Green, *Religion in the Age of Decline*, p. 91.

46. J. A. Hargreaves, 'The Church of England in Late-Victorian Halifax, 1852–1914', *THAS* (1992) pp. 27–8.

47. Hargreaves, Ph.D. thesis, pp. 406–9.

48. A. E. Dingle, *The Campaign for Prohibition in Victorian England. The United Kingdom Alliance, 1872–95* (London: 1980).

49. E. Webster, 'Leisure and pleasure in nineteenth century Halifax', *THAS* (1989).

50. C. Binfield, *So Down to Prayers: Studies in English Nonconformity, 1780–1920* (Dent, London, 1977) p. 147.

51. Hargreaves, *Halifax in Old Picture Postcards*, pp. 21, 22, 55, 80, 84, 96.

52. D. Taylor, 'Annals of the Parish of Halifax', *THAS* (1972), p. 122.

53. *Yorkshire Weekly Post*, 16 June 1910.

54. M. Blatchford, *The History of Halifax Industrial Society* (Halifax Industrial Society, Halifax: 1901), p. 10.

55. Wadsworth, *Halifax. A Commercial and Industrial Centre*, p. 35.

Notes to Chapter 6

1. K. Laybourn, *Britain on the Breadline* (Sutton Publishing, Stroud: 1998); J. Stevenson and C. Cook, *Britain in the Depression* (Longman, London: 1994).

2. T. R. Hornshaw, 'Calderdale and the wars of the twentieth century, 1899–1945', *THAS* 6 (1998), pp. 117–131; J. J. Mulroy (ed.), *The Story of the Town that Bred Us* (J. J. Mulroy, Halifax: 1948), pp. 71–4; D. Albon, *Copley and District, 1935–50* (Halifax: n.d.), p. 34; *Calderdale at War* (Calderdale Museums Service, Halifax: 1982), pp. 2, 13. I am grateful to Mr Derek Albon for sharing with me his reminiscences of Halifax during the Second World War.

3. Hornshaw, *THAS* 6 (1998), p. 131.

4. Census, 1921, 1931; J. Reynolds and K. Laybourn, *Labour Heartland* (Bradford University Press, Bradford: 1987), pp. 5–10.

5. Reynolds and Laybourn, *Labour Heartland*, p. 10; J. H. Waddington, *Essays and Addresses* (Halifax: 1939), p. 26.

6. Alderman J. Radcliffe, speech on election as mayor, 9 November 1938, Calderdale Central Library, Horsfall Turner Collection.

7. Reynolds and Laybourn, *Labour Heartland*, Table 1.6, p. 23.

8. N. Watson, *Holdsworths of Halifax* (unpublished typescript), pp. 38–40; P. Bentley, *O Dreams, O Destinations* (Gollancz, London: 1962), p. 109; E. Webster, *Dean Clough* (Dean Clough Publications, Halifax: 1988), p. 21.

9. 60th Annual Report Halifax Chamber of Commerce, 1921, pp. 8–9; Bentley, *O Dreams, O Destinations*, pp. 156–7; Watson, *Holdsworths*, p. 40.

10. S. Constantine, *Social Conditions in Britain, 1918–1939* (Methuen, London: 1983), pp. 42–3; Watson, *Holdsworths*, p. 43.

11. *Annual Report Halifax Chamber of Commerce*, 1925, p. 2; 1928, p. 8.

12. Bentley, *O Dreams, O Destinations*, pp. 134–7; Watson, *Holdsworths*, p. 43; Webster, *Dean Clough*, pp. 17, 22; *Halifax Chamber of Commerce Journal*, June 1926, vol. vi, no. 67; Mulroy, *Story of the Town that Bred Us*, p. 118.

13. Reynolds and Laybourn, *Labour Heartland*, p. 100.

14. Watson, *Holdsworths*, p. 43; Webster, *Dean Clough*, p. 22.

15. Constantine, *Social Conditions*, p. 43.

16. Watson, *Holdsworths*, p. 47.

17. Webster, *Dean Clough*, p. 25; Reynolds and Laybourn, *Labour Heartland*, p. 12; *Kelly's Directory of the Textile Industries* (London: 1928), p. 565.

18. Watson, *Holdsworths*, p. 50.

19. Census, 1921 and 1931; Reynolds and Laybourn, *Labour Heartland*, p. 12.

20. Watson, *Holdsworths*, pp. 53–4.

21. Reynolds and Laybourn, *Labour Heartland*, p. 11; P. Bryan, *Wool, War and Westminster* (Tom Donovan, London: 1993), p. 29; Watson, *Holdsworths*, p. 45; *Kelly's Directory*, p. 565.

22. Reynolds and Laybourn, *Labour Heartland*, p. 11.

23. Census, 1921 and 1931; Reynolds and Laybourn, *Labour Heartland*, p. 12.

24. *Commercial Year Book of the Halifax Chamber of Commerce* (London: 1918), p. 47.

25. G. P. Wadsworth in *Halifax Publicity Week, October 10–17, 1931* (Halifax Chamber of Trade, Halifax: 1931), p. 9; P. Saunders, 'Halifax: Town of Industries and Hills', *Trade and Engineering* (October, 1936);

S. Constantine, *Unemployment in Britain Between the Wars* (Longman, London: 1980), p. 19.

26. E. Webster, *From Rule of Thumb to CNC* (E. Webster, Halifax: 1997), pp. 25, 30, 36, 55, 70, 74–5; *Butler, 1868–1968* (Butler Machine Tool Co., Halifax: 1968), pp. 5–6; *With the World at War We Were not Idle* (G. H. Gledhill and Sons, Halifax: n.d.), p. 4; S. Glynn and A. Booth, *Modern Britain* (Routledge, London: 1996), p. 69.

27. *Annual Report Halifax Chamber of Commerce*, 1921, p. 9; 1925, p. 2.

28. Webster, *From Rule of Thumb to CNC*, pp. 36, 76.

29. *Annual Report Halifax Chamber of Commerce*, 1928, p. 8; Webster, *From Rule of Thumb to CNC*, pp. 53, 66–7, 85, 87; Census, 1921; 1931.

30. Webster, *From Rule of Thumb to CNC*, pp. 70, 77, 81–2, 92, 96.

31. Ibid., pp. 70, 82, 94, 97; *With The World at War, We Were Not Idle*, pp. 5, 8, 10, 13.

32. Webster, *From Rule of Thumb to CNC*, p. 55.

33. G. W. Crutchley, *John Mackintosh* (Hodder and Stoughton, London: 1921), p. 114.

34. Ibid., pp. 63–4, 113–17; A. A. Thomson, *By Faith and Work* (Hutchinson, London: 1966), pp. 50–1, 62, 66, 91, 93f.

35. Glynn and Booth, *Modern Britain*, pp. 65, 81–2; Census, 1921, 1931; Hobson, *Halifax*, p. 77; Bryan, *Wool, War and Westminster*, p. 157.

36. M. Hartley and J. Ingleby, *Life and Tradition in West Yorkshire* (Smith Settle, Otley: 1990), pp. 65, 139; *Halifax County Borough Directory, 1936* (Cade Publications reprint, Halifax: 1998), p. 403.

37. J. A. Hargreaves, '"The Catseye Man": Percy Shaw of Halifax, road stud manufacturer, 1890–1976', *THAS* 4 (1996), pp. 126–34.

38. Hobson, *Halifax*, 87–9; Thomson, *By Faith and Work*, p. 76.

39. Hobson, *Halifax*, pp. 82–3, 106–14; R. K. Bacon, *The Life of Sir Enoch Hill* (London: 1934).

40. Hobson, *Halifax*, p. 93.

41. Ibid., pp. 95–6.

42. Ibid., pp. 73, 82, 117–18, 121.

43. *Halifax Chamber of Trade, Shopping Festival and Exhibition* (Halifax Chamber of Trade, Halifax: 1936), p. 3.

44. Waddington, *Essays and Addresses*, pp. 11–12.

45. W. Pickles, *Sometime Never* (Werner Laurie, London: 1951), p. 89.

46. Census, 1921, 1931.

47. Ibid.; Hobson, *Halifax*, p. 75; *Halifax Equitable Benefit Building Society Jubilee* (Halifax Equitable Building Society, Halifax: 1921), p. 144.

48. Webster, *Rule of Thumb to CNC*, p. 89.

49. J. Stevenson, *British Society, 1914–45* (Penguin, London: 1984), p. 307; B. Keith-Lucas, *English Local Government in the Nineteenth and Twentieth Centuries* (Historical Association, London: 1977), pp. 26–9; B. J. Barber and M. W. Beresford, *The West Riding County Council, 1889–1974* (West Yorkshire Metropolitan County Council, Wakefield: 1979), pp. 84–5; *Halifax Official Handbook* (Halifax Corporation, Halifax: 1939), pp. 18–24.

50. Barber and Beresford, *West Riding County Council, 1889–1974*, pp. 242–6; Keith-Lucas, *English Local Government in the Nineteenth and Twentieth Centuries*, pp. 31–2; Halifax Extension Bill, 1935, Calderdale Central Library, L3117.

51. *Local Government Journal and Officials' Gazette* (April 1935), p. 109; *Halifax Official Handbook*, pp. 18–21; *Halifax County Borough Directory*, p. lxxii; H. B. Priestley, *Halifax in the Tramway Era* (Turntable Publications, Sheffield: 1977), p. 4; Mulroy, *Story of the Town that Bred Us*, p. 33; D. Bell, *Hebble Remembered* (Becknell Books, King's Lynn: 1983).

52. *Annual Report Halifax Chamber of Commerce*, 1925, pp. 21–2; Waddington, *Essays and Addresses*, p. 12; *Halifax County Borough Directory*, p. xl; *Local Government Journal and Officials' Gazette* (April, 1935), pp. 107–11.

53. Hartley and Ingleby, *Life and Tradition in West Yorkshire*, p. 35; Webster, *Dean Clough*, p. 22.

54. K. Laybourn, *The Evolution of British Social Policy and the Welfare State* (Keele University Press, Keele: 1995), pp. 122–6; E. Webster, 'Halifax Schools, 1870–1970', *THAS* (1972), pp. 37–46; *Halifax Official Handbook*, pp. 23–4; Bentley, *O Dreams, O Destinations*, p. 87; Bryan, *Wool, War and Westminster*, pp. 29–30.

55. Webster, 'Halifax Schools', p. 40; Bentley, *O Dreams, O Destinations*, p. 115; *Halifax Official Handbook*, p. 23.

56. *Halifax County Borough Directory*, p. lv; P. Bentley, *O Dreams, O Destinations*, p. 114; J. Cockcroft, *Not a Proper Doctor* (Pennine Heritage, Hebden Bridge: n.d.), p. 38.

57. J. G. Washington, 'The origins and development of the Royal Halifax Infirmary', *THAS* 4 (1996), pp. 78–81; R. Chew, *100 Years of Caring. A History of the Royal Halifax Infirmary* (Calderdale and Kirklees Health Authority, Halifax: 1996), pp. 11–14; J. A. Hargreaves, *Sowerby Bridge in Old Photographs* (Smith Settle, Otley: 1994), p. 175.

58. *Halifax Official Handbook*, pp. 11–16, 23; *Halifax County Borough Directory*, p. li.

59. Reynolds and Laybourn, *Labour Heartland*, p. 27; Laybourn, *Britain on the Breadline*, Table 3.3., p. 86; Halifax Housing Committee, Housing Statistics, August 1929; *Halifax Official Handbook*, 1939, p. 11; 1947, p. 40; Reynolds and Laybourn, *Labour Heartland*, p. 29; *Daily News and Westminster Gazette*, 4 March 1930.

60. Thomson, *By Faith and Work*, p. 42; J. Wild, 'Some local people of note', II, *THAS* (1977), p. 64; Webster, *From Rule of Thumb to CNC*, p. 89; R. Rooney, B. Lewis and R. Schuhle, *Home is Where the Heart is* (Yorkshire Arts Circus: 1989), p. 36.

61. Reynolds and Laybourn, *Labour Heartland*, pp. 47–50, 141, 144–7; *Halifax Courier and Guardian Historical Almanack*, 1925–1939.

62. D. Beddoe, *Discovering Women's History* (Longman, London: 1998), p. 176; 'Women civic leaders', *Halifax Courier Yearbook*, 1965; Bentley, *O Dreams, O Destinations*, p. 114; Mulroy, *The Story of the Town that Bred Us*, p. 118; *Halifax Courier*, 4 August 1998; J. G. Washington, 'The history of the Halifax General Hospital, 1897–1987', *THAS* 6 (1998), pp. 105, 107.

63. K. Laybourn and J. Reynolds, *Liberalism and the rise of Labour* (Croom Helm, London: 1984), pp. 183–5, 191–2, 196–8; *Labour Heartland*, p. 37.

64. J. Wild, 'Some local people of note', II, *THAS* (1977), pp. 75–6.

65. Reynolds and Laybourn, *Labour Heartland*, p. 85; *Halifax Courier*, 28 July 1998.

66. *Labour Heartland*, pp. 98, 123; F. W. S. Craig, *British Parliamentary Election Results, 1918–1949* (Postal Reference Publications, Glasgow: 1969), p. 140.

67. *Yorkshire Post, The Daily Telegraph*, 28 June

1945. I am grateful to Sophie Clapp, Archivist, Churchill Archives Centre, Churchill College, Cambridge, for providing me with details of the visit.

68. Reynolds and Laybourn, *Labour Heartland*, pp. 118, 139; *Halifax Courier*, 1 August 1997.

69. Bentley, *O Dreams, O Destinations*, pp. 116, 205–6, 208; Reynolds and Laybourn, *Labour Heartland*, pp. 141, 144–7.

70. *Halifax Courier*, 19 May 1998.

71. Crutchley, *John Mackintosh*, pp. 210–11.

72. Hargreaves, 'Religion and society in the parish of Halifax, c1740–1914', unpup. Ph.D. thesis, Huddersfield Polytechnic, 1991, p. 410; *Methodist Times*, 11 July 1929.

73. Waddington, *Essays and Addresses*, pp, 33–4.

74. T. Hughes, *Remains of Elmet* (Faber, London: 1979), p. 8.

75. S. J. D. Green, *Religion in the Age of Decline* (Cambridge University Press, Cambridge: 1996), pp. 372–90; *Halifax Courier*, 22 September 1998.

76. Watson, *Holdsworths*, pp. 40–43, 55; Hardcastle, *Thrum Hall Story*, p. 82; Hobson, *Halifax*, pp. 110–11; J. Hudson, *Wakes Week* (Alan Sutton, Stroud: 1992).

77. J. A. Hargreaves, *Halifax in Old Picture Postcards* (European Library, Zaltbommel, Netherlands: 1989), pp. 11, 72, 137; Bentley, *O Dreams, O Destinations*, pp. 111–12.

78. Hardcastle, *Thrum Hall Story*, pp. 49, 64–88; Hargreaves, *Halifax in Old Picture Postcards*, p. 123.

79. W. Pickles, *Have Another Go* (David and Charles, Newton Abbot: 1978), pp. 25–6; Bentley, *O Dreams, O Destinations*, pp. 112–13; Hardcastle, *Thrum Hall Story*, p. 74.

80. *Halifax County Borough Directory*, p. 420; Mulroy, *Story of the Town that Bred Us*, p. 61.

81. Mulroy, *Story of the Town that Bred Us*, p. 61;

J. Priestley, *English Journey* (Folio Society reprint, London: 1997), p. 162; *Halifax Courier*, 21 September 1998; *Halifax Choral Society*, Halifax, 1992; R. A. Edwards, *And the Glory* (W. S. Maney and Son Ltd, Leeds: 1986), pp. 48, 113.

82. Bentley, *O Dreams, O Destinations*, pp. 137, 147, 173; L. Schroeder, foreword, J. Wren, *Yorkshire Hill-Folk* (Halifax Courier, Halifax: 1928); Waddington, *Essays and Addresses*, p. 46.

83. Bentley, *O Dreams, O Destinations*, p. 173; E. Evens, *Through the Years with Romany* (University of London Press, London: 1946), pp. 118–28; Pickles, *Have Another Go*, pp. 56–62, 120; M. Pickles, *Married to Wilfred* (Odhams Press, London: 1956), pp. 58–60, 99–107.

84. *Halifax Courier*, 13 July 1990; I. Chilvers, H. Osborne and D. Farr, *The Oxford Dictionary of Art* (Oxford University Press, Oxford: 1988), pp. 411, 466.

85. D. Cant, 'Jackson of Coley (1867–1931), master woodcarver', *THAS* 2 (1994), pp. 95, 100; *Halifax Chamber of Trade, Shopping Festival and Exhibition*, p. 35; *Halifax County Borough Directory*, pp. 479–80.

86. Hobson, *Halifax*, pp. 90–91, 102.

87. *Halifax Courier*, 18 August 1998; *Halifax Official Handbook*, 1947, pp. 18–19; A. Betteridge, D. Bridge and P. H. Thornborrow, *Calderdale Architecture and History* (Ryburn, Halifax: 1988), pl. 105; S. Gee, *Around Halifax* (Chalford Publishing Company, Stroud: 1996), pp. 13, 21.

88. Mulroy, *Story of the Town that Bred Us*, p. 61; *Halifax Shopping Week*, pp. 97, 107; Priestley, *English Journey*, p. 162; Hughes, *Remains of Elmet*, p. 124; E. Pontefract and M. Hartley, *Yorkshire Tour* (J. M. Dent, London: 1939), p. 117.

Notes to Chapter 7

1. *Halifax Courier*, 22 March 1948.

2. *Census, Yorkshire West Riding* (HMSO, London: 1963 and 1973); *Census Digest, Calderdale MBC* (Halifax: 1983 and 1993); Yorkshire and Humberside Economic Planning Council and Board, *Halifax and the Calder Valley* (HMSO, London: 1968), pp. 15–18.

3. *Halifax Courier*, 9 January 1988; *Calderdale*

Trends, Autumn 1990 and Summer 1993; *Census Digest, Calderdale MBC* (Halifax: 1983 and 1993).

4. *Calderdale Report*, 1982–3, p. 7; *Calderdale Trends*, Winter 1990 and 1993.

5. *Calderdale Trends*, Winter 1997.

6. *Calderdale Report*, 1995–6; *Halifax and Calder Valley. An Area Study*, pp. 12, 33.

7. *Calderdale Report*, 1982–3, p. 7.

8. *Calderdale Report*, 1990–1, p. 2; 1991–2, p. 5; 1992–3, p. 9; 1995–6, p. 10; *Halifax Courier*, 9 October 1990, 1 February 1991.

9. *Calderdale Report*, 1994–5, p. 12.

10. A. Marwick, *British Society since 1945* (Penguin, London: 1982), pp. 29–30.

11. *Halifax and the Calder Valley*, pp. 12, 126, 128.

12. *Halifax Courier*, 30 December 1994.

13. N. Watson, *Holdsworths of Halifax* (unpublished typescript), chapters 4–7.

14. E. Webster, *Dean Clough* (Dean Clough Publications, Halifax: 1988), pp. 28–9, 32–3.

15. Webster, *Dean Clough*, p. 33; *Halifax Courier*, 20 September 1986, 19 February 1988.

16. I am grateful to Mr B. Butler for supplying me with information about Joseph Horsfall and Sons Ltd.

17. E. Webster, *From Rule of Thumb to CNC* (E. Webster, Halifax: 1997), pp. 11, 13–15, 17, 26, 36–7, 39, 47–53, 73, 77, 80, 83, 92, 97–8, 100, 103–4, 109; *Halifax and Calder Valley*, pp. 12–13; *Halifax Courier*, 30 December 1994, 9 October 1995, 4 December 1995, 22 September 1998, 5 December 1998; *Calderdale News*, 4 January 1996.

18. *Halifax Courier*, 16 October 1986, 11 April 1991.

19. P. W. Robinson, 'Stone Trough Brewery', *THAS*, 1989, p. 18.

20. O. Hobson, *A Hundred Years of the Halifax* (Batsford, London: 1953), p. 144; *Calderdale Trends*, Autumn 1994; *Halifax Courier*, 9 December 1986; P. Pugh, *The Strength to Change* (Penguin, London: 1968), pp. 9, 84, 100, 102, 182. I am grateful to Sir James Birrell and Mr David Gilchrist for providing me with additional information.

21. *Halifax Courier*, 20 October 1983. I am grateful to Karen Hales of Royal Sun Alliance and Chris Johnstone of Provident Insurance and Colonnade Insurance Brokers, for supplying me with this information.

22. *The Sunday Times*, 6 April 1997, 19 April 1998; *Calderdale Community Foundation Annual Report*, 1993. I am grateful to Jane Gaze for providing me with information about Gartland, Whalley and Barker.

23. *Halifax in Calderdale. A Strategy of Prosperity*, Civic Trust, 1984, pp. 8–13, 65–6; *Calderdale Tourism Impact Study* (Ecotec, Birmingham: 1990), p. 20; *Halifax Courier*, 14 July 1998.

24. *Calderdale the Challenge* (Civic Trust, London: 1986), pp. 19–20; *Halifax Courier*, 14 July 1998.

25. *Halifax Courier*, 6 October 1993, 2 December 1993, 14 July 1998; *Halifax Civic Trust Report*, 1995.

26. *Halifax Courier*, 11 November 1998, 28 January 1999; *Halifax Shopping Guide*, Halifax Town Centre Forum, 1998.

27. *Halifax Courier*, 7 April 1987.

28. *Halifax Courier*, 9 December 1986.

29. *Calderdale Report*, 1986–7, p. 7; M. Middleton, *Cities in Transition* (London: 1991), p. 205; A. Holden, *Charles* (Weidenfield and Nicolson, London: 1988), pp. 145–55; J. Dimbleby, *The Prince of Wales: A Biography* (Little, Brown, London: 1994), pp. 367–8; *Vision in Calderdale* (Calderdale Partnership, Halifax: 1989).

30. *Halifax Official Guide* (Halifax County Borough, Halifax: 1972).

31. C. B. Phillips and J. H. Smith, *Lancashire and Cheshire from AD 1540* (Longman, London: 1994), Table 5.15, p. 371; *Halifax in Calderdale*, p. 8; B. J. Barber and M. W. Beresford, *The West Riding County Council, 1889–1974* (West Yorkshire Metropolitan County Council, Wakefield: 1978), pp. 253–4.

32. *Calderdale Report*, 1989–90, p. 2; 1990–1, p. 2; 1991–2, p. 2; 1993–4, p. 7.

33. E. Webster, 'Halifax Schools, 1870–1970', *THAS* (1972), pp. 46–49; *Calderdale News*, 19 March 1998; C. C. Robinson (ed.), *Birth and Rebirth* (Hipperholme Grammar School, Halifax: 1997), pp. 12–14; P. Clark, *Back from the Brink* (Metro, London: 1998), p. 3–5. I am grateful to Mr C. C. Robinson for information about Hipperholme Grammar School.

34. *The Sunday Times*, 25 October 1998, p. 44; *Halifax Courier*, 9 October 1995.

35. Clark, *Back from the Brink*; *Calderdale Report*, 1996–7, pp. 29–30.

36. *Calderdale College. A Century of Achievement*, Halifax, 1993; D. Harpwood, *Golden Years of Halifax* (True North Books, Halifax: 1998), pp. 35–9; *Halifax Courier*, 7 May 1988.

37. *Halifax Courier*, 15 July 1998.

38. *Halifax Courier*, 9 December 1989.

39. *Annual Report of League*, 1958; *Halifax Courier*, 6 July 1988.

40. *Halifax and the Calder Valley*, pp. 71, 73, 77;

Halifax Guide, 1972, p. 65; *Halifax Courier*, 15 June 1989.

41. *Halifax and Calder Valley*, p. 143; *Yorkshire Life*, March 1970; *Calderdale Trends*, Spring 1992; *Halifax Official Guide*, 1972, p. 55; *Calderdale; What Future?*, Halifax, 1972, p. 6; *Calderdale Report*, 1995, p. 55–6; 1997, p. 51; N. Danziger, *Danziger's Britain: A Journey to the Edge* (Harper Collins, London: 1996), p. 56; *Halifax Courier*, 18 January 1999.

42. *Halifax Courier*, 22 March 1948. P. Brears and S. Davies, *Treasures for the People* (Yorkshire and Humberside Museums Council: 1989), pp. 60–1, 77–8.

43. *Halifax Courier*, 4 January 1973; *Halifax Courier*, 26 October 1998; *Halifax Official Guide*, 1972.

44. *Halifax Courier*, 26 October 1998; *Halifax Official Guide*, 1972. I am grateful to Mrs Betty Brooksby for information about concerts at the Victoria Theatre.

45. *Calderdale Tourism Impact Study*, p. 5; *Halifax Courier*, 23 January 1999.

46. M. Middleton, *Cities in Transition*, p. 207.

47. *Halifax Courier*, 10 May 1970, 14 May 1971, 5 May 1972, 11 May 1973.

48. *Halifax Courier*, 6 May 1976, 5 May 1978, 3 May 1979; M. Middleton, *Cities in Crisis*, p. 207.

49. *Calderdale Report*, 1992–3, p. 3; Middleton, *Cities in Crisis*, p. 207; *Halifax Courier*, 1 June 1995.

50. *Halifax Courier*, 8 May 1998.

51. *Halifax Courier*, 7 May 1999.

52. *Halifax Courier*, 12 Nov 1998; *Halifax Courier and Guardian Historical Almanack*, 1945, pp. 25–29.

53. *Halifax Courier and Guardian Historical Almanack*, 1951; R. Davenport-Hines, *The Macmillans* (Heinemann, London: 1992), p. 242.

54. R. Waller and B. Criddle, *The Almanac of British Politics* (Routledge, London: 1996), p. 414.

55. *Halifax Courier and Guardian Historical Almanack*, 1947; *Epworth Review*, January 1985, p. 5; *Halifax Circuit Directory*, 1998.

56. J. Peart-Binns, *Eric Treacy* (Ian Allan, London: 1980), p. 141.

57. M. Morris, *Social Enterprise. A study of the activities of voluntary societies and voluntary workers in an industrial town* (National Council of Social Service, London: 1962), pp. 13, 107–8; *Changes*, November, 1998, Calderdale Community Church, Halifax, pp. 3–4; J. M. Turner, *Modern Methodism in England, 1932–98* (Epworth, Peterborough: 1998), p. 76; *Halifax Courier*, 16 April 1997, 12 November 1997; *Halifax Courier*, 30 October 1995. I am grateful to Mrs Dorothy Moore for information about the Christian Contact Centre.

58. A. Hardcastle, *The Thrum Hall Story*, pp. 89, 91, 99–100, 105, 126–8; *Halifax Courier*, 4 May 1987.

59. *Halifax Official Guide*, 1972, pp. 98–9; *Halifax Courier*, 28 October 1998.

60. R. A. Edwards, *And the Glory* (W. S. Maney, Leeds: 1986), p. 113; *Yorkshire Post*, 19 January 1999; *Halifax Courier*, 29 February 1992; Hardcastle, *Thrum Hall Story*, p. 112.

61. *Yorkshire Life*, Mar 1970; E. Royle, 'Historians and the Making of the English Working Class, 1963–1988', *THAS* (1989), p. 81; J. A. Hargreaves, 'Planting the liberty tree', *THAS* (1988), pp. xviii–xx; J. Harber, 'Edward Thompson (1926–93)', *THAS* 2 (1994), pp. 125–8.

62. N. Pevsner, *Yorkshire: the West Riding* (Penguin, London: 1959), p. 229.

63. *Halifax and the Calder Valley*, p. 137.

64. *Halifax Courier*, 4 January 1973; *Nairn's Journeys*, BBC Television, Manchester, 1975.

65. *Halifax in Calderdale. A Strategy for Prosperity*, Civic Trust, 1984, p. 1.

66. Pevsner, *Yorkshire, the West Riding*, pp. 229, 231; *Halifax in Calderdale*, 1984, pp. 11–13; *Context*, Association of Conservation Officers, 18, Spring 1988, p. 6; *Quality of Life in Britain's Intermediate Cities* (Glasgow: 1989).

67. Halifax Civic Trust Report; E. A. H. Haigh (ed.), *Huddersfield. A most handsome town* (Kirklees Leisure Services, Huddersfield: 1992), pp. 330, 353; G. Firth, *A History of Bradford* (Phillimore, Chichester: 1997), pp. 134–5.

Index